Behold the Child

American energy and optimism. Sam Patch, a folk hero renowned for his spectacular leaps, jumping from a church steeple. From The Wonderful Leaps of Sam Patch *(New York n.d).*

GILLIAN AVERY

Behold the Child

AMERICAN CHILDREN AND

THEIR BOOKS 1621–1922

THE JOHNS HOPKINS UNIVERSITY PRESS

BALTIMORE, MARYLAND

In memory of Ruth Baldwin

1918–1990

1 3 5 5 7 9 10 8 6 4 2

Copyright © Gillian Avery 1994

First published in the United Kingdom 1994
by The Bodley Head Children's Books

First published in the United States of America 1994
by The Johns Hopkins University Press
2715 North Charles Street
Baltimore, Maryland 21218-4319

ISBN 0-8018-5066-5

A catalog record for this book is available from the
Library of Congress

Printed in Great Britain

Contents

List of Illustrations

Illustration Acknowledgements

The author and publishers would like to thank the following for permission to reproduce the illustrations in this book:

American Antiquarian Society; pp. ii, 3, 43, 49, 51, 55, 74, 95, 133, 159

Baldwin Library, University of Florida; pp. 76, 103, 149, 174

Bodleian Library, Oxford; pp. 7, 24, 41, 79, 88, 118, 127, 130, 139, 140, 144, 171, 178, 185, 188, 195

British Library; pp. 15, 31, 44, 111, 112, 135

Congregational Library, Boston; pp. 20, 101

Fine Arts Museums of San Francisco; p. 17

Rare Book Department, Free Library of Philadelphia; pp. 14, 18, 39, 53, 68, 73, 75, 109

Gallimard 1978, Illustration by Nicollet for *Enfantimages*; p. 196

Library of Congress, Washington D.C.; pp. 32, 100

Margaret Woodbury Strong Museum, Rochester, New York; p. 176

Maryland Historical Society, Baltimore; p. 37

Betsy Beinecke Shirley; pp. 8, 66, 72, 158, 160, 165

Behold the child, by nature's kindly law
Pleased with a rattle, tickled with a straw:
Some livelier plaything gives his youth delight,
A little louder, but as empty quite:
Scarfs, garters, gold, amuse his riper stage,
And beads and pray'r-books are the toys of age:
Pleased with this bauble still, as that before;
Till tired he sleeps, and life's poor play is o'er.

Alexander Pope

Preface

The origins of this book lie in a visit made in 1982 to Gainesville, Florida, for the formal opening of the Baldwin Library, the huge historical collection of English and American children's books assembled by the late Ruth Baldwin and presented by her to the University of Florida. I had queries of my own to settle while I was there, but when I asked for the best history of American children's books – I had been able to find nothing in England – I was told that there was none, that there were monographs and studies of small areas, but as yet no full account of what had been provided for American children to read over the centuries, nor of the development of an American style. That there was a very distinctive American style I discovered during that week at Gainesville when I read Baldwin books during the whole of the time the library was open, which was – since Ruth Baldwin was in charge of the books she had given and responded generously to a visitor's enthusiasm – from early morning until midnight.

I found that in the absence of a fuller guide, Jacob Blanck's *Peter Parley to Penrod* (1961), which contains bibliographical descriptions of representative juvenile books, provided signposts, of a sort, to favourite authors of the last century.·Some of the books were names known to me – Cornelia Meigs and her co-authors had included American writing in *A Critical History of Children's Literature* (1953) – but many were completely new. All were of absorbing interest, and I began to feel a missionary zeal: I wanted these authors to be remembered, and if there was no history to give them a context, then perhaps I could attempt one. For it is a sad fact that even the names of major American writers are now forgotten, so that specialists from American universities and library schools, well read in English authors of the last century, have never heard, say, of Samuel Goodrich, Jacob Abbott, Horace Scudder or Susan Coolidge, nor of Catharine Sedgwick from whose domestic fiction in the early decades of the nineteenth century so much later work stemmed

In defiance of its title, when the *Dictionary of American Children's Fiction 1859–1959* was published in 1985 it found space in the course of some six hundred pages for barely more than a dozen books from the pre-1900 period. The even larger *Writers for Children*, published from New York in 1988, confined itself to much the same expected handful of authors: Washington Irving, Louisa Alcott, Mark Twain, Frank Baum and a few others for whom there already exists an abundance of biographical and critical material. I discovered Mary Lystad's *From Dr Mather to Dr Seuss* (1980) after my own work was under way. This statistical analysis of a random sample of a thousand books published during the course of two centuries is admirable, but is not the literary history that I had searched for.

I had started in the Baldwin Library by noting the titles selected by Blanck. Since many of these were unobtainable in England, it was clear that the greater part of the initial reading would have to be done in American libraries. A generous grant from the Leverhulme Foundation helped with this, and in 1983 and 1984 I was able to work in the Free Library of Philadelphia (the home of the Rosenbach Collection), the Library of Congress, the Congregational Library in Boston (where there is a superb collection of Sunday school books published by the Massachusetts Sabbath School Society), and the Jordan Collection in the Boston Public Library.

I also made my first visit to the American Antiquarian Society. I had noted in D'Alté Welch's *Bibliography of American Children's Books Printed prior to 1821* the location MWA (Massachusetts Worcester Antiquarians) after the titles of all the early books I most wanted to see, but Worcester seemed at first inaccessible for someone based in Boston. Eventually I made my way out by the reluctant bus which is the only means of public transport, and presented myself in Salisbury Street with just three hours before I had to turn round and go back again. In 1983 my plans for the book were nebulous to the point of near-invisibility, and had the Society been discouraging that day I would not have attempted another visit – and might even have given up the whole project. But Frederick Bauer (since retired) not only listened with sympathy to my faltering apologia, but found a small collection of books that could be studied in the short time before I had to run for the bus. In 1984 I returned (always with the same limited time), and in 1985 applied for and was granted a fellowship, which meant that I could live in the Society's Goddard-Daniels house and work in the library daily for all the hours that it was open.

No study of early American children's books could be attempted without recourse to the American Antiquarian Society's holdings. Their cut-off point is 1876, and they are strongest in pre-Civil War publications, but nearly all the material for the early chapters of this book could be found in their library. Of all libraries that I have visited this one provides (except for its limited opening hours) the most perfect working conditions: material can be fetched from the stacks within minutes, all the reference books needed are at one's elbow, and above all there is the help of a highly knowledgeable and generous staff who draw one's attention to items that might otherwise have been overlooked. My indebtedness to the Society is overwhelming, and I am proud to have been elected one of their very few English members.

At the Baldwin Library, where I first saw American children's books in any quantity, the volumes are shelved with their English contemporaries, and it was the contrast between the two traditions that struck me from the very first. I have found that this initial impression has dictated the shape the present book has taken: while trying to chart the history of American children's reading, I have compared their books with those being offered to English children. Not only are the English classics well enough known to provide some sort of anchorage in unfamiliar seas, but the differences between the two approaches reflect fascinating differences in the respective cultures.

Most writing on early English children's books has been influenced ultimately by F. J. Harvey Darton's *Children's Books in England*, first published in 1932. For American books there is no Darton, and I am uneasily aware that in some chapters I have been trying to piece together an overall impression from perhaps a too random selection of books. But my feeling has always been that if I could provide a skeleton outline of the first three centuries, it would be a starting point, and others could take it further forward. I have deliberately included a much greater diversity of material in the first chapters, bringing in religious instruction and schoolbooks, as well as books not primarily written for children though read by them, because until the last century most young readers would have been far more familiar with these than with any recreational books of their own. Nearly all histories exclude such matter – even Welch in his bibliography and William Sloane in his account of seventeenth-century children's books. Indeed, the books to which most authorities choose to confine themselves give only a partial picture.

In later chapters I have used memoirs of childhood to give some idea of social background and reading habits. I have taken the history up to the first decades of this century and *The Rootabaga Stories*, Carl Sandburg's memorable evocation of the Midwest in the form of nonsense as Edward Lear would have understood it (nonsense and fantasy in America for generations had to struggle against fears that they represented the worst form of fiction). The books of the post-1920s have been fairly thoroughly covered already, and there is a notably good summary by Sally Allen McNall in *American Childhood* (1985).

Many friends in the US have helped and encouraged me, and have been generous in the uniquely American way with their hospitality, information and gifts of material. I am well aware that without them it would have been impossible to write this book. Paul and Ethel Heins, former editors of the *Horn Book Magazine*, have been munificent hosts, providing me with a Boston base, driving me to libraries and on sightseeing trips and effecting introductions, and I have learned more than I can say from talking to them. I remember with particular gratitude Paul's guided tour of old Boston, which gave me the feel of the city that plays such a dominant part in this book. Peggy Coughlan of the Library of Congress has been another generous host, has given unlimited time to my queries, drawn my attention to rarities which otherwise would have escaped my notice; my desk in the Library was kept supplied with treasures until I had to be dragged from them to catch the plane home. *Yankee-Doodle's Literary Sampler* (1974), the compendious anthology of prose, poetry and pictures which she and Virginia Haviland selected from children's books in the Library, has been one of the most useful books in my own reference library.

Robert Bator in Chicago, the best of all correspondents, has since 1979 given me a running commentary on the American scene, and has annually gathered up and dispatched a consignment of juvenile books of the sort unobtainable in any library here. I am particularly indebted to him for the boys' fiction he found for chapter 7. Selma Richardson of the University of Illinois Graduate School of Library Science at Urbana–Champaign, under whose auspices I first visited the US in 1979, has been unfailingly generous, as has been her predecessor Alice Loehrer, who showed me Chicago and introduced me to many friends. With Thelma Minard in New Hampshire I could at last get some idea, after exclusively urban experience of America, of the rural background against which so many children's books of the past were set, and I first saw several of the Sunday school books referred to in chapter 4 in the now disused church of North Wilmet of which she is custodian. Billie Levy, whose extensive collection of illustrated books has now been given to the University of Connecticut, has been lavish with hospitality, taken me to literary sites in Hartford, given me books and introduced me to people she felt could help. I am particularly grateful for the way she located a copy of James Kirke Paulding's *A Christmas Gift from Fairyland* in the library of Trinity College, Hartford. Virginia Reynolds has shown much kindness and arranged for me to visit the library at Princeton. John Seelye, of the University of Florida, has been a stimulating presence when we have coincided at the AAS, has lent me his house in Gainesville so that I could work at the Baldwin Library, and has given me

my most treasured possession – an early *New England Primer*. Betsy Beinecke Shirley has been a most generous and unfailing source of help with illustrations; chapters 3 and 6 have drawn heavily on her magnificent collection of American children's books (many of which have already been given to the Beinecke Library at Yale). Susan Gannon has found material for me from the Scudder papers at Harvard. At home, Caroline Dawnay over a long period has given me much appreciated support; it is mostly due to her persistence that this book makes its appearance. Sue Phillpott has put the manuscript into its final shape with her customary meticulous care, on many occasions saving me from myself. Sylvia Gardner, now in charge of the Opie books at the Bodleian Library, has searched for many specific illustrations for me. Michael Dudley at the Ashmolean Museum has photographed from my own books.

There are so many friends in Worcester and Gainesville who have made my visits memorable that it is hard to know where to begin, but to Marcus McCorison, late President of the American Antiquarian Society, and to all his staff I must repeat my deep sense of indebtedness – in particular to Joanne Chaison, Head of Readers' Services, who has given expert help and advice over illustrations. I shall for ever be grateful to Sam Gowan of the University of Florida Libraries whose invitation to make the presentation speech at the opening of the Baldwin Library initiated this whole project, and to Ruth Baldwin herself, who presided over its first tentative beginnings and made me aware of the unmined richness of American children's books of the past.

Oxford, 1993

Introduction

Sam Patch, shown on the frontispiece leaping from a church steeple, seems to embody two of the dominant qualities of American children's books of the last century – unbounded energy and optimism. Sam, a folk-hero of his time whose exploits are described in a later chapter, turned his one great talent to sound commercial profit, and in his vigour and resolution resembled many a storybook boy (though unlike most of them he finally overreached himself and came to disaster).

This same sense of purpose characterizes the first published American discourse, preached by Robert Cushman to the second contingent of Pilgrims in Plymouth, Massachusetts, in 1621. He exhorted his congregation in a way that was to become very familiar in the years that followed, stressing the need for industry, plain living and individual effort. Warming to the theme of idleness and enumerating some aspects of it, he went on: 'Such idle Droanes are intollerable in a setled Common-wealth, much more in a Common-wealth which is but as it were in the bud.' Two hundred and fifty years later, though the commonwealth was established and hugely prospering, American Sunday school writers were still urging a single-minded industry and purposefulness in which all distractions were to be avoided.

But in the preface to the published sermon Cushman made an assertion that was disputable even then: 'New-England [is] called, not onely ... because Captaine Smith hath so entituled it in his Description, but because of the resemblance that is in it, of England the native soile of English-men.' No doubt he said this partly to comfort the homesick and the apprehensive, but from the start the differences between the two cultures, if not the landscapes, were marked. Back in Old England there was nothing like the same concentration of purpose – Cushman in effect admitted this in his derogatory remarks about the recent Virginian settlers. And the differences extended to the children. In a new country where everyone, even the youngest, had a part to play in the household economy, and where

opportunities seemed limitless, children grew up very fast; from early days travellers remarked on their assurance and independence. But it was not until the 1840s that these cultural differences become discernible in children's books.

At first the New World had mostly imported or pirated the books that it gave to its young. Then the Revolutionary War obliged publishers to find writers nearer home for their schoolbooks. These they took seriously; the colonists had long been aware of the importance of education, but there was now a growing realization that they should develop their own style of teaching, better suited to a new country than was the outmoded dependence on classical learning to be found in British schools. In 1783, in his introduction to the book that was to standardize American spelling, Noah Webster says with passion that America viewed the vices of the British 'with abhorrence, their errours with pity, and their follies with contempt'.[1] Among the follies he included the supremacy of Greek and Latin in the school curriculum and the neglect of the English language. This he sought to remedy, and indeed his *Grammatical Institute of the English Language* long played a fundamental part in American education.

But though he defiantly writes of his country's new identity, 'the United States', and repeats the word 'American', there is little evidence of radically different social ways in the passages he composed for his readers. Indeed, the leisured courtliness of the 'familiar Phrases, and easy Dialogues, for young beginners' have a markedly Old World flavour:

> Sir, your most humble servant.
> I have the pleasure to be yours.
> I hope you are very well.
> I am very well, Sir, I thank you.
> How do they do at your house?
> They are all well.
> And you, Madam, how do you do?
> Pretty well. Very well.

It was natural that American writing for the young should make a beginning with schoolbooks. It was some time before conditions would be ripe for recreational books. As Webster had written, 'It commonly requires length of time and favourable circumstances to diffuse and establish a sentiment among the body of the people.'[2] It took another war, that of 1812, to goad publishers into looking for native talent. And even when this was found, early stories show little national feeling. They are remarkably similar not only to each other, but to their English models too. There is no strong sense of place, no apparent difference in manners or daily life, and it is usually difficult to decide whether a publication with, say, a Boston, a Hartford or a New Haven imprint has been composed by a local author or copied from a forgotten English book.

So for the first century and a half, and more, of the history of American children's reading, nearly all their books had been written in England. In these early years, covered in Part I of this book, *Ties with England*, it is instructive to discover which works were popular in the new colonies, which influenced American writing, and which – like fairytales and romantic legends – were frowned upon or had little appeal. To the seventeenth century, though it produced little in the way of children's books, I have devoted a long chapter, since it is crucial to what came later. Culturally New England was the dominant colony then, and it was not just the Puritans' emphasis on hard work, thrift and material gain, but their deep-rooted distrust of leisure and of the imagination, and their abhorrence of fiction (the 'sporting lie' as they termed it), that shaped later attitudes. But there was an additional, positive quality: the concern with home and the family. For Puritans, the home and the parents presiding over it had the sanctity and the authority that the Church and the priest had held in past ages, and the domestic novel owed much to this – as Horace Scudder, himself the child of a Calvinist home, was to note two centuries later. The fact that this is a genre at which American writers have always excelled must be attributed to those early beginnings in seventeenth-century New England.

Part II, *An American Style*, shows a parting of the ways. From the late 1820s American children's books began to take their own course. The scene becomes recognizably New World, and likewise the child characters. In the magazine *Juvenile Miscellany* for September 1826, for instance, in a story called

'The Little Rebels' – we are told it is founded on fact – we meet the prototypes of the assured, forthright, articulate children who are so characteristic of the nineteenth-century story. It is the time of the Revolutionary War; the scene is Boston Common, where a crowd of boys form up and march with drum and fife and colours to the English general in his tent:

'We come to complain of the insults and outrages of your soldiers. They break our kite strings, ruin our skating pond, and steal our drums from us. We have spoken more than once, to no purpose; and now we have come to say, that we cannot, and we will not endure it any longer.' *General* [aside to his aide]: 'Good heavens! liberty is in the very air, and the boys breathe it.'

The 1820s also saw the advent of Samuel Goodrich's Peter Parley books, in which the narrator, Parley, dispenses information in a manner that was to become immensely popular with his readers. The Parley style was didactic, but more informal than the turgid little compilations of facts that hack writers in England were producing about this time, and other American writers took it up. Goodrich also conducted a fierce ideological war against fairy-tales and nursery rhymes. A true child of the New World, he felt that a rational, properly educated generation should have no dealings with these relics of a credulous past. And the great nineteenth-century educator Jacob Abbott, though never as vehement as Goodrich, was also dismissive of fairy-tales. His Rollo, who idly wishes for an Aladdin's lamp, is convinced by his father's calm reasoning that it would not make him any happier, and that one's own honest toil brings the greatest reward.

It is interesting that the same years that saw the emergence of Peter Parley also saw the development of the Father Christmas legend. Early New York publishers might not know how to spell the Santa Claus that the Dutch settlers had brought over with them but, judging by the ferocity with which one of them attacked 'old Santa-Claw' in 1814 as a preposterous lie, he was a well known figure even then – the only 'fairy' that immigrants were to bring over from the Old World. The first Christmas book featuring Santa Claus with his flying sleigh and reindeer was published in New York in 1821, a year before Clement C. Moore wrote his poem 'A Visit from St Nicholas'. After that, the idea of

"NOW TO FILL THE STOCKINGS AS QUIETLY AS POSSIBLE."

Santa Claus – an American contribution to fairy legend. From A Christmas Alphabet
Published by the McLoughlin firm c. 1900.

the Christmas Eve descent down the chimney to fill children's stockings was ineradicable, whatever the rationalists might say.

The rational approach favoured by Goodrich and Abbott and their kind had been characteristic of English writing for the young in the eighteenth century; it is to be found in works as various as *Little Goody Two-Shoes* and the educational treatises composed by Richard Lovell Edgeworth and his daughter, the great Maria. But by the middle years of the next century the pendulum in England was swinging back. Fairy-tales had been rediscovered. For a century or more they had been associated with the ignorant, the foolish, those who knew no better. But the scholarly compilations of the Grimm brothers – a translation of some of the stories appeared in England in 1823 – seemed to make the genre respectable in a way that the previous century's translations of Charles Perrault's fairy-stories did not. (This may in part have been due to the fact that the English traditionally equate the French with frivolity, the Germans with high seriousness.) Further respectability was bestowed on fairy-tales by the writings of Hans Andersen, first translated in 1846. The bittersweet flavour of the Andersen tales, strongly infused with moral reflection, was very much to Victorian taste, and he had many imitators.

Andersen had American admirers too, notably Horace Scudder who in the 1860s succeeded in persuading him to contribute to the *Riverside Magazine for Young People*, which Scudder edited. But one is conscious through most of the century of many authors' and publishers' misgivings about fairy-stories. Though there were occasional ventures into fantasy, some of them of great distinction, like James Kirke Paulding's *A Christmas Gift from Fairyland* in 1838 and Christopher Cranch's *The Last of the Huggermuggers* in 1855, these were to disappear unremembered, and the genre did not become popular until Frank Baum wrote *The Wonderful Wizard of Oz* in 1900.

The place of fantasy in American juvenile fiction was to some extent taken by humour. Comic supermen of the Davy Crockett and Paul Bunyan sort had greater appeal than romantic heroes. George Wilbur Peck's 'Bad Boy', uproariously funny to 1880s readers, could be considered a version of Crockett – who according to the *Crockett Almanac* of 1837 told Congress complacently, ' "I'm a leetle the savagest crittur you ever did see" ', then proceeded to hurl

all manner of abuse at the Members. Joel Chandler Harris's *Uncle Remus*, the first collection of American popular legends to make any mark, was originally marketed as humour, and America took more readily to Mother Goose's nursery rhymes than to fairy-tales. For fairies to be popular, it seems they had to be comical, like Palmer Cox's Brownies, and it is the humorous verse, such as John Trowbridge's 'Darius Green and his Flying Machine', that stands out in anthologies. (Some thirty years before the Wright brothers succeeded in launching themselves into the air, young Darius tries to fly and comes a cropper. As he picks himself up he says, ' "Wal, I like flyin' well enough, but the' ain't sich a thunderin' sight/ O' fun in't when yo' come to light." ')

Earlier in the century Samuel Goodrich had waged a war against nonsense and fantasy, which he sought to replace with fact. His vast output of informative Peter Parley books flitted lightly over a broad spectrum of topics geographical, historical and zoological, some of which he knew a little about, some nothing. But he opened windows to children who had no expectation of seeing the sights he described, and in his way fed their imagination. The relaxed Parley method of purveying information continued in the form of travelogues, at the peak of their popularity in the 1870s, in which authors – many of them distinguished – worked gobbets of history and geography and general culture around engravings that happened to be part of their publishers' stock. This rarely resulted in memorable literature, but the books were popular. 'It is not difficult to understand the ready appreciation of such writing on the part of parents and educators ... [They] felt they were giving their young people something of undisputed value.'[3]

Sunday school books played a large part in the reading of Victorian children on both sides of the Atlantic. But each country had its distinctive style, and except for such extravaganzas as Susan Warner's *The Wide, Wide World* and Maria Cummins' *The Lamplighter* (which most people now would consider romantic escapism rather than literature of an 'improving' kind), and the harrowing stories of London street waifs such as Hesba Stretton's *Jessica's First Prayer*,[4] there was not much two-way traffic; the difference in social expectations was too great. The English Sunday school fiction tended to stress the importance of doing one's

DARIUS GREEN AND

What 's he got on ? I van, it 's wings !

An' t' other thing ? I vum, it 's a tail !

An' there he sets like a hawk on a rail !

Steppin' careful, he travels the length

Of his spring-board, and teeters to try its

strength.

Now he stretches his wings, like a monstrous

bat;

Peeks over his shoulder, this way an' that,

Fer to see 'f the' 's any one passin' by;

But the' 's on'y a ca'f an' a goslin' nigh.

46

'Darius Green and his Flying Machine', a famous comic poem by J. T. Trowbridge written thirty years before the Wright brothers took flight in 1903. This edition of 1910 is illustrated by Wallace Goldsmith (Boston and New York, 1910).

duty in that state of life to which it should please God to call his children, as the Church of England catechism put it. Readers were discouraged from supposing that they could move to a higher level of society. Flora Thompson described the daily scripture lessons at her Oxfordshire village school in the 1880s. The rector, she said, 'spoke to them from a great height, physical, mental and spiritual'.

The children must not lie or steal or be discontented or envious. God had placed them just where they were in the social order and given them their own special work to do; to envy others or to try to change their own lot in life was a sin of which he hoped they never would be guilty.[5]

And though by the time she left school attitudes were changing a little and the new teacher told them about boys who had risen on their own merits, this still differed markedly from the rags-to-riches theme characteristic of so much American Sunday school writing, where individual effort could bring untold wealth, and the doctrine 'If I do no wrong, something good will come to me' prevailed. Even temperance literature took on a different hue. English tracts on the subject were sometimes tear-jerking, more often dull, but they were never best-selling shockers like T. S. Arthur's *Ten Nights in a Bar-Room* (1854) with its arresting descriptions of delirium tremens and of savage violence – ' "I caught a single glance at his face. It was covered with blood, and every feature seemed to have been

literally trampled down, until all was a level surface." ' Like others in this field, Arthur discovered
that the promotion of godliness could be a rich
source of profit and need not cramp an author's
style.

The influence that the *McGuffey Eclectic Readers*
exerted on the minds of American schoolchildren
in the last century has been often discussed. But
Sunday school libraries also played a large part in
shaping the American character. From the start it
had been the practice of *all* respectable American
parents to send their children to Sunday school,
whereas in England the schools were more for the
poor and ignorant and did not expect to take the
offspring of the prosperous, educated classes. For
many, the Sunday school library provided the only
fiction acceptable to authority, and the message that
dominated the welter of 'virtuous twaddle', as one
indignant clergyman called it in 1870, was that any
pleasure that distracted a child from getting on in
life was wrong and must be avoided. The manifold
prohibitions ranged from circuses to storybooks,
and it is ironical that William Cardell's *The Story
of Jack Halyard* (1825), whose hero execrated such
English books as Mother Goose and worshipped
Benjamin Franklin, should itself be condemned as
a distraction in a Sunday school life of President
Garfield fifty-five years later.[6]

And here we have a clue to the factors underlying
nineteenth-century differences between American
and English children's books. Victorian England –
those in it who could afford to do so – had a high
regard for leisure. There was until the First World
War a sizeable section of upper-class society which
had nothing whatever to do but enjoy itself. This
emphasis on leisure, which went with a spirit of
amateurism, affected not only those with inherited
wealth, but the professional classes as well. American visitors who were appalled by the destitution
of the city poor, and deplored the immense gulf
between rich and poor, still could admire the placid
tempo of life led by the more fortunate. 'He is
satisfied if he is slowly accumulating; takes life
easy and enjoys himself as he goes along,' said one
observer in the 1840s of the typical English businessman. He contrasts this with the hustle of his
own country: 'Of how many Americans can it be
said, they started on nothing – worked hard – got
suddenly rich – became dyspeptic – just got ready
to enjoy life – lost their fortune by speculating, or
– were blown up in a steam-boat?'[7]

Given a leisurely approach to adult life, it was
only to be expected that the upper- and middle-class
English childhood was prolonged. More than this,
it was spent in seclusion, separated from the adult
world. For girls it did not end until they emerged
from the schoolroom at eighteen; for boys it could
be said to last all through their university days.
During those sequestered years the young undoubtedly were made to work at lessons, but they
played with an intensity – imaginative games in
the nursery, team games at school, field sports for
the country gentry – perhaps rarely equalled in
their adult life. Authors such as Charles Lutwidge
Dodgson (Lewis Carroll), Robert Louis Stevenson,
Kenneth Grahame, George MacDonald, Andrew
Lang, J. M. Barrie, from a wide variety of backgrounds, all created their own imaginary worlds
in childhood, which profoundly affected their writing in adult life.

Young Americans, on the other hand, mingled far
more with the adult world. These immigrants' lives
changed as soon as they reached the other side of
the Atlantic, as can be seen from *Our Cousins in
Ohio* (1849), a little book pieced together by the
Quaker writer Mary Howitt (1799–1888) from the
diaries of her sister Emma Alderson. The Aldersons
left England in 1842 and settled near Cincinnati
where they lived in comfortable prosperity, in con-
siderably easier circumstances than the Howitts
back in England. Meggy and Herbert Howitt lead
sheltered nursery lives, described by their mother
in *The Children's Year* (1847). They play at being
grown-up with their toy stove and their Swiss
Family Robinson house. Nine-year-old Willy Alderson, Florence who is eight and Nanny who is six,
on the other hand, all have their share of duties in
a household where there is no thought of a separate
child world. Before they can play they have not only
their lessons to prepare, but there is the corn to
husk, potatoes to dig, the cows to fetch, the pigs to
feed.

This type of sturdy, self-reliant child, accustomed
to associating with adults on an equal footing,
fascinated some English travellers. But the precocious assurance repelled others, one of whom noted
in 1875:

I have never discovered that there were any American
children. Diminutive men and women in process of growing
up into big ones, I have met with, but the child, in the
full sense attached to that word in England, a child with

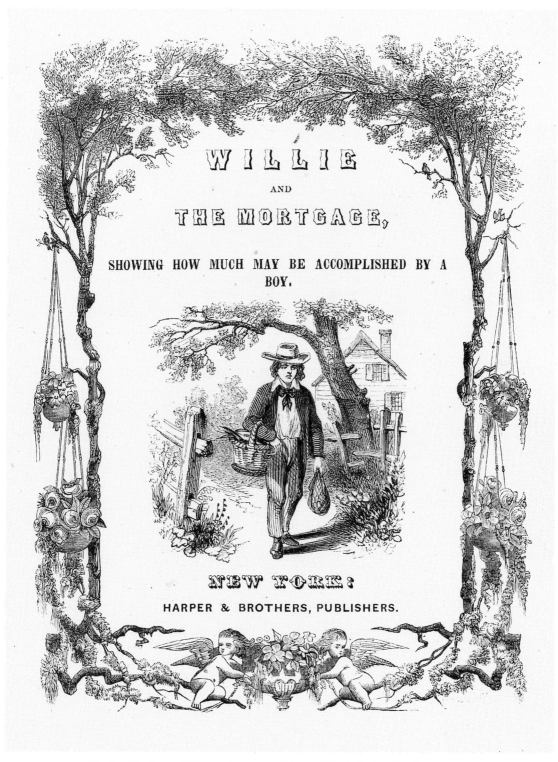

Sturdy self-reliance. Title-page from one of Jacob Abbott's books (New York, 1854).

its rosy cheeks and bright joyous laugh, its docile obedience and simplicity, its healthful play and its disciplined work, is a being almost unknown in America.[8]

This author and most of her English contemporaries had the same ideals for childhood: it should combine the spontaneity of Rousseau's Émile with the innocent joy of Blake, carefully trained on a framework of Victorian order and Christian duty. A separate nursery world was a phenomenon peculiar to England, and to upper- and middle-class nineteenth-century England at that, but many seemed to suppose it was the way that right-minded parents had reared their young since the beginning of time. They also considered that any country affluent enough to be able to afford a leisured nursery environment for its children was wrong-headed, if not totally perverse, if it chose to make adults of them as soon as it could.

The long, encapsulated childhood of the Victorians certainly helped nurture imaginative writing, but it was less conducive to the evolution of the family story. The works of Charlotte Yonge, Mary Louisa Molesworth, Juliana Horatia Ewing were limited in their appeal. They turn far too much on the middle-class mores of the time, on long-discarded prejudices and taboos, on class distinctions – now meaningless, but which once seemed of cosmic significance. And since English children were not allowed to penetrate the kitchen regions, Victorian domestic stories lacked a social dimension. They seem rarefied now, and must always have been so regarded by American readers.

But the strong sense of home that is noticeable in American writing, the image of a family gathered round the hearth, with the doors barred and windows shuttered against the hostile world outside, made for domestic stories with a universal appeal. The kitchen here is the focal point, the source of warmth and companionship, as well as of food and comfort. Food for the prosperous English was something that was prepared by unseen hands and sent upstairs three times a day. It might be palatable, or it might not; the consumers appeared to have little control over the results, short of hiring a new cook, which was always a troublesome and uncertain business. But in an American farming family all members of the household collaborated in the growing and preparation of the food, and the consumption of it might be remembered with passionate intensity:

Six months had passed since the prairie soil was broken for the corn, and now we should see it no more till it came into the house in the form of golden meal, all ready for the bread pan, baked in the oven, and set steaming hot on the table for breakfast or supper, about an inch thick, as yellow as rich gold, the top baked to a brown crust, the whole cut into good-sized squares in the pan. We cut the pieces through the middle and spread them with fresh home-made butter; and this, with home-cured bacon, and eggs laid in the sweet-smelling hay of the old barn, by hens fattened on corn, surpassed any dish I have ever eaten.[9]

And celebrations and family occasions centred on food, which had an enormous appeal to English children, habitually reared in conditions of considerable austerity.

They also warmed to the optimism in American books. Debilitating illness and death stalked through too many English stories; heroes and heroines wasted away with unspecified spinal ailments; if the poor did not die they nevertheless remained poor. English authors did not allow themselves the fairy-tale intervention of rich benefactors such as that gratifyingly bestowed by Margaret Sidney on the five little Peppers and their mother (1881), or by Alice Hegan Rice upon Mrs Wiggs of the Cabbage Patch (1901). There was, besides, in the later nine-

Thanksgiving Day – arrival at the old home.
Illustration by Winslow Homer, a regular contributor
to Harper's Weekly *and the* Riverside Magazine, *in*
Harper's Weekly, *27 November 1858.*

teenth century an American informality that English readers found very appealing. It is best seen in periodicals such as *St Nicholas* and *Harper's Young People*, which not only attracted the best writers of the day but never condescended or hectored, as their English contemporaries were apt to do. Though the long-lived *Boy's Own Paper* and the *Girl's Own Paper* commanded loyalty and respect, they never achieved the international circulation of the American magazines; the gaiety and high spirits are missing, and the editorial responses in the correspondence columns too often have a repressive *de haut en bas* quality.

This informality is also noticeable among the characters encountered in stories; Part III of this book, *Differing Ideals*, compares American and English aspirations for their young. American heroines in the latter half of the last century were allowed a far greater degree of high spirits and independence than English contemporaries – qualities that were evident in real life too. The historian Alexis de Tocqueville, who visited the United States in 1831, said that he had been 'frequently surprised, and almost frightened, at the singular address and happy boldness with which young women in America contrive to manage their thoughts and their language'.[10] An English visitor some thirty years later reported much the same, adding that he did not recollect 'to have seen a bashful girl in the United States'.[11] English girls who were unremittingly chaperoned and obliged to observe elaborate codes of propriety were fascinated by such heroines as Ellen Montgomery in Susan Warner's *The Wide, Wide World*, who by the mere expedient of designating a young man her 'brother' was permitted to spend hours alone with him and even to receive his caresses. Tomboys and 'romps' featured in American stories long before they were countenanced in England, and the poise noted by so many travellers can be found in heroines as various as Frances Hodgson Burnett's Sara Crewe (essentially American, though the book's setting is English), and the small Kentucky girl who tells her grandfather she is called the Little Colonel because she has got ' "such a vile tempah, and I stamps my foot" ', just like him.[12]

While an English girl could feel part of the *Little Women* family and relish the good fortune of the five little Peppers, as well as absorbing practical detail about American schools, pastimes and small-town life from such books as *What Katy Did, Rebecca*

"YOU ARE NOT KIND."

Assured, forthright and articulate; Sara Crewe confronts her headmistress. From Frances Hodgson Burnett: Sara Crewe *(London and New York, 1888).*

of *Sunnybrook Farm* and *Daddy Long-Legs*, their brothers never to the same extent identified with American boys. Indeed, apart from Mark Twain, American boys' authors were hardly known in England. Part of the trouble probably lay in the patriotic sentiments – xenophobic so far as English books were concerned – that made the boys' literature of both countries virtually unexportable. There was also the speed at which American boys grew up. Already young capitalists, they were supporting their families and carving out a future while English boys, still dependent on pocket money, were tumbling around playing fields. Besides, while the American boy was encouraged to strike out for himself, the ethic on which all books for British boys were founded was loyalty to the group.

Nor did the English male understand the nostalgic yearning for vanished boyhood that became fashionable in certain American books at the turn of the century – the conviction that the prison-house closed around one after the age of twelve. A French analyst in the 1950s observed the same great difference between her French and American patients. For the former, 'the diploma which certifies the end of studies suddenly liberates the child'. But for Americans it was adult life that threatened their freedom, the pre-adolescent years that were most enviable: 'The adults dream of their lost childhood – the golden age which they can only find in regression.'[13] The English child of prosperous parents was different again. Unlike his French counterpart he had been encouraged to play all through his early life, and as he entered adolescence he still had many years of freedom ahead. Those from a poor home were unlikely to want to return to childhood; as with the French, release would only come when they had left school.

It is Booth Tarkington's three *Penrod* stories, the first of which was published in 1914, which bring the American style closer to the British one. Here is a boy growing up in a small Midwestern town, who has no responsibilities and the sort of leisure that his middle-class English contemporaries would have expected but which certainly had not hitherto been a commonplace in American boys' books. He also has an intense imaginary life – again, a rarity. There had been plenty of 'Bad Boys' since Thomas Bailey Aldrich had begun the fashion for stories about mischievous lads in 1870, but readers and writers alike had been aware that all too soon the carefree feet must 'Like a colt's for work be shod', as John Greenleaf Whittier put it in 'The Barefoot Boy'. Tarkington's Penrod, however, has no thought of any future; education is not the key to advancement but 'a dreadful burden', and he dreams his life away. And as far as his family are concerned, his dreaming is far more desirable than the bursts of activity which inevitably lead to mayhem. What is even more remarkable is that in 1922 an English writer, Richmal Crompton, should have taken over virtually the whole scenario for her own Bad Boy series. Up to then cultural differences would have precluded this.

The year 1922 – and Carl Sandburg's *Rootabaga*

Stories – is the point to which I have taken this history. These last are perhaps the most strikingly original of any writing for American children, influenced by no predecessor, like nothing but themselves. They celebrate the American landscape and way of life, but they do it with fantastic imagery and extravagant nonsense. They represent the 'sporting lie' at its extreme limits; they have departed as far as it is possible to depart from the doctrine of usefulness preached by Robert Cushman back in 1621, and by his contemporaries and successors.

NOTES

1. Noah Webster: *A Grammatical Institute of the English Language*, Part I (Hartford, Conn., 1783), introduction.

2. ibid.

3. Virginia Haviland: 'The Travelogue Storybook of the Nineteenth Century', *The Hewins Lectures 1947–1962* (Boston, 1963), 27.

4. Hesba Stretton [Sarah Smith]: *Jessica's First Prayer* (London, 1867).

5. Flora Thompson: *Lark Rise to Candleford* (London, 1945), 173.

6. William Thayer: *From Log Cabin to White House* (Boston, 1880).

7. C. Edwards Lester: *The Glory and the Shame of England* (London, 1841).

8. Thérèse Yelverton: *Teresina in America* (London, 1875), 263.

9. Francis Grierson [Benjamin Shepard]: *The Valley of the Shadows: recollections of Lincoln County, 1858–63* (Boston and New York, 1909), 109.

10. Alexis de Tocqueville: *Democracy in America* [1835] (trans. Henry Reeve, London, 1862), II, 238.

11. Thomas Grattan: *Civilized America* (London, 1859), II, 57.

12. Annie Fellows Johnston: *The Little Colonel* (Boston, 1895).

13. Françoise Dolto: 'French and American Children as Seen by a French Analyst', in *Childhood in Contemporary Cultures*, ed. Margaret Mead and Martha Wolfenstein (Chicago, 1955).

Part One

TIES WITH ENGLAND

1. Children of Godly Ancestors

THE NEW COLONIES

'Nothing in our more diffuse civilisation,' wrote William Sloane in his account of seventeenth-century children's books, 'quite holds the pivotal position, the centrality, which religion held in seventeenth-century England and America. To man's relation with God all the other circumstances of his life were peripheral . . . This centrality of religion, which gave the period its peculiar hue and makes it for us at once remote and strangely fascinating, gave it also an extraordinary singleness of purpose.'[1] He did not include schoolbooks in his survey, but the same purpose would have been found in education. Young children learned their letters from hornbooks, on which the alphabet and syllabary were followed by the invocation to the Trinity and the Lord's Prayer. They moved straight from this to their catechism and the Bible. In grammar schools the Latin texts they read were for the most part moral precepts culled from classical writers. Even the standard Latin grammar – written by William Lily in the previous century – was prefaced by a code of conduct.

Thus it is no surprise to find that religious books dominated the libraries brought out by the settlers to the new colonies across the Atlantic. In New England – where so many of the newcomers had made the perilous journey solely because of their religious beliefs – this might be expected. But it was the same with more hedonistic immigrants in the Chesapeake Bay region. A third of the books listed in the 1690 inventory of the property of Colonel John Carter of Lancaster County, Virginia, for instance, were religious works.[2] As for the Dutch settlers on the banks of the Hudson, Anne Grant, writing of life in the early years of the next century, said that the children then learned to read from the Bible and a few Calvinist tracts, which was the extent of most households' libraries.[3]

Curiously, it would seem that Quakers sometimes had the most eclectic theological libraries. They did indeed hold that devotional books were profitless – 'Much Reading is an Oppression of the Mind, and extinguishes the natural Candle,' William Penn told his children[4] – and the earliest immigrants to Pennsylvania in 1682 brought out with them only the Bible and two or three Quaker texts. But from this developed a remarkably non-sectarian view: William Penn in 1693 was recommending to a young Quaker friend such religious classics as St Augustine's *City of God* and Thomas à Kempis' *The Imitation of Christ*, as well as the works of Anglican and Puritan contemporaries.[5]

But undeniably the dominant intellectual force in the early colonial years lay in New England – sometimes too much so, in the opinion of their neighbours. Anne Grant, in her description of early Albany, NY, said with some irritation that the New Englanders had sailed from their native land 'foaming with religious and political fury. They might be compared to lava, discharged by the fury of internal combustion . . . This lava . . . takes a long time to cool, and when at length it is cooled, turns to a substance hard and barren.'[6] The New Englanders from the start took a lofty view of the other colonies. Robert Cushman, preaching to the settlers in 1621, commented that there were many Virginians 'which, whilest they lived in England, seemed very religious, zealous and conscionable; and have now lost even the sap of grace, and edge to all goodnesse; and are become meere worldlings'.[7] Though there were plenty of people of their cast of thought in England, there were also many others – even at the height of Puritan zealotry during the Commonwealth of 1649–60 – who were apathetic or sulkily hostile to the new austerity which proscribed all entertainment and pleasure. The readiness with which England returned to its normal self on the restoration of the monarchy is proof enough of that.

But the New Englanders had a concentrated purpose, a zeal and a determination that mark them out from any other group of immigrants before or since. Two additional factors gave them an ascendancy over settlers further south: the environment

The arrival of the Pilgrims. From The Pilgrims,
or First Settlers of New England *(Baltimore and
Philadelphia, 1825).*

was healthy, and they had tended to immigrate in family units, a factor which permitted them to achieve quite early on an enviable stability and continuity. Indeed, their strong family life was evident from the very start, and it made its mark on their later literary culture and was specially noticeable in their children's books. Since the New England spirit shaped so many of these, it seems important to consider the Puritan outlook.

The Puritans were Calvinists. In England the spirit of the Anglican Church was against the Calvinist system, even though Calvinistic doctrine had infiltrated the Thirty-nine Articles. Calvinism, which had already for a long time been very strong in Scotland too, held that faith alone, not works, could redeem mankind; that natural man was wholly vile, corrupt

and inclined towards evil, that without God he could do nothing that was good. The purest Calvinism asserted that the human race had, after the Fall, been destined to eternal damnation, but that through the redeeming grace of Christ, God had consented to save from hell a certain pre-ordained number. But the first New England Puritans did not regard God as quite so arbitrary in his dealings with them. Their faith was a blend of pessimism about total human depravity, and of optimism that with will and effort, greater even than was needed to cultivate their harsh new land, they could achieve salvation. They were God's people, their congregations *were* the elect, and God had entered into a covenant, the Covenant of Grace, promising that he would save those who surrendered to him.

Puritanism had also a materialistic side. In England it had always made special headway among merchants, tradesmen and the self-employed, who attributed their prosperity and ascendancy over papist countries to the fact that Protestantism had purged religion of 'the slavery and incumbrances' of antiquated doctrines and ceremonies. To them thrift, industry and the accumulation of wealth were the cardinal virtues, and poverty very nearly a crime. William Ames, a divine they much revered, commended riches as useful and profitable, and declared that voluntary poverty was 'a madness to bee condemned ... Because this is to tempt God, if anyone having wherewithall to maintaine himselfe, shall cast away that, expecting sustenation from God'.[8] Not for Ames the lilies of the field.

This ruthlessness, this almost religious veneration for success, the certainty that prosperity could be equated with godliness and therefore rose and fell with the behaviour of the population, was part of New England from the very start, as was the detestation of idleness. Idleness was a lust of the flesh that brought both material and spiritual disaster, and when John Cotton, who had emigrated to the Massachusetts Bay Colony in 1633, set out in a religious work the reasons for *not* being idle, it was the material disadvantages that he stressed most.[9] Puritans were habitually uneasy about leisure and felt that every moment should be purposeful: 'Pastime also carieth many from their calling, and likewise from thrift. He that loveth pastime shall be a poore man,'[10] declared one of the books on household government very popular on both sides of the Atlantic. This theme was to dominate American Sunday school books throughout the nineteenth century; the more relaxed attitudes of the south stood no chance against it, so far as books for the young were concerned.

The Puritan way of life was to remain a force in New England for many generations to come. Lucy Larcom (1824–93) in her autobiographical *A New England Girlhood* (1889) emphasized that, though much of the grimness of earlier times had departed, she and her generation were all children of the Puritans:

The religion of our forefathers overhung us children like the shadow of a mighty tree against the trunk of which

we rested, while we looked up in wonder through the great boughs that half hid and half revealed the sky. Some of the boughs were already decaying, so that perhaps we began to see a little more of the sky than our elders; but the tree was sound at its heart. There was life in it that can never be lost to the world.

Then, as two centuries before, their elders saw to it that even the youngest children were instructed in the doctrines of their faith, and Lucy remembered that the thought of God when she was small seemed as natural as the thought of father and mother: 'The second strand in New England life then was

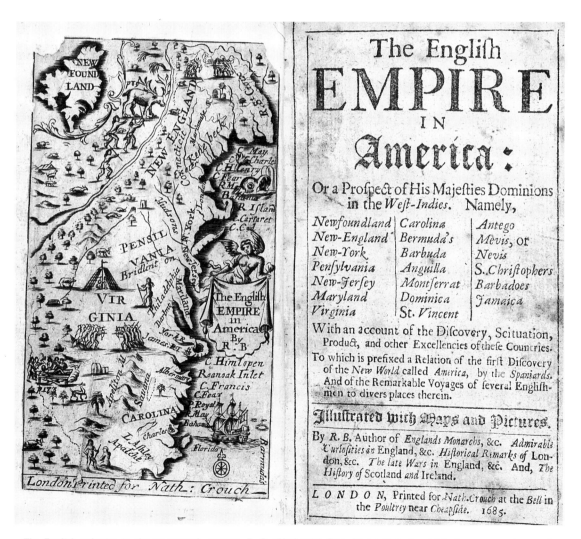

The English colonies in the seventeenth century. R. B. (Nathaniel Crouch) wrote and published many popular works for young readers.

work. We were taught to work almost as if it was a religion; to keep at work, expecting nothing else. It was our inheritance, handed down from the outcasts of Eden.' It was an ethic that was to persist long after her generation.

Horace Scudder, born fourteen years after Miss Larcom, summarized the Puritan attitude to childhood. His father's family had settled on Cape Cod in the early eighteenth century. They had preserved much of the attitudes of their forebears, and at a time when the Massachusetts churches were sharply divided by the move to Unitarianism, the Scudders stayed resolutely with orthodox Congregationalism. Horace was aware of the drawbacks of a Puritan upbringing. He wrote of the weight of personal responsibility that offered little scope for the wantonness and spontaneity of childhood – which was in effect, he said, a time of probation and suspense, accompanied by much parental anxiety and an overemphasis on the child's salvation that inhibited natural development at a natural pace. But he came from a very happy family, and though he had long been a member of the Episcopal Church by the time his *Childhood in Literature and Art* was published in 1894, he spoke eloquently of the debt that society owed to the Puritan ethic. It might have robbed childhood of its freedom, but it had laid great stress on the importance of the family:

The narratives of domestic life under puritanic control are often full of a grave sweetness ... Nor could the intense concern for the spiritual well-being of children, and religious passion reinforcing natural affection, fail to give an importance to the individual life of the family, and prepare the way for that new intelligence of the scope of childhood which was to come later to an England still largely dominated by puritan ideals.[11]

The Puritan concept of family life – though he was writing here of literature in England – was to be seen at its fullest in American domestic chronicles.

CHILDHOOD, THE FAMILY AND SALVATION

Inevitably we base our impression of seventeenth-century American childhood on New England experience, since these are the only records we have. New Englanders were zealous for the spiritual welfare of their children, and catechisms and sermons urging them to emulate their godly ancestors were among the earliest publications of the colony. We have two major diaries, kept by Samuel Sewall and Cotton Mather, plus the latter's account of his exemplary brother Nathanael, so that though we have no record of children's own experience we know fairly well what adult aspiration for them was.

Much was expected of them. Puritan children were dedicated to God from their first moments, often in the womb. 'When 'tis become Sensible to you, that you have conceived, you will do well, without any Delay, to carry even this Embryo to the Lord,' Cotton Mather told mothers, reminding them that they themselves might not survive the birth. 'Your Death has entered into you, and you may have conceived that which determines, but about Nine Months more at the most, for you to live in the World.'[12] It was customary to baptize infants on the first Sabbath of their life, but baptism was only a sign of the covenant, which was conditional upon faith and repentance. Only when they had experienced the reception of divine grace and were 'savingly converted' could they become full participants in the Covenant of Grace and partake of the Lord's Supper.

On the subject of the fate of children who died in infancy, too young to have experienced conversion, theologians for the most part remained silent. Michael Wigglesworth in *The Day of Doom* (1662), learnt by heart by many children, represented Christ as an implacable and merciless judge consigning such infants to eternal damnation:

Then to the Bar they all drew near who dy'd in
    infancy
And never had, or good or bad, effected pers'nally.
But from the womb unto the tomb were
    straightway carried,
(Or at the least, ere they transgrest) who thus
    began to plead.
'How could we sin who had not bin? or how is
    his sin our
Without consent, which to prevent we never had
    the pow'r?'

But Christ answers that Adam's fall is theirs too, and he rebukes their temerity in questioning his decree: 'You sinners are, with such a share as sinners may expect. / Such you shall have, for I do save none but my Elect.'

A New England family, 1670: David, Joanna and Abigail Mason. Attributed to the Freake-Gibbs painter (active 1670–4).

Wigglesworth's relentless application of strict Calvinist doctrine was not the norm. Cotton Mather, for instance, the father of many children who died in infancy, spoke of them with great tenderness. Likening the death of a child to the tearing off of a limb, he asked: 'Was the Infant whose decease we do deplore, one that was very pretty, one that had pretty Features, pretty Speeches, pretty Actions? Well, at the Resurrection of the Just we shall see the dear Lambs again.' He concluded with verses of his own composition, less lame than usual. The image of the child as a flower – to become a cliché later – was not common then:

> I pausing on't, this sweet refreshed my thought,
> Christ would in Glory have a Flower sweet, prime,
> And having Choice chose this my Branch forth
> brought:
> Lord tak't; I thank thee, Thou tak'st aught of mine.[13]

But those who were of an age to choose God and had not so chosen were given terrible warning:

The Waters of Baptism will be turned into Rivers of Brimstone, for the Torturing of thy Soul! O thou impious Deserter... God will dash thee against the Stones, more furiously than the Brats of Babylon, and crush thee between the Millstones of His Wrath more terribly than the Offspring of Ethiopians. Truly, such Baptised Rebels, God will Baptise them over again; he will Dip them, and Drench them, in that Burning Lake, from whence the smoke of their Torment shall ascend for ever and ever.[14]

Precisely how long the innocence of childhood could be deemed to last was never, so far as I can discover, exactly formulated, but Mary Livermore (born in 1820, brought up as a strict Baptist in Boston) supposed it to be seven years. Her father accepted the Calvinist faith 'in its entirety and severity' and expounded it to his family with power and eloquence, so that Mary before she was ten had all the doctrine at her fingertips. When she was seven she was shown her newly born sister: 'A great rush of affection welled up within me at the sight of the little one, and an infinite feeling of pity as I thought what her doom might be. "Oh, mother" I cried, "don't let's keep the baby; let's send her back to God! What if she doesn't grow up to be a Christian, and is lost!" '[15]

Countless were the sermons addressed to children on the subject of what was known as early piety. Whatever the preachers' convictions might be about God's ultimate plan for the very young, they knew it was an imperative duty to urge conversion on them all, regardless of age. None knew when death might overtake a child; all must be prepared. 'Man's Life is the Shadow of Smoak, the Dream of a Shadow; one doubteth whether to call it a Dying Life or a Living Death,' the author of *Apples of Gold*[16] told his readers. This book of religious instruction, imported by Boston booksellers from London, was pressed into the hands of thousands of children, as was Joseph Alleine's *Allarum to the Unconverted*, which under its later title of *A Sure Guide to Heaven* was to remain a classic into the nineteenth century.

But sermons on early piety were directed at parents as well as children, for the family unit was assuming a new importance. The writers of books about family government described it again and again as a church and a commonwealth in which the father was responsible for the spiritual welfare of each member. 'A Holy Family is a place of Comfort; a Church of God,' Richard Baxter wrote

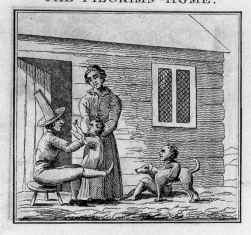

6

THE PILGRIMS HOME.

And soon the Pilgrim's hut arose
    Amid the savage wild;
And round its door at evening close
    Sat Father, wife and child:

The holy scriptures made the light
    Their feeble steps to guide;
They asked a blessing morn and night,
    And cared for nought beside.

Family life. From The Pilgrims, or First Settlers of New England *(Baltimore and Philadelphia, 1825).*

in *The Poor Man's Family Book* (1674), an English work very popular in New England. In the post-Reformation family the father stood in place of the priest, and must organize the family worship. Baxter instructed him to call the family together twice daily to read a chapter of the Bible and 'some leaves of some other good Book'. If the family could sing, he prescribed a psalm; if not, the psalms should be read. 'Then in Faithful fervent Prayer, call on God through Jesus Christ, in his Spirit. And so at Evening.'

Cotton Mather's diary records the anxious care he bestowed upon his children's spiritual welfare. Since it was written for the edification of his family and ultimately for the public eye, it cannot be considered a spontaneous record, but the reader is forcibly struck by two things: firstly, his deep concern and affection for the children. The fact that they are referred to by diminutive names – Cresy, Sammy, Nibby, Katy – shows an unexpected informality, an intimacy that could not have been feigned just for posterity. Secondly, we notice the lack of allowance made for child, or indeed human, nature. Here is that blend of pessimism and optimism that has been noted before: pessimism about human depravity, optimism that children could profit from and even enjoy a regime more suited to the cloister than to everyday life. Mather kept continual watch on them, and catechized them each night on their behaviour during the day. He never let Cresy – young Increase* – 'spend many minutes with me without entring upon a Point of Conversation, that may instruct him, and enrich him'.[17]

There are frequent references to the papers that he made his children write for him on such topics as their destiny and purpose in life. He resolved that on their birthdays he must 'discourse very proper and pungent Things unto them, relating to their eternal Interests, but also to oblige them to consider, first, What is their main Errand into the World; and then, what they have done of that Errand. And such of them as are old enough to write, shall give me some written thoughts upon these Things.'[18] Such play as they were allowed must be sanctified, and lessons derived from it. He believed that 'table-talk [should be] facetious as well as instructive', but that the two elements should be continually intermixed, and therefore proposed to introduce at meals 'some sentence of the Bible, and make some useful Remarks upon it'.[19]

How American children of this period played and what they played at is not recorded. They must have kept up the games and the songs of the old country, for William Wells Newell, collecting these two hundred years later, asserted that in 'this minor but curious branch of folk-lore, the vein in the United States is both richer and purer than that so far worked in Great Britain'.[20] Keith Thomas in a recent essay has recorded some of the activities of children in Tudor and Stuart England.[21] But the fleeting glimpses of the small pleasures of childhood that we get from American writings are incidental, as in the homely analogy used by Thomas Hooker, the Connecticut theologian, in a sermon to illustrate

how the reprobate is responsible for his fate. (We notice the same tenderness that Cotton Mather used when he wrote of his children.)

Looke as it is with a childe that travels to a Fair with his father, or goeth into a crowd: hee bids him doe not gaze about and lose mee, the childe is careful to keepe his father within sight and view, and then if hee bee weake and weary, his father can take him by the hand, and lead him, or take him into his armes and carry him; or if there bee any thing hee wants or would have, his father can buy it for him.[22]

The qualities that later generations were to associate with children, and to delight in – carefree high spirits and capacity for enjoyment – were not what Puritans wished to see in them. The ideal child was certainly not a playful one, but old beyond her years. Cotton Mather said of a child that had died of 'bladders in the windpipe' (diphtheria) when she was five and a half: 'so gracious and intelligent were her expressions and behaviour, both living and dying, and so evident her faith, in Christ, [that it] was a luculent commentary on that marvellous prophecy, that the child should dye an hundred years old'.[23] And he enthusiastically described his young brother Nathanael, who had died in 1688 at the age of nineteen, as 'an Old Man without Gray Hairs upon him'.[24]

It is interesting to consider Nathanael Mather, for he and others like him were continually held up to seventeenth-century children as exemplars: 'From his very Childhood, his Book was perhaps as dear to him as his Play, and hence he grew particularly acquainted with Church-History.' His learning was prodigious and embraced all subjects, so that he was 'admirably capable of arguing about almost every Subject that fell within the Concernments of a Learned Man'. In adolescence he had passed through a phase of apostasy, but when he was sixteen 'God visited him with sore Terrors and Horrors in his wounded Soul, the Anguish whereof he thought intollerable.' He was a melancholy youth, given to fits of terrifying despair and tormented by 'Horrible Conceptions of God, buzzing about his mind'. He was full of loathing for what he conceived as his depravity, and wrote when he was sixteen,

---

* Cresy was always an anxiety. Born in 1699, by the time he was eleven his father was fearing that he would be ensnared by 'vicious and wicked lads'. In adolescence he habitually consorted with disorderly and riotous company, and in 1717 a 'Harlot big with a Bastard, accuses my poor Cresy, and layes her Belly to him'. He was to perish in a shipwreck, but his father put his death to good use in a sermon.

A nineteenth-century evangelical family assembled at domestic worship: 'the father, the priest *of the household ... is now addressing his beloved children.' From* The Well-Spring, *9 February 1844 (Massachusetts Sabbath School Society).*

on a day of fasting and prayer, that 'of the manifold Sins which I was guilty of, none so stick upon me, as that being very young, I was whittling on the Sabbath-day; and for fear of being seen, I did it behind the door'. In the end he so devoured books, his brother said, that 'it came to pass that Books devoured him'. His neglect of exercise ruined his health, and his weak body could sustain him no longer. Inactive and morbidly reflective, Nathanael was as remote as could be from the pioneers who were hewing out a new country. Nevertheless, his admiring elder brother presented him to the children of New England as 'a Mirrour, wherein you may see what *should* be done, so what *may* be done by a Young Person'.[25]

Nathanael was also dead, and it is perhaps not unfair to say that the Puritans expressed more pleasure in their dead and dying children than in their living ones. There is no doubting their love for them, but there was always the dread that a child might alienate himself from salvation. One could not even trust in apparent conversions, for these had often been proved to be false dawns. But dying in a state of grace, if we are to believe the many accounts, was by far the most joyful moment of a lifetime. 'Children are certain cares but uncertain comforts,' wrote Samuel Clarke. 'They may prove as Augustus his three children did, whom he called ... his three Ulcers, or Cankers.'[26] Nearly two hundred years later, in a famous American tract – *Agnes and the Little Key* (the key is of her coffin) – addressed to bereaved parents in 1858, the Rev. Nehemiah Adams reminded parents of this. He told the story of a clergyman praying by the bed of a sick child, and of his dismay that the mother was unable to submit to the possibility that the child might die. 'He and that mother both lived to see that child perish on the gallows by the hand of the public executioner, at the age of twenty-five.'

Cotton Mather devotes three pages to the triumphant dying of his daughter Katherine. His sister Jerusha had already died such a death:

It is the Portion of Some, to go away Triumphing into the Heavenly World . . . And so our dying Jerusha, when she certainly knew that she was to Dy, she said unto those about her; Here is a Strange Thing! When I was in Health, Death was a Terror to me. But now I know, I shall Dy, I am not at all afraid of it . . . This is a Wonderful Work of God! I know, that . . . I shall shortly be in the Heavenly Jerusalem, with an innumerable Company of Angels, and among the Spirits of Just Men made Perfect. Said she, I see things that are Unutterable! Then she Sang for Joy.[27]

The Puritan way of death was to have a great impact on children's books, as will be discussed later in the chapter.

INTELLECTUAL LIFE

To the original settlers the chances of replenishing their libraries when they were on the further side of the Atlantic must have seemed remote. Before they left England they had to think of all the contingencies that were likely to arise in a totally alien environment, a land none of them had seen. They needed a firm foundation of reference books, for they had to provide for both spiritual and physical needs – on a Virginia plantation the head of the household might have to stand in place of clergy, as well as acting as physician and lawyer. They could well be called upon to be experts in matters as diverse as architecture, surveying and farriery, and to understand about budding and grafting, bees and cider presses. They also had to consider what their family's future educational needs might be.

One English schoolmaster early in the century tried to anticipate this latter need. In 1622 John Brinsley, headmaster of Ashby-de-la-Zouch school in Leicestershire, wrote *A Consolation for our Grammar Schools* with 'ruder countries and places' in mind. He specifically named Ireland, Wales and Virginia, his concern being, he said in the dedication, 'for their soules and eternal happiness'. Interestingly, he also gave some thought to the native American, and begged the Virginian settlers 'that there be no wrong offered to the poor savage' – it was his spiritual destiny that he had in mind: 'if through the wickedness or offensive carriage of Ministers or people, minding nothing but for their owne advantage, these poore soules shall take occasion

to conceive evill of the Lord and his religion, all this hope is utterly overthrowne.'

Although in 1671 Sir William Berkeley, then governor, thanked God that there was not a printing press nor a free school in the colony (he strongly disapproved of education for the masses), there had from early days been efforts to provide an educational system. Within ten years of the first settlement of Jamestown James I had commanded the English bishops to collect money for the founding of schools. The first schemes collapsed in the disastrous Indian massacre on Good Friday 1622, which almost wrecked the colony. But in the decades that followed we can deduce from benefactions in wills that settlers were striving to set up schools. In 1635 a certain Benjamin Symmes, for instance, left two hundred acres of land and eight cows for the foundation of a school, which survived until the nineteenth century. Such schools as these were not ambitious; they taught only reading, writing and simple arithmetic, with perhaps a little Latin, and parents who wanted more had either to provide their children with private tutors or send them to England – a perilous journey then, from which many never came back. Even the College of William and Mary, established by royal charter in 1693, was in its early years little more than a grammar school. In 1697 James Blair, first president of the College, said in the *Account of the Present State of Virginia and the College* (published in 1727) that as far as education went Virginia was 'one of the poorest, miserablest, and worst countries in all America that is inhabited by Christians'. (Blair came from Scotland, which had always prided itself on its educational system.)

One early settler, at least, went out with hopes of establishing an English-style grammar school. The Rev. John Goodborne, an Anglican clergyman, took a library of 191 titles with him in 1635. Among these were two books of educational theory: Roger Ascham's *The Scholemaster*, which had been published in 1570, and John Brinsley's *Ludus Literarius* (1612), this being the quaint term then for a grammar school (whose activities, as plenty pointed out, were normally far removed from any sort of game).

Ludus Literarius laid down the aims of a grammar school, its course of studies and timetable, and listed the texts that Brinsley used in his own school. It was a strenuous day that started at six o'clock in the morning (he conceded that this was earlier than the norm), and ended at half-past five with prayers. He recommended fifteen-minute breaks for recreation, at nine and at three. These, he admitted, 'may be offensive, as they who know not the maner of them, may reproch the schoole, thinking they do nothing, but play'. However, he felt that otherwise the boys' minds would focus on games instead of on their work. He also suggested that pupils should have part of an afternoon during the week for recreation, though 'clownish sports or perilous, or yet playing for money, are in no way to be admitted'.

The curriculum centred on Latin, with Greek for the boys in their final two years. Though there might be a little elementary arithmetic, the writing of English was not taught, nor history or geography nor any modern language. Ideally, children should not enter the grammar school until they could already read the New Testament perfectly and had been grounded in Latin grammar; but often, Brinsley admitted, they did have to be taught the rudiments there. Grammar schools also saw to it that their pupils received proper religious instruction.

Brinsley was himself a Puritan – 'very severe in his life and conversation,' one of his pupils remembered – and after falling out with his bishop over doctrinal matters was obliged to leave his post. He was an authority much respected in New England, and the grammar schools set up there followed the English model as outlined in *Ludus Literarius*. The New Englanders were more successful than the Virginians in starting an educational system, and within ten years of the founding of Massachusetts Bay there was a vigorous intellectual life, with a college, a printing press and schools. At least 130 university men had come to New England by 1646 – a high proportion in a population no greater than 25,000 – and in addition there were men who had received the classical education provided by English grammar schools. The first freshman class at Harvard began their studies in the summer of 1638, and in 1647 Massachusetts declared that every town of fifty families should appoint a common schoolmaster to teach children to read and write. It was also decreed that towns of a hundred families or more should establish a grammar school. (Connecticut adopted the law in 1650, though it later modified it.) In theory the schools followed the same course of studies as Brinsley had outlined. In practice there were only a handful who were able to do so; the schools took such Latin scholars as came along, but for the most part gave only elementary instruction.

The Boston Latin School was one of the few that gave the full classical education, and it is interesting to see what books the seventeenth-century boy who went through the system on either side of the Atlantic would have read by the time he was reckoned to be ready to proceed to university. He would have spent his first three years mastering Latin grammar, and reading Aesop's fables, compilations of Latin conversation, and moral maxims such as were to be found in Cato's *Disticha* and in the popular *Sententiae Pueriles* (Sentences for Children). The fourth year proceeded to Erasmus' *Colloquies* and Ovid's *de Tristibus*. The fifth year continued with these and began Cicero's Letters, Latin prosody and composition. The sixth year read more Cicero, began Virgil, composed Latin verse, began Greek and rhetoric. The seventh and last year, by which time the boy might be sixteen, studied Cicero's Orations, Virgil, Horace, Juvenal and Persius. In Greek they read Homer, Hesiod, Isocrates and the New Testament. From this it will be gathered how abstract school reading was for the younger pupils. Apart from Aesop in the early years there was no narrative content in any of the texts until the sixth year began the *Aeneid*. Even the moral maxims they studied were ill-adapted to youth, as can be seen from examples from *Sententiae Pueriles*:

Nothing is more absurd than a lecherous old man.
Nothing is more pleasant than old age, that may take its ease.
There is an old contest betwixt the Mother-in-Law and the Daughter-in-Law.
We learn our wives' faults after marriage.

This system of education seemed immutable, and was to persist throughout the next century in both the New and the Old Worlds. 'All men covet to have their children speake latin,' Ascham had said in *The Scholemaster* in 1570, and two hundred years later this was still true. Even educational reformers like John Locke in 1693 looked upon it as 'absolutely necessary for a gentleman'.[28] One would have thought that Latin would play no part in the Quaker education, but though Friends had debated the question for over a century, it was still being taught in Pennsylvanian schools in the eighteenth century. However, when John Wilson resigned from the grammar school in Philadelphia in 1769 he wrote passionately to the overseers:

Is it not monstrous? That Christian Children intended to believe and relish the Truths of Gospel should have their early and most retentive years imbued with the shocking Legends and abominable Romances of the worst of Heathens, should be obliged to be Pimps to the detestable Lusts of Jupiter and Mars, attend the Thefts and Villany of Mercury or follow Aeneas on his Murdering Progress.[29]

This may have been the reason why younger boys were kept so long on moral maxims before they were allowed to move on to Ovid.

Nevertheless, many of those who went through this system remained devoted to the classical authors. William Byrd of Westover in Virginia (1674–1744), who had been educated in England at Felstead Grammar School, daily read Latin and Greek – sometimes two books of Homer before breakfast. With Cotton Mather and James Logan of Philadelphia, he was reckoned to own one of the most extensive colonial libraries of the early eighteenth century. John Goodborne, already mentioned, took many classical works with him, including those of Homer, Thucydides, Plutarch, Virgil, Horace and Ovid. John Winthrop, Governor of Connecticut, already in 1640 had a collection of a thousand books half of which were in Latin. In the seventeenth century readers still had infinite faith in the power of Greece and Rome to provide a basis for education, to impart wisdom and to inspire at times of crisis. Thus in England Sir Thomas Browne (1605–82) gave Plutarch's *Lives of the Noble Greeks and Romans* to his son Tom to read when the boy joined the navy. And more than a hundred years later, in 1777, John Adams wrote from Philadelphia to his son John Quincy, then ten years old, that at this time when their country was engaged in war it was specially important to prepare for 'that Part which may be allotted you to act on the Stage of Life. There is no History, perhaps, better adapted to this usefull Purpose than [*The History of the Peloponnesian War*] of Thucidides.'[30]

Of books to amuse, by contrast, there were very few, nor at first were there many among those ordered from the old country. In New England many of the immigrants had brought out volumes of poetry, and seventeenth-century 'commonplace books' kept by Harvard students have stanzas from Cowley, Herrick, Cleveland and Spenser copied into them.[31] Drama was of course excluded so far as

the Puritans were concerned, and seems to have been rarely represented in any library. The inventory of Edmund Berkeley of Middlesex County in Virginia, who died in 1718, is one of the earliest to list Shakespeare's works. But it has to be remembered that no English authors were yet considered classics in the way that Latin and Greek literature was.

Some readers would have enjoyed history. The *Jewish Antiquities* of Flavius Josephus (first translated into English in 1602), Ralegh's *History of the World* (the ancient world only), Plutarch's *Lives of the Noble Grecians and Romans* in Sir Thomas North's translation of 1579, Foxe's *Book of Martyrs* (published as *Actes and Monuments* in 1563) – all these are often to be found in inventories of colonial libraries, and were long held to be suitable reading for the young. Increase Mather, recording the death of his daughter Jerusha in 1711, said that she had been a great reader since she was four, in 'Historical Books, as well as Theological', and these probably included Plutarch, Josephus and Ralegh.

Nor would she have been particularly unusual in this. Recreational books for children are a very recent phenomenon, and did not reach significant proportions until the nineteenth century. Children of previous generations became literate and often highly literary without recourse to them. They enjoyed the sort of narratives to be found in Josephus and Foxe, and the fact that these were often bloodthirsty and macabre made their appeal even greater. But these books were, of course, available only to the few; most colonial households would have had to rely on the Bible alone. Michael Wigglesworth's *The Day of Doom*, though, reached a huge public. All 1800 copies of the first edition of 1662 were sold within the first year, which meant that in New England alone one in every twenty-five persons bought a copy. Everything about this lugubrious work in halting ballad metre is remarkable – its profound pessimism, its length and stereotyped imagery, its record as a best-seller, and the fact that it was the first work of imagination to emanate from the new colonies.

A narrative that long enjoyed Protestant favour was Nathaniel Bacon's *A Relation of the Fearful Estate of Francis Spira* (London, 1638; Boston, 1682).* It was evidently well known in New England,

---

* One of the improving books named in the publisher Newbery's adaptation of Richardson's *Clarissa* (reduced from three thousand pages to 135), a version very popular in eighteenth-century America. In an episode that does not occur in the original *Clarissa*, the Harlowe parents hurl it after the daughter they aver is obstinate, contumacious and erring, and one infers that young readers would recognize the title as required Sunday reading.

for Samuel Sewall records in his diary the anguish that it caused Betty, aged fourteen. On 22 February 1696 she came to him weeping, afraid that she would go to hell and was 'like Spira, not elected'. This narrative that so terrified her opens with the rhythms of a fairy-tale: 'In the year 1548, when the glorious Sunne of the Gospel was but newly risen in Europe; in the daies of the raigne of Edward the Sixth of that name King of England . . . in the town of Cittadella, there lived one Francis Spira, a Civil Lawyer, an Advocate of great rank and esteeme.' Spira, a papist, becomes convinced by Lutheran teaching, but strong pressure is brought to bear on him by his Church, and he recants. He falls into a stupor of despair (an almost clinical description of depression is given in the course of

a hundred-odd pages) during which the curious gather round him as though he were some sort of prodigy, and attempt to convince him that God is merciful. To no avail. Worn to nothing but sinews and bones, 'dreadful of Hell, yet coveting death . . . like a living man in Hell . . . he departed this present life'. In spite of what Betty thought, there is no talk here of God's elect; Spira's predicament was quite different and could bear no parallel to hers.

Although books for mere amusement would have had a low priority in a new country, by the 1680s booksellers' invoices are evidence that there was a market for them in Boston.[32] Admittedly, theology formed a large proportion of the imports. And there was a fair number of classical texts, dictionaries, treatises on medicine, law, accountancy, shipbuild-

Youth before and after conversion. Double frontispiece from Benjamin Keach: War with the Devil, *13th impression (London, 1728). This verse dialogue urging youth to repent was popular with Puritan families on both sides of the Atlantic.*

ing, navigation, cookery and farriery; and cate- chisms and schoolbooks in quantity. In these records there is a sprinkling of what we would call 'stories' and they, 'histories'. *Dr Faustus* was easily the most popular, and was to be printed in Boston in 1733, one of the first pieces of fiction to come from an American press. But there was a certain respect- ability about the book's theme; indeed, it was in- cluded in a consignment of otherwise theological texts dispatched to the Rev. Thomas Shephard in the 1680s. And among such items as *The Assembly's Catechism*, *Warnings to the Unclean* and *Call to Delaying Sinners* we find occasional copies of the medieval romances that had been part of popular literary culture in England for centuries – the *History of Parismus, Prince of Bohemia*; *Fortunatus*; *Valentine and Orson*; *The Destruction of Troy*; *Guy of Warwick*.

An invoice of books imported by the Boston bookseller John Usher about 1682 does contain an exceptionally large clutch of such matter, and the list is worth recording since it gives us some idea of popular English reading of the time:

1 destruction of troy; 1 Valentyn and Orson; 6 Guy of Warwick; 6 Reynard Fox; 12 dr Faustus; 6 [Tom a] Lincoln; 12 Joviall Garland; 12 Crown Garland; 6 Jack Newberry; 6 Garland of Delight; 6 fortunatus; 6 royall arbours; 8 S[c]oggins jests; 6 history of Joseph; 6 Devill and Dives; 6 Book of Knowledg; 4 Mandevill Travels.[33]*

Stories such as the first five – of chivalry, marvellous deeds, magical events, talking animals – were old even in the fifteenth century, when Caxton trans- lated *Recuyell of the Historyes of Troye*. Originally enjoyed by cultivated readers and the lower orders alike, by the seventeenth century they had become relegated to the unsophisticated and to children, who cherished them and kept them alive. In England they were to be found in chapbook versions well into the nineteenth century. Together with the bal- lads about characters such as Robin Hood and Tom Thumb, fairy-tales and traditional rhymes like Cock Robin and Simple Simon, they were part of the fabric of popular culture. The importance of such elements in a country's literary history is incalcul- able, and even if we restrict our attention to chil- dren's books it is clear that the direction that these took in England, with a unique preponderance of

fantasy and nonsense, must have been largely dic- tated by the make-believe of the past.

In medieval times such stories had been accept- able: Edward IV had directed that his six-year-old son should listen at dinner to 'such noble stories as behoveth a prince to understand and know', and in 1477 Caxton had presented the child with his *History of Jason* – a mingling of classical legend and medieval romance with a strong love interest. After the Reformation preachers and schoolmasters took a far more severe view. The stories, to their mind, were a relic of the bad old days 'when Papistrie, as a standyng poole, covered and over- flowed all England'.[34] 'Suffer these bookes to be read,' Roger Ascham warned, 'and they shall soon displace all bookes of godly learnyng.'[35]

Such denunciations were habitual throughout the sixteenth and seventeenth centuries. But the genre flourished despite the condemnation of higher author- ity. The ordinary Englishman, habitually conservat- ive and resistant to what is said from the pulpit, clung to his 'fayned fables, vayne fantasyes, and wanton stories' (as Hugh Rhodes' *Boke of Nurture* put it in 1577). A few were bold enough to challenge the moralists' view. Writing in 1709, Richard Steele said that his small godson was steeped in the old romances such as *Guy of Warwick* and *Bevis of Southampton*. Steele commended his enthusiasm and his informed views on such characters, con- sidering that 'by this Means [he] had his Thoughts insensibly moulded into the Notions of Discretion, Virtue and Honour'.[36] The anonymous English author of *The Father's Legacy, or counsels to his children* (1678) had taken the same line. Indeed, he felt that for children romance was in many ways preferable to real history:

True History represents to us only things as they are, with all their faults, their events depend more on Fortune than Reason, and the narration becomes very often very tedious, because it gives account of not extraordinary success; when on the contrary every thing in a romance is great, there Virtue and Vice are extream, and always recorded according to the measure of merit. A Thousand rare and unforeseen Adventures there, surprise the Reader, and keep him always in breath, in expectation of some other novelty which may prove still more wonderful. In fine, the Soul elevates itself by this reading, and it comes often to pass that being instructed by the excellent qualities of some imaginary

* 'Garlands' were books of ballads; 'Scoggins jests' was a compilation of jokes over which at least one moralist had shaken his head; the 'royall arbours' consisted of poems and songs.

Hero, it regains in effect some real impression of them; or some horror of Vice, from the borrowed shape of the villainous.

To the seventeenth-century Puritan, however, fiction did not only deflect the reader from more profitable occupation, there was an additional, very grave objection. It was untrue, therefore a lie, and therefore damnably wicked. Puritans customarily divided lying into three categories: the pernicious lie, made for evil intent; the officious lie, intended to prevent some danger or procure some good; and the sporting lie, 'which is to make one merry, or to pass away Precious Time'. 'All these sorts of Lying are Sinful,' *The School of Good Manners* affirmed in 1715. In this its compiler, Eleazar Moody, a Boston schoolmaster, was echoing the habitual Puritan ruling. The theologian Thomas Gouge (1609–81), for instance, had been similarly severe on the 'sporting lie': 'Beside that it is a sin against truth, it is also an unwarrantable, and an idle misspending of precious time, which ought rather to be redeemed.'[37]

This abhorrence of fantasy was still often expressed in nineteenth-century America. In a little undated booklet called *Letters to Little Children, by their Father* published by the American Tract Society, we find the following reflection on any departure from the strictest truth:

My dear little George... at the house where the coach stopped to change horses, there is a very large wooden lion over the door. It is painted red, like your great humming top; and it has a very long tail. One of the men, who sat beside me in the coach, said that this lion wagged its tail every morning at eight o'clock. And he laughed, and seemed to think that he had said something very clever. But I thought it was very silly, and very wicked too.

' "Is it a true book, John?" ' asks the grandmother in Charles Dudley Warner's *Being a Boy* (1877), ' "Because if it isn't true, it is the worst thing that a boy can read." '

And those of a later generation, like the Rev. Heman Humphrey, Congregational clergyman and president of Amherst College, Massachusetts, from 1823 to 1845, felt that while all fiction might not necessarily be evil, it was nevertheless a dangerous area: 'Absolutely to proscribe *all* fiction, would, perhaps be going too far. I think I could select a

dozen volumes, beside Robinson Crusoe, which I should be willing to have my children read in their minority.' But he warned that even one work of fiction could lead to an insatiable appetite for it. Of Shakespeare he said: 'I am sorry that most of his plays were ever written. I believe it will appear in the Great Day, that they have done more harm than good ... It is scarcely possible they should pass through the youthful mind and imagination, without leaving a stain behind.'[38]

Though the Boston booksellers had imported some of the old romances, these never became part of colonial culture. But America made its own contribution to heroic legend – the Indian captivity story. Treating of almost supernatural endurance and courage, incorporating moments of tenderness, tragedy and triumph, it was not only true but uplifting, and must have made stories like *Fortunatus* and *St George and the Dragon* seem alien and irrelevant. The first captivity story, published in 1682, told of Mary Rowlandson's capture during the later stages of King Philip's War:* *The Sovereignty and Goodness of God, Together with the Faithfulness of His Promises Displayed: Being a Narrative of the Captivity and Restauration of Mrs Mary Rowlandson.* It had a happy ending, for after eleven weeks and five days she was ransomed and allowed to return to her people. It is related in spare, sinewy prose that owes much to the style of the Authorized Version – King James' Bible of 1611. Children must have found it a compelling story, not least for the appearance of children in the narrative. There is the six-year-old wounded in the raid in which Mary Rowlandson had been captured, who dies in her lap, and her son Joseph whom she unexpectedly meets during her eighth move, and who comforts her by reading from the Bible.

One eighteenth-century captivity story even had a child as the central character: *Memoirs of Odd Adventures, Strange Deliverances, etc., in the Captivity of John Gyles, Esq., Commander of the Garrison on St George's River* (1736).[39] Gyles was only ten years old when he was captured in Maine by French and Indian forces. He spent six years among the Eastern Indians and almost three among the French (during which time he stood firm against French attempts to make him a papist – a frequent theme in captivity stories) before he was released and reunited with the surviving members of his family.

---

* New England's most devastating Indian war, 1675-6. King Philip was the name given by the settlers to the Indian leader.

John Gyles' memoirs are adorned with accounts of animals, Indian customs (including preparations for war) and legends, which must have made them particularly attractive to children.

Captivity stories and *The Pilgrim's Progress* were for Puritan families virtually the only narratives acceptable, beyond those in the Bible. Many in later years felt that the lack of distracting fiction had been a great blessing; it meant, for one thing, that the young had grappled with the works of the great divines. Others felt that this absence had shaped the American character, and looked back wistfully, like the Rev. Franklin Eddy in 1882, to a time when a household might possess no books beyond the Bible and a hymn-book:

It has been said of the late Abraham Lincoln, our martyred President, whose early life was spent amidst the hardships of our then western frontier, and whose principal books were the Bible, Pilgrim's Progress, Aesop's Fables, and the biographies of Washington, Franklin and Clay, that 'the poverty of his books was the wealth of his life'. And if we notice the dissipating effect of our many books and papers, we shall easily understand the philosophy of this wise and truthful remark.[40]

It was not as simple as that, as anyone knows who has read of Lincoln's early life and his craving for books – any books. But it was a fine rhetorical statement that appealed to many.

BOOKS FOR CHILDREN

From the very early days, New England printing presses directed books at the young. It was vital that every child should know the essentials of his faith for, according to Calvinist belief, to be ignorant was to be damned. In *The Pilgrim's Progress*, for instance, Christian and Hopeful meet at the end of their journey a boy called Ignorance. Christian is not satisfied with his understanding of God's purposes and tells him: ' "Ignorant thou art of what justifying righteousness is, and as ignorant how to secure thy soul through the faith of it from the heavy wrath of God." '[41] And in the closing paragraphs of the book, while Christian and Hopeful are rejoicing in the heavenly city, Ignorance is bound hand and foot and cast into hell. To avoid this terrible end every child had to be drilled in the elements of Christian dogma as defined in an approved catechism, and in 1642 the General Court of Massachusetts decreed that all masters of families should catechize their children and servants at least once a week in the principles of religion.

The earliest catechism – for which in 1629 the Massachusetts Bay settlers voted three shillings to purchase '2 dussen and ten'[42] – was in all probability that of William Perkins, a theologian of the previous century held in high repute by Puritans. For all its engaging introduction, listing the misapprehensions, or 'errors', commonly held among the ignorant,* it was not ideal, being somewhat diffuse, and, with 135 questions and answers, decidedly on the long side. However, it was printed many times in England, reprinted in New England at least once, in 1682, and translated by John Eliot into the Massachusetts Indian language in 1654.

Wilberforce Eames lists the first New England catechism as that of Hugh Peters of Salem.[43] He had come out in 1635, and in 1641 went back to London where he prepared and published a catechism for his congregation, giving it the title of *Milke for Babes, and Meat for Men*, anticipating by five years the title of John Cotton's catechism *Milke for Babes, Drawn out of the Breasts of both Testaments. Chiefly for the Spirituall Nourishment of Boston Babes in either England.* The title had already been used in England by the Puritan divine, William Crashaw, in *Milke for Babes. Or, A North-Countrie Catechisme. Made plaine and easie, to the Capacitie of the Countrie People.* The word 'babe' in all these titles referred to the uninstructed generally, not merely to children, and it must be remembered that at this time children were regarded as different from adults only in that they generally had lower capacities.

Many New England congregations devised their own catechisms; Increase Mather in 1679 referred to no fewer than five hundred variants.[44] There was also the *Westminster Shorter Catechism* formulated by the Westminster Assembly (the synod appointed by the Long Parliament to reform the English Church) between 1643 and 1647. It seems

* *Works*, 761. No. 17 of the 'errors' said: 'That a man which commeth at no sermons, may as well believe, as he which heares all the sermons in the world'; no. 19: 'That it was a good world when the old Religion was, because all things were cheape'; no. 20: 'That drinking and bezeling in the Ale-house or Taverne, is good fellowship, and shewes a good kinde nature, and maintaines neighborhoode.'

to be this one – beginning 'What is the chief end
of man?' 'Man's chief end is to glorify God and to
enjoy Him for ever and ever' – that was recalled
in memoirs with religious awe. For the catechism
came to occupy for the New Englander the same
sort of position as the Torah for the Jews, and the
reciting of it was almost sacramental. In 1840 Heman
Humphrey spoke with emotion of the 'aged disciple,
just on the verge of heaven ... feasting his soul
upon the definitions of *justification, adoption, sanc-
tification*, and the like, which three quarters of a
century before in the nursery were imprinted indelibly upon his memory'.[45] Some forty years later
another clergyman reminded his congregation how
the New England character had been hammered
out upon the anvil of the Westminster Catechism:

The catechism was as truly a classic as any other book.
It was taught everywhere, in the family, in the school, in
the church; indeed it was the principal intellectual and
religious pabulum of the people. We had it for breakfast,
and we had it for dinner, and we had it for supper. The
entire town was *saturated* with its doctrines, and it is
almost as much so at the present day.[46]

It seems likely that for many American children
reading would have stopped with the Bible and the
catechism. If there was leisure and it was a bookish
household, they might be given one of the theological works that dealt with conversion. Thomas
White, an English preacher, specifies some of these
in *A Little Book for Little Children*, first published
in Boston in 1702 (in London some thirty years
earlier). After telling his readers to abjure 'Ballads
and Foolish Books', he lists what they ought to read
in addition to the Bible: 'the Plain-man's path way
to Heaven ... get the Practice of Pietie, Mr Baxter's
Call to the Unconverted, Allen's Allarum to the
Unconverted; read the Histories of the Martyrs that
dyed for Christ; and in the Book of Martyrs . . .
Read also often Treatises of Death, and Hell, and
Judgement, and of the Love and Passion of Christ.'*

Although White was addressing himself to very
young children who had not yet learned to read,
the books he prescribed were adult theological
treatises. We do notice in the last three decades of

The death of a Protestant martyr. From The New
England Primer *(Boston, c. 1820). This account of the
burning of John Rogers appears in almost all known
editions of the primer.*

the century a dawning realization that children
ought to be approached in a different way from
adults, and writers begin to wheedle rather than
command or threaten. White is one of the first to
address them tenderly. He calls them his 'dear
pretty children' and speaks of their 'pretty little
hands lifted up in prayer', while still expecting adult
understanding of them in theological matters. The
coaxing manner creeps into schoolbooks too, so
that in 1694 an English schoolmaster, who signed
himself only by the initials 'J.G.', called his reading

* Arthur Dent: *The Plaine Mans Path-way to Heaven: wherein every man may clearly see whether he shall be saved or damned* (1610); Lewis
Bayly: *The Practise of Pietie* (1613) – as popular in Virginia as it was in New England; Richard Baxter: *Call to the Unconverted* (1657) – the
74th edition appeared in 1821, and John Eliot translated it into the Massachusetts Indian language in 1664; Joseph Alleine: *Allarum to the
Unconverted* (1671), a very popular work, later reissued under the title *A Sure Guide to Heaven*. The Book of Martyrs must refer to Foxe's
Actes and Monuments.

primer *A Play-Book for Children*, and devised sentences about animals and birds and practical matters within a child's experience.

At first books for 'the first enterers', as John Brinsley called them, were imported, but after the 1680s the colonies had their own primer. Exactly what the earliest *New England Primer* contained there is now no means of discovering, since all the early editions have disappeared and the earliest one to survive dates from 1727, printed by Kneeland & Green in Boston. (It was first printed in Boston sometime between 1686 and 1690.) Its bibliography is vast and complex and its history is investigated in many specialist works.[47] It is known that Benjamin Harris, a rabid anti-papist who had fled from London in 1686, was selling copies at his London Coffee House in Boston, and was advertising a second edition in 1691. How much Harris had to do with the compilation of the primer has never been established, but the contents of the 1727 edition are nowhere near so ferociously polemical as *The Protestant Tutor*, which he had published in London in 1679 and which Samuel Green printed in Boston in 1685. The original primer probably contained the usual alphabet, syllabary, Lord's Prayer, Ten Commandments, a catechism, and the names and order of the books of the Bible.* The account of the death of John Rogers, the first martyr in the persecutions of Queen Mary's reign, taken from *The Protestant Tutor*, may well have been included from the start, and appears in nearly all extant editions. Other famous features were probably added later, such as the dialogue between Christ, Youth and the Devil, and the famous rhymed picture alphabet with its sonorous reminder: 'In Adam's Fall / We sinned all.'

Over the many decades of its popularity, the contents of the primer varied. In general it was religious, with hymns, prayers, precepts and the catechism. In this New England was imitating the ancient shape of a primer: the medieval and Tudor primer was not a speller but a liturgical book with psalms and prayers. Some New England Primers were gentler than others; occasionally they have a more secular tone. More verse was added over the years, including the famous 'Now I lay me down

to sleep'. This first appeared in 1737, in an edition published by Thomas Fleet, and was to be found in almost all subsequent editions, as were the lines on human mortality which began:

> In the burying place may see
> Graves shorter there than I.
> From death's arrest no age is free
> Young children too may die.

This image of a grave shorter than oneself was a very potent one, and often recurs in subsequent children's books. Isaac Watts' hymns became popular, especially the 'Cradle Hymn' which begins 'Hush! my Dear, lie still and slumber' – giving a mild and childlike touch to a book that is otherwise conspicuously austere.

The subjects of the illustrated alphabet also varied, sometimes predominantly religious, sometimes more secular. Its effect on children who rarely saw pictures is almost impossible for us to imagine in a world where images are toppling the printed word. The thumb-nail engravings were crude, blurred and often baffling, but the very mystery was appealing. Of a later version of the alphabet George Livermore in 1849 recalled a Harvard professor telling him that in 'Young Timothy Learned Sin to fly', where Sin is represented by a devil, he supposed that Sin ('a strange-looking biped with a switch tail and wings') was a little dog whom the boy had fitted with wings, and was teaching to fly. The professor's ancestors would have been in no doubt about what 'sin' meant.

The *New England Primer*, part of nearly every American child's culture until the nineteenth century, bit deep into the consciousness of many generations. During the time that it was popular – some one hundred and fifty years – there were not many children's books. When George Livermore contributed his articles on the Primer to the *Cambridge Chronicle* in 1849, a correspondent wrote to recall how as a boy he had so longed for a copy that a sympathetic storekeeper had agreed to accept his kitten in exchange.

The dialogue between Christ, Youth and the Devil which featured in many editions of the primer[†] was

---

* These are the contents of John Eliot's *Indian Primer* of 1669, a unique copy of which survives in Edinburgh.

[†] It appears in the ninth edition (?1710) of *Instructions for Children: or The Child's and Youth's Delight*, a catechism and spelling book devised by Benjamin Keach, an English Baptist minister, and first published in 1693. He had already written a poem of a somewhat similar nature, *War with the Devil* (1673); but in this, a dialogue between Youth, Truth and the Devil, Truth triumphs and Youth is savingly converted.

profoundly pessimistic. The youth himself is brightly hopeful that there is still time for repentance:

> Moreover, this I also know,
> Thou can'st at last great mercy show.
> When I am old, and pleasure gone,
> Then what thou say'st I'll think upon.

But Christ says grimly that it is already too late, that he will not live to be old. Death thereupon carries him off, and the poem concludes:

> Thus ends the days of woful youth,
> Who won't obey nor mind the truth;
> Nor hearken to what preachers say,
> But do their parents disobey.
> They in their youth go down to hell,
> Under eternal wrath to dwell.

Dramatic poetry of this sort was a concession. In the past children had been expected to make their way to salvation helped only by the sort of theological works named by Thomas White (see page 28). But by the turn of the century, as has been said, attitudes towards books for children were changing. The difficulty was what to give them to read. 'Children are naturally taken with Histories,' Cotton Mather was to say in 1708; 'Now, instead of Corrupt Stories and Idle Fables, Why should we not single out the Histories in the Holy Scriptures for them? Only, it would be adviseable always to Clench the Histories, with some Admonitions of Piety, which are to be gathered from them.'[48] It seems from this that even in the best-regulated families it was difficult to keep children cloistered from 'idle fables'. It would also appear that Mather felt the difficulty of presenting some of the Old Testament to the young.

Indeed, Nathaniel Crouch in *Youth's Divine Pastime* (the third edition was published in London in 1691) had shown what sensational material there was in the holy scriptures. Subtitling his work 'Remarkable Scripture Histories, turned into English Verse. With Forty Curious Pictures proper to each Story. Very Delightful for the Virtuous Imploying the Vacant Hours of young Persons, and preventing Vain and Vicious Divertisements', he seems deliberately to have sought out some of the more salacious

episodes of the Old Testament, such as the story of Jezebel, that of David and Bathsheba, of Joseph and Potiphar's wife, of the Levite dismembering his concubine (dead after a gang rape), of the ravishing of Dinah, and of Lot's incest. Crouch, writer, editor and publisher, whose works were often imported by Boston booksellers, was one of the first to realize what money lay in purveying piety to the young. Like some of the Sunday school publishers two centuries later, he specialized in sensational material – only, in his case, plundered from other men's books.

But what, beside the Bible, could young children safely be given to read? John Brinsley, discussing the needs of the younger grammar school pupils in 1612, could only suggest 'courtesy books' – 'full of precepts of civilitie' – which, he averred, children took a delight in. But by the closing years of the century there are signs that more thought was being given to the question. In England, for instance, John Locke, in *Some Thoughts Concerning Education* (1693) – a work which gives detailed instructions about the rearing of children, their physical health, their upbringing and schooling – said that 'some easy pleasant book' should be given to the child once he knew his letters. Not the customary Lord's Prayer and creeds, he thought; these were better learnt by heart from repetition. He was also adamant that the Bible was not suitable, 'either for the perfecting of their Reading, or principling their Religion'. Indeed, he thought no worse book could be found, since much of it must be incomprehensible: 'And what an odd jumble of Thoughts must a Child have in his Head, if he have any at all, such as he should have concerning Religion, who in his tender Age reads all the Parts of the Bible indifferently, as the Word of God without any other Distinction.'[49]

But at this date there was little or nothing available, and he could recommend only Aesop, with pictures in it if possible, and *Reynard the Fox*. Illustrated Aesops were a rarity, hardly seen outside the bibliophile's library, and there was no edition for children except the Latin texts used by the grammar schools.* Nor was *Reynard the Fox* – a medieval beast epic popular in Caxton's time – available in a version for children. Locke admitted the dearth of material:

---

* In 1703 Locke supervised, perhaps partially wrote, a version of Aesop 'in English and Latin, Interlineary'... with Sculptures'. It was a schoolbook, but nevertheless was the first illustrated Aesop for the young.

14

15

tenance wore the expression of great distress by reason of the pain which she endured, but never did a word of complaint fall from her lips. While she was yet able to sit up a good part of the day, it was proposed to her to have her chair put by the window, that she might be diverted by looking into the street. She declined in every instance, and never seemed at a loss for any amusement. If any of the family, or of her friends who came to see her, in their conversation talked about worldly or trifling things, she would express her disapprobation, though with much meekness and mildness. She desired to hear the conversation of pious persons, and was always pleased to have them pray with and for her. Such as she knew would not speak upon the subject of religion, but divert her mind and talk about the common things of the day, when she heard they were down stairs, she would say, " I hope they will not come up; I have done with the world."

She was persuaded, from the first of her

During her last illness, which lasted twelve weeks, this dear child manifested the greatest patience and submission. Often her coun-

In the style of Janeway (1). From Memoir of Mary Gosner of Philadelphia *(American Sunday School Union, 1832).*

What other books there are in English ... fit to engage the liking of Children, and to tempt them to read, I do not know: But am apt to think, that Children, being generally delivered over to the Method of Schools, where the fear of the Rod is to inforce, and not any pleasure of the Imployment to invite them to learn, this sort of useful Books, amongst the number of silly ones that are of all sorts [presumably popular romances and ballads], have yet had the fate to be neglected; and nothing that I know has been considered of this kind out of the ordinary Road of the Horn-Book, Primer, Psalter, Testament, and Bible.[50]

He overlooked, however, one piece of writing that was to the known liking of children, and was acceptable even in the Mather family. This was a work by an English nonconformist preacher – James Janeway's *A Token for Children, Being an Exact Account of the Conversion, Holy and Exemplary*

Lives and Joyful Deaths of Several Young Children. The first part appeared in 1671, the second the following year. In 1674 Janeway, not yet forty, died of consumption. *A Token* was not printed in New England until 1700, but Boston booksellers' invoices show that it was being imported in fair numbers in the 1680s.

To get some idea of why this compilation of pious deaths was so extraordinarily popular among the young, one has to bear in mind that it was the first book they had encountered that told stories of children. Up till then they had been given books with titles such as *Repeated Warnings, The Young Man Spoken To, The Sins of Youth, The Vain Youth Summoned to Appear before Christ's Bar.* But here in Janeway were thirteen children manifestly more holy than their elders, some of them as young as five years old, gloriously holding the stage. And there was dialogue and domestic detail, too – scanty no doubt, but enough to clothe the incidents with some sort of reality.

'"Away then all that is the world,"' said Jacob Bicks, dying of 'a very sore sickness upon the sixth of August, 1664... "Away with all my pleasant things in the world; away with my Dagger for where I go there is nothing to do with Daggers and Swords; men shall not fight there but praise God."' '"I know I shall be marked,"' said eleven-year-old John Harvy, sickening with the plague in 1665; '"I pray let me have Mr Baxter's Book, that I may read a little more of Eternity before I go into it."' This was the child who grieved that his new suit had ribbons, and told his mother that she was mistaken if she thought such things pleased him. John also would 'intreat his Mother to have a care of gratifying a proud humour in his Brothers and Sisters, he did tell them of the danger of pride'.

This was another characteristic of the Janeway children: they exhorted their peers and their elders, and were not rebuked for it. When they came to die the sorrowing family would cluster in the bed-chamber, awed by this glimpse of a heaven that the dying saw so clearly, and cherishing the words that fell from them. '"God is the best Physitian,"' said Charles Bridgman, '"into his hands I commend my spirit, O Lord Jesus Christ receive my soul; now close mine eyes. Forgive me, Father, Mother, Brothers, Sisters, all the world. Now I am well, my pain is almost gone, O Lord receive my Soul unto thee."'

It was not the first time that youthful holiness had been recorded. In 1646 Samuel Clarke had included a few young martyrs in *A Mirrour*, and Thomas White cited some examples of early piety in *A Little Book for Little Children*, though choosing

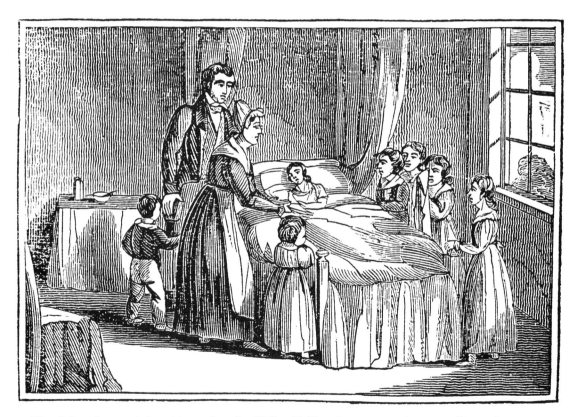

"Her clothes she gave to her sister, and as she did it, said, 'Now, I suppose, mother, you will cry when you see them, but I do not want you should.'"

In the style of Janeway (2). Frontispiece from Amos Augustus Phelps: Memoir of Ann Elizabeth Pierce *(Massachusetts Sabbath School Society, 1833).*

to give far more space to lengthy accounts of the torturing and death of infant Jewish martyrs as described by Josephus. White's book well might have influenced Janeway, though he omitted martyrs and dealt only with children whose examples his readers could reasonably aspire to emulate. He himself claimed no sort of originality for his work. Indeed, he admits that the story of Charles Bridgman is taken from 'Mr Ambrose his Life's Lease'. And if we turn up *Life's Lease* in the works of the Puritan divine, Isaac Ambrose, we find an account of this 'sweet rose, cropt in its blossoms, no sooner budded but blasted', which Janeway simplified a little and shortened. None of the children seems to have been personally known to him; some of them died when he himself was a child; two – Susanna and Jacob Bicks – lived in Holland. Twice he acknowledges that friends of the child in question had told him the story, and in the preface to the second part he speaks with indignation of the people who disbelieved his account of 'a child that began to be serious between two or three years old'. He had it, he said, from 'Mrs Jeofries in Long-Lane in Mary Magdalen Bermondsey Parish, in the County of Surry . . . and as a reverend Divine said, Such a Mother in Israel, her single Testimony about London, is of as much authority almost as any one single Minister'.

In the twentieth century Janeway has been called morbid, chilling, soul-battering; even his Victorian biographer in the *Dictionary of National Biography* refers to the compilation with evident distaste as 'extraordinary'. But three hundred years earlier the theme had not been extraordinary at all, though it was the first time that children had featured so prominently in any literary work. Far from being chilling, it is triumphant. These are *good* children, going to their heavenly reward, and it shows them enjoying the sort of dignity and esteem that few could have experienced in their lifetime, and all must envy. Moreover, Janeway forbears to sermonize, to point out the difference between good children and bad. Certainly, the preface asks readers which sort they are, but asks with the same tenderness that White had used. Janeway tells his readers that they should not lie, or take the Lord's name in vain, or keep bad company; that they should obey their parents cheerfully, be diligent in reading the scriptures and learning their catechism. 'Think a little by your self about God and Heaven . . . Labour to get a dear love for Christ.' And having

suggested that they ask their fathers to buy them 'Mr White's Book for little Children', he concludes:

O children, if you love me, if you love your Parents, if you love your Souls; if you would escape Hell fire, and if you would live in Heaven when you dye, do you go and do as these good Children; and that you may be your Parents joy, your Countreys honour, and live in Gods fear, and dye in his love, is the prayer of your dear Friend, J. Janeway.

The thirteen narratives are set down with the same simplicity. No doubt, not knowing any of the children personally, Janeway invented the dialogue in many but the most conscientious parent could not take exception. *A Token* was read even in families where fiction was anathema. It was one of the most powerful pieces of writing ever produced for children, all the more since it stimulated their own imaginings. 'I felt as if I were willing to die with them if I could with equal success, engage the admiration of my friends and mankind,' one boy reader recalled.[51]

The impact of this profoundly influential book was felt for generations. Cotton Mather saw its possibilities and added accounts of New England piety to the Boston edition:

About this Time, our Booksellers reprinting the Excellent Janewayes token for Children, I was willing to charm the Children of New England unto the Fear of God with the Exemples of some Children that were exemplary for it, in this Countrey, and being furnished with six or seven remarkable Narratives [one being about his brother Nathanael], I put them into shape and gave the little Book unto the Booksellers. Tis Entituled, A Token for the Children of New England.[52]

One would guess that a famous early example of the genre, *A Legacy for Children, being some of the last expressions and dying sayings of Hannah Hill, Jnr. of the city of Philadelphia* (1714), published 'at the ardent desire of the deceased', was directly inspired by the child's having read Janeway. Such organizations as the American Tract Society and the Massachusetts Sabbath School Society continued to publish quantities of books in this vein during the first half of the nineteenth century.

But the influence of Janeway – derived maybe second-or even third-hand – shows in far less obvious ways than mere factual examples of early piety. It spreads out like the ripples on a pool. One might guess that Dickens, when he came to describe the deaths of Paul Dombey and Little Nell, remembered something of the emotion he had felt as a child reading tracts about the deaths of children who, unlike him, were admired and valued. It must have been Janeway, at several removes, who was responsible for the mawkish and by now purposeless deaths that clogged third-rate English fiction in the later Victorian period, written by people who had experienced in childhood a heady emotion from identifying with little dying evangelizers. Fewer children died in American fiction, but there were cohorts of pious little girls like Susan Warner's Ellen Montgomery and Daisy Randolph, and Martha Finley's. Elsie Dinsmore, who exhort and convert. Inadvertently, Janeway had begotten a whole genre of fiction.

NOTES

1. William Sloane: *Children's Books in England and America in the Seventeenth Century* (New York, 1955), 11.

2. Louis B. Wright: *The First Gentlemen of Virginia* (San Marino, Calif., 1940), 239.

3. Anne Grant: *Memoirs of an American Lady* (London, 1808), I, 33.

4. *Fruits of a Father's Love, being the advice of William Penn to his children* (London, 1726), 41.

5. Frederick B. Tolles: *Meeting House and Counting House* (Chapel Hill, NC, 1948), 145.

6. Grant: op. cit., I, 197.

7. [Robert Cushman]: *A Sermon Preached at Plimmoth in New-England, December 9, 1621* (London, 1622).

8. William Ames: *Conscience with the Power and Cases Thereof* (London, 1639), 252.

9. John Cotton: *A Practicall Commentary . . . on the First Epistle Generall of John* (London, 1658), 129.

10. Robert Cawdrey: *A Godly Forme of Household Government*, ed. John Dod and Robert Cleaver (London, 1614).

11. Horace Scudder: *Childhood in Literature and Art* (Cambridge, Mass., 1894), 128.

12. Cotton Mather: *Elizabeth in her Holy Retirement* (Boston, 1710), 17.

13. Cotton Mather: *Right Thoughts in Sad Hours* (London, 1689), 47–55 passim.

14. Cotton Mather: *The Duty of Children* (Boston, 1719), 71.

15. Mary A. Livermore: *The Story of My Life* (Hartford, Conn., 1897), 61.

16. Thomas Brooks: *Apples of Gold* (London, 1657).

17. Cotton Mather: *Diary* (Massachusetts Historical Society, Boston, 1911), II, 49.

18. ibid., II, 219.

19. ibid., II, 651.

20. William Wells Newell: *Games and Songs of American Children* (New York, 1884), editor's note.

21. Keith Thomas: 'Children in Early Modern England', in *Children and their Books*, ed. Gillian Avery and Julia Briggs (Oxford, 1989).

22. Quoted in Perry Miller: *The New England Mind: the seventeenth century* (Cambridge, Mass., 1954), 357.

23. Cotton Mather: *Magnalia Christi Americana*, ed. Thomas Robbins (Hartford, Conn., 1853), II, 64.

24. [Cotton Mather]: *Early Piety Exemplified in the Life and Death of Nathanael Mather* (London, 1689), 3. Though the preface 'To the Reader' is signed by Samuel Mather, what follows is the work of his father.

25. ibid., passim.

26. Samuel Clarke: *A Mirrour or Looking Glass Both for Saints and Sinners* (London, 1671; originally published 1646), 407.

27. Increase Mather: *Memorials of Early Piety, occurring in the holy life and joyful death of Mrs Jerusha Oliver* (Boston, 1711), 48.

28. John Locke: *Some Thoughts Concerning Education* (London, 1693), 193.

29. Quoted in Jean Straub: 'Quaker School Life in Philadelphia before 1800', *Pennsylvania Magazine of History and Biography*, vol. 79 (1965), pp. 138–9.

30. *The Book of Abigail and John: selected letters of the Adams family 1762–1784*, ed. L. H. Butterfield (Cambridge, Mass., 1975), 188.

31. Samuel Eliot Morison: *The Puritan Pronaos* (New York, 1936), 46 *et seq.*

32. Worthington Chauncey Ford: *The Boston Book Market 1679–1730* (Boston, 1917).

33. Thomas Goddard Wright: *Literary Culture in Early New England 1620–1730* (New Haven, Conn., 1920), 225.

34. Roger Ascham: *The Scholemaster* (London, 1570), 27.

35. ibid., 28.

36. *Tatler*, no. 95 (London, 17 Nov. 1709).

37. Thomas Gouge: *The Young Man's Guide*, in *Works* (London, 1706), 396.

38. Heman Humphrey: *Domestic Education* (Amherst, Mass., 1840), 94–9 passim.

39. Both these narratives are included in *Puritans among the Indians: accounts of captivity and redemption 1676–1724*, ed. Alden T. Vaughan and Edward W. Clark (Cambridge, Mass., 1981).

40. Franklin Eddy: *The Sabbath-School Centenary* (Hamilton, Ohio, 1882).

41. John Bunyan: *The Pilgrim's Progress* (Penguin English Library, ed. Roger Sharrock, London, 1965), 188.

42. Paul Leicester Ford: *The New England Primer* (New York, 1897).

43. Wilberforce Eames: *Early New England Catechisms* (Worcester, Mass., 1898).

44. Increase Mather: introduction to James Fitch: *First Principles of the Doctrine of Christ* (Boston, 1679).

45. Humphrey: op. cit., 160.

46. The Rev. Dorus Clarke, in a lecture at Westhampton, Mass., 1878. This address was printed in full in Paul Leicester Ford: op. cit., 277–81.

47. Paul Leicester Ford: op. cit.; George Livermore: *The Origin, History and Character of the New England Primer* (Cambridge, Mass., 1849; reissued New York, 1915); Charles F. Heartman: *The New England Primer issued prior to 1830* (3rd edn, New York, 1934). It is also covered in Charles Carpenter: *History of American Schoolbooks* (Philadelphia, 1963).

48. Cotton Mather: *Corderius Americanus* (Boston, 1708), 9.

49. Locke: op. cit., 187.

50. ibid., 185.

51. William Godwin, 1756–1836; cf. C. Kegan Paul: *William Godwin, his Friends and Contemporaries* (London, 1876), I, 7.

52. Cotton Mather: *Diary* (Massachusetts Historical Society, Boston, 1911), I, 369.

2. The Eighteenth Century: Dick Whittington, Goody Two-Shoes and Benjamin Franklin

A CHANGING CLIMATE

On 27 September 1713 Cotton Mather wrote mournfully in his diary: 'I am informed that the Minds and Manners of many People about the Countrey are much corrupted by foolish Songs and Ballads, which the Hawkers and Peddlars carry into all parts of the Countrey.' Nor were these necessarily foreign imports. The colonies now had time for light reading, and in Boston at least were printing their own. Thomas Fleet, an Englishman born in Shropshire in 1685, had arrived in New England about 1712. In his *History of Printing in America* (1810) Isaiah Thomas recorded that by 1713 Fleet was printing 'small books for children and ballads. He made a profit on the latter, which was sufficient to support his family reputably.'

'Small books for children' at that date probably meant educational material – catechisms and primers – but 'ballads' give some indication of popular taste. Many London ballads, some with ancient themes, were reprinted in the colonies. The romance of 'Fair Rosamond', the beloved of Henry II who had died about 1176, and of Jane Shore, mistress of Edward IV, had an extraordinary hold on the popular mind. (Indeed, when Cecil Sharp was collecting songs in the Appalachians early this century he found many sagas of English medieval kings still being sung.) New England also made ballads out of topical events. Criminals, their exploits and execution were a favourite theme, and Benjamin Franklin's literary career began with a ballad, 'On the Taking of Teach' (a pirate), put out in 1719 when he was only thirteen. ('Wretched stuff,' Franklin was to comment in his autobiography, adding that it was his father's pronouncement that verse-makers were generally beggars that had saved him from trying to be a poet.)

Ballads about criminals and their ends could be said to carry a moral, but there were many that had none at all and were cheerfully bawdy. Mather's lamentation about his countrymen's fondness for 'foolish Songs' suggests that this had only just come to his attention. Whether there had been a rapid decline, or whether the godliness that Mather remembered had been only an illusion, the fact is that by 1744 Dr Alexander Hamilton, an immigrant of Scots origin who had settled in Annapolis, was much struck by the worldliness of Boston. The Great Awakening – that series of religious revivals that the colonies experienced about the middle of the century – had passed over the city without much permanent effect that he could perceive; the enthusiasm it had generated was slackening, and there was an abundance of diversions available: 'Assemblies of the gayer sort are frequent here, the gentlemen and ladies meeting almost every week at concerts of musick and balls. I was present at two or three such, and saw as fine a ring of ladies, as good dancing, and heard musick as elegant as I had been witness to anywhere.'[1] He commented on the hospitality of Bostonians, and the abundance of 'men of learning and parts', but added dourly that the people were 'more captivated with speculative than with practical religion. It is not by half such a flagrant sin to cheat and cozen one's neighbour, as it is to ride about for pleasure on the Sabbath day, or to neglect going to church and singing of psalms' – a comment that might equally well have been made about Hamilton's own countrymen.

We gain the same impression of a worldly society from the diary of Anna Green Winslow,[2] who was sent from Nova Scotia in 1771 to her aunt in Boston to get a fashionable education. Dutifully she records sermons, which clearly make no impact whatsoever on her: 'Mr Bacon read his sermon on R.iv.6. I can remember he said, that before we all sinned in Adam our father Christ loved us...Aunt has been upstairs all the time I have been writing and recollecting this – so no help from her.' But her thoughts most of the time ran on her social life, which was full and varied, and above all on fashions

A Maryland brother and sister. Henry and Eleanor Darnall c. 1710, by Justus Engelhardt Kühn.

in which she took an intense interest, particularly when it came to her own clothes, over which she seems to have been much indulged.

Dr Hamilton found Boston a far more entertaining place than Philadelphia, and though by 1744 it had seen itself supplanted by Philadelphia in size and prosperity, it had a cosmopolitan outlook that the latter lacked, and a gentrified class with plenty of leisure. At the end of the century Nathaniel Dwight in his *System of the Geography of the World*, a popular school geography, was writing of New Englanders as spending much time in amusing themselves: dancing, he said, was a favourite diversion, along with sleigh-riding in winter, skating, ball games, shooting and fishing. Neither Dwight nor Hamilton cared for Pennsylvania. Dwight took a moralistic view, declaring that the inhabitants were 'very ignorant and superstitious . . . impatient of good government, order and regularity'. (Local prejudice is much in evidence in the geography books of this period.) Hamilton found the Pennsylvanians tiresomely sedate. No doubt because of this seriousness, eighteenth-century Philadelphia produced less in the way of recreational books than Boston and New York.

But throughout the colonies life was becoming much easier. 'The first drudgery of settling . . . which confines the attention of people to mere necessaries is now pretty well over,' Franklin said in 1743, 'and there are many in every province in circumstances, that set them at ease, and afford leisure to cultivate the finer arts, and improve the common stock of knowledge.'[3] A new demand for polite literature was developing, and now that parents had more time for their children they desired books for them.

But what sort of parents, what sort of children? Colonial society was racially and socially very various. They might be New England farming children, or the sons and daughters of Boston merchants; Irish apprentices in Philadelphia, or German schoolchildren in Maryland; wealthy planter families in the South, or slave children on the plantations. In an issue of the magazine *Juvenile Miscellany* of 1827 Lydia Child illustrated the cultural difference between town-bred elite and farmers' boys. She called her dialogue 'Conversation between a little boy of olden times and a Boston boy of 1827', but it might equally well have been a country boy and a town boy. Theodore says:

I rise at seven or eight o'clock and read my Virgil or Horace before I go to school. I have history and geography and mathematics to attend to in the forenoon. In the afternoon I ride out on horseback, or in the carriage with my father. I go to see all the museums and pictures, and if I suffer for exercise, I go to the gymnasium now and then.

Jacob, on the other hand, goes into the fields barefoot and labours there all day, and for him there are only six weeks of school a year at the most. We get an idea of the sort of books he might have known from the following advertisement, inserted by Moses Johnson of Keene, New Hampshire, in the *Cheshire Advertiser* of 22 March 1792:

Moses Johnson, informs all little Misses, and other his Customers that he receives all kinds of Cotton or Linen Rags . . . 1½lb. Rags will buy a Primer or Story Book, one yard of Ribbon, two Thimbles, two Rings . . . 4lb. will buy a pair of handsome Buckles, or the famous history of Robinson Cruisoe [*sic*], who lived 28 years on an uninhabited island . . . [The book] will help [my young friends] very much in learning to read, and perhaps give them a taste for history of larger extent and importance, such as geography, husbandry, revolutions of countries, &c. - and for the encouragement of which, all kinds of Books, Stationary at a much less advance than any other Goods; good Writing-Paper for 10d per quire, Spelling Books 1s, Bibles 3s, Watts's Psalms and Hymns 2s6d, Morse's Geography 4s6d and other books equally cheap.[4]

Johnson's attitude towards reading was one of hard-headed practicality. A religious education was taken for granted – which his stock of bibles and Isaac Watts' hymns demonstrates. Otherwise, the purpose of books was to help you get on in life; they were a rung on the ladder of learning.

However, he did advertise storybooks, time-wasting though they might be, and we get some idea of what these might have included from Joseph Buckingham's account of his childhood reading. Buckingham, later to become a distinguished and pugnacious newspaper editor, was born in Windham, Connecticut, in 1779 and brought up in conditions of abject poverty. The last of ten children, he had lost his father when he was three. But his elder brothers

when they came home 'sometimes brought me a picture-book, and at the age of six I was the owner of Robinson Crusoe, Goody Two-Shoes, Tom Thumb, and perhaps half-a-dozen other books of a similar character.'[5]

Such books were certainly being printed by then in the colonies. In *The Friar and the Boy*, for instance, published in Boston by Andrew Barclay in 1767, there was an advertisement for *Robinson Crusoe,** Goose's Tales [sic], Arabian Nights, History of Mother Bunch, Tom Thumb, Jack the Piper, Jack Horner* and *Jack and the Giants*. None has survived. They would have been very small and frail, and since children possessed so few of them they would have had more handling than their flimsiness could endure. One of Buckingham's brothers was a sailor, so it is conceivable that he brought him storybooks from England, though it seems more likely that they were local products.

What is interesting is that Buckingham thought that this sort of reading was commonplace, even though his mother was 'a firm believer in the doctrines of the Puritans'. *Tom Thumb* was a fairy-tale much denounced by Puritan preachers, there being something about this mischievous and daunt-less little creature that they found peculiarly subversive. *Goody Two-Shoes*, which little Joseph had also been given, was often fated to be ranked with fairy-tales, though it is in fact a moral tale of a peculiarly eighteenth-century cast, first published by John Newbery in London in 1765, and by Hugh Gaine in New York in 1775 (its first recorded American publication). Indeed, if we had to name the patron saints of mid-eighteenth-century juvenile reading we well might put forward Goody Two-Shoes, alias Margery Meanwell, and Dick Whittington. (The latter had been an English folk hero for centuries, but was particularly popular with American readers at this time.) Through diligence and perseverance both rose from very modest beginnings to the sort of dignified comfort that it was then assumed all young persons desired. Little Margery is an orphan, and the gift of two shoes – for before she had only one – so excites her that she is nicknamed Two-Shoes. She teaches herself to read, and sets up as a 'trotting tutoress', rapidly gaining the respect of the community for her wisdom and

---

* Though this was first published in 1719, it was a long time before it appeared in the colonies. The American Antiquarian Society possesses a *Robinson Crusoe* printed in Boston by Fowle & Draper between 1757 and 1762. There may have been earlier editions which have not survived.

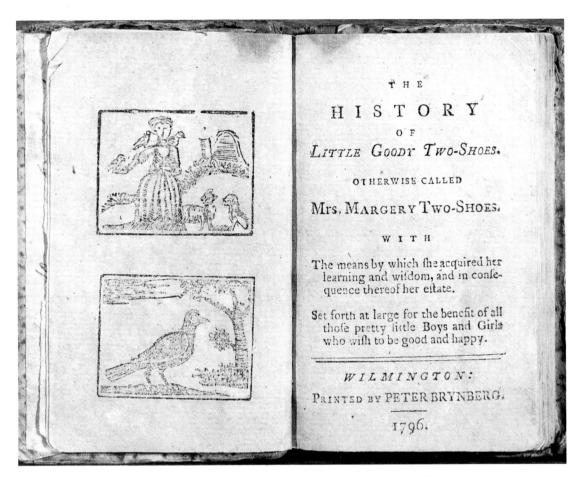

The title-page from a 1796 edition of Little Goody Two-Shoes *published in Wilmington, Delaware.*

good counsel. She marries a wealthy widower, 'is made a Lady', and finishes as a notable philanthropist. The original title-page said that her history was 'set forth at large for the benefit of those'

> Who from a State of Rags and Care,
> And having Shoes but half a pair;
> Their Fortune and their Fame would fix,
> And gallop in a Coach and Six.

This cheerfully materialistic philosophy appears to have suited Newbery's customers both at home and abroad, for we find it repeated over and over again in his books for the young.

Though by the 1760s all thirteen of the original American colonies possessed a printing press, they were still largely dependent on the old country for their writers, and were to remain so for some time

to come. As late as 1825 Thomas Jefferson wrote to a friend: 'Literature is not yet a distinct profession with us. Now and then a strong mind arises, and in intervals of leisure from business, emits a flash of light. But the first object of young societies is bread and covering; science is but secondary and subsequent.'[6]

In colonial Virginia such records as we have suggest that plantation owners were conservative in their reading, and clung to the authors of their fathers' and grandfathers' time. Philip Fithian, a graduate of Princeton, spent 1773–4 in Virginia as tutor to eight children (Robert Carter's two sons, one nephew, five daughters). Writing to his own tutor, he described his employer's library thus:

It consists of a general collection of law books, all the Latin and Greek classicks, vast numbers of Books on

Divinity chiefly by writers who are of the Established Religion [Fithian himself was preparing for the Congregational ministry; the Carters were Church of England]; he has the works of almost all the late famous writers, as Locke, Addison, Young, Pope, Swift, Dryden, & in short, Sir, to speak moderately, he has more than eight times your number.[7]

The 'late famous writers' were all long dead – Dryden and Locke some seventy years before – and from the bibliographical inventory included as an appendix to Fithian's letters we get the impression of an inherited library to which the then owner had added nothing. Fithian's pupils do not seem to have been bookish; there is far more talk of music and dancing than of reading. He taught all eight of them together, from the oldest son who was making his way through Sallust and the Greek grammar to the little ones who were learning to read and spell. There is no mention of any children's books except 'an old Book of Esop's Fables done into English verse'; the oldest daughter, a fifteen-year-old, during lesson time reads from the *Spectator*, a journal of her grandfather's youth.

Robert Carter's library resembled many in Virginia, and also in England among the squirearchy of the time. So the interest that some colonists took in recently published children's books is unexpected. As early as the 1740s we find subscribers from Boston, South Carolina and Virginia named in Thomas Boreman's *Gigantick Histories*. Boreman, a bookseller with a shop on Ludgate Hill and in the Guildhall in London, was publishing this series of light-hearted guides to popular sights in the city between 1740 and 1743. They are among the earliest recreational books for children, and it might be said that they were floated on their readers' pocket money. You could have your name printed in the list of subscribers by sending sixpence to 'T. Boreman in Guildhall in London', and in the third history, which describes St Paul's Cathedral, we find American children listed: 'Miss Nabby Davenport / Master Sammy Mather / Miss Polly Oliver / Master Natty Rogers / All of Boston, New England / Master Allick Hume / Master Bobbie Hume / Both of South Carolina'. In the third volume of the Westminster Abbey set we find the name of Master

Gavin Corbin of Rappahannock in Virginia. His loyalty is still evident in the volume devoted to the giant Cajanus, for which Boreman could produce only 106 subscribers; he was obliged to put a brave face on it by crediting Cajanus himself with taking up a hundred copies. Boreman's venture seems to have been a very small one – he commented gloomily at one point that success and he had long been strangers.

However, the vivacity and ebullience of the *Gigantick Histories* may possibly have inspired John Newbery. A far more astute businessman whose interests included patent medicines as well as bookselling and publishing, he moved to London at about the same time as Boreman's little series was coming to a close. Newbery's books were to be extensively pirated by American publishers throughout the eighteenth century, but he himself had been early aware of potential American markets. On 15 November 1750 he had inserted in the *Pennsylvanian Gazette* a column of advertisements of children's books. This was enterprising indeed, since he had embarked on juvenile publishing only six years before. They were of an improving nature. *A Museum for Young Gentlemen and Ladies* or *A private tutor for little Masters and Misses*, published that same year, was an assemblage of miscellaneous facts, together with equally miscellaneous rules for behaviour, finishing with 'Dying Words and Behaviour of Great Men, when just quitting the Stage of Life; with many other useful Particulars, all in a plain familiar Way for the Youth of Both Sexes'. *The Pretty Book for Children* was subtitled 'an easy guide to the English tongue', and two other books listed are similarly educational – a French primer, and *The Royal Battledore* (a 'battledore' being an elaboration of a hornbook, to teach young children their letters).

But two years later his *Lilliputian Magazine,** a medley of stories, verses and riddles, offered more entertaining material. (We know that it reached America, because the list of subscribers included forty-nine from Maryland.) It also launched what must have been the first international children's club, the Lilliputian Society, and for this it deserves to be remembered. 'We whose names are hereunto subscribed, members of the Lilliputian Society,

---

* Newbery, it seems, intended that this periodical should appear at regular intervals; but apparently failing to get enough response, he bound up the first three parts together and sold them as a single volume. See S. Roscoe: *John Newbery and his Successors* (Wormley, Herts., 1973), 166–70.

(142)

N. B. There are many Thoufands of young Gentlemen and Ladies, who, by fubfcribing to this Work, are become Members of this Society, and have entered into the Agreement above fpecified; but as their Names are too numerous to be here inferted, we are obliged to omit them till the Publication of the next Volume.

JAMES TRUELOVE, *Sec.*

A LIST of Subfcribers, from *Maryland,* which came too late to be inferted in the proper place.

MASTER Tommy Addifon, of Prince George's County, Maryland
Mafter Harry Addifon
Mafter Jacky Addifon
Mifs Nancy Addifon
Mifs Nelly Addifon
Mafter Walter Beall, Frederick County
Mafter Tommy Beall
Mafter Brooke Beall
Mafter Jerry Beall
Mafter Sammy Beall
Mafter Ifaac Beall
Mifs Amelia Beall
Mafter Randolph Brandt, Charles County
Mafter Dicky Brandt
Mafter Dicky Brooke

Mifs

(143)

Mifs Sally Brooke, Prince George's County
Mifs Jane Contee
Mafter Billy Cooke
Mifs Rachael Cooke
Mafter Watty Dent
Mafter Dicky Dent
Mifs Nancy Dobfon
Mafter Dulany, in Annapolis
Mafter Lloyd Dulany
Mifs Becky Dulany
Mafter Matthew Everfield, Prince George's County
Mafter Charles Everfield
Mifs Debby Everfield
Mafter Fitzchew, Calvert County
Mafter Tommy T. Greenfield, St. Mary's County
Mifs Rachael T. Greenfield
Mifs Gantt, Calvert County
Mafter Sammy Hepburn, Marlborough
Mifs Nancy Hepburn
Mafter Tommy Hawkins, Prince George's County
Mifs Betfy Hawkins
Mifs Chloe Hanfon, Charles County
Mifs Jenny Hanfon
Mifs Fanny Jenning, Prince George's County

Mafter

Some of John Newbery's Maryland subscribers. From the Lilliputian Magazine *(London, 1752).*

and proprietors in this magazine', its manifesto began. Members promised to say their prayers, keep the Sabbath holy, to love their parents and brothers and sisters, and 'THIRDLY, we agree to live in the strictest friendship, to promote each other's interest and happiness, and the interest and happiness of all mankind, but especially those that are poor and distressed.' There is something touchingly childlike about its ardent idealism, not to be found in any other Newbery publication, and the members must have been bitterly disappointed that the periodical ended almost as soon as it began.

The Newbery firm kept up its presence in the colonies after the death of its founder in 1767. An undated entry for 1773 in the diary of Colonel Landon Carter, a Virginian plantation owner, records the following purchases:

Poetical description of Beasts, 6d, by Charley Chatter.
Half a dozen for my Grand Children.
Mother Bunche's Fairy tales, and all Newbury's [sic] collection of little books for young children.
The Young Gentleman and Lady's Philosophy, vol. 2.[8]

This is interesting on more than one count. It shows that recreational books for children were now accepted, and also that American buyers were fully abreast of what was available. The three named were very recent publications; the first two – both Newbery – had appeared only that year, and the third, subtitled 'a continued survey of the works of nature and art', by Benjamin Martin, in 1772. But children would own, at best, only a handful of such books, and were expected to move on to standard reading at a very early age. In England in 1766, for instance, the Rev. John Ash, adapting a manual of grammar for children under ten,[9] appended a reading list comprising adult theology, history and general information. Even in the section 'Books of Amusement and Imagination' there is nothing resembling a story except *Robinson Crusoe* and Aesop's *Fables*. It was not until the next century that children's books became cheap enough to be commonplace.

RELIGIOUS BOOKS

By the eighteenth century large numbers of Americans played no part in organized religious life. Even in New England, the best-churched region, with its tightly knit communities and compulsory church attendance, it is probable that not more than one person in seven was a full church member. And the further South, the weaker the religion. ' "Shall I see you in church tomorrow?" ' one speaker asks another in the model dialogue that Noah Webster appends to Part I of his *Grammatical Institute* (1783). ' "If I am well I shall attend," ' comes the reply. ' "I think it a duty for us all to attend religious worship" ' – the implication being that it is no longer inescapable.

Nevertheless for most children the Bible was still their earliest reading book. Joseph Buckingham had read the Bible with his mother, and then when he was apprenticed to a farmer at the age of seven his new family saw to it that he read at least one chapter every day, and often two or three: 'I have no doubt that I read the Bible at least a dozen times before I was sixteen years old, with no other omissions than the jaw-breaking chapters of the Chronicles.' Looking back on this in 1852, and aware that he must tread carefully or he would offend many of his readers, he wondered whether this indiscriminate reading of the Bible was wise, since there was so much in it that children could not understand or benefit from. The book of Revelations, for instance, terrified him, and he used to bury himself in the bedclothes to try to blot out the pale horse of death.

Noah Webster, in Part III of the *Grammatical Institute*, spoke out against the use of the Bible as a reader in schools. The style was so different from the present day, and 'such a common use of the Bible is a kind of prostitution of divine truth to secular purposes'. If it were read with seriousness just two or three times a week in school, 'then

the awful solemnities of inspiration would escape profanation from the levity and wickedness of schoolboys'.

From an early date there were summaries of the Bible, aimed no doubt at youth. The first miniature version was the work of John Taylor (1580–1653), a Thames bargee who referred to himself as the 'water-poet' and was noted more for his boisterous humour than for his piety. In 1614 he produced *Verbum Sempiternum*, a verse summary of the Old and New Testaments later known as the Thumb Bible. It was printed in America in about 1760.[10] Many publishers then took it up, including Thomas Fleet, son of the first Thomas. It was *The Holy Bible in Verse*, however, that reached the colonies first. This rendering by Benjamin Harris, which appeared in England in 1698, was published in Boston in 1717. (Only four editions have survived, though many more were published.) It was designed as a mnemonic – the title-page says 'Done into Verse by B. Harris for the Benefit of those of weak Memories' – but you would have to know the original text reasonably well to be able to make sense of this sort of shorthand:

> K. David dies and leaves the Throne
> Unto the Wise King Solomon;
> Who's very rich and wealthy grown
> Most wisely judgement passes on
> The Harlots and does soon discover
> Who of the living Child was Mother.

The main appeal to children must have been that it was illustrated, the crude postage-stamp-sized woodcuts having been taken from an edition of the *New England Primer* that has not survived.

The History of the Holy Jesus 'by a Lover of [children's] Precious Souls' was an altogether more sophisticated and attractive work. What is more, it was a wholly American product, deriving from no English original. Advertised in the *Boston News Letter* of 31 January 1745 (though the earliest extant edition is the third, of 1746), it was one of the most popular New England books of the period: the bibliographer D'Alté Welch records over forty editions before the end of the century. The illustrations, naive as they are, show a tremendous advance on the often undecipherable scrawls in the *New England Primer*. There is an abundance of detail, and the fact that Christ is dressed like Cotton Mather and shown preaching to ladies in muslin aprons

GENESIS XI. *ver.* 4. 21

The People of the [world] said, Go to, let us build a [city] and a [tower] whose Top may reach unto Heaven.

The People of the *World* said, Go to, let us build a *City* and a *Tower* whose Top may reach unto *Heaven*.

A Curious Hieroglyphick Bible, *'Designed Chiefly To familiarize tender Age, in a pleasing and diverting Manner, with early Ideas of the Holy Scriptures'. Published by Isaiah Thomas in 1788 from T. Hodgson's London publication of 1783.*

and gentlemen in skirted coats probably did not surprise its original readers, who would rarely, if ever, have encountered religious art in any form. The engravings show a rare glimpse of colonial life. The woodcut that accompanies the crucifixion – 'Behold the Rock in Pieces rend / The Earth did quake likewise' – shows an early-eighteenth-century township with its steepled meeting-house and two-storey frame houses tumbling around its distraught citizens. And the illustration of Lazarus at the rich man's gate and the feasting within gives a close-up of such a house and its interior. It is altogether a fitting first book for America to produce for its young; the combination of religion and domesticity foreshadows the fiction of the nineteenth century.

Probably the only eighteenth-century children's classic from which a present generation (and certainly all Victorian children) could quote is Isaac Watts' *Divine Songs*. First published in England in 1715, the earliest American edition extant (described as the seventh) is a Boston one of 1730. It was to go through over three hundred editions in America, where for nearly two hundred years it stamped itself indelibly on the juvenile mind. Indeed, it could

not be escaped. Even if children were unaware of the name Watts, they would find his verses in their schoolbooks and their home books; they would recite them at Sunday school and as a Sunday task, and would hear them quoted by their elders in rebuke or exhortation. Individual songs were used in many of the *New England Primers*, in *McGuffey* and many other readers, and were printed, mostly unacknowledged, as ballast in thousands of tracts and children's chapbooks. These songs were invested with almost sacramental qualities. Children died repeating them; conversions were attributed to them; with the Bible and the catechism they were an inevitable part of Protestant childhood. In 1825, 110 years after their original publication, an English primer carried this verse:

> What sweet-er book to me be-longs
> Than Dr Watts's book of Songs?
> Oh! I could learn them all the day,
> I'm sure I love them more than play.

The trouble is that there are comparatively few of them: only twenty-seven of the 'divine songs',

From The History of the Holy Jesus, *5th edition (Boston, 1748). Woodcut accompanying the description of the crucifixion.*

with a few 'moral songs' added (two in the earlier editions, rising to the full complement of seven later).* So in the absence of other hymns for children they were to become wearisomely familiar. As Harvey Darton says: 'Very few poems can survive the ordeal of being recited by children in public year in, year out, to the mortification of the reciters and the weariness of the audiences.'[11] It might also be mentioned that Isaac Watts' nephew, James Brackstone, in 1746 was ejected from church 'for damning and cursing [his uncle] in a shocking manner and for declaring he would no longer be a member of his church'.[12] Perhaps long years of being associated with such a household object of veneration had taken their toll.

For ten years Dr Watts was a nonconformist minister in London, but collapsing under the strain in 1712 he was carried off to convalesce in the household of Sir Thomas Abney, one of his congregation. There he lived until his death in 1748, writing many educational works and books of religious instruction, and outstaying his host (who died in 1722) by twenty-four years. The *Divine Songs* were dedicated to the three Abney daughters, Sarah, Mary and Elizabeth; the presentation copy inscribed to Elizabeth is in the Pierpont Morgan Library. In the preface Watts speaks of the usefulness of verse as a teaching aid: 'There is something so amusing and entertaining in rhyme and metre, that will incline children to make this part of their business a diversion.' 'What is learnt in verse, is longer retained in memory,' he claimed, 'and it may often happen, that the end of a song, returning in the mind, may be an effectual means to keep off some temptations.' He hoped that his songs would be 'a constant furniture for the minds of children', but could never have foreseen how even Lewis Carroll's parodies of them would be parodied in their turn, and that they would become part of the cultural background of all English-speaking people, who still can quote such lines as 'birds in their little nests agree' and 'for Satan finds some mischief still for idle hands to do', though now without the faintest notion of who wrote them.

Watts' verse does not have the grandeur of Mrs Barbauld's *Hymns in Prose* (see below), nor her observation of nature. His opening song, 'Of Praise to God', for instance, is thin and not particularly memorable:

> How glorious is our heavenly King
>> Who reigns above the Sky.
> How shall a Child presume to sing
>> His dreadful Majesty?

But he did choose to begin his collection with songs of praise rather than the more usual reminders of human depravity and the need for conversion. Then follows more sombre verse, in a style that all Protestant children of Watts' time would have known well:

> There is a dreadful Hell,
>> And everlasting Pains;
> There Sinners must with Devils dwell
>> And Darkness, Fire and Chains.

There are the usual warnings about bad company, swearing, sartorial pride and idleness, which echo what all the moralists of the time were saying and were to continue to say for many more decades.

It is perhaps hard to see why these verses lasted, when children's books so rarely survive their generation. Many of them lack any distinction; memorable images like that of the sluggard – 'As the Door on its Hinges, so he on his Bed / Turns his Sides and his Shoulders, and his heavy Head' – are rare, and some verses limp along with faulty metre and dubious rhymes. But *Divine Songs* presented a new approach. Nobody before had told quarrelling children that they were like barking dogs, and nobody in a semi-sacred work had endorsed Locke's view that play was an essential part of childhood; the last verse of the song about idleness begins 'In Books, or Works or healthful Play / Let my first Years be passed.' With the last song, 'A Cradle Hymn', Watts did achieve poetry rather than just verse, and succeeded in conveying to children a sense of God's loving care in a way that had eluded him in the poems that preceded it:

> Hush! my Dear, lie still and slumber,
>> Holy Angels guard thy Bed!
> Heavenly Blessings without Number
>> Gently falling on thy Head.

Another English writer who was very popular in America was Anna Laetitia Barbauld (1743–1824). She came of a Dissenting family, and her views

---

* The title *Divine and Moral Songs* was not used until some seventy five years later.

were wider and more tolerant than many of her contemporaries in the established Church of England. She had been unusually well educated; her father ran a school of his own where she had been taught Latin and Greek, and in 1774 she had married one of his pupils, the Rev. Rochemont Barbauld. They had no children, but adopted a nephew, Charles, for whom his aunt wrote *Lessons for Children*, a series of graded books the first of which, for children of from two to three years, appeared in 1778. This gives us one of the best pictures that we have of Georgian childhood. We see Charles hiding from Papa under Mamma's apron, riding on Papa's cane, having his hair combed, being given his tea: 'Where is the toast and the muffin? Here is some bread for you. Little boys should not eat butter. Sop the bread in your tea. The tea is too hot, you must not drink it yet. You must wait a little.' We are shown Charles' toys: 'See, here is Betty come from the fair. What has she brought? She has brought Charles a gun, and a sword, and a hammer, and some gingerbread.'

As Charles grows older he becomes capable of following connected stories, and these are provided for him. They reflect the mood of the times in that they are not works of imagination, but they contain – and this was uncommon then – anecdotes concerning real children, like the little girl who killed a brood of nestlings through mistaken kindness. The *Lessons* were first published in Philadelphia in 1788 and remained popular all through the early decades of the next century. Like Watts' hymns, they were reprinted over and over again, and excerpts and imitations are to be found in countless American primers for the next forty years or more.

Though Mrs Barbauld's *Hymns in Prose* (1781) were also popular, they did not have the universality of Watts' *Divine Songs*, probably because they could not be recited so easily, but also because their appeal would be more to those with literary tastes. Nevertheless, they remained in print through most of the nineteenth century, and the power and majesty of the prose must have affected the impressionable child in a way that Watts never could. Her themes were the beauty of the natural world, and the love of God. She wrote of death too, but approached it in a very different manner from Watts, whose language and imagery were those of the Puritan preachers. She dwelt not on corruption, but on renewal:

I have seen the sun set in the west, and the shades of night shut in the wide horizon...gloom and darkness brooded around – I looked, the sun broke forth again from the east, he gilded the mountain tops; the lark rose to meet him from her low nest, and the shades of darkness fled away...Thus shall it be with thee, O man!...A little while thou shalt lie in the ground, as the seed lieth in the bosom of the earth; but thou shalt be raised again.

The Barbauld work that best reflected the mood of young America was *Evenings at Home*, a collection of didactic stories and dialogues written with her brother John Aikin. (She was the minor collaborator, but the work was often associated with her alone.) Dr Aikin's political and religious views – his message of tolerance, his denunciation of war and his questioning of the accepted English class structure – though hardly the norm in England, were the orthodoxy in America, and, once American literature got under way, were to be found in many books for the young. But that mood had been discernible much earlier. In *A Serious Poem on Various Subjects* which Ebenezer Drayton, a schoolmaster in Newport, Rhode Island, wrote in 1769 as a copy-book exercise we find:

> Fear not, Quakers, Moravians,
> Newlights, or Presbyterians,
> Baptists, Churchmen (by Possession)
> No matter which, be a Christian:
> Thy Neighbour love, thy God obey;
> In secret never mind to pray:
> Let all Mankind have thy Good Will;
> The Poor, the Sick, thy Help and Skill.

The same sentiments are apparent in Dr Aikin's 'Differences and Agreement; or Sunday Morning' in *Evenings at Home*, where a father takes his son to all the different congregations – Roman Catholic, Quaker, Methodist, Baptist – and teaches him that, while all differ on how to worship, all agree about the nature of charity.

Dr Aikin's career as a physician was greatly hampered by his political opinions, and Sarah Trimmer, who represented the ultra-conservative point of view in the English educational world then, took strong exception to much of *Evenings at Home*. She told readers of her journal, the *Guardian of Education*, that this 'very ingenious and amusing miscellany' should be read 'under the care of a judicious parent or teacher', since 'the leaven of Modern

Philosophy is as dangerous in these days, as that of the Scribes and Pharisees in our Saviour's time'.[13] She was very uneasy about the theme of religious toleration, but took even greater offence at 'Things by their Right Names' and 'The Price of Victory' – both strictures on war. 'Whoever believes the Scriptures,' she said vehemently, 'must know that war is often both *lawful* and *necessary*.'[14] (England was embroiled in the Napoleonic Wars at the time, and it was strongly felt by Mrs Trimmer and her like that Rousseau and his fellow-philosophers had been largely responsible for the turmoil in France.) As a final thrust she pointed out that war was character-building; many soldiers were profligate and their sufferings brought them to a sense of their sins.

But her sense of outrage was most aroused by 'The Colonists', to become a favourite American piece, often reprinted without acknowledgement. Here a schoolmaster questions his pupils about the professions they would choose in the new colony he proposes to found. The boys who variously offer farming, milling, carpentry, farriery, masonry, shoe-making, tailoring or medicine are all commended. But the silversmith is told to stay at home, the barber is warned that there will be little work, the lawyer that nobody will be rich enough to employ him. Finally, a gentleman offers himself:

'A gentleman! And what good can you do us, sir?'

'O, sir, that is not at all my intention. I only mean to amuse myself.'

'But do you mean, sir, that we should pay for your amusement?'

'As to maintenance, I expect to be able to kill game enough for my own eating, with a little bread and garden stuff, which you will give me. Then I will be content with a house somewhat better than the common ones; and your barber will be my valet.'

'And pray, sir, what inducement can we have for doing all this for you?'

'Why, sir, you will have the credit of having *one gentleman* at least in your colony.'

Like Dr Aikin's patients, Mrs Trimmer was incensed by these Jacobin sentiments: 'Of what use can this lesson be, but to fill boys' heads with schemes for emigrating from their native country, and to bring certain professions and ranks into disrepute, we cannot conceive.'[15] Her indignation stemmed partly from a fear lest England should experience the same reign of terror as France, so

that she saw traces of republicanism in the most surprising places. Richard Edgeworth's suggestion in *Practical Education* (see pages 65–6) that children should make their own beds seemed sinister to her, and she disapproved of such stories as *Little Goody Two-Shoes* and *Primrose Prettyface* because they gave the lower orders ideas about moving out of their station (and might even tempt impressionable boys to marry beneath them). Trimmer was not alone in holding that the organization of English society and its elaborate stratification, with a leisured elite at the top and an abundance of willing servants, was as sacred and God-ordained as the Church of England. So many of the comments of English travellers who visited America in the nineteenth century were based on this premise.

Barbauld's writings remained classics in America for many decades. 'All unite in cordially approving this lady's writings', said Lydia Child in *The Mother's Book* in 1832, and in her reading list she recommended three Barbauld works. In her own *Evenings in New England* (1824) she had quoted a child who commented, 'How I do wish Mrs Barbauld would write another volume of *Evenings at Home*', and she hoped that her own work, unashamedly modelled on Aikin and Barbauld, would by introducing 'American scenes and American characters...give a delightful locality' to the stories. But perhaps because she was too much dominated by her model, Mrs Child failed to achieve anything that now seems distinctively American.

THE EARLY DAYS OF COLONIAL PUBLISHING

One of the earliest importers of Newbery books was Hugh Gaine of New York. Like Newbery he was a purveyor of patent medicine, with premises at the sign of the Bible and Crown. After the Revolutionary War, when the British troops left New York, he thought it expedient to forgo the Crown. In those years he was apparently Whig and Tory by turns, whichever seemed the best bet. Newbery books were clearly profitable and he took much of the London firm's output, until he felt confident enough to print them himself. In the *New York Mercury* in 1762 he announced 'divers diverting books for infants'. They were all Newbery titles, but some had been slightly reworded, and a noteworthy change occurred in the subtitle of *Food for the Mind*, which now read 'a new Riddle Book for the use of Good Boys and Girls in *America*'[16] – an early example of the new sense of national identity, though it is ironic that it should have come from this notorious turncoat.

All Gaine's books of the 1760s have disappeared. Of those years when so little has survived, there is preserved in the Huntington Library in California the earliest known storybook for children published in America, *A New Gift for Children* – D'Alté Welch dates it speculatively at 1756. Wretchedly printed (by Daniel Fowle of Boston) and with paper covers only, half the front cover has gone. The stories, adapted from English originals, have more interest than most of the little moral fables of the time, and we sometimes even feel that we are reading about real children. Even though the heroine of 'The Generosity of Confessing a Fault' is called Miss Fanny Goodwill, she does behave as if she is flesh and blood, and her papa takes her on his knee, kisses her and calls her his 'little charmer'. However, the woodcuts obviously come from other, not very appropriate, sources; Miss Fanny's maid, with musket and cocked hat, and holding a powder horn, looks as though she is manning the barricades.

The first New England publisher who made the reprinting of English children's books a serious business was Isaiah Thomas. He plundered the London publisher John Marshall's lists as well, but his name is forever associated with Newbery. Born in 1749 of a family that had established itself in Boston as early as 1640, he lost his father when he was three. He was apprenticed when he was seven to Zechariah Fowle, an indifferent printer – he was to learn more from Fowle's partner, Samuel Draper, and from a neighbouring printer, Gamaliel Rogers. From the first, Thomas showed great aptitude for the craft, and, standing on a bench so that he could reach the type cases, he set up his first piece of work, a ballad, before he had learnt to read. When he was only eight he had done the casework for 12,000 copies of the *New England Primer*, and at thirteen he not only printed the *New Book of Knowledge* but made the woodcuts. He broke with his shiftless master before his indenture was up; he was already, in his teens, an independent – some might say imperious – character. After some years of wandering he was back in Boston in 1770. Five years later his patriotic paper, the *Massachusetts Spy*, brought him into such trouble with the British authorities that he was obliged to flee, with his

press and type, to Worcester, some forty miles west. There he stayed for his remaining fifty-six years, creating an empire of newspapers, printing works and bookstores (including one in Albany and one in Baltimore). By the end of his life Thomas had published more than nine hundred books over a wide range – bibles, English novels and political works, ballads, legal and medical works, schoolbooks and children's books.

The last he did not take very seriously; they were just part of an astute businessman's policy of trying every market. He started off cautiously enough in 1784 with a psalter, 'being an introduction for children to the reading of the Holy Scriptures'. He followed this up the next year with a handful of schoolbooks, including the *New American Spelling Book* which he brought out in a vain effort to compete with Noah Webster, whose speller and grammar were achieving such spectacular success. But by the 1790s he was publishing Webster too.

Along with these he included translations of two dialogues from Mme de Genlis' *Theatre of Education* – *The Beauty and the Monster* and *Hagar in the Desert*. De Genlis' sub-Racine moral playlets, whose characters declaim lofty sentiments in lofty prose, were much favoured by English seminaries for young ladies, and the fact that Isaiah Thomas, who had a keen eye for his markets, thought that he could sell these turgid pieces is an indication that New England in the 1780s, despite the setbacks and privations of the Revolutionary War, had a sufficiency of such young ladies being genteelly educated.

The 1780s were Thomas' most productive years for children's books; he published twenty-nine different titles in 1786 and 1787 – and this is to exclude school textbooks. None of these titles was new. All, with the exception of *The History of the Holy Jesus*, had English origins, and some of them dated from several decades earlier, such as *A Little Pretty Pocket-Book* which appeared forty-three years after its original publication. To this compilation he appended 163 maxims from *The School of Good Manners*, an approved New England book – perhaps hoping that the stricter sort of buyer would thereby be induced to overlook the maypole dancing described in it, a pastime once held in abhorrence by Puritan opinion.

He made only cursory alterations to the English originals, and was often inconsistent. The good little girl addressed on the title-page of *Nurse Truelove's New Year's Gift* (1786), taken from a Newbery publication of some thirty years earlier, is promised a ride in the 'governour's gilt coach', as there are no lord mayors in New England. But Thomas' attention slipped after that, and he apparently did not notice, or did not care, that in the story itself Miss Polly Friendly becomes 'a great Lady Mayoress'. So superficial were his alterations, that the landscape and the society in all his books are English. There are squires and tenants and clergymen of a recognizably Anglican cast; there are primroses and cowslips in the hedges, larks and linnets in the sky, and the robins are the Old World redbreasts, not the American robin. But the mid-eighteenth-century stories of the Newbery sort were otherwise particularly suitable for transplanting. Their emphasis on industry and effort and on the material advantages that accrue therefrom, their accounts of ragged children like Goody Two-Shoes, Dick Whittington and Peter Pippin who attain their coach and six, and their optimism, were what the new colonies wanted to read about. In England at that

time there was not nearly so much difference between what the rich and the poor read as there was to be in the next century, when two wholly different juvenile cultures grew up, each with its own system of ethics, neither of which applied to the United States.

Isaiah Thomas' juvenile list was thus not adventurous, and the fact that the first collections of nursery rhymes to be published in America – *Mother Goose's Melody* (?1785) and *Tommy Thumb's Song Book* (1788) – appeared from his press seems accidental. He had similar good luck in achieving a first with fairy-tales. In 1789 he published *An Approved Collection of Entertaining Stories. Calculated for the Instruction and Amusement of All Little Masters and Misses. By Solomon Winlove Esq.* This portentous title concealed what would seem to be the first American printing of *Cinderella*, and an early printing of *Little Red Riding Hood*.

None of the turbulence of the 1780s is reflected in any contemporary book for children. Enthusiasm

An early story of the Revolutionary War. Enoch Crosby, an informer for the Americans, escaping from his British captors. From Whig against Tory, or the military adventures of a shoemaker *(Hartford, 1832).*

for the results achieved by the Revolutionary War is occasionally expressed. Thus in a 1796 edition of *Goody Two-Shoes* published in Wilmington, Delaware, this note is appended to the account of the tyrannical behaviour of the landlord: 'Such is the state of things in Britain. AMERICANS, prize your liberty, guard your rights and be happy.' But we have to wait for a long time before there is any account of the war itself. Lydia Child's 'little boy of olden times', Jacob (see page 37), tells Theodore of 1827 what it was like when the men had all gone to the wars, leaving only women and children to produce the food; when there were no candles, and the children went to bed hungry and cried. Other contemporaries of Mrs Child, perhaps remembering what fathers and grandfathers had told them of the war, wrote accounts that do have the flavour of real experience. One of the earliest books on the war written for children is the anonymous *Whig against Tory* (New Haven, 1831), a stirring account of how Enoch Crosby, a Massachusetts shoemaker, acted as informer for the American forces. And an undated and anonymous Sunday school book of the earlier nineteenth century recalls:

My grandfather said that when Cornwallis surrendered his men were all dressed splendidly, even to the common soldiers, with their red coats and powdered hair; and as they passed through our lines, half our men barefoot and their clothes a bunch of rags about them, he heard them mutter between their clenched teeth, 'To be obliged to submit to such scoundrels!'[17]

The same writer recorded how a pair of pantaloons was made by the women of the family for a soldier son, in forty-one hours from the time the wool was taken from the sheep. And the farm now being left without any men, the women and children harvested the corn and potatoes, pulled the beans, stored the apples and gathered the pumpkins.

But what colonial America did provide for its children was schoolbooks. By the end of the eighteenth century these were nearly all written by their own countrymen, and here we get glimpses of the New World scene so lacking in recreational books. Little Joseph Buckingham was initially sent to school with a copy of Thomas Dilworth's *A New Guide to the English Tongue*, then the standard book of English grammar, first published in 1740 and in its fifty-fourth edition by 1793 – one of the English textbooks on which American schools relied until

the 1780s, when the Revolutionary War dried up supplies. It was then that American schoolbooks made their debut. The three great classics of this period were Noah Webster's *Spelling Book*, Jedidiah Morse's *Geography Made Easy* (1784), and Nicholas Pike's *Arithmetic* (1788). Webster had devised his speller while he was in charge of a school in Orange County, New York, finding that Dilworth was unsatisfactory. It was to form Part I of the three-volume *Grammatical Institute of the English Language* (a cumbrous title suggested by the then president of Yale University), consisting of speller, grammar and reader, in which he sought to standardize and simplify American spelling and pronunciation. It became the most famous American work of its kind, printed in Hartford, Boston, Albany, New York and Philadelphia, and also, as has been seen, by Isaiah Thomas in Worcester. Usually issued in boards covered with blue paper, the speller was known as 'the old blue-back'.

Webster's was followed by a flood of others which were often given the name of the part of the country where they were printed – Pennsylvania, Vermont, Boston, and so on. More often than not they consisted of gleanings from other books, frequently English. Watts' hymns were a favourite, of course, and extracts from Mrs Barbauld's *Lessons for Children*. This last could be easily adapted to fit American children, as with *The Child's Spelling-book* (Hartford, 1798), whose compiler quoted directly from Barbauld but also added something of his own, applicable to American schools:

How cold it is! Where are the little girls and boys? Have they not yet come from school?

Here they come, here they come. Who was at the head of the class to-day? Rachel. And did she get the bow? Yes papa, here is the pretty bow. And will papa give me a penny for bringing home the bow?

Yes, Rachel shall have a penny. No, pennies are out of date. She shall have a cent.

In New England, Caleb Bingham's schoolbooks were to become almost as popular as Webster's. *The Child's Companion*, as well as spelling and advice and moral reflections, included fables and stories. There is, for instance, a conversation between Charlotte and Sophia in which the former reveals the reason why she wants to learn how to spell: when trying to inscribe 'For Sally Chapman' in a book that she was going to give to her cousin,

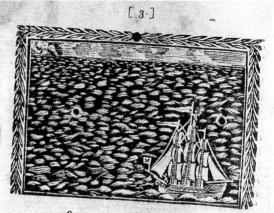

ADVERTISEMENT.

THE compiler of this work has been repeatedly requested by the Instructors of schools, to publish a small book, containing familiar stories in plain language, for the benefit of children, when they first begin to read without spelling. It is said, with much truth, that most of the books published, are written on subjects and in a stile above the capacities of beginners. The following stories are selected and thrown into an intelligible form, to remove in part the common complaint, and assist young beginners in reading. It is hoped these few stories will not be useless, but serve as a step by which children will rise with more ease to the American Selection, or other books used in schools.

[3.]

STORY OF COLUMBUS.

ABOUT three hundred years ago, this country was not known to the people in Europe. Indians only lived here, and the face of the earth was covered with woods. Columbus, a learned and brave man, believed he might find land by sailing from Europe westward, across the ocean; he requested several kings to let him have ships and men to go on a voyage for this purpose, some of whom refused to encourage him, because they thought his scheme wild and foolish. But at last the king and queen of Spain were persuaded to assist Columbus, and they furnished him with three ships and ninety men. He sailed from Spain on the third day of August, in the

From Noah Webster. The Little Reader's Assistant *(Hartford, 1791).*

she had written 'For Sale Cheap Mon.' and had been misunderstood. But perhaps the most interesting feature is the twelve-page appendix of 'Improprieties in Pronunciation common among the people of New-England', which shows how people spoke then – 'vige' for voyage, 'spumful' for spoonful, 'warnut' for walnut, and so on. Bingham's *The American Preceptor* (Boston, 1794), which went through sixty-eight editions, and *The Columbian Orator* (Boston, 1797) were for older pupils, and contain extracts for speaking and reading from leading European writers, all tending to promote Augustan virtues – lofty good sense, justice and magnanimity. There are some patriotic speeches, too, and the occasional glimpse of native shrewdness, like this advice to a young tradesman: 'Remember that time is money. He who can earn ten shillings a day by his labor, and goes abroad, or sits idle one half of that day, though he spend but sixpence during his diversion or idleness, ought not to reckon that the only expense.'

Anthony Benezet, a French Huguenot who emigrated in 1731 and became a Quaker, compiled *The Pennsylvania Spelling Book* (Philadelphia, 1779), the product of many decades of teaching children both black and white, with homely sentences about country life: 'The sun is up, my boys, / Get out of bed. / Go see for the cow; / Let her eat her hay.' And a later Pennsylvanian reader, *Easy Lessons for Young Children* (Philadelphia, 1794), gives a rare glimpse of eighteenth-century Philadelphia. William's Papa takes him to town; they put up their horse in a livery stable and go to see the library and the museum: 'Then he and his papa went to see Mar-ket street meet-ing house, which is a ve-ry fine place in-deed, and mount-ed to the gal-le-rys; af-ter-wards they went to the con-gress hall and saw the Pre-si-dent de-li-ver an ad-dress to both hou-ses of con-gress amid ma-ny fine gen-tle-men.' This same book encourages the disadvantaged to strike out for themselves. Ralph the poor boy is taught by his benefactor to hedge and ditch, to plough, sow and reap, to thresh and drive a team, clean a horse and feed the pigs. He is given a quarter-dollar for each day's work, buys two new shirts, a pair of shoes and a good coat, and feels well set up.

The most patriotic sentiments come in *The Child's Instructor... by a teacher of little children in Philadelphia* (third edition, New London, 1794). This is a winning compilation by one John Ely that has reading lessons on such attractive topics as games – 'What will you play? Will you play hide and whoop? or blind hob or chuckers, or ball? Or will you whip the top, or jump the rope, or shoot marbles?' Its story about an ardent little patriot is so delightful that it should be quoted in full:

Once Billy came running to his mamma; he was almost out of breath: he said that general Washington was coming to town, and they were going to fire the great guns. Hark! says he, do you hear the drums? Then his mamma said to him, Come Billy, can you say a speech for these ladies? Billy would always do as he was bid; he made his bow and began:

Americans! place constantly before your eyes, the deplorable scenes of your servitude. Begin with the infant in his cradle: let the first word he lisps be WASHINGTON.

O Washington! thrice glorious name!
  What rewards can man decree;
Empires are far below thy aim,
  And sceptres have no charm for thee.
Virtue alone has thy regard,
And she shall be thy great reward.

The ladies were all delighted to hear Billy speak so well. One said he should be a parson, another said he should be a lawyer, and another said he should be president of the United States. But Billy said he could not be either unless his mamma gave him leave.

Geography in colonial days was regarded as more of a diversion than a serious school subject, and Jedidiah Morse's *Geography Made Easy*, dedicated to 'The Young Masters and Misses Throughout the United States', with its travellers' tales that frequently lapse into fantasy, is a precursor of the sort of geographical fiction that Samuel Goodrich would purvey fifty years later in his Peter Parley books. There are plenty of anecdotes about people, animals and places, and a wealth of wholly unscientific information such as the following:

Grey Squirrels sometimes migrate in considerable numbers. If in their course they meet with a river, each of them takes a shingle, piece of bark, or the like, and carries it to the water; thus equipped they embark, and erect their tails to the gentle breeze, which soon wafts them over in safety; but a sudden flaw of wind sometimes produces a destructive shipwreck.

Here was a frequently repeated fable that we meet in the medieval bestiaries, and that Beatrix Potter makes use of in *Squirrel Nutkin*. Morse adds that 'the greater part of the males of this species is found castrated'.

Nathaniel Dwight, in *A Short but Comprehensive System of the Geography of the World* (Hartford, 1795), also assembled some startling facts. These must have been as entrancing as fairy-stories to readers looking for marvels, such as the fountain near Grenoble with 'a flame which will burn paper, straw, etc. but will not burn gunpowder', or the elk of Poland 'which is said to be destroyed in the winter by flies who get into his ears and destroy his brain'. Dwight was very partisan. Of Connecticut inhabitants he said fiercely: 'They are more enlightened and better educated than those of any state.' He was perhaps retaliating against Morse, who had remarked that they were 'intemperately fond of law suits and little petty arbitrations' (a view deleted after the first edition).

History was not a school subject, and such histories as there are are surprisingly empty of accurate facts. *The Life of Gen. Washington* (Philadelphia, 1794), for instance, gives no account of the part he played in the recent war 'because the impression which [it] made is yet fresh in every mind', and most of the writer's attention is given to the way Washington runs his estates, and his achievements as a farmer. And *The History of America, abridged for the use of children of all denominations* (Philadelphia, 1795), which Rosenbach in his *Early American Children's Books* supposes is the earliest history for American children, is eloquent in Washington's praise, but has nothing to say about his life. 'The greatest economy was used in the portrait [wood]cuts,' Rosenbach notes: these fall into two groups, those where a tricorn hat (with or without a cockade) is worn, and those where the subject wears a periwig. Thus Christopher Columbus, wearing a tricorn, stares out left, and Americus Vesputius, almost identical, stares right.

But political feeling and patriotic fervour were

Columbus's first interview with the Natives of America.

From the first American history for children: The History of America, abridged for the use of children of all denominations *(Philadelphia, 1795).*

high, even if there was not yet a tradition of historical writing – as one school catechism demonstrates:

'What advantages had the inhabitants of the United States in forming the present federal constitution of government?'

'The greatest by far that any people ever had; and it can scarcely be expected that any should ever have greater.' *Conclusion.* That it is a land of liberty, peace and plenty; an asylum for the persecuted and oppressed from all parts of the globe; a land of happiness; a people planted and preserved by the Lord. Such another country, in all respects, is not to be found on earth.[18]

Noah Webster in his *Little Reader's Assistant* (1791) included, along with instruction on grammar and husbandry (he was writing for farmers' children), some of the earliest stories of American

history. Despite the gruesome details, it is a book full of compassion. The Indians and the African slaves have been cruelly used, he says, and he concludes with a sorrowful description of the wretched state of the latter:

Shall this barbarous and unlawful practice always prevail? Are the negroes brutes? Or are they men like ourselves? Have not the negroes the same right to steal us, our wives and children, transport us to Africa, and reduce us to bondage, as we have to enslave them? If there is justice in heaven, vengeance must fall upon the heads of men who commit this outrage upon their own kind.

Schoolbooks such as these were, of course, for a privileged minority only. When Joseph Buckingham at the age of seven was indentured to a farmer, he found there was very little indeed to read: 'At that time a farmer in Connecticut was not expected to keep much of a library.' There was the Bible and Dr Watts' psalms and hymns, of course, and a volume or two of sermons, plus Philip Doddridge's *Rise and Progress of Religion,* a few theological pamphlets and Michael Wigglesworth's *The Day of Doom,* which caused him 'many an hour of intense mental agony'. But in addition there was 'a regular file of *Almanacks* for near or quite fifty years. Some of them were dated as far back as 1720, and some were made by 'Nathaniel Ames, Philomath'. These periodicals I read often, and with never-relaxing interest. They contained many fragments of history, scraps of poetry, anecdotes, epigrams &c.'

Almanacs, indispensable to all country-dwellers, were for the great majority the only secular reading available. Paul Leicester Ford memorably evoked the early farmhouses:

the low-ceiled kitchen, with its great broad fire-place, around which the whole family nightly gathered, – seated on settles whose high backs but ill shut off the cold drafts that entered at doors, windows, and the chinks in the logs or clab-boards ... the mother and daughters knitting, spinning, or skeining with an eye to the youngsters; the sons making or mending their farming tools, or cleaning their rifles and traps; while the grave and probably rheumatic sire studies the last printed sermon or theological tractate, newspaper, or political squib, 'Death-bed Confession' or 'Last Dying Speech' but most probably the weather predictions contained in the most valued of all publications – the Almanac.[19]

An Almanack for New-England for the Year 1639 had been (if one excludes a broadside) the first work printed in the British colonies. Almanacs were far from being mere calendars: they contained weather forecasts, homely adages, scraps of verse, lists of remarkable events and a wealth of practical information. They were the poor man's newspaper, encyclopaedia and *Reader's Digest* all in one, and had a universal appeal that nothing else has subsequently achieved. Like the Bible, they were reading for the whole family.

And it is the sentiments of the almanacs, of 'Poor Richard's' in particular, that we pick out as the unifying element in the mass of very various books read by American children in the eighteenth century. Exhortations to frugality, temperance and industry were a familiar Puritan message, as we have seen. Benjamin Franklin, 'religiously educated as a Presbyterian', remembered how his father 'frequently repeated a proverb of Solomon, "Seest thou a man diligent in his calling, he shall stand before kings, he shall not stand before mean men." I from thence considered industry as a means of obtaining wealth and distinction, which encouraged me.'[20] Here was the essential spirit of so many eighteenth-century children's books, both English and American – not least of *Goody Two-Shoes*, which was subtitled 'The Means by which she acquired her Learning and Wisdom, and in consequence thereof her Estate'. And when in 1733 Franklin began his series of almanacs – which, since they were published under the name of Richard Saunders, were popularly known as 'Poor Richard's Almanacs' – he 'filled all the little spaces that occurred between the remarkable days in the calendar with proverbial sentences, chiefly such as inculcated industry and frugality as the means of procuring wealth and thereby securing virtue – it being more difficult for a man in want to act always honestly, as (to use here one of those proverbs) "it is hard for an empty sack to stand upright." '[21]

Franklin's name was particularly linked with youth; indeed, it might be said that by the nineteenth century he was being invoked in much the same way as Timothy had been by Puritan preachers – as the virtuous example that youth should perennially keep before them. Naturally, he had at least one primer named after him. Samuel Willard's *Franklin Primer*, published in Boston in 1802, was adorned with a bust of Franklin who, the author (still in his twenties at the time) said, was 'a man

whose manner of life from his youth up, is worthy the most minute observation, and imitation of the rising generation'. And the sixth edition of 1806 spoke of 'his care ... for the education and emolument of the American Youth'.

Franklin did not originate all 'the sayings of Poor Richard'; he took them from such sources as Bacon and La Rochefoucauld, from the Book of Proverbs and other collections of maxims, expressing them in an easy, homespun style that made them not only memorable but very attractive. 'Poor Richard' had the common touch; he seemed to speak to each individual, using images and analogies that the ordinary man immediately understood:

> Plough deep while Sluggards sleep
> And you shall have Corn to sell and to keep.
> Three removes are as bad as a Fire.
> Keep thy Shop and thy Shop will keep thee.
> I never saw an oft removed Tree
> That throve so well as those that settled be.
> Now I have a Sheep and a Cow Every body bids
>   me Good-morrow.
> Handle your Tools without Mittens. Remember
>   the Cat in Gloves catches no Mice.[22]

This style of pithy advice was, of course, imitated. Noah Webster, for instance, took it up in *The Prompter*, subtitled 'a commentary on common sayings and subjects, which are full of common sense, the best sense in the world'. His remarks on slovenly practices such as farmers turning their cattle out into the streets 'to run at large and waste their dung' have a crisp Yankee practicality about them, as has 'When I pass along the road and see a house with the clap-boards hanging an end by one nail, and old hats and cloths stuffed into the broken windows, and the fences tumbling down or destroyed, I conclude the owner loves rum.'

Franklin's maxims are in the same spirit as that first sermon preached in 1621 by Robert Cushman, in which he spoke with abhorrence of those who would not help themselves: 'let the roofe of the house drop thorow, they stirre not; let the field be over-growne with weeds, they care not, they must not soile their hands'. Franklin spoke of his debt to Cotton Mather's *Essay to do Good*. His approach to morality was utilitarian:

I grew convinced that *truth, sincerity* and *integrity* in dealings between man and man were of the utmost

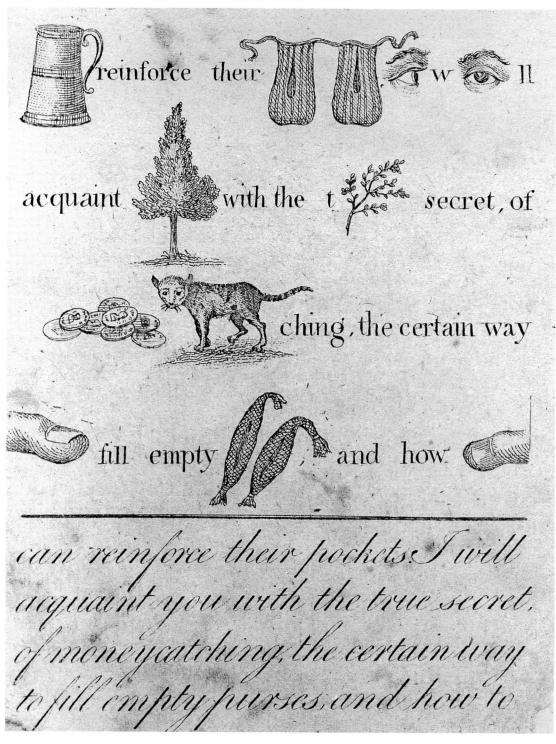

Maxims of Benjamin Franklin, in hieroglyphic form. From The Art of Making Money Plenty, in Every Man's Pocket *(New York, 1811).*

importance to the felicity of life ... Revelation had indeed no weight with me as such; but I entertained an opinion that tho' certain actions might not be bad *because* they were forbidden by it, or good *because* it commanded them, yet probably these actions might be forbidden *because* they were bad for us, or commanded *because* they were beneficial to us in their own nature.[23]

And in his journal Franklin listed the qualities that ought to be cultivated, and how his own perform-ance stood – the sort of self-examination that had always been recommended to zealous Puritans.

Poor Richard's maxims for a profitable life were collected and published under the titles of *The Way to Wealth* and *The Art of Making Money Plenty*. The prefatory remarks to the latter were clearly to be absorbed by American Sunday school heroes (as will be seen in chapter 4):

At this time when the general complaint is that money is so short it must be an act of kindness to inform the moneyless how they can reinforce their pockets, I will acquaint you with the true secret of money catching, the certain way to fill empty purses, and how to keep them always full. Two simple rules well observed will do the business.
1. Let honesty and industry be thy constant companions.
2. Spend one shilling every day less than thy clear gains. Then shall thy pockets soon begin to thrive, thy creditors will never insult thee, nor want oppress, nor hunger bite, nor nakedness freeze thee. The whole hemisphere will shine brighter, and pleasure spring up in every corner of thy heart. Now therefore, embrace these rules and be happy.

Among the illustrated Franklins are a hieroglyphic *Art*, published by Samuel Wood of New York in 1811, with the text written out alongside the printed version in copybook copperplate – no doubt for imitation – and an even prettier undated English version of about the same date, *Franklin's Morals for the Entertainment and Instruction of Youth*, 'neatly engraved on copper plates', with the maxims circling the engravings. Franklin was regarded as one of the most important mentors of American youth. In 1783, fifty years after the first 'Poor Richard' almanac, a Quaker acquaintance wrote to him in France urging him for the sake of the young people of America to publish his journal: 'I know

of no character living, nor many of them put together, who has so much in his power as thyself to promote a greater spirit of industry and early attention to business, frugality and temperance with the American youth.'[24]

'My friend Franklin taught me early habits of industry and frugality,' Samuel Goodrich's Peter Parley told children in the next century; 'he in-structed me never to eat my breakfast until I had earned it; he taught me to profit by experience ... The moral maxims of my old friend "Poor Richard" have made such an indelible impression on my mind that they never can be effaced.'[25] They made a similar impression on William Henry Venable, born in 1836. Recalling his boyhood on a farm in Southern Ohio, he spoke of the days when

the strenuous and inexorable mandates of *Poor Richard's Almanac* were virtuously and strenuously enforced and obeyed as if they were holy Scripture, and when even young children learned by heart, with the purpose of making them rules of conduct, such prudential maxims as 'God helps them who help themselves;' 'The sleeping fox catches no poultry;' ... 'He that by the plow would thrive himself must either hold or drive;' 'Rather go to bed supperless, than to rise in debt.'[26]

From which it will be seen that for many households Franklin had replaced the Westminster Catechism as the child's guide to a way of life. And in a Presbyterian Sunday school book of 1876 with the title of *Wat Adams, the Young Machinist and his Proverbs* we find little Wat, whose second name is Franklin, reared on the *New England Primer* ('now becoming so scarce as to be looked upon as a relic') and *Poor Richard's Almanac*, 'which so pleased the little boy that he was never weary of repeating the old maxims with which it abounded'. These maxims governed his life and earned him the name of 'Old Proverbs'.[27]

In England Franklin was particularly popular with the independent-minded artisans of the textile towns of Lancashire and Yorkshire, and *The Way to Wealth* was to be found in the libraries of many mechanics' institutes. *The Whistle*,* a much reprinted two-page homily of Franklin's on paying too great a price for the object of one's desire – sometimes bound

---

* This pamphlet, originally inscribed *The Whistle: a true story. Written to his nephew* and dated 1779, was one of the few pieces composed and printed by Franklin on the private press set up by him in his house at Passy, during his residence there as minister to France. A copy of this 'excessively rare bagatelle', as A. W. Rosenbach describes it, is owned by the Library Company of Philadelphia.

in with his *Advice to a Young Tradesman* (1748) –
is a recollection of an episode in his own childhood,
when he gave all the money he had to a boy who
had a whistle that he coveted. 'As I grew up, came
into the world, and observed the actions of men, I
thought I met with many, very many, who gave
too much for the whistle.'

Some twenty years later a writer who called
himself 'Giles Grinder' wrote an extended sequel
to this – *Pleasing and Instructive Lessons on Turning
the Grindstone:*[28]

I remember when I was a little Boy, one cold winter
morning, just as I was starting for school, I met a man
with a smiling countenance, with an axe on his shoulder.
Good-morning, my lad, said he, has your father got a
grindstone? Yes, sir, said I, and scampered with all my
might to show him where it was. You are a fine little
man, said the gentleman – Will you get a little hot water
and turn for me a few minutes?

Pleased and flattered, the boy does so, and afterwards collects a beating from the schoolmaster and
another from his parents; and he has to repent too
late that 'I had been turning the grindstone'. He
exhorts his readers to remember to avoid people
who have axes to grind, and finishes with this
anecdote: 'When I arrived at that age when the
boys feel uneasy and the girls feel queer, I paid
my addresses to Patty Prude. Her hair was curled,
her face painted and her tongue ran smooth as oil,
when in my presence; but in the kitchen – o lack
a day – it sounded like the crank of a – aye, aye,
I began to look out for the – grindstone.' While
owing much to Franklin, this is interesting as a
very early example of the homely domestic narrative
New Englanders were to make their speciality.

NURSERY RHYMES OR
FAIRY-TALES?

We have to accept that children in the eighteenth
century put childish things behind them at an early
age. The opening number of the *Youth's News Paper*,
which enjoyed a life of six weeks in New York in
1797, ran this editorial:

My dear Young Friends,
    You undoubtedly see in many corners of your houses
News Papers, but the first idea, the sight of them impress

you with, is, this belongs to our parents, though it would
be useful for you to peruse them, and your parents in all
probability be delighted in hearing you read, as it would,
at least, much aid your promptness in reading; yet the
size of these large papers, the perplexity of the stile, the
multiplicity of the matter they contain, and the number
of advertisements which have no relation at all to your
concerns, deter you.

The matter that the editor selected as attractive
to young readers dwelt much upon calamity – mad
dogs, deaths by lightning and drowning and fire,
statistics of death and burial, and such snippets as
'At a circuit court in the city of Albany last week,
14 persons were found guilty of the most detestable
crimes and received their sentence accordingly.'
This catalogue of disaster was interspersed with
geographical information, accounts of natural phe-
nomena, and reflections on the beauty of the American constitution – so much better than the English
one which was 'usage and some old laws, made
by kings, who should not speak in the eighteenth
century'. The contents of the *Children's Magazine*,
'calculated for the use of Families and Schools' and
published from Hartford in 1789, are similar, and
include advice 'on the best method of recovering
from the dreadful effect of dram drinking' and 'rules
for a life of business'.

It was much the same in England. *A Collection
of Pretty Poems for the Amusement of Children Three
Feet High* (Newbery, 1756?) set out to amuse its
young readers with reflections on the folly of going
to law and the vanity of ambition, on courtship
and on politicians. *The Exhibition of Tom Thumb*,
published by Isaiah Thomas in 1787 from *Tom
Thumb's Exhibition* which Francis Newbery had
put out in the previous decade, shows a Hogarthian
world. 'Squire Thumb's Perspective Glass' makes
people who look through it see their vanities and
self-indulgence in their true light, as well as the
end in store for them. Thieves go to the gallows;
the young rake surrounded by harlots, pimps, game-
sters and sharpers is shown through the glass what
it will all come to – himself in rags 'with scarcely
a shoe to his foot, dedewing [*sic*] his face with a
plentiful shower of tears and stamping on the ground
and ringing his hands like a madman. His attendants
are a surly bailiff and his followers, who have just
arrested him for a large debt ... [and] are now
dragging him to a gloomy prison.' Sally Pretty-face,
on the other hand, a model young girl, is seen in

the glass 'in a fine gilt chariot, in company with a Gentleman who, I make no doubt, is hereafter to marry her'. (Sally has played her cards well: he is the *eldest* son of a nobleman. Properly instructed young English ladies were keenly aware that from the point of view of inheritance only the eldest son counted.) 'Thus you see what an excellent thing it is for little masters and misses to be good children and behave as they ought. It is the safest and shortest, and I might have added the most reputable way to riches and honour in this world, and to true and everlasting felicity in the next.' (The priorities here should be noted.)

In 1836 the introduction to *The Fairy-Book*, a scholarly collection of fairy-tales published from New York, was to look back at the previous century as blessed, for children, by the productions of the Newbery firm. Its anonymous editor was Giulian Crommelin Verplanck (1786–1870), New York lawyer and politician, also remembered for his scholarly editing of Shakespeare. In his introduction he blessed the memory of 'good, wise, generous, public-spirited Mr Francis Newbery', for the glittering little books of his youth where, inside red, green and gold covers, he had found tales of wonder and enchantment. But, as too often happens with recollections of past joy, memory had exaggerated. There were two Francis Newberys, the son and the nephew of the firm's founder, John. Neither, in fact, was a particularly agreeable character and, more important, neither initiated much in the juvenile line. Francis the son, working with the stepson Thomas Carnan under the imprint of Newbery & Carnan (occasionally Carnan & Newbery), for the most part reissued John Newbery's books; they did, however, publish Perrault's *Histories or Tales of Past Times*. After 1780 Francis the son left the publishing side and occupied himself with the patent medicines that were the other part of the business. *Thoughts on Scurvy*, *Essay on Ulcerated Legs* and *Nature of Agistment of Tithe* were typical of the nephew's list, and though he did put out a handful of children's books, *Mother Bunch's Fairy Tales* among them, it was by no means the abundance that Verplanck remembered. In any case he had died six years before Verplanck was born, whereupon his widow Elizabeth took over the business.

The Fairy-Book spoke wistfully of the eighteenth century as a happier age than the 1830s; as a time when fancy reigned and there was not only Newbery, but in New York 'the worthy Hugh Gaine, at the sign of the Bible and Crown, in Pearl street, and the patriotic Samuel Loudon, and the genuine unadulter-ated New Yorker, Evert Duychink [Duykinck], besides others in Boston and Philadelphia, who trod in the steps of Newbery, and supplied the infant mind with its first and sweetest literary food'. But when we look at what has survived from those years, fantasy certainly does not predominate – either in England or in America. There were a few decades of relative freedom, when children's books had escaped the single-mindedness of Puritan teaching and had not been overtaken by educationalists seeking to cram information into their readers: 'geological catechisms, entomological primers, and tales of political economy – dismal trash, all of them,' remarked Verplanck dolefully of the children's books of the 1830s.

What we do find in the middle years of the eighteenth century is a cheerful random quality. The lists of the Newbery firm in London and of Isaiah Thomas in Massachusetts epitomize this spirit: they range from schoolbooks to collections of riddles, from nursery rhymes to Isaac Watts, and if there is a common ethic that runs through the publications of the period it is the Goody Two-Shoes one of 'Be good, and you will prosper.' Take Nathaniel Coverly, publishing in Boston from 1771. His list includes many editions of Watts, staple American favourites such as *The History of the Holy Jesus* and *The Prodigal Daughter* (an improving ballad from England about the awful consequences of indulging a daughter); *Goody Two-Shoes*, *Robinson Crusoe*, an abridgement of Fielding's *Amelia*, a few collections of little moral fables, and some nursery rhymes and riddles. The books published by William Durell of New York in the 1790s have the same flavour, and include *Dick Whittington* and Thomas Day's priggishly instructive *History of Sandford and Merton*.

The eighteenth-century climate in both England and America was better suited to nursery rhymes than to fairy-tales. As Iona and Peter Opie have demonstrated,[29] few of the former except lullabies and those that were part of games were originally written for children. Instead, over the centuries verses have been wrenched out of ballads, popular songs, plays, street cries, love lyrics, barrack-room and alehouse songs; then preserved by children long after their beginnings were forgotten, their lack of context giving them an appealing inconsequentiality, often a certain mystery. These 'nursery rhymes' are ruthless, often violent, but generations of illustrators have contrived to prettify them and soften the impact of such tragedies as 'Humpty Dumpty' and 'Goosey Gander', and by representing characters such as 'Jumping Joan' as children have

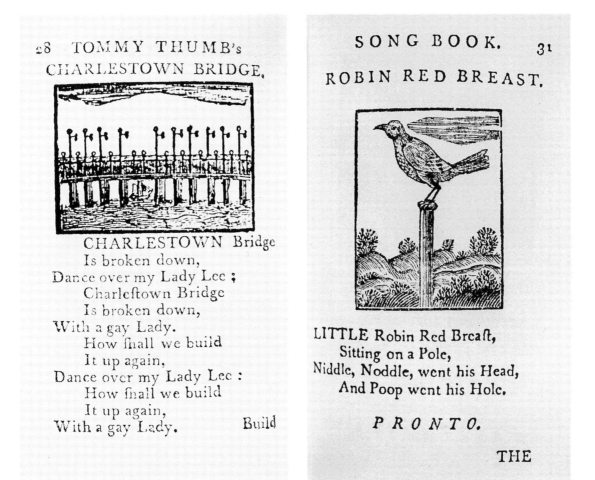

28 TOMMY THUMB's
CHARLESTOWN BRIDGE,

CHARLESTOWN Bridge
Is broken down,
Dance over my Lady Lee ;
Charleftown Bridge
Is broken down,
With a gay Lady.
How fhall we build
It up again,
Dance over my Lady Lee :
How fhall we build
It up again,
With a gay Lady.   Build

SONG BOOK.   31
ROBIN RED BREAST,

LITTLE Robin Red Breaft,
Sitting on a Pole,
Niddle, Noddle, went his Head,
And Poop went his Hole.

PRONTO.

THE

Two pages from Tommy Thumb's Song Book *(Worcester, Massachussetts, 1794).*

removed the original sexual connotation. Over the years, too, the cruder and more suggestive rhymes have been jettisoned. But in the eighteenth century children were not sheltered, and grew up quickly. Thus what strikes us about the earliest compilations of these traditional rhymes is the adult content and a feeling that we are close to their origins.

Tommy Thumb's Song Book is always reckoned to be the first collection of nursery rhymes. Though these had been sung to children for generations, nobody had thought of assembling them in print, until 'Nurse Lovechild', possibly Mary Cooper, the publisher herself, put out her little book in London. Mrs Cooper advertised it in 1744 but no copy has survived, and we can only surmise that the book of that title issued by Isaiah Thomas in 1788 was taken from her publication, or from a pirated version of it.

Thomas, who, as we noted earlier, usually made little alteration to the texts he appropriated but occasionally put in American references, altered 'London Bridge' to 'Charlestown Bridge'. But he kept the random and irrelevant musical directions that Mrs Cooper, who was also a music publisher, scattered over the pages – 'Vivace', 'Encore', 'Affetuoso' and so on (she was to do the same in the book's sequel).

Tommy Thumb's Song Book was aimed at the youngest children, 'to be sung to them by their nurses, until they can sing themselves', and it is interesting to see how far Nurse Lovechild's care for them extends. She gives tender instructions that they must not be frightened, but is not otherwise concerned to censor what is repeated to them. Thus 'Mistress Mary' finishes: 'Sing Cuckolds all in a row', and 'Robin Red Breast' appears in its original state:

> Little Robin Red Breast,
>   Sitting on a Pole,
> Niddle, Noddle, went his Head,
>   And Poop went his Hole.

as does

> O rare Harry Parry!
> When will you marry?
> When Apples and Pears are ripe;
> I'll come to your Wedding
> Without any Bidding,
> And lie with your Bride all Night.*

A few months later Mary Cooper followed up her first *Tommy Thumb* with *Tommy Thumb's Pretty Song Book*, voll. [*sic*] II, of which only one copy is known – now in the British Library in London. It is a deliciously pretty little book whose copper engravings of children playing (printed alternately in red and black) are sometimes at strange odds with the coarseness of some of the language. Though it contains favourites that have lasted such as 'Hickere, Dickere Dock', 'Sing a Song of Sixpence', 'Little Tom Tucker' and 'Mistress Mary', there are drinking and wenching songs, and abusive chants which have long ago been discarded. This 'voll. II' was not printed in America, so far as is known.

The Famous Tommy Thumb's Little Story-Book† is the first surviving American book to include rhymes. It contains the story of Tom Thumb, some fables, and a few rhymes – 'Cock Robin' among them. It had been published in England in about 1760, and was printed by W. M'Alpine of Boston in 1768. There was a time when some conjectured that the earliest collection of nursery rhymes was of Boston origin, published by Thomas Fleet in 1719 (predating any such English publication by twenty-five years), and that 'Mother Goose' herself was an American figure. This legend was launched by John Fleet Eliot, great-grandson of Thomas Fleet. In 1860 he wrote an article in the *Boston Transcript* claiming that his great-grandfather, who had married an Elizabeth Goose (Vergoose or Vertigoose),

having had to listen *ad nauseam* to his mother-in-law crooning old rhymes to her grandchildren, had eventually been driven to print them, giving her name to them and putting on the title-page a wood-cut of a goose. Eliot stated that a gentleman (who unfortunately died before the article was written) had seen Fleet's book in the library of the American Antiquarian Society. Repeated searches have failed to find what is now accepted to be a ghost volume.‡

But the figure of Mother Goose is an ancient one, long predating Fleet's supposed invention of her. She is portrayed in the frontispiece of Perrault's *Histoires* of 1697 as an old woman telling fireside stories to children. This role of storyteller she had apparently long held in France. In 1768 the Newbery firm advertised *Histories or Tales of Past Times*, 'told by Mother Goose', and used her again as 'author', this time of nursery rhymes, when they published *Mother Goose's Melody* twelve years later.[30]

It was this Newbery book, first published by Isaiah Thomas (conjecturally in 1786), that brought Mother Goose to America to preside over the rhymes hitherto associated with Tommy Thumb. The immediate impression is that a refining process has been at work with the fifty-one rhymes that constitute Part I. Either society was becoming more fastidious, or there was an instinct developing that children should be sheltered from adult improprieties. Exhortations to drink remain, as, for example:

> Round about, round about
>   Maggotty Pye [magpie].
> My Father loves good Ale,
>   And so do I.

This had appeared in *Tommy Thumb's Song Book*. But in general we notice that the rhymes have been laundered for the benefit of children – purged of their grosser elements.

Only a fragment remains of Isaiah Thomas' first Worcester edition, which lacks even the title-page. The second Worcester edition, of 1794, follows Newbery closely, except that in 'Se saw sacara down, /

---

* Later editors have ingeniously sat Robin Red Breast on a rail, so that the last line can run 'Wiggle, waggle went his tail'. The last line of 'Harry Parry' has been altered to 'Dance with your bride all night', or 'Dance and sing all night'.
† The terms 'Tom Thumb' or 'Tommy Thumb' were widely used by eighteenth-century publishers to designate books for small children.
‡ The legend is summarized in Iona and Peter Opie: *The Oxford Dictionary of Nursery Rhymes* (1951), 37–9. It is told at length in an article by Codman Hislop in *Colophon* (New York, autumn 1935), but the author had not seen either the 1697 edition of Perrault's *Histoires, ou contes du temps passé* nor the English translation of 1729, in both of which the legend 'Ma Mère l'Oye' or 'Mother Goose' appears in the frontispiece.

Which is the Way to London Town?' Thomas substitutes Boston. What is additionally interesting about the Worcester printing is that Part II carries, as the London one did, the songs of 'that sweet Songster and Nurse of Wit and Humour, Master William Shakespear'. Shakespeare was not at all a commonplace in New England at that time, and it was not until 1794 that one of his plays was published in Boston.

Neither the Puritan nor the utilitarian outlook favoured what we must loosely call 'fairy-tales', nor those stories of ancient heroic deeds referred to in the previous chapter. In England the latter survived in chapbook form, but came to be associated with the uneducated and unsophisticated. Tales from *The Arabian Nights' Entertainments – Sinbad, Ali Baba* and *Aladdin* – were at first known chiefly from chapbook versions which had begun to appear in 1712. It was the same with Perrault stories such as *Cinderella, Blue Beard, Puss in Boots* and *Little Red Riding Hood*. Many literary men, when they came to write their memoirs in the next century, recalled what this sort of literature – bought with hard-earned halfpennies and read over and over again – had meant to them. But it was not the sort of reading that educated parents in the eighteenth century bought for their children.

In the American colonies the climate was even less favourable. It is interesting that *The Child's New Play-Thing*, a delightful reader published by Mary Cooper in England in 1743 and in Boston in 1750, included not fairy-tales but old legends such as *St George and the Dragon, Fortunatus, Guy of Warwick* and *Reynard the Fox*, describing them as 'Stories Proper to raise the Attention and excite the Curiosity of Children'. *Fortunatus* (together with *Red Riding Hood, Cinderella* and an assortment of moral tales) reappeared in *An Approved Collection of Entertaining Stories* by 'Solomon Winlove', which Isaiah Thomas, having filched it from Francis Newbery, published in 1789. But these tales never achieved anything like the popularity in America that they did in Britain; 'the population had gotten

beyond the elementary tastes and childlike intelligence required for the enjoyment of such works,' one chapbook historian surmised.[31]

But they do seem to have been known. Caleb Bingham in *The Columbian Orator* (1797) composed a recitation for 'a very small boy' to speak. It begins: 'I am a monstrous great student. There is no telling the half of what I have read.' He goes on to list his favourite stories:

The Arabian Tales, Tom Thumb's Folio through, Winter Evening tales, and Seven Champions, and Parismus and Parismenus, and Valentine and Orson, and Mother Bunch, and Seven Wise Masters, Robinson Crusoe and Reynard the Fox, and Moll Flanders, and Irish Rogues, and life of St Patrick, and Philip Quarle and Conjuror Crop and Aesop's Fables, and Laugh and be Fat, and Tony Lumpkin's Elegy on the Birth of a Child.

Only two of these – *Tom Thumb's Folio* and *Crop the Conjuror** – were written specifically for children; all were favourite chapbook titles, and though Bingham (a schoolmaster) was mocking such books as suitable only for girls and very little boys, he must have assumed they were well enough known for an audience to recognize.

However, a knowledge of fairy-tales was far from universal then. Samuel Goodrich – alias Peter Parley – born in 1793, had apparently very little to read as a child except the *New England Primer* and the theology in his father's library. Then when he was ten his father brought him 'Gaffer Ginger,[†] Goody Two-Shoes, and some of the rhymes and jingles, now collected under the name of Mother Goose'. He was amazed at their foolishness, but his real outrage came a little later when he read

Little Red Riding Hood, Puss in Boots, Jack the Giant-killer, and some other of the tales of horror, commonly put into the hands of youth, as if for the express purpose of reconciling them to vice and crime. Some children, no doubt, have a ready appetite for these monstrosities, but to others they are revolting; until by repetition and familiarity, the taste is sufficiently degraded to relish them.

---

* *Tom Thumb's Folio*, 'To which is prefixed, An Abstract of the Life of Mr Thumb, and an Historical account of the wonderful Deeds he performed. Together with some Anecdotes concerning Grumbo, the great Giant'. London, Newbery, ?1767; Boston, Thomas and John Fleet, *c*. 1780. *The Wisdom of Crop the Conjuror* 'exemplified in several Characters of Good and Bad Boys with an impartial Account of the Celebrated Thomas Trot, who rode before all the Boys of the Kingdom until he arrived at the Top of the Hill, called Learning'. Published by Isaiah Thomas in 1786.
[†] Probably *The History of Giles Gingerbread*, a favourite chapbook tale resembling *Goody Two-Shoes*, about a little boy who teaches himself to read and achieves prosperity.

As for *Puss in Boots,*

that seemed to me without meaning, unless it was to teach that a Good Genius may cheat, lie and steal...I never liked cats, and to make one of the race – sly, thieving and bloodthirsty by instinct – the personification of virtue, inclined me, so far as the story produced any moral effect, to hate virtue itself.

One might have predicted that Goodrich would have abhorred *Blue Beard*, but not that he would have found *Jack the Giant Killer* rather worse:

He, too, was a good genius, but of course – according to the taste of this species of composition – a great liar. Surely – such is the moral of the tale – we must learn to forgive, nay, to love and approve, wickedness – lying, deception and murder – when they are employed for good and beneficent purposes.[32]

Usually regarded with amusement as an example of Goodrich's literal-mindedness and dislike of products of the imagination, this is one of the few recorded instances of the impact that traditional fairy-stories might make on somebody who had been entirely sheltered from all such things. It was a state of affairs less possible in Europe, where over the centuries such stories had been absorbed into the popular consciousness, and is one reason for the differences between English and American writing for children in the next century.

NOTES

1. Alexander Hamilton: *Hamilton's Itinerarium*, ed. Albert Bushnell Hart (St Louis, Mo., 1907), 178.

2. *Diary of Anna Green Winslow*, ed. Alice Morse Earle (Boston, 1895).

3. Quoted in Clarence L. Ver Steeg: *The Formative Years 1667–1783* (New York, 1964), 232.

4. Lawrence Wroth: *The Colonial Printer* (Portland, Me., 1938), 145.

5. Joseph Buckingham: *Personal Memoirs* (Boston, 1852), I.

6. Letter to J. Evelyn Denison, 9 Nov. 1825, in *The Writing of Thomas Jefferson*, ed. A. A. Lipscomb and A. L. Bergh (Washington, DC, 1903), XVI, 129.

7. *The Journal and Letters of Philip Vickers Fithian 1773–1774*, ed. Hunter Dickinson Farish (Williamsburg, Va., 1943), 34.

8. *The Diary of Colonel Landon Carter of Sabine Hall 1752–1778*, ed. Jack P. Greene (Charlottesville, Va., 1965), II, 786.

9. John Ash: *The Easiest Introduction to Dr Lowth's English Grammar* (London, 1766).

10. A so-called seventh edition printed by 'S.P.', identified by D'Alté Welch as Samuel Parker.

11. F. J. Harvey Darton: *Children's Books in England* (3rd edn, Cambridge, UK, 1982), 109.

12. Wilbur Macey Stone: *The Divine and Moral Songs of Isaac Watts* (New York, 1918).

13. *Guardian of Education*, vol. 2 (1803), p. 350.

14. ibid., p. 346.

15. ibid., p. 350.

16. Rosalie V. Halsey: *Forgotten Books of the American Nursery* (Boston, 1911), 67. Welch, however, can trace no edition or advertisement for this book earlier than Isaiah Thomas' of 1794.

17. *Eunice Locke's Story* (no imprint, n.d.).

18. Elhanan Winchester: *A Plain Pictorial Catechism. Intended for the use of schools in the United States of America* (Greenfield, Mass., 1796).

19. *The Sayings of Poor Richard. The prefaces, proverbs and poems of Benjamin Franklin. Originally printed in Poor Richard's almanacs for 1733–1758.* Coll. and ed. Paul Leicester Ford (Brooklyn, NY, 1890).

20. Benjamin Franklin: *The Autobiography*, ed. Max Farrand (Berkeley and Los Angeles, 1949), 98.

21. ibid., 117.

22. *Franklin's Morals, for the Entertainment and Instruction of Youth* (London, n.d.).

23. Franklin: op. cit., ed. Farrand, 71.

24. ibid., 88.

25. [Samuel Goodrich]: *Peter Parley's Christmas Tales* (New York, 1838).

26. William Henry Venable: *A Buckeye Boyhood* (Cincinnati, 1911), 5.

27. Mary D. R. Boyd: *Wat Adams, the Young Machinist and his Proverbs* (Philadelphia, 1876).

28. Welch conjectures, 'possibly an apprentice's token printed *c.* 1800–1810'.

29. Iona and Peter Opie: *The Oxford Dictionary of Nursery Rhymes* (Oxford, 1951).

30. Entered at Stationers' Hall in 1780. The earliest surviving dated edition is one published by Francis Power, John Newbery's son-in-law, in 1791.

31. Harry Weiss: *American Chapbooks* (Trenton, NJ, 1938), 5.

32. Samuel Goodrich: *Recollections of a Lifetime* (New York, 1856), 166.

Part Two

AN AMERICAN STYLE

3. *Rational Ideas*

THE EDGEWORTH INFLUENCE

'It is delightful to contemplate the great progress of American literature,' wrote Samuel Breck on 9 February 1828.

I remember forty years ago, when all our books were imported, and we possessed absolutely no native literature. A meagre magazine was published monthly in Boston, adorned principally with conundrums, acrostics, enigmas, &c., which were a source of puzzle and industry to all the young fellows and girls of the town. In the other cities of the Union nothing of a higher character was attempted for six or eight years after the close of the Revolutionary War.[1]

There was by this time native literature for children too. But English books were still important, and though American booksellers had long ago realized that it was far more profitable to print their own versions of them they often made little effort – as we saw in the case of Isaiah Thomas – to adapt the text. *Lives of Eminent Men*, published in Philadelphia in 1812, is a compilation of writings on English worthies of the previous century, in which Lord Chatham's American policies are described entirely from the English point of view. Even a reader which called itself *American Popular Lessons** was shamelessly subtitled 'chiefly selected from the writings of Mrs Barbauld, Miss Edgeworth and other approved authors'. The reading lists which Lydia Child gave in *The Mother's Book* in 1828 are largely made up of English authors. And dominating these lists and all other imports were the works of Maria Edgeworth who, if Goody Two-Shoes and Dick Whittington were the patron saints of eighteenth-century children's books, might be called the patroness of the 1820s.

Her writing for the young was probably more influential in America than in her own country. In England, though she was admired, she and her father Richard were regarded by many as dangerously radical, in the same league as Mrs Barbauld and Thomas Day, the author of *Sandford and Merton* – all of them supposedly working to bring about the downfall of the social order. The lack of religious content in her writing was also criticized. But the Edgeworth system of education and Maria's stories in particular seemed to have been designed for a new, young country. The emphasis was on science and practical matters rather than the culture of ancient civilizations, and the Edgeworth ideal of alert, independent, socially minded young people, taking an informed interest in the world about them and learning from experience, became the model for American heroes and heroines.

The Edgeworth attitude to fairy-tales and works of imagination, too, were thoroughly in the American mood. They were held to belong to the past; they were irrational, unproductive, and irrelevant to modern needs. The chapter on books which Maria contributed to her father's *Practical Education* dismissed fairy-tales as 'not now much read'. Two years earlier, in 1796, writing an introduction to her *Parent's Assistant*, Richard Edgeworth had taken issue with Dr Johnson, who had recommended that children should be given tales of giants and fairies and castles and enchantment:

Supposing that they do prefer such tales, is this a reason why they should be indulged in reading them? It may be said that a little experience in life would soon convince them, that fairies, and giants, and enchanters, are not to be met with in the world. But why should so much valuable time be lost? Why should we vitiate their taste, and spoil their appetite, by suffering them to feed upon sweetmeats? It is to be hoped, that the magic of Dr Johnson's name will not have power to restore fairies.

---

* Edited by Eliza Robbins, and published in 1820. Edward Hale (1822–1909) recalled reading it in his childhood.

Children playing with sensible toys of the sort recommended by Richard and Maria Edgeworth. Frontispiece to Jacob Abbott Ellen Linn *(New York, 1852).*

Besides, he felt, children should have outgrown fiction by the age of nine.

Richard Lovell Edgeworth was an Anglo-Irish landowner who in the course of four marriages fathered twenty-two children, Maria being a daughter of his first wife. He was a man of parts, a Fellow of the Royal Society, versed in all aspects of science and dedicated to improving himself and his fellow-men. Maria, who strove to please him and to be a worthy daughter, seems to have taken a deprecating attitude to her own writing for children, feeling that it was only justifiable if there were useful ends. Edgeworth's views on the upbringing of children were set out in *Practical Education* (1798), in which father and daughter collaborated, and Maria illustrated the theories in *Early Lessons**

– tales of Harry and Lucy, Rosamond and Frank, their moral development, and the lessons that they learn about the world around them. Much of the Edgeworth educational system holds good today: children played with sensible toys designed to teach them useful skills, and they learned through their own experience and experimentation. But their unflagging zest for acquiring knowledge now seems unnatural. Hilaire Belloc parodied the type in Charles Augustus Fortescue ('Who always Did what was Right, and so accumulated an Immense Fortune') – 'He sought, when it was in his Power / For information twice an hour.'[2]

In the wake of the Edgeworths came a deluge of juvenile books which sought to edify and instruct through conversation. Maria had raised hers to a

---

* This series began in 1801. *Harry and Lucy* shows the daily life of a small brother and sister (the first stories having in fact been composed by Richard Edgeworth and his second wife, Honora); *Rosamond* concentrates more on its heroine's moral development; in *Frank* a six-year-old learns about the natural world. Twenty years later, after the death of her father, Maria Edgeworth wrote sequels to all three for older children, finishing with *Harry and Lucy Concluded* (1825).

literary level, and had made Harry, Lucy, Frank and Rosamond credible children. 'We read of those children almost as if they had been personal friends,' Edward Hale wrote in *A New England Boyhood*. But her imitators, with the honourable exception of Jacob Abbott, produced neither readable fiction nor good instruction.

The Edgeworth system, mingled with a little Rousseau, seems to have been responsible for an American curiosity, Enos Hitchcock's *Memoirs of the Bloomsgrove Family* (1790). Here in 'the ancient Bloomsgrove mansion' Rosella and Osander Bloomsgrove receive a very rarefied and privileged education. And though 'in America children are generally reared up in a domestic state, and by their parents', these two are provided with a personal servant each. Like Edgeworth children they learn from their daily experiences (though Harry, Lucy, Rosamond and Frank were less pampered and far more self-reliant). They have gardens, where they watch 'the opening tulip, the expanding rose, the blushing violet, the unfading amaranth'. This is not a Virginia plantation, as one might expect from the luxury and the number of servants, but New England of the Enlightenment. Here a benevolent God watches high-minded parents present to their children the concept of a Supreme Being 'in the most pleasing and amiable light':

The parents... were happy in finding that [this religious system] prevented them from entertaining any of those frightful notions of the Deity, which were formerly thought to constitute the essence of religion... In those days, where superstition reared its sable standard, and taught men that, to serve God with fear and dread was the only acceptable manner of worshipping him, the Deity was represented as severe and unforgiving... But as man acquired more rational notions of the Deity, the gloom of superstition dissipated, as vapors before the rising sun.

Enos Hitchcock (1744–1803) was a Congregational clergyman, though 'distinctly on the way to Unitarianism', as the *Dictionary of American Biography* puts it: 'orthodox doctrines of election, original sin and imputed righteousness found no place in his sermons'. His attitude that attendance at public worship was 'the best school of good manners' makes an interesting contrast to the religious teaching described in the first chapter of this book.

The stories by Maria Edgeworth collected under the title of *The Parent's Assistant*[3] set out to illustrate moral truths, and in doing so succeeded in turning a genre to which every other writer gave the kiss of death into small literary masterpieces. Edgeworth virtues were very much to the American taste. She extolled diligence, honesty and perseverance, and often used cottage life to show these qualities. Undoubtedly, there are stories of fashionable life in the collection, but the memorable characters are those like Simple Susan, the farmer's daughter whose virtue and simplicity triumph over the wiles of a scheming lawyer; Lazy Lawrence, who progresses from shiftlessness to crime; and the two little orphans Paul and Anne whose honesty earns them a blanket for their grandmother and their chance to learn a trade. These stories were constantly reprinted, and her *Moral Tales* were standard reading for older girls. Mrs Child in *The Mother's Book* recommended Edgeworth for every age, from five to sixteen. Children, she said, were enthusiastic about Miss Edgeworth's stories. 'If ever I am big enough,' she quoted one little Bostonian as saying, 'I will go to England on purpose to see Miss Edgeworth; and if I am not suffered to go to her house, I will stand in the street till I see her go by.'[4] Young ladies were not so keen. Caroline Redwood in Catharine Sedgwick's *Redwood* says scornfully that the village library has not a single novel 'unless it be some of Miss Edgeworth's, which scarcely deserve the name of novels.'[5]

For throughout the nineteenth century the word 'novel' sent *frissons* through those responsible for the nurture of the young. 'It is a misnomer to call such productions "works of taste",' concluded a Massachusetts Sabbath School publication. 'If they shine, it is only as the rotting log, or putrescent carcase, which is phosphorescent because decaying.'[6] Edgeworth novels, however, seem to have occupied an entirely separate level, and in the ever-recurring discussion of the admissibility of fiction hers was often cited as one of the very few instances where there was any good to be gained from reading it. ' "I do not disapprove of narrative fiction, simply as fiction," ' pronounces a careful aunt in 1843. ' "Valuable truths are not less valuable when pleasingly told..." ' ' "I'm sure that's true," ' says her niece. ' "Miss Edgeworth's Moral Tales did me a great deal of good." '[7] It was the moral and instructive content that appealed to those in authority; the literary excellence, if they did recognize it, would have seemed irrelevant.

MOTHER GOOSE: HER DEFENDERS AND DETRACTORS

Fairy-tales did not flourish in the Edgeworth-domin-
ated years. It was becoming old-fashioned to object
to them on the score of their untruthfulness, though
the anonymous author of *False Stories Corrected*,
published by Samuel Wood of New York in 1814,
was moved by this fact. He set out to persuade
children of the folly of believing in such things as
ghosts, together with other mythical creatures less
likely to trouble them – phoenixes, centaurs, harpies,
griffons and the like. 'Many false stories . . . are told
merely for sport or pastime. This also is wicked;
it is lying, and of course reprehensible.' He was
particularly fierce against those who believe in

old Santa-claw, of whom so often little children hear such
foolish stories; and once in the year are encouraged to
hang their stockings in the chimney at night, and when
they arise in the morning, they find in them cakes, nuts,
money, and placed there by some of the family, which
they are told old Santa claw has come down chimney in
the night and put in.

In a companion volume published the same year,
True Stories Related, the author asks in Edgeworth
fashion what advantage can be derived from stories
of 'Hobgoblins, Enchanted Castles, Fairies, Sylphs,
Magical Wands, Wishing Caps, &c., &c.', and asserts:

It is certainly paying a very poor compliment to the
understanding and taste of children, to suppose they are
not capable of being pleased with anything but Fiction
and Romance, and that therefore their little volumes must
be filled with such stuff as the battle of Tom Thumb with
the Bumble-Bee, the exploits of Gulliver among the Lilli-
putians, the Descent of Sinbad into the Valley of Diamonds
&c.

Samuel Goodrich, as has already been related,
was outraged at an early age by the violence and
terror in fairy-tales. He condemned them as 'monstrous, false and pestilential' and pronounced that
just as no one would feed children with blood and
poison, so no one should administer 'cruelty and
violence, terror and impurity'.[8] Others raised different objections: fairy-tales were not useful, they
stood in the way of progress, and they were un-

*Children learning that stories about fabulous creatures
are all lies.*

genteel. All these arguments are advanced in *The
Fairy Tale*, a little tract published in Providence,
Rhode Island, in 1831.[9]

'I wonder what makes Pa dislike Fairy Tales so much,
mother; I am sure they can do us no harm, while we
know they are all false.'
'Is there no harm in wasting your time in the perusal
of nonsensical, and often wicked stories, Julia?'
'Wicked, mother?'
'Yes, Julia, often wicked, though you are not old enough
to understand their coarse allusion to sacred things;

besides, my child, time is too precious to waste it on that which will neither make us wiser or better. Remember, that life is but a span – a moment – a flash – and I am sure you will think with regret of your wasted hours.'

Julia's mother does not object to outdoor play since this is exercise necessary to health, but in a purposeful life fairy-tales can have no part. They are sweetmeats (as Richard Edgeworth saw them), possibly poisonous ones (as was Goodrich's view). But she added an objection of her own: they were not genteel. Julia's mother, though uncertain of her grammar, is very conscious of the low standing of such tales, which no doubt she associated with the crudely printed little versions of such stories as *Sinbad*, *Blue Beard* and *Cinderella* sold by pedlars to people who knew no better: ' "Few people of talents, at the present day, write fairy tales; and such nonsense as you was reading, Julia, is never read by well-educated people." ' And to show her daughter what fiction should be like she reads her an allegory about Intemperance and Luxury and Licentiousness, where Holiness and Prayer triumph, and Industry and Invention make 'a black powder which blows rock away very easy', this powder representing 'the force of industry accomplishing any desirable object'.

The Fairy-Book of 1836, mentioned in the previous chapter, is a pioneer work that includes, as well as eight tales from Perrault's *Histoires*, stories by Mme d'Aulnoy, Mme Leprince de Beaumont and other French writers. Its editor, Verplanck, who unlike Goodrich had been reared in a tradition of fairy-tales, saw them as stimulating courage and daring in boys, gentleness and compassion in girls. Washington, he averred, must have been formed by them: 'At any rate, I feel quite positive that he would not have been the first and greatest President of the United States, had he never read "Whittington and his Cat".' And, he pointed out with great truth, the stories of Miss Edgeworth 'are but the histories of Giles Gingerbread and Goody Two-Shoes grown up and living among the people of our own days'.

In his mock-serious championship of the traditional tales Verplanck speaks passionately of their antiquity, their influence on Shakespeare and the poets, and rejects 'the sage opinion that they are not true, and that children ought not to be allowed to read anything but the truth'. They have, he insists, an essential moral truth; indeed, history itself 'as commonly taught to the young in dry chronological tables and meager catalogues of musty names [does not] contain one quarter so much of living reality'.

There was another prevalent objection: 'Many worthy people think that this kind of literature is suited only to the old countries, and of course that our American children have nothing to do with such knowledge.' William Cardell, who in *The Story of Jack Halyard*[10] set out to write a story with 'doctrines and sentiments intended to be American', said as much about nursery rhymes: '[*Mother Goose's Melody*] was a parcel of silly rhymes, made by some ignorant people in England about a hundred years ago. The book was written in bad English, and full of plumping long stories from beginning to end.' His hero feels the same: ' "It is strange," ' says Jack, who has just read 'Hey Diddle Diddle' with much contempt, ' "that a child of common sense can take delight in reading such falsehoods, and believe that dishes can hop, and dogs laugh, and cows jump higher than eagles can fly." '

Samuel Goodrich, who, as we have seen, felt that children should be presented with rational ideas rather than nonsensical verse, spoke with grief about English efforts to revive the rhymes: 'A quaint, quiet, scholarly gentleman, called Mr Felix Summerly* – a dear lover of children – was invented to preside over the enterprise, to rap the knuckles of Peter Parley, and woo back the erring generation of children to the good old orthodox rhymes and jingles of England.'[11] He was thankful to add that the enterprise went bankrupt (this was wishful thinking), though regrettably it did not stop James Orchard Halliwell, the English antiquarian, from devoting the weight of his scholarship to these same foolish rhymes.[12] Goodrich's sorrow at this insensate folly was expressed in his magazine *Merry's Museum* in August 1846, in a dialogue between a boy and his mother, who realizes too late that 'these foolish rhymes stick like burrs... and the coarsest and vilest seem to be best remembered'. She recommends her son to learn 'good, sensible things' instead. But these turn out to be Watts' hymns – ' "I hate 'em," ' says Timothy tersely, and goes on shouting the jingle he has composed:

* Sir Henry Cole (1808–82) edited the Home Treasury series, begun in 1843, whose purpose was 'to cultivate the Affections, Fancy, Imagination, and Taste of Children'. The character of the series, said the prospectus, 'may be briefly described as anti-Peter Parleyism'.

Higglety, pigglety, pop!
The dog has eat the mop;
The pig's in a hurry,
The cat's in a flurry –
Higglety, pigglety – pop!

'And, because in spite of everything, he was a bit of a genius, Goodrich had unwittingly added to the store of nursery rhyme literature,' the Opies comment, triumphantly including the verse in *The Oxford Dictionary of Nursery Rhymes*. (And should anyone think that composing nonsensical jingles is easy, they have only to consider the many people who have tried and failed. The New Englander Eliza Follen compiled *Little Songs for Little Boys and Girls* in 1833, hoping to 'catch that good-humored pleasantry, that musical nonsense which makes Mother Goose so attractive to children', while excluding its 'vulgarisms and other defects'. But the result was banal.)

Sara Josepha Hale (1788–1879) was another American who unwittingly contributed to the Mother Goose corpus. She had included 'Mary had a little lamb'* in *Poems for Children* in 1830. The preface to this expressed her disapproval of the traditional rhymes: 'I know little children love to read rhymes and sing little verses, and such manner of spending their time is not good.' She wanted to teach her readers, instead, to love truth and goodness. She was an earnest lady whose verses in *The Wise Boys* (1860) told of oppressively sensible children such as Fred, who always thinks before he acts and reasons 'there's caution needed here' – with the result that he meets with great success in trade and 'grows richer every year':

At length he built a country-house,
And kept his coach, and grew
Wiser and richer, for he still
Kept forethought in his view.

Despite Peter Parleyism, Mother Goose rhymes seemed to settle easily in America. Other publishers took over *Mother Goose's Melody* from Isaiah Thomas. In an abridged chapbook version, printed in Windsor, Vermont, in 1814, a verse of 'Yankee Doodle' has been added – a rare topical touch:

Father and I went down to Camp
Along with Captain Goodwin,
And there we saw the men and boys
As thick as hasty pudding.
With fire ribbons in their hats,
They look'd so taring fine O,
I wish I had just such a one
To give to my Jemimo.†

Then, about 1825 Edmund Munroe and David Francis, Boston booksellers and publishers, put out *Mother Goose's Quarto, or Melodies Complete*, and though it was only a small book (about 128 pages) it was the largest collection of rhymes that had yet appeared. It contained most of the *Mother Goose's Melody* rhymes that Isaiah Thomas had reprinted from Newbery, but added others, some from the English *Songs for the Nursery* (Benjamin Tabart, 1805). It included a pedlar's song which gives a glimpse of children's toys of the time – 'babies', pipes, 'trunks to fill with weekly pence', plumed horses, windmills, toy soldiers, guns and horses.

The *Quarto* was not an influential book in itself, but its successor was. Munroe and Francis published *Mother Goose's Melodies* in 1833, basing it largely on the *Quarto*, which it condensed into ninety-six pages. It was highly popular and there were many subsequent editions. The cover engraving shows a goose dressed like a nurse, with attentive goslings all around her, and the preamble, 'Hear what Ma'am Goose says', tells readers to pay no heed to the old women who say that 'my enchanting, quieting, soothing volume' ought to be laid aside for more learned books. The adult flavour so evident in Mary Cooper's *Tommy Thumb's Song Book* of some ninety years before has disappeared; some of the rhymes have been unobtrusively reworded and others omitted. The attractive wood engravings (some of them in the first edition by Dr Alexander Anderson‡) have also done much to make the rhymes childlike.

We also find an example of the arbitrary way in which over the centuries verses have been

---

* It first appeared above Mrs Hale's initials in the magazine *Juvenile Miscellany* in September 1830.

† The *Oxford Dictionary of Quotations* (1980) attributes the song to Edward Bangs (fl. 1775), the *Oxford Companion to American Literature* to a Dr Shuckburgh, a British army surgeon in the Revolutionary War. The earliest known printing is in a Scottish collection of verse of c. 1778.

‡ Alexander Anderson (1775–1870) has been called 'the father of wood-engraving in the United States'. A great admirer of Bewick, he used the same white-line technique to produce sophisticated engravings.

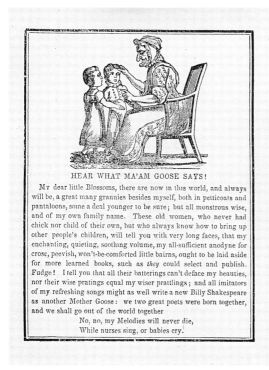

HEAR WHAT MA'AM GOOSE SAYS!

My dear little Blossoms, there are now in this world, and always will be, a great many grannies besides myself, both in petticoats and pantaloons, some a deal younger to be sure; but all monstrous wise, and of my own family name. These old women, who never had chick nor child of their own, but who always know how to bring up other people's children, will tell you with very long faces, that my enchanting, quieting, soothing volume, my all-sufficient anodyne for cross, peevish, won't-be-comforted little bairns, ought to be laid aside for more learned books, such as *they* could select and publish. Fudge! I tell you that all their batterings can't deface my beauties, nor their wise pratings equal my wiser prattlings; and all imitators of my refreshing songs might as well write a new Billy Shakespeare as another Mother Goose: we two great poets were born together, and we shall go out of the world together

No, no, my Melodies will never die,
While nurses sing, or babies cry.

Preface to Mother Goose's Melodies, *published by Munroe and Francis (Boston, 1833).*

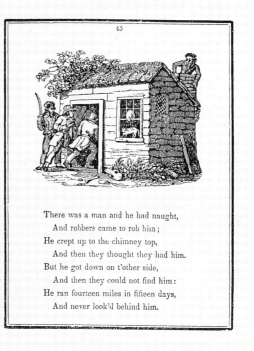

There was a man and he had naught,
    And robbers came to rob him;
He crept up to the chimney top,
    And then they thought they had him.
But he got down on t'other side,
    And then they could not find him:
He ran fourteen miles in fifteen days,
    And never look'd behind him.

Illustration by Alexander Anderson for Mother Goose's Melodies.

wrenched out of context and declared to be 'nursery rhymes'. On page 71 there are three, of which one begins:

> Pibroch of Donnel Dhu,
>   Pibroch of Donnel,
> Wake thy voice anew,
>   Summon Clan-Connel.
> Come away, come away,
>   Hark to the summons,
> Come in your war array,
>   Gentles and commons!

This is in fact taken from a ballad by Sir Walter Scott, though presented in isolation like this it is mysterious, not least because of the Scots names. It was a curious inclusion, and one that did not survive. The *Melodies* bear all the marks of their English origins. 'See saw, sacradown' still asks the way to Boston town, as Isaiah Thomas had printed it, but otherwise the rhymes celebrate such places as Charing Cross and Banbury Cross, St Ives, and the bells of London churches. There are robins and

cuckoos, and kings and queens. But in *Chimes, Rhymes and Jingles*, the third of the Munroe and Francis Mother Goose collections, published about 1845, there is a Santa Claus rhyme:

> Tite, tite prickly pears
> Jolly Santa Claus, what are your wares?
> 'A silver cup for Johnny Bowlyn –
> His name engraved around the rim.
> A doll for Annie, a drum for you –
> I have something for every shoe.'

This must surely have American origins. Santa Claus was known in New York in the early years of the nineteenth century, since children in 1814 were being warned of the foolishness of belief in 'old Santa-claw' (see page 68). Dutch settlers had brought the gift-giving St Nicholas with them, but in 1814 there was obvious doubt about how his name was spelt. Other variants were Sinterklaas, San Claas, Sancte Claus. The author of *A New Year's Present*[13] calls him 'Old Santeclaus'. This little eight-page book published in New York in 1821 is the

The steady friend of virtuous youth,

The friend of duty, and of truth,

Each Christmas eve he joys to come

Where love and peace have made their home.

From the first known American Christmas book: The Children's Friend. Number III. A New-Year's Present *(New York, 1821).*

first known American Christmas book. Issued anonymously, it was in fact written and illustrated by Arthur J. Stansbury, a former Presbyterian minister. The little illustrations, clearly the work of an amateur hand, include one of a sleigh drawn by a single reindeer, with a tall chimney stack in the background, accompanied by the rhyme

> Old Santeclaus with much delight
> His reindeer drives this frosty night.
> O'er chimney tops, and tracks of snow,
> To bring his yearly gifts to you.

It is likely that Clement Moore, who was a friend of the publisher William Gilley, had this in mind when he wrote 'A Visit from St Nicholas' a year

later as a gift for his own family. This poem, the first American children's classic, was to set the scene for Christmas Eve in perpetuity.*

THE BEGINNINGS OF AN AMERICAN MODE

The Fairy-Book in 1836 spoke gloomily of the reading matter then available to American children as 'something halfway between stupid story-books and bad school-books'. But before the moralists and the educationalists reached out chilling fingers to grasp children's leisure reading, there had been a last kick from the more robust traditions of the previous century. In the main this came from Philadelphia, that city which Dr Alexander Hamilton had found so staid sixty years before. By the beginning of the nineteenth century it had the largest population (some 70,000 inhabitants) in the United States, with New York not far behind with 60,000, and Boston standing at only 25,000. Its earlier books for children had been predominantly serious – schoolbooks, catechisms and the like – with very little in the way of entertainment; and from 1824 Philadelphia was associated with the American Sunday School Union. But for the first two decades of the century the city excelled in its production of picture books of a boisterous sort, nearly all originating in England and often commemorating in both illustration and text a sturdily independent rural life that was rapidly disappearing, in England though not in America. The name of the engraver William Charles, who also had his own publishing and bookselling business, is the one that so often appears on such books as *The Adventures of Old Dame Trudge, Dame Trot and her Comical Cat, The History of Mother Twaddle* and *Tom the Piper's Son*, all pirated from English originals.

Of Scots origin, Charles reputedly left Edinburgh to escape prosecution for his caricatures of the clergy there.[14] He arrived in New York in 1801, then moved a few years later to Philadelphia; there are picture-books bearing his name, published from Philadelphia as early as 1808. A prudent businessman, he did not confine himself to a single style – though it has to be said that humour predominates. He published for all tastes: fairy-stories such as *Cinderella, Jack the Giant Killer* and *Blue Beard,*

---

* Betsy Beinecke Shirley has summarized the development of the Santa Claus legend in 'Visions of Santa Claus', *American Book Collector,* 9 December 1986.

and a modicum of poetry and moral tales as well. One feels, nevertheless, that his heart lay really in such works as *Pug's Visit; or the Disasters of Mr Punch* (1809) and its sequel *Punch's Visit to Mr Pug* (1810). Both are crudely farcical:

Punch yawn'd as he said Wife I grow melancholy,
  By sitting at home with no creature but you.
Let's send for friend Pug and we'll make ourselves jolly,
  Have supper and crack a good bottle or two.

Pug, a monkey, is enthusiastic, and the three of them carouse until Pug is too drunk to go home. (We see him vomiting in a corner.) Mrs Punch proposes they should all three sleep in the bed, and is so enchanted by the sight of the monkey in her husband's clothes that she elopes with him.

Usually Charles made little alteration to the English texts, but in *Peter Pry's Puppet Show. Part the Second* which his widow Mary published in 1821 (William having died the previous year at the age of forty-four) there is a rousing burst of American patriotism. The first illustration is accompanied by:

Here's Johnny Bull from England come,
  Who boasts of being a sailor,
But yankey tars will let him know
  He'll meet with many a failure.

Even more than for his spirited humour, William Charles should be remembered for his use of colour in children's books. From 1814 onwards he issued most of them both plain and coloured, as London firms such as John Harris were doing.

Many other Philadelphia firms were publishing children's books at this time. Jacob Johnson, for instance, produced a large output of mostly sedate items of an improving nature – little books of information and moral tales from England. William Morgan seems to be the only other publisher who went in for books of the exuberant sort that was Charles' speciality. (He also used many of the Charles plates.)

Some thirty years after Charles' time were produced, also in Philadelphia, some of the most distinguished illustrated books of the period, published by the American Sunday School Union, who are not usually associated with books of such high quality. *City Sights for Country Eyes, Common Sights in Town and Country, Common Sights on Land and Water* and *The Child's Book of Animals*, all published

American patriotism, in a page from Peter Pry's Puppet Show. Part the Second *(Philadelphia, 1821).*

in the mid-1850s, are large picture-books illustrated with lithographs made 'from life' by Augustus Kollner (see page 178). His forte was horses, and there is one on nearly every page; these are beautifully finished pieces of work, showing scenes of mid-century America with an elegance that was most unusual at that date. (The accompanying text, presumably composed by an ASSU hack, is often inappropriate and always very moral.)

A very early example of a wholly American picture-book came from New York in about 1806. *Some Very Gentle Touches to Some Very Gentle-Men*, dedicated to 'all the little Girls & Boys, of the City of New-York', illustrates a common hazard of the early American city – the pigs that ran through the streets, throwing down the passers-by and dowsing 'each Lady that passes'. The mayor and corporation did apparently nothing to control this nuisance:

In this City so fair
Resides, Mr Mayor
But he tis supposed always rides.
For if he should foot it
Where these dirty snouts root it
Tis hop'd he would feel their fat sides.

A New York hazard. From Some Very Gentle Touches to Some Very Gentle-Men. By a humble country Cousin of
Peter Pindar Esq. *(c. 1806).*

Another early American picture-book was published in Baltimore in 1825 – a rhymed account, illustrated by splendidly vigorous copperplate engravings, of the settlement of New England: *The Pilgrims, or First Settlers of New England* (see pages 14 and 18). Much stress is laid upon their home life. We see them, always wearing their steeple-crowned hats – labouring to clear the forest, putting up their first huts, and enjoying the idyllic domestic harmony that ensues.

Editions of London street cries were frequently reprinted, but it took a surprisingly long time for American publishers to produce their own versions. Then in 1808 Samuel Wood brought out *The Cries of New-York*, which is American through and through – not just in scene but in sentiment too. We learn much about contemporary living conditions, such as the prohibition on throwing 'offal of any kind ... dead rats, cats or shells' into the streets in the summer. (They had instead to be handed to the bell-man, who came along in his cart. 'Such parts as are fit for hogs and cows to eat, he preserves, and discharges the rest off the end of the dock, into the river.') One of the first features of the city to be described in the book is the fire alarm (European visitors remarked how often that was to be heard). We are told what commodities were sold in the streets, and how much they cost. The occasional homily is thrown in, including the expected one on industry. Does not the little radish-seller lead a better life than 'the gentleman hog'? the reader is asked. And warnings are given about the time and money that are wasted in idle gossip round the tea-table. More unexpected is the castigation of slavery. Remarks on stealing water-melons lead the writer to reflect: 'astonishing is it, that a professed christian whose principle tenet is, that we are bound to do, as we would be done by, especially an American, whose political creed is, "all men are born free and equal", should so widely differ in practice, as to rob a fellow creature of the most precious gem in nature, LIBERTY.'

Samuel Wood (1760–1844) of New York[15] was one of the first publishers to specialize in American material. Until he was forty he was a schoolmaster, but in 1803 set up as a bookseller in Pearl Street – then as much a centre of the book trade as Paternoster Row was in London. He bought a small printing press and embarked on the first of his huge output of toy books with *The Young Child's A B C, or, First Book* in 1806. As befitted a school-

One of Samuel Wood's moral publications: The Cries of New-York *(1808).*

master and a Quaker, his publications were soberly instructive and contained nothing that approached fantasy. (It was he, indeed, who published *False Stories Corrected* and *True Stories Related* mentioned earlier, and since we know that he wrote many of his titles himself we may suspect that he was responsible for these too.) The general tone of his publications may be summarized by the moral reflection that accompanies the picture of the ant in *The Instructive Alphabet* (1814): 'Thus all their proceedings are conducted apparently by the utmost

THE

New-York Preceptor;

OR,

THIRD BOOK.

" 'Tis education forms the youthful mind :
Just as the twig is bent, the tree's inclin'd."

NEW-YORK :

PUBLISHED BY SAMUEL WOOD & SONS,
NO. 261, PEARL-STREET ;
A'nd Samuel S. Wood & Co. No. 212, Market-street,
Baltimore.

An early New York schoolbook.

prudence and persevering principles of forethought
and economy – an instructive lesson to man –
especially to youth.'

But to compensate for all this seriousness, the
little books were profusely illustrated, many of them
with wood engravings by Dr Alexander Anderson.
In them we sometimes glimpse a distinctively
American scene; a tranquil domesticity of a kind
that was to be such a feature of later-nineteenth-
century books for the young – *The Seasons* (1810)
closes with an account of the farmer's year brought
to a prosperous end. The sheep, the hogs and
pigs, the turkeys, geese and ducks are all bedded
down, the winter's stock of fuel has been brought
in:

Now [the farmer] sits himself down to rest, and perhaps
enjoys the agreeable company of his neighbour in friendly
chat…and they regale themselves with the fruit of the
orchard and the juice of the same, while the little folks
are busied in cracking the nuts that the autumn winds
blew from the trees, and their little fingers gathered; and
the old dog and cat come in for their share of the comforts
of the fireside.

Contemporary with Samuel Wood in New York,
and with a list that was very similar, was the
publisher Mahlon Day (1790–1854).[16] More light-
hearted than either was Solomon King (1791–
1832),[17] who flourished in New York between about
1821 and 1832, and specialized in chapbooks and
children's books illustrated with copper engravings.
His toy books include nursery rhymes, fairy-tales,
comic verse and accounts of subversive heroes such
as Robin Hood and 'Glenwar the Scotch bandit'.

The famous series of toy books known as 'Cobb's
Toys' comes somewhere between Wood and King
so far as frivolity is concerned. Lyman Cobb (1800–
64) was a famous educator remembered for his
work *The Evil Tendencies of Corporal Punishment*
(1847). Firm in not wanting pupils to 'become
disgusted or fatigued' with monotonous reading, he
produced a series of graded readers of which the
Dictionary of American Biography says 'it must be
admitted that by the time the *New Sequel or Fourth
Reading Book* (1843) was reached, an excessive
aridity and formality had crept in'. A typical story
(number 11 in the second series, *Pretty Stories for
Pretty Children*) tells of Charles and Robert, who
make their way to school no matter whether it
rains, hails or snows, because they are determined
to have learning 'and to become wise men in the
world'. But John, in spite of their urging, can never
summon up the resolution to go to school. And so,
while they rise to be 'great men in their native
state, John became a poor worthless creature'.

The firm of Sidney Babcock in New Haven who
were publishing from 1825 put out books with a
distinctive character. In 1833 one of their publications assured customers: 'At Babcock's in Church
street, / There are hundreds of Toys / Full of beautiful
Pictures / For good girls and boys.' We find the
same mood in the little duodecimo books with their
pink, blue and yellow paper covers. Many of them
describe day-to-day events in the lives of happy
children, as in *The Four Seasons* where a little boy
wishes that every season would last for ever, or
the children in *Woodbine-Arbor; or The Little Gar-
deners* (1850) who build an arbour, invite their
parents to visit them and present them with the

produce of their own gardens. The illustrations, many drawn by the prolific Alexander Anderson, showing little boys in skeleton suits and the girls in the low-necked dresses of the period, are often very attractive.

It was largely the War of 1812 that sent publishers of recreational books in search of home talent, just as the Revolutionary War had encouraged the growth of American schoolbooks. In a preface to *Original Tales*,[18] a New Year's gift book of 1813, the publisher speaks of the 'restrictions of commerce between the United States and Great Britain' which have emboldened him to lay these stories before the public. Nevertheless, even here the setting is London, and only in the last few pages, in a story called 'The Juvenile Geographers', does the author reveal his allegiance to America, giving an account of its geography, constitution and the liberty that Americans enjoy.

Nancy Sproat (1766–1826), who also wrote as 'A Lady of Boston' and Goody Lovechild, is possibly the first American children's author to write under her own name.[19] Her little verses are of no great distinction, though 'The Blackberry Girl' appeared in many nineteenth-century school readers and was famous enough to be printed on handkerchiefs and aprons. It tells of Phebe, who tries to earn enough money for a new bonnet for church by selling blackberries, then spills them, and as she sits crying by the empty basket is seen by 'a pretty little Miss' who takes off her own bonnet and gives it to her. Mostly Sproat is concerned to tell cautionary tales. She did not rise to the same literary level (modest though this was) of her English contemporaries Jane and Ann Taylor, whose *Original Poems* (1804–5) and *Hymns for Infant Minds* (1810) she probably had in mind.

Lydia Child's attempt in 1824 to write a Barbauld-style book, *Evenings in New England*, produced nothing markedly different from her English model. But in the following year William Cardell (1780–1828) – of whom little is known except that he was a teacher and the author of two children's books – produced a story, one of the earliest of its kind, that is both manifestly American and patriotic. *The Story of Jack Halyard, the Sailor Boy* was designed, he said, for American children in families and schools. (We have already referred to his views on the unsuitability of nursery rhymes, page 69.) Its hero, who lives with his family on a small farm in New Jersey, is a likeable lad, called 'little General

Washington' by his schoolmaster because of his honour and manliness. He displays flaws as well as virtues, that we are to encounter in much subsequent moral fiction. He is a hard worker and an early riser, for 'he read in Dr Franklin's almanac, among the sayings of Poor Richard, that laziness kills more people than hard work'. But at the age of five he experiments with rum and makes himself drunk; he also fires a gun at his little brother and nearly kills him. Life on the farm comes to an end when Jack's father dies, the family moves to New York, and Jack goes to sea. On his third trip to Liverpool as a cabin boy, a lady asks him what he is reading. He tells her it is called *The Federalist*: 'It explains the principles of our government, and contains much useful information; besides ma'am, I have another reason for liking it; it is an American book.' Several voyages later Jack is prosperous enough to buy back his father's farm, for like so many of his countrymen at this time Cardell took an idealistic view of the farmer: ' "Of all men, I think," said Mr Halyard, "the American Farmers are the most independent, and the most happy." '

The Happy Family; or Scenes of American Life, published three years later (the year of his death), has the flavour of actual experience. Certainly, it is larded with lofty moralizing and many gobbets of information, but there is an abundance of fascinating practical detail about settler life in this account of a family leaving Massachusetts and trekking over the mountains to Ohio. Here, after unflagging work with the axe and spade, they become comfortably wealthy, own a fine house and a horse and carriage, and the father is instrumental in establishing a library company, whose 'collection amounts to four hundred well-chosen volumes'. Cardell was moved to write this book, he says in the preface, when he saw an apparently respectable woman in a bookstore selecting for her children 'volumes of falsehood, nonsense and bad English' (presumably nursery rhymes). He did not wish to proscribe English books; 'But it is absurd that they should be made, among our children, the main standard of feeling and thought. Parents who take the trouble to examine, can hardly fail to observe, that extensively as these juvenile books are multiplied, the greater part contain very little American, except occasionally... the word *American*, in a title page.' It would be some time, though, before there was any abundance of recognizably American books.

The best-known tale of these early days – America's own folk-story – is the tale of young Washington and the hatchet which Mason Locke Weems (1759–1825) put into the so-called fifth edition (1806) of *The Life and Memorable Actions of George Washington*. Like folk-stories of other cultures, it was not specifically intended for children, but was taken over by them. Weems, who came from a well connected Maryland family, had been ordained in England as an Anglican clergyman, but he was a most uncharacteristic one – a robust and colourful individual who took to the roads south of Philadelphia, peddling books for the great entrepreneur Mathew Carey. And he had the contempt of a new country for the learning of the past. Washington's education, he asserted, was of 'the proper sort. Dead languages, pride and pedantry, had no charms for him, who always preferred sense to sound, the kernel to the shell. A grammatical knowledge of his mother tongue – the mathematics – geography – history – natural and moral philosophy, were the valuable objects of his youthful studies.' Weems threw in a characteristically American castigation of idleness, which, he pronounced in a torrent of eloquence, was the root of all evil, from King David's adultery with Bathsheba to the Trojan War, from the most recent suicide to 'horrid uproar' on the eve of national holidays. But he possessed the common touch, and this, rather than his purple patches, is what has ensured his place in the American pantheon. The story of the five-year-old Washington learning generosity is not so well known as his refusal to lie. Little George had demurred at sharing an apple with his brothers and sisters. His father showed him an orchard strewn with windfalls. 'With his little naked toes [George] scratched in the soft ground ... then lifting his eyes filled with shining moisture, to his father, he softly said "Well, Pa, only forgive me this time, see if I ever be so stingy ever more."

PETER PARLEY AND THE QUEST FOR KNOWLEDGE

It is fitting that Samuel Goodrich (1793–1860) should in effect open the history of American children's recreational books. We have seen something of what had been provided for their reading in the seventeenth and eighteenth centuries: first, the attempts to guide their souls, then, as people gradually

acknowledged that there was a place for entertainment, the lighter type of English imports that were favoured. Now came a New England genre of writing that evolved out of the wish to promote mental improvement – information informally and zestfully imparted, over a huge variety of topics ranging from Athens to zebras, on which Goodrich could invariably express himself in a most readable and friendly manner. It was the 'travelogue' style, a type of writing that America was to make particularly its own. In his memoirs Goodrich paid tribute to the philanthropic British lady of letters, Hannah More. Many of her Cheap Repository Tracts, a series of popular religious pamphlets, were sold in America, though the English rural society they described must have made Americans congratulate themselves that such conditions were not to be found in their own country. But in fact Goodrich's own writings owe far more to Mrs Barbauld and the Edgeworths, with their emphasis on useful knowledge, their dismissal of the products of the imagination as, if not dangerous, then irrelevant to modern society.

It is ironical, therefore, that his huge output of facts was based on a piece of fiction which the stricter might well have called a lie – the character he created of Peter Parley. 'Here I am!' he wrote in his first book, *Peter Parley's Tales of America*, in 1827 when he was in his early thirties. 'My name is Peter Parley: I am an old man. I am very gray and lame. But I have seen a great many things, and had a great many adventures, and I love to talk about them.' This was accompanied by the little engraving that was to become famous – of a white-haired old man wearing a dark buttoned coat, and supporting himself on a cane. There were to be minor variations: sometimes he was shown holding a wooden crutch, or resting his gouty foot, swathed in bandages, on a soft chair. There is a frontispiece picture of him thus in *Peter Parley's Method of Telling about Geography* (1830), abjuring boys to take care – if they run against his gouty toe he'll not tell them another story. In the opening number of *Parley's Magazine* in 1833 he wrote, 'I cannot undertake to become the editor as you desire, for my quill is nearly worn to the stump, and the hand that guides it, must soon cease from its labors.' It was apparently an image that appealed to children, and they were more than a little shaken if they met Goodrich in the flesh to find that the real Parley was a smart man in early middle age. When Goodrich's other children's magazine, *Robert Merry's*

Museum, sent its readers photographs of Goodrich, one girl wrote reproachfully from Virginia that his readers had been enticed into 'an affectional correspondence' and that they blushed to think how familiar they had been.[20]

Goodrich was born in Ridgefield, Connecticut, the son of a Congregational minister who also worked his own small farm. It was not a bookish milieu: 'All could read and write, but...beyond the Almanac and Watts' Psalms and Hymns, their literary acquirements had little scope. There were, I think, four newspapers, all weekly. There were, however, not more than three subscribers to all these in our village. We had, however, a public library of some two hundred volumes.'[21] The school he attended used little except the *New England Primer*, and no doubt it was this meagre fare that filled him later with the desire to provide more and yet more histories and geographies for schools.

While he admired the values of hard-working rural communities such as the one in which he spent his youth, he aspired after a broader scene, and in 1816 began a publishing and bookselling business in Hartford. It collapsed in 1823 but in 1826 he began again in Boston, and the following year saw the publication of his first Peter Parley book. This was followed by *Tales of Peter Parley about Europe* (1828), *Parley's Winter Evening Tales* (1829) and *Parley's Juvenile Tales* (1830). By 1856 he could claim in his *Recollections* that he had produced some 116 different titles, of which he had sold seven million copies. He had also founded two children's magazines, which purveyed information in the same genial manner.

There were not many topics on which he did not aspire to instruct – astronomy, ancient history, natural history, trades and manufactures, geography, mythology. And he poured out streams of facts, whether he knew anything about the subject or not. His information was nearly always attractively presented, often compelling, though usually misleading and frequently wrong. 'The people of Italy are called Italians,' announces *Tales of Peter Parley about Europe*; 'They live in a delightful climate and are very fond of music. Here is a picture of an Italian playing on a guitar; he is serenading a lady. The inhabitants of Germany are called Germans. They consist of several nations. They are generally very industrious. *The finest part of Germany is Austria* [my italics].' In view of this and other assertions, such as that tigers in India 'fight dreadful

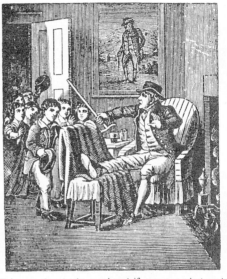

PETER PARLEY
Going to tell about Geography.

Take care there! take care boys! if you run against my toe, I'll not tell you another story!

Peter Parley's gouty foot, from Samuel Goodrich's Peter Parley's Geography for Children *(Hartford, 1830).*

GEOGRAPHY FOR CHILDREN. 63

13. Denmark and Sweden are cold countries, and not so pleasant as some other parts of Europe. They are not fruitful, but the people are intelligent and generally happy. The people of Denmark are called Danes; those of Sweden are called Swedes.

Sweden.   *Norwegian.*

14. Norway is a very cold and mountainous country, and the people live principally by hunting and fishing. Bears are very numerous in Norway, and here is a picture of a Norwegian killing a bear.

15. Russia is a vast country, but it is neither a beautiful nor a fruitful country. The people of Russia are generally ignorant, and many of them poor and unhappy.

Peter Parley's Method of Telling about Geography *(Rochester, NY. 1835)*.

battles with the lion',[22] it is hardly surprising that
the *London and Westminster Review* commented
tersely that Goodrich was 'a bad dealer in slip-slop'
and that 'we have a right to insist that he shall
know what he is talking about'.[23] The trouble was
that his brief generalizations, right or wrong, were
so memorable; the stereotypes they presented must
have remained engraved on readers' minds for a
lifetime. Take this lyrical summary from *The Tales
of Peter Parley about Asia,* infinitely more delightful
than the usual facts about imports and exports or
mineral resources contained in the geography catechisms of his time:

Persia lying to the west of Afghanistan, is inhabited by a
nation, who are fond of poetry and fine horses. To the
north of Persia is Independent Tartary, a country of lofty
mountains, and inhabited by a nation of bold and daring
robbers. To the west . . . is a great salt lake, called the
Caspian Sea. On the western border of this lake are the
Caucasian countries. The people here are remarkable for
their beauty. Many of the women are carried to Turkey,
and sold for slaves.

England was one of the countries that he actually
had visited, though even here he was apt to get
his facts wrong, declaring, for instance, that the
British Museum was in Trafalgar Square. His feelings about the country were mixed. He was probably
remembering the wretchedness of the rural poor
as described in his favourite Cheap Repository Tract,
The Shepherd of Salisbury Plain, when he wrote:
'The Lords and Ladies, indeed, live in luxury and
magnificence, but within the very sound of their
revelry and mirth, the poor cottager and the beggar
often lie down and die for the want of food.'[24] But
he had a fondness for picturesque English traditions,
and was convinced of the superiority of the Protestant ethic: 'It is only in countries where the
Protestant religion predominates, that the people
have been raised, by education, and freedom of
enquiry, to that pitch of intelligence and virtue,
which are indispensible to the success of liberal
institutions.'[25] His own country, he naturally
thought, had no rival, 'if we regard the general
happiness of the great mass of the people'.[26] His
was an uncomplicated philosophy. Man was designed to be happy: 'And how can we be happy?
The answer is easy, to do good, and to do it the
right way.'[27] His story 'The Little Gardener'[28] de-
velops his point a little further. A destitute Irish

boy sits weeping in the city of Boston, faint with
hunger, wet, homeless. A kind man hears his story
and takes him home. 'I need hardly tell you the
rest of Peter's story. He lived with the man who
had brought him home, and by his good conduct,
won the favor of all who knew him . . . And so, my
little reader, all persons, however poor, may get to
be happy, if, like this little boy, they are good and
industrious.' For there was no reason why in America, that land blessed above all others, everybody
should not prosper; and prosperity meant happiness.

Goodrich was a kindly man – prosy no doubt,
and with a keen commercial instinct allied to a
thirst for moralizing. Even natural history he
presented with a moral slant: 'The tiger is one of
the most graceful and beautiful, yet one of the
fiercest and most bloodthirsty of animals. It seems,
therefore, that external beauty is no proof of corres-
ponding good qualities in the character and disposition.'[29] But he had a genuine fondness for
children: 'They are the great blessings of the household,' he asserted in his *Recollections.* 'Without
children, the world would be like a forest of old
oaks, gnarled, groaning and fretful in the desolation
of winter.' He wanted them to be happy. It was
simple: all they had to do was work hard, acquire
education, be kind to animals, study nature. And
he did succeed in pleasing them, as spontaneous
remarks scribbled in their copies of his books attest:
'This is Good Book' appears in one now in the
American Antiquarian Society's library. 'I am Betty;
Peter Parley is my friend', 'I love Peter Parley',
'Happy New Year, my dear Peter Parley' are among
the comments found in others. A fan letter in
Parley's Magazine is typical:

I write this letter to tell you a story of myself. I read all
your little books about America, Asia, Africa and other
places, and I wanted to see you very much. I learnt from
them many things, that I did not know before, and I
thought if I could see you, you could tell me something
more. Besides, I wanted to know how you look, and hear
you talk; and I thought you would let me sit down with
the little boys and girls that come to hear your stories,
and then I should have been very happy.[30]

Something of the pervasive influence that the books
had on the young of his time, and the omniscience
with which they were credited, can be seen from
a little Methodist Sunday school story of 1848.
' "Poor little blue-bird," said Tommy. "I pity you

this cold winter morning... You are a foolish little bird, or before this time you would have been, in the warm, sunny south. If you would study Peter Parley's geography as I do, Mrs Bluebird, you would know of a land where Jack Frost never goes." ,[31]

It is with Goodrich that the mainstream of English and American writing for children divides. Undoubtedly there were periods in England when pressure from religious moralists and educationalists drove works of imagination underground so far as children were concerned, but the tradition was strong enough to persist nevertheless, and to surface when the climate was more favourable. But while England in the 1830s and 40s was witnessing what might be termed 'gentrification' of the traditional stories, in that they were being removed from the chapbooks and put into a format acceptable to the drawing-room, America was in the grip of facts. Knowledge was the key to prosperity and would open up the future. *Youth's Mental Casket and Literary Star*, a periodical published from New Jersey, spelt out the message when in 1841 it warmly recommended geological cabinets for the young. These would, it averred, increase wealth because a knowledge of geology would help people discover valuable minerals: 'Many farms have been made worth double, some ten times as much as they were before.' As an afterthought, the writer pointed out the moral benefit that would accrue: 'If each of the two millions of families in our republic, had a Cabinet of Nature and Art, there probably would not be one theatre, or one tippling-shop, in one of the United States.' Knowledge, it seems, had replaced early piety as the parental goal for children.

To the English with literary tastes, Goodrich was a dull dog; 'the strangest antidote to hilarity', Harvey Darton called him (though the name of Peter Parley and the style seemed attractive enough to some for there to be several English imitators – to Goodrich's indignation). He is, nevertheless, an important figure who brought colour and interest into children's lives and made them curious about distant places. His books were a substitute for fantasy, opening windows for many young Americans.

PERIODICALS FOR THE YOUNG

'America is a world of newspapers,' wrote a Scottish observer in 1870. 'More dailies are published in the single state of New York than in all England, Scotland and Ireland put together... The newspaper is half the life of an American.'[32] Many other visitors noticed how even the lowest ranks in society read them, and supposed this was all part of the independence that the English, in particular, found so unnerving. Mrs Frances Trollope in 1832 observed this universal newspaper habit (of all the many travellers' accounts of the United States her *Domestic Manners of the Americans* is the most carping and disparaging):

This, I presume, is what is meant by the general diffusion of knowledge, so boasted of in the United States... Throughout all ranks of society, from the successful merchant, which is the highest, to the domestic serving man, which is the lowest, they are all too actively employed to read, except at such broken moments as may suffice for a peep at a newspaper.[33]

Her son was to say later that the average consumption of newspapers by an American must amount to about three a day.[34] Clearly, there was plenty of scope here for juvenile journals.

But the contents of most of those available before the 1860s seem to confirm the European observers' comments on the precocious maturity of American children. The *Juvenile Gazette: Being an Amusing Repository for Youth*[35] pitches all its humour at an adult level, and carries news items such as 'Snelson, the robber of the Virginia Bank, has been seen near Quebec.' One of its very infrequent pieces of fiction features two boys, deadly rivals at school, who fight a duel with pistols. In the *Juvenile Magazine; or Miscellaneous Repository of Useful Information*[36] we encounter another lad of the same kidney: 'George got drunk, kicked up a riot, lost his eye in the brawl, was obliged to pay a large sum to an inhabitant of the town he had maimed for life; and to crown all, was expelled. "How can *you* keep yourself out of all these scrapes?" said he to his brother.'

Perhaps it was predictable that Thomas G. Condie, who was not yet fourteen when he founded the *Juvenile Port-Folio and Literary Miscellany* in Philadelphia in 1812, should have given it a very lofty tone – adolescents on the whole find life a serious matter. Of his poetry contributors he said: 'Scarce is a Youngster freed from the trammels of the School, than he conceives himself a Scott, a Byron or a Moore, in Embryo, and pants for a niche in the Muses' Temple.' The magazine contained poems and moral tales, musings on such subjects as 'Deceit', 'The Acquirement of Virtuous Habits in Youth', 'Punctuality', 'Bets and Oaths', and an occasional joke – though he experienced difficulty, he said, in procuring 'a sufficiency of *chaste* wit and humour'. It was very different indeed from the light-hearted nonsense of another magazine founded in England by an adolescent – *The Rectory Umbrella*, produced in 1850 by the young Lewis Carroll. But unlike this last, the *Juvenile Port-Folio* was a commercial venture, and a remarkably professional one. It came out weekly and lasted for four years, achieving at its peak a circulation of over six hundred. Admittedly, in the early stage young Condie had the assistance of his father, but the latter died of 'a severe and lingering *Pulmonary Consumption*' in 1814, and thereafter the boy presumably managed by himself. This type of precocious business sense is perhaps where American youth differed most from English contemporaries.

One of the most chilling of the journals produced for the miniature businessman was the *Juvenile Key*, published from Brunswick, Maine; it ran for about three years before being reissued in a larger format as the *Family Pioneer and Juvenile Key*.[37] The first number appeared on 18 September 1830 and bore the names of Z. J. and J. W. Griffen, two children, then aged seven and nine, of the newspaper's proprietor Joseph Griffen. Not only had they done most of the typographical work, said their father, they were also involved in the make-up, promotion and distribution of the initial two hundred copies. (What they were paid is not revealed, but in the twelfth issue the subscribers, who so far had not had to pay, were told that money was now needed 'for the hard earned wages of the printers'.) Zerui'ah-Juan and Joseph Warren Griffen – dedicated as they were to usefulness – were shining examples of the sort of child that the *Juvenile Key* held up as its ideal. Little boys were told to eschew such trivialities as hoops, kites and playing ball, and girls were to abandon jumping the rope and gadding about the streets; for 'as soon as the little boy is strong enough to lift a hammer, hatchet, hoe or shovel, he should be taught to use these implements in places where he may at least think he is doing some good service', while girls should of course be usefully employed in the home. As for reading and learning, they should limit themselves to practical matters which would make them good

farmers and mechanics. The paper specialized in disaster – violent deaths, executions, murders, revolution in France, massacre in Ireland, oppression in Poland – which it reported with a considerable amount of lurid detail, but with an absence of moral comment that was unusual for those days. There was little religion, and though alcohol, tobacco and holiday fireworks were all opposed, it was upon the grounds that these inhibited work and the acquisition of wealth.

Griffen made work into a religion in itself, but, as has already been seen, there was a general American distrust of play. It was shared by Lydia Child, who expressed herself very forcefully in *The Frugal Housewife*, even if she was not so exacting in the *Juvenile Miscellany* (see page 83), which was aimed at a class with more leisure. As far as farm children were concerned, however, it was a great deal better for them 'to be picking blackberries at six cents a quarter, than to be wearing out their clothes in senseless play'. Six-year-olds could 'knit garters, suspenders and stockings... make patchwork and braid straw... make mats for the table and mats for the floor... weed the garden, and pick cranberries from the meadow, to be carried to market'. She deplored the practice of allowing children to 'romp away their existence till they get to be thirteen or fourteen'.

By far the longest-lived juvenile periodical of that time – indeed, of all time, for at its demise in 1929 it was 102 years old – was the *Youth's Companion*. It was founded in Boston in 1827 by Nathaniel Willis (1780–1870) as an offshoot of his religious paper, the *Recorder*. Willis (known as Deacon Willis to distinguish him from his very different son, also Nathaniel and also a journalist) was, as the *Dictionary of American Biography* has it, 'known during his long life for his rigid and formal piety', and the *Youth's Companion* reflected this throughout his editorship, which lasted thirty years. (He sold it in 1857 to Daniel S. Ford and John W. Olmstead.) While not as severe as the Massachusetts Sabbath School Society's *Well-Spring* (see page 104), it did reflect the orthodox Congregationalism of the time. It excluded all visual appeal, all pleasures of the imagination – not so much consciously as because it would never have occurred to the editor that these were of the slightest consequence.

Deacon Willis seems to have had great ambitions to exert a formative influence. He wrote in the first number, in April 1827:

This is a day of peculiar care for Youth...The human mind is becoming emancipated from the bondage of ignorance and superstition. Our children are born to higher destinies than their fathers; they will be actors in a far advanced period of the church and the world. Let their minds be formed, their hearts prepared, and their character moulded for the scenes and duties of a brighter day.

But this opening grandiloquence was not sustained in the rest of the little paper. In its four unillustrated pages of deplorable small type there is nothing to distinguish it from other publications of the time. And though Willis had promised that it would be something new, 'not a Sabbath School Magazine' nor yet a literary magazine that provided only for amusement, the early issues could be easily mistaken for the former. There are many articles on temperance, obituaries of pious children, items of natural history and discussions of the sad effects of disobedience, procrastination and the like. The first number is typical, containing a deathbed scene of a six-year-old, a child's prayer for his minister, and 'advice on marriage'. With this piety went shrewd New England business sense. A model child is told how to lay out his monthly shilling: sixpence to a juvenile benevolent society, one cent to Sabbath School missionaries, three cents for another juvenile magazine, and the remaining two cents 'to pay for the second volume of [the *Youth's Companion*] in advance, and so get it for two cents a month'. But from its success and survival in those early years under Willis we have to infer that this was the sort of reading that many Boston parents desired for their young.

Nevertheless there were parents who wanted something better, and Mrs Child's bi-monthly *Juvenile Miscellany* met this need. It was aimed at the same sort of public that had been attracted by Edgeworth principles in England: the parent (in this case the mother – fathers appear only rarely in the pages of the *Miscellany*) with leisure to devote herself to the education of her young. Essentially a Boston journal – Boston settings feature in its stories – it made its first appearance in that city in September 1826. There were none of the trumpet blasts with which Deacon Willis had heralded a new dawn, but the *Juvenile Miscellany* was far more innovatory than his paper both in its use of fiction to entertain the young and in its compassionate attitudes to those who had received little such attention before – native Americans, Africans, the

poor, the physically handicapped. It published much about American achievements (there is perhaps the earliest description of a railway to appear in children's literature – the Quincy Railway built to carry stone from the quarries for Boston's Bunker Hill Monument), and about great Americans. Among the poems was one composed by Lydia Child herself which, though not particularly distinguished, is remembered because it celebrates America's first festival – 'The New-England Boy's Song about Thanksgiving Day'. But the importance of the *Miscellany* lies in its fiction and its emphasis on the domestic scene.

Lydia Child was only twenty-four, a teacher at a private school in Watertown, Massachusetts, when she began publishing the *Miscellany*, but she had already written two novels – *Hobomok* (1824), about seventeenth-century Salem and the love of an Indian youth for a settler's daughter, and *The Rebels; or, Boston Before the Revolution* (1825). She was deeply concerned with the plight of oppressed races and it was her anti-slavery views that were to start the magazine's decline, ending with its demise in 1836.

She had already discussed slavery issues in *Evenings in New England* (where she took a less decided attitude than she was later to adopt in her famous 1833 manifesto, *Appeal in Favor of that Class of Americans called Africans*). In response to the suggestion that Southerners must be very cruel to keep slaves, she maintained that the system was their misfortune rather than their fault, and was now not easy to change. (She added that slaves were unfit for freedom – a view she was later to discard.) In the *Miscellany* her views were slipped into articles where the unwary might not expect them – an essay on dogs discussed the use of bloodhounds in Santo Domingo to pursue escaped slaves – or were more openly vented in stories which attacked the assumptions of racial inferiority on which slavery (not necessarily American slavery) was based. 'The St. Domingo Orphans', for instance, in which two white children are mistaken for West Indians, showed the futility and danger of a system that derives from difference in colour. Writing for younger children she stressed, as in 'The Little White and the Little Black Lamb', that the outer colour was as nothing compared to the inner nature of a child: 'God loves George and Thomas and me, when we are good children. And God loves the little white lamb and the little black lamb, when they are good lambs.'[38] Though her feelings on

American slavery were strongly held, her comments were usually oblique. Only in one story, 'Jumbo and Zairee', did she include a full frontal attack: 'Shame on my country – everlasting shame! History blushes as she writes the page of American slavery, and Europe points her finger in derision.' Even so, since it was a story for children, she brought matters to a happy conclusion: Jumbo and Zairee and their father, an African prince, are bought by a benevolent former slave-owner and dispatched to their own country. This story was published in 1830, but it was not until 1834 that growing antagonism to abolitionist views brought the *Miscellany*'s circulation to such a low ebb that Lydia Child was forced out of the editorship in favour of Sara Josepha Hale.

Mrs Child also had a strong sense of the wrongs suffered by the original inhabitants of the American continent. In the introduction to *The First Settlers of New-England. By a Lady of Massachusetts* (1829), she spoke of her conviction that the treatment of the Indians by the white settlers had throughout been 'in direct violation of the religious and civil institutions which we have heretofore so nobly defended, and by which we profess to be governed'. 'To what purpose,' she concluded, 'is the multitude of our sacrifices and vain oblations, our sabbaths and calling of assemblies, and solemn meetings, whilst we omit to "do justice and show mercy" to the oppressed?' And she included in the *Miscellany* an unsigned story, almost certainly written by herself, about two lost children who are returned to their home by a kind Indian woman.

As a schoolmistress, she had from the start decided views on how children should behave. 'I seldom meet a little girl, even in the crowded streets of Boston, without thinking with anxious tenderness, concerning her education, her temper, and her principles,' she wrote in the opening number. But her views – and those of her contributors – on their behaviour were expressed gently, encouragingly. If children really wished to be good, God would help them. There is little of the hectic pursuit of success (in the achievement either of early piety or of worldly wealth) that we find in so much of what had gone before and was still to come. Admittedly, in the early *Evenings in New England* we find a story, 'The Young Bookseller', containing the industry-plus-luck formula which was to be such a prominent feature of the American moral tale. The hero provides for his mother and sister out of his modest earnings; then, 'in a few years [his employer] died, leaving all his business to young Mr Adams, together with a legacy of fifteen thousand dollars'. But the children that we meet in the pages of the *Miscellany* are largely from families already prosperous, and they are intent upon learning not how to make their way in the world but how to improve their characters. The calm security of their lives, the affection that surrounds them, their childishness, are new in American writing.

A religious background is implicit rather than expressed, and the Calvinism that had pervaded so much improving literature of the past is noticeably absent. Indeed, in *The First Settlers of New-England* Mrs Child had made it clear that she thought Calvinist doctrines were 'odious', in their teaching that the elect could not err and gloating over the agonies of the non-elect. The story in the *Miscellany* that opens 'Come, little girls, those of you who like to hear of good children . . . listen to the story of Emily Walters' is not a story of early piety, hectic conversion and death but of a good, affectionate little girl, who likes to play. When her baby sister dies, her mother kisses her and tells her that the baby is happy now and will never more have pain or sickness.

The mothers in the *Miscellany* are more demonstrative than Maria Edgeworth's, but they speak with the same irritating reasonableness. When Emily Heard roars at having her face washed, thinking that she can thereby extract a new doll from her mother, Mrs Heard merely tells the maid to let her go to the party with a smutty face.[39] Mary and Frances rush full of excitement to their mother to tell her that their father has given them a garden, but their mother asks why they expect that a bit of ground and a few roots and seeds will make them happy. (She is right, of course; it does not.)[40]

The periodical attracted distinguished contributors, among them Lydia Sigourney, the 'Sweet Singer of Hartford', a versifier so popular that the journal *Godey's Lady's Book* paid her an annual retainer of $500 just to list her name on its title-page; Sarah Josepha Hale, whose 'Mary had a little lamb' first appeared there; Catharine Sedgwick, Eliza Leslie and the English Mary Howitt. Indeed, it could be said to have launched a new species in America – the literary lady who wrote for children. When Sara Josepha Hale took over the editorship of the *Miscellany* the magazine became a monthly, but ceased publication altogether in April 1836.

One of the contributors to the *Miscellany*, Caroline Gilman (1794–1888), a minor lady of letters who wrote reminiscences of life in both the North and the South, founded her own children's periodical. Born in Boston, she moved with her husband, a Unitarian minister, to Charleston, South Carolina, where, although she felt that the women of the North and the South were far more united by a common sense of the importance of family life than they were divided by political antagonisms, she later committed herself to the Southern cause. She began *Rose Bud* in August 1832, in response, she claimed, to a request from one of her children. Although inevitably didactic, given the temper of the times, the paper carried jokes and riddles as well as the usual informative articles, accounts of topical events, and stories and verse of an improving sort. This is one of the earliest papers to include a section for younger readers, with an easy vocabulary, large type and words divided into syllables, and she also included book reviews. The first issue is notable for an unusually frivolous piece of verse, 'The Little Boy's Complaint about Butter':

> As soon as I become a man,
>   I'll have a pie as tall as you,
> With doors and windows like a house,
>   And lin'd with plums
> All through and through.

Rose Bud was not long-lived. Its name was changed in 1833 to *Southern Rose Bud*, and from volume two onwards it took on an increasingly adult character, becoming the *Southern Rose* in 1835 in recognition of 'the advanced years of its early subscribers'. It ceased publication in 1839, Caroline Gilman explaining that 'she would prefer some mode of publication less exacting than the rigorous punctuality of a periodical work'.[41] *Rose Bud* will be remembered as the first juvenile periodical in the South.

A FEMALE MODE ESTABLISHED

The *Juvenile Miscellany* was the first periodical for the young with signed contributions by women. Thenceforward women were to dominate the field of juvenile fiction. These early writers were, as Anne Scott MacLeod has pointed out,[42] from relatively prosperous Protestant middle-class back-

grounds. Nearly all were born in New England or the Middle Atlantic states – a Southern writer or a Southern imprint was rare before 1860. They were highly educated, and many were of 'old stock' American heredity. Catharine Sedgwick (1789–1867), one of Mrs Child's more distinguished contributors, was in these respects typical. She was born in Stockbridge, Massachusetts, in the Berkshire Hills. Her father, who was to become Speaker of the House of Representatives and a judge of the Massachusetts Supreme Court, had a lofty sense of his superiority to the commonalty, whom he habitually referred to, his daughter said, as 'Jacobins', '*sans culottes*' and 'miscreants'. 'He dreaded every upward step they made, regarding their elevation as a depression, in proportion to their ascension, of the intelligence and virtue of the country.' 'Social lines were very firmly drawn in that old colonial society, before the plough of the Revolution went through it,' commented one of Catharine Sedgwick's biographers.[43] She herself was far more egalitarian: 'It is certainly a false notion in a democratic republic, that a lawyer has any higher claim to respectability – gentility if you please – than a tanner, a goldsmith, a printer, or a builder... Talent and worth are the only eternal grounds of distinction.'[44]

Her influence on the domestic novel (described in chapter 6) would be a dominant one. She was already the author of *A New-England Tale* (1822) and *Redwood* (1824), both for adult readers, but found time to write for children too. *The Travellers* (1825) is one of the very earliest travelogues. The rest of her work for the young, mostly written when she was in her fifties, strikes a rather hectoring note. In *Morals of Manners; or Hints for our Young People* she laid down a code which included deference to one's elders and cleanliness, and devoted many pages to denouncing the practice of spitting. She spoke with horror of not only pavements, bar-rooms, floors and carpets defiled with spittle, but even churches: 'I have seen gentlemen – so-called – in a new church... spitting at the right hand and the left.' She finishes with a passionate appeal to the young to reform, since 'we are blamed, satirized, laughed at, as a nation, for this vile habit'. She had much to say on health matters, advocating daily washing, plenty of exercise in the open air, and plain food.

She also had strong views (discussed at more length in chapter 6) on what constituted true gentility, and equally strong views on the selfishness and general worthlessness of men. Nearly all the fathers in her juvenile tales are shiftless drones supported by excellent wives. Poverty made her impatient; it was caused only by vice or disease, and was unnecessary: 'If the moral and physical laws of the Creator were obeyed, the first of these causes would be at an end, and the second would scarcely exist. Industry and frugality are wonderful multipliers of small means.' Conversely, virtue, good habits and manners brought money. These pronouncements occur in *The Poor Rich Man and the Rich Poor Man*, a tale whose moral can be guessed without much difficulty but which is interesting for the domestic touches, an area where Miss Sedgwick excelled. Modest comfort was within the reach of every American, she was sure:

This is, above all others, the country of self-made men. Here the rewards of ingenuity, enterprise, and industry, are attainable by all. No class is crushed by inevitable want or ignorance... What makes a man, in the highest sense of the word, is the full development of his faculties; and in the United States he who is true to himself has the power of this development.[45]

Catharine Sedgwick was wary of anti-slavery sentiments. Writing to one Mrs Channing in 1860, she remarked that while she was in sympathy with the humanitarian aspect, she did not wish her name to be associated with 'a party whose measures are sometimes violent';[46] and though in some of her novels she does refer to slavery, she avoids the topic in her children's stories. She showed, however, unexpected compassion towards the Irish immigrants, whose desperate plight in those early years shocked and often outraged the pride of a country confident that poverty and ignorance were left behind in the Old World.[47]

Eliza Lee Cabot Follen (1787–1860) was another writer with impeccable New England ancestry. She was a woman of considerable purpose, who married a man nine years younger than herself (Charles Follen, a political refugee from Germany, and Harvard's first professor of German literature) and inspired him to offer himself for ordination. A prominent member of the Massachusetts anti-slavery group, she was deeply interested in social and religious problems. She edited the American Sunday School Union's the *Child's Friend*, a conventional and undistinguished little periodical, from 1843 to 1850. She is now remembered for what, in fact, she did *not* write, the verses 'Three little kittens, they lost their mittens', which appear at the end of her *New Nursery Songs for All Good Children* (though they are there described as 'traditional', their authorship is often attributed to her).[48] Her best-known book, *The Well-Spent Hour* (1827), is an infusion of religious principles into an Edgeworth approach to education. Here Kitty, learning to spend one hour well, goes on to make all her time profitable. When she momentarily wavers in her purpose, her mother questions her about her motives until Kitty is shamed into abandoning pleasure and going back to her self-imposed task. The moral instruction is interspersed with bursts of not always accurate information. Her London editor rewrote the chapter on the eye, which, he had found, was not in accordance with medical fact.

Mrs Follen was discreet with her abolitionist views. *The Well-Spent Hour* did not introduce the subject of slavery, though in *A Sequel to the Well-Spent Hour* there is a reference to the noble loyalty of a negro woman to her slave husband. Similarly in *Twilight Tales* (1858), she writes of a little negro boy who returns good for evil and thus abashes a white contemporary. Her strongest comment is to be found in *The Little Pedler of Dust Sticks*, in which Henry the little Hamburg pedlar (who grows to prosperity through steadiness) is angered by American slavery: 'He felt that slavery brought labor into discredit, and his heart ached for the poor slaves, who are cut off from all knowledge and improvement.' Further than this she did not go, and it may be noted that she was allowed to continue at her post with the *Child's Friend*.

Her contemporary, Anna Maria Wells (1795–1868), whose *Poems and Juvenile Sketches* appeared in 1830, was a pleasant minor versifier in the Jane and Ann Taylor style. Like them, she took a mildly moral attitude towards children, and made it plain that she preferred them when they were good. But she was able to remember how it felt to be a child:

> My own Mamma!
> My dear Mamma!
>   How happy I shall be,
> To-morrow night,
> At candle-light,
>   When she comes home to me.

This informality is particularly attractive at a time when so many felt that writing for children must involve lecturing them.

Eliza Leslie (1787–1858) of Philadelphia was a writer of more individuality. She was primarily an author of occasional pieces in journals such as *Godey's Lady's Book*, but a very successful one, and the fact that she, like Catharine Sedgwick, from time to time turned her hand to juvenile writing shows the increasing prestige attached to that literary form. The *Stories for Adelaide* (1829) are admittedly of a cautionary nature, but there are some delightful domestic details, as of Eliza, who yearns for a leghorn hat to wear by the seaside instead of the pink gingham bonnet (with wire and canes to keep it in shape) that her mother makes for her. And, in *The Quilting*,[49] a moral tale that makes the distinction between true and false gentility, she gives an evocative account of the quilting-bee, and the splendid supper that follows. Her *American Girls' Book* (1831) is a valuable source of games and pastimes popular then.

She was also the author of an early travelogue, *The Young Americans: or sketches of a sea voyage* (1829). Here is a wealth of social detail and interesting comparisons of American children with their English contemporaries. Matilda, the spoilt child of a Virginian planter, is sent to live with her English aunt, the description of whom echoes many French and American comments on English upper-class women: 'Mrs Massingham was a very tall woman, with a large figure and large features. She was fair, and had a florid but not a delicate complexion, a very wide mouth, with a long upper lip, and prominent white teeth, round staring blue eyes, and two masses of flaxen curls.' She is arrogant and contemptuous, and has the lowest opinion of the American way of life. She is not a real lady of fashion, readers are told, but she is apparently typical of many English people, who are 'prone to offend our feelings by their indications of ignorance of almost everything relating to America'.

Matilda is indignant at the nursery regime imposed on her in her aunt's house: ' "Two years ago, I came out, and now I am to go in again, and to be dressed and treated like a child, till I am eighteen." ' Her handsome dresses and jewellery are taken from her, she now wears muslin frocks with short sleeves and no trimming, and her hair is cropped. She dolefully contrasts the strict order here with the mayhem at home, ' "where the children dance on the mahogany tables and roll over the Brussels carpet, eating gingerbread, spread an inch thick with butter. Why, one of their favourite amusements is to cut slits in the sofas, and pull out the horsehair, and to stand on chairs and pick the gilding off the looking-glasses and picture frames." ' There is no gingerbread for English children, Matilda finds; her diet consists mostly of bread and butter, and if there is fish or meat it is boiled. Another child in the book is disposed to like her English contemporaries rather better than Matilda does, though she marvels at the rigours with which they are brought up, adding: ' "Charles thinks they cannot take care of themselves half so well as the juvenile Americans" ' – one of the earliest instances of this observation, which was to become a commonplace.

JACOB ABBOTT AND A NEW GENERATION

Jacob Abbott (1803–79) was the first writer to make the American domestic scene familiar to English readers, and to produce characters – Rollo and Beechnut, for example – with enough life in them to step out of the page. Undoubtedly, he took over from the Edgeworths; if it had not been for Harry, Lucy, Rosamond and Frank there would have been no Rollo, and undoubtedly like them Abbott considered that the purpose of fiction was to infuse useful principles. All the same, Rollo has always seemed a tangible presence: a sturdy little boy, sometimes wilful but always likeable, whose doings, even though comparatively humdrum, have the power to engage the reader.

Abbott was even more prolific than Goodrich; bibliographies of his work list 180 volumes of which he was sole author, and thirty-one more of which he was joint author or editor. At the age of twenty-five he had founded the Mount Vernon School in Boston, one of the pioneer institutions in America for the education of young women. A typical Abbott feature was the way it relied for good order on the honour and conscience of the pupils. In 1833 he resigned from the school and became minister of the Eliot Congregational Church in Roxbury, Massachusetts, but a year later he had given up the charge to his brother, and thereafter he devoted most of his life to writing, though he did help to found and run two other schools.

THE EXPEDITION PREPARING TO START.

Busy, purposeful children. Frontispiece to Jacob Abbott's The Engineer, or How to Travel in the Woods
(New York, 1856)

His books are up-market; he was addressing himself to the same sort of public as Mrs Child and the Edgeworths, to middle-class parents who had leisure for their children. Behind his writing one senses the presence of the wise schoolmaster – patient, tolerant and good-humoured, but concerned to improve his pupils. He set about this discreetly: realizing that children respect the opinions of older children and are more ready to listen to their advice than to an adult's, he made a practice of introducing a youthful sage, very often a hired boy like Beechnut or Jonas, who offers counsels of prudence to impetuous little boys. Jonas, though not so well remembered as Beechnut, had a whole series of books named after him. There are female preceptors too: Mary Bell, aged only twelve, and Juno, 'a nice and tidy-looking coloured girl', who later sets up her own Sunday school class. Though these young people may seem preternaturally wise, they are flesh and blood, not mere personifications of virtue like Goody Two-Shoes. What is more, they are likeable, for Jacob Abbott had the rare gift of making goodness seem both credible and attractive.

His ideal child differs from the standard evangelical hero discussed in the next chapter. Religion is more often implied than obtruded. His books seek more to inculcate social virtues such as obedience, forbearance, tolerance, diligence and orderliness. His aim was to produce capable, self-reliant children who questioned, discovered and thought for themselves. There was a characteristically American slant to this – knowledge brought money:

'Father, Jonas says that the more anybody knows, the more money he can earn. Is this true?'

'...He has better pay; and so he can live in a more comfortable house, and educate his children better, and have more books to read, and travel more. And just so it is in all branches of learning. Those who have the most extensive knowledge, have, generally, the lightest work, and yet the best pay.'[50]

In Abbott's world, children learn early to manage money. The two in *Florence and John* (1860) get a half-dollar weekly allowance, and if they propose an expedition they themselves have to pay part of the cost of hiring a carriage, and must undertake all the arrangements – the buying of the rail tickets, deciding upon a hotel. Moreover, they must agree to accept the consequences of their mistakes or else hand the control back to their mother. This was

very different from the dependence of the upper- or middle-class English child; a visitor in 1852 expressed her astonishment at seeing a six-year-old in New York studying the regulations for travel on an omnibus and instructing his younger brothers.[51] Florence and John's mother also allows them to make what many would consider dangerous experiments, telling herself that she must be brave about it or else they will grow up 'cowardly and weak, and good for nothing'.

Unlike some of his contemporaries, Abbott saw the need for play. To form good, healthy constitutions, he said, boys must run about a lot, and 'have a great deal of frolicking and fun'.[52] The father in *The Engineer: or How to Travel in the Woods* (1856) explains to his children how 'hunters, emigrants and travelers' make their way through 'the wild regions of the Western country of America', and in the final chapter Stanley and Dorie are allowed to make a day's expedition with their friends in the snowy woods. They set out on sledges, build a hut, make a fire and cook food. And on the way home 'they pretended to have an alarm from the Indians' and rush pell-mell down the hill.

Many of Abbott's books contain inspired suggestions for amusing children, and he is careful to include detailed directions with them. *Work for Autumn*, in a series of books that suggest occupations for all the seasons, presents particularly delightful possibilities: the children haul out an old stove to a deserted sugar-house and make beechnut candy, stew apples, roast potatoes and toast bread, while the boys gather wood and haul it on their sled. Everybody keeps journals, and they prepare pictures for an art gallery of their own. Elsewhere, some children are helped to make a box full of amusements, to be locked away and only opened when one of them is convalescing from an illness.[53]

The first two Rollo books (of a series which came to number some twenty-eight volumes) were *The Little Scholar Learning to Talk* and *Rollo Learning to Read*, both published in 1835. Rollo's childhood is more interesting than his priggish youth. Presumably when his character is in need of no further moulding, he is taken by his uncle on a twelve-volume tour of Europe, 'with the satisfied consciousness of hailing from a land far superior to those inhabited by foreigners'.[54] Rollo aged five is an engaging little boy, with not much thought beyond his own concerns, unwilling to concentrate on anything for very long, loftily confident of his ability to achieve anything he chooses, apt to cry when things go wrong. Rapidly he learns to be both sensible and useful. At six he asks, ' "When shall I learn to work?" ', to which his father replies, ' "I have been thinking that it is full time now. You are about six years old, and they say that a boy of *seven* years old is able to earn his living." ',[55] Lacking the perseverance, he fails at the first task he is given – sorting nails – but his father keeps him to it:

'Now, I am going to give you one hour's work to do, every forenoon and afternoon. I shall give you such things to do, as are perfectly plain and easy, so that you will have no excuse for neglecting your work or leaving it. But yet I shall choose such things as will afford you no amusement; for I want you to learn to *work*, not play.'

Set to picking up stones, Rollo plays several times, and instead of beefsteak and apple pie he has bread and water for dinner. But he learns to persevere, and 'in the course of a month Rollo became quite a faithful and efficient little workman'.

Rollo is every little boy, sometimes endearing, sometimes irritating. While he is acquiring practical skills and knowledge about the world around him – like Richard Edgeworth's, Abbott's interest lay in science and in practical matters – he is also quarrelling with his little brother and learning restraint, self-control and self-denial. This Abbott presents as merely reasonable and expedient behaviour if one is to live happily with others, rather than as an inescapable moral law.

He takes the same line with fairy-tales. When the seven-year-old Rollo chatters to his father (engaged in pruning an apple tree) about Aladdin and how he wishes he had just such a lamp, his father soberly convinces him that he would soon get tired of calling up quantities of beautiful gardens. Similarly, he would rapidly tire if he were allowed to look at all the pictures in his father's books of prints and engravings, instead of seeing them one at a time. However, as 'a very valuable experiment in intellectual philosophy' he proposes to allow Rollo to do this and thus learn 'the value of moderation, and the uselessness of Aladdin's lamps in all human enjoyments'.[56]

He did, in fact, attempt one fairy-story himself, *Minigo*,[57] about a firm and sensible fairy cast in much the same mould as Beechnut and Jonas, with all their ability to make an errant child instantly

feel ashamed. He felt bound to preface it with a reminder surely not needed by American children, that fairies were 'fictitious and imaginary', though the principles they sought to inculcate in his book were sound.

Mild schoolmaster though he seems, Abbott insisted upon two things at least – diligence and instant obedience. Like boys, girls had to learn early to be useful. Mary, wanting to earn money for buying wool to make mittens for cousin John, is told by her mother that she will be paid if she can teach her six-year-old sister Luly to darn: ' "I will consider that she has learned as soon as you can show me two holes as big as a postage stamp that she has darned neatly." ' And Mary is given valuable practical advice on how to entice a small child into learning and how to keep her attention.[58]

Obedience had to be absolute, and given cheerfully; a reluctant, delayed response was almost as bad as disobedience. Nor should authority give its reasons for a command: this 'almost always leads to a debate, which usually ends in making matters rather worse than they were before'. (Abbott addresses parents and teachers as much as children; he is severe on indulgent mothers who ruin their children's lives, as well as on over-stern schoolmasters. Authority should always be good-natured.[59]

Nevertheless, he is prepared to make obedience seem attractive. The resourceful and sagacious Beechnut (alias Antoine Bianchinette, the French hired boy), who teaches the children in the Franconia books so many valuable lessons, expects that they all should heed them. Suspecting that a young visitor will not do so – ' "City girls are very seldom taught to obey" ' – he gives a test command, and when she disobeys he tells her that he now knows he is unable to trust her. All the children are awed by Beechnut's superior wisdom as well as by his ingenuity and many skills. Whatever he does for the children he contrives to present in some unconventional or curious way that frequently astonishes them, and always gives them pleasure. His authority is gentle but absolute:

Beechnut never scolded; he always punished the boys he had dealings with, for their faults and delinquencies. It is true the boys were not obliged to submit to his punishments, but they generally did so of their own accord for the punishments were always reasonable and just, and Beechnut was, moreover, very good-natured, though still very firm, in inflicting them.[60]

The recalcitrant boy who will not co-operate with the others is tried by a good-natured court-martial, and being found guilty is sentenced to be marooned on a rocky islet (from which, naturally, he can easily swim ashore); after this, he is willing to submit. Abbott understood that in children's books the outcome should be happy.

Abbott's Franconia is a village in New Hampshire, where reside Phonny and Beechnut, Mary Bell and her friend Caroline ('a young lady, thirteen years old'); Malleville and Wallace are visitors from the city. The author states his purpose in the preface to each book in the series, his overall aim being to present 'quiet and peaceful pictures of happy domestic life'. There is remarkably little adult presence; Beechnut fills the role of guide and guardian. What drama there is – such as the death of Ellen Linn's father in a snowstorm – is recounted in the same leisurely, unemotional style accorded to the blueberrying expeditions, the building of a diving pier, the maple-sugaring. Pace and drama are not characteristics of Abbott's writing. When Beechnut is arrested on a false charge of arson the episode appears to be no more than an exercise to explain the processes of the law. 'Pleasing pictures of still life in the country,' a reviewer in the *Presbyterian* pronounced of *Malleville*; and the books are no less pleasing for their gentle goodness.

The difference between Jacob Abbott's approach and that of so many of his contemporaries can be seen from *The Child at Home*, a volume of moral reflections written by his brother John, a Calvinist pastor. It opens with a long account of a parental visit to the condemned cell and of an errant daughter's anguish. The second chapter recounts the bitter remorse of dying children; in the third we meet the girl who has denied eating apples but whose lie is shown up when an emetic is administered, and the disobedient boy who ends up in the state prison. These child characters are far more typical of their time than Rollo.

Nathaniel Willis in 1827 had proclaimed a new dawn for American children, with his *Youth's Companion*, but the magazine had failed to distinguish itself from anything that had gone before. It was Jacob Abbott who showed how a new generation might be moulded. Many of his methods are now standard practice in teaching, and it is easy to forget how innovatory he was. His writing has a rare humanity, tolerance, and gentleness which make it stand out among children's books of any age.

NOTES

1. Samuel Breck: *Recollections* (London, 1877), 306.

2. Hilaire Belloc: *The Bad Child's Book of Beasts* (London, 1923).

3. The 1796 edition of *The Parent's Assistant*, described as the 'Second Edition' though it is the first one known, included the following stories: 'The Little Dog Trusty', 'The Orange Man', 'Tarlton', 'Lazy Lawrence', 'The False Key', 'The Purple Jar', 'The Bracelets', 'Mlle Panache', 'The Birthday Present', 'The Mimic', 'Old Poz' and 'The Barring Out'. Eight more stories were added to the 1800 edition: 'Simple Susan', 'The Little Merchants', 'The Basket Woman', 'The White Pigeon', 'The Orphans', 'Waste Not, Want Not', 'Forget and Forgive' and 'Eton Montem'; and three ('The Little Dog Trusty', 'The Orange Man' and 'The Purple Jar') were removed and put into *Early Lessons*.

4. [Lydia Mary Child]: *Evenings in New England. By an American Lady* (Boston, 1824).

5. C. M. Sedgwick: *Redwood* (London, 1824), I, 182.

6. *A Book for the Eldest Daughter. By a Lady* (Massachusetts Sabbath School Society, Boston, 1849).

7. Anna Bache: *The Fire-screen* (Philadelphia, 1843). Dedicated to 'The Young Ladies of this Country'.

8. Samuel Goodrich: *Recollections of a Lifetime* (New York, 1856), 172.

9. *The Fairy Tale. By the author of 'The Sandfords, or Home Scenes,' 'Sarah and her Cousins', &c.* (Providence, RI, 1831).

10. William S. Cardell: *The Story of Jack Halyard, the Sailor Boy, or the Virtuous Family. Designed for American Children in Families and Schools* (New York, 1825).

11. Goodrich, op. cit., 312.

12. Halliwell's collection *The Book of Nursery Rhymes Complete* was in fact published in Philadelphia in 1846.

13. *Children's Friend, Number III. A New Year's Present for the Little Ones from Five to Twelve* (New York, 1821).

14. Harry Weiss: *William Charles* (New York, 1932).

15. Harry Weiss: 'Samuel Wood & Sons', *Bulletin of the New York Public Library*, vol. 46 (1942).

16. Harry Weiss: 'Mahlon Day', *Bulletin of the New York Public Library*, vol. 45 (1941).

17. Harry Weiss: 'Solomon King', *Bulletin of the New York Public Library*, vol. 51 (1947).

18. This appeared anonymously but was in fact by the American Daniel Fitz.

19. An article by Alice Sproat Emery in the *Bulletin of the New York Public Library*, vol. 55 (1951), collects the facts that are known about her.

20. Daniel Roselle: *Samuel Griswold Goodrich* (Albany, NY, n.d., *c.* 1968), 40.

21. Goodrich: op. cit., 54.

22. *Peter Parley's Method of Telling about Geography* (Boston, 1830).

23. *London and Westminster Review*, vol. 33 p. 49.

24. *Peter Parley's Tales about Great Britain* (Baltimore, Md., 1832).

25. *Lights and Shadows of American History* (Boston, 1844).

26. ibid.

27. *What to Do and How to Do It* (New York, 1844).

28. *Peter Parley's Short Stories for Long Nights* (Boston, 1853).

29. *Peter Parley's Tales of Animals* (Boston, 1836).

30. *Parley's Magazine* (New York and Boston, 1833), vol. 1, no. 3.

31. *The Bluebird* (Sunday School Union of the Methodist Episcopal Church, New York, 1848).

32. David Macrae: *The Americans at Home* (Edinburgh, 1870), II, 369.

33. Frances Trollope: *Domestic Manners of the Americans* (London, 1832), I, 128.

34. Anthony Trollope: *North America* (London, 1862), I, 421.

35. Published from Providence, RI, 1827-8.

36. Published by Benjamin and Jacob Johnson, Philadelphia, 1802-3. Since much of this appears to have been lifted from an English publication, it is only fair to point out that this boy too may have been English.

37. A full account of its publishing history is given in *Children's Periodicals of the United States*, ed. R. Gordon Kelly (1984), 149-52.

38. The fullest account of the anti-slavery articles in the *Juvenile Miscellany* is to be found in Carolyn L. Karcher: 'Lydia Mary Child and *The Juvenile Miscellany*', in *Research about Nineteenth Century Children's Books*, ed. Selma K. Richardson (Urbana-Champaign, Ill., 1980). It is also discussed in Anne Scott MacLeod: *A Moral Tale* (Hamden, Conn., 1975).

39. 'The Rural Feast', *Juvenile Miscellany*, vol. 2 (1827).

40. 'Mary and Frances', ibid., vol. 5 (1830).

41. *Southern Rose*, 17 Aug. 1839.

42. MacLeod: op. cit., 32.

43. Seth Curtis Beach: *Daughters of the Puritans* (London, 1967), 5.

44. *Home* (New York, 1835).

45. *Facts and Fancies for School-day Reading. A Sequel to Morals of Manners* (New York and London, 1848).

46. Mary Michael Welsh: *Catharine Maria Sedgwick* (Washington, DC, 1937), 129.

47. 'Mill Hill', *A Love-token for Children* (London, 1838).

48. For example, in *The Oxford Book of Children's Verse in America*, ed. Donald Hall (New York, 1985).

49. The copy in the Philadelphia Free Library, bound in with a story by Mrs Sherwood and published in London, states that both originally appeared in *The New Year's Token* of 1835.

50. *Rollo's Vacation* (Boston, *c.* 1838).

51. Mary Lundie Duncan: *America as I Found It* (London, 1852).

52. *Stuyvesant* (New York, 1853).

53. *Cousin Lucy at Play* (Boston, 1842).

54. Alice M. Jordan: *From Rollo to Tom Sawyer* (Boston, 1948), 76.

55. *Rollo at Work* (Boston, 1838).

56. *Rollo's Experiments* (Boston, 1839).

57. *Minigo; or The Fairy of Cairnstone Abbey* (New York, 1857).

58. *Mary Gay; or Work for Girls* (New York, n.d.).

59. *John Gay; or Work for Boys* (New York, 1864).

60. *Beechnut* (New York, 1850).

4. Doctrine and Virtuous Twaddle: Religious Education and Sunday School Fiction

CALLS FOR CONVERSION

'The provision for Sunday reading, outside of the Bible, was not very great in those days,' wrote Bishop Thomas Clark (1812–1903) of his Calvinist childhood:

All that I can remember...were a volume of religious anecdotes, not over-cheerful. Foxe's 'Book of Martyrs' still less so with its terrific pictures. Hannah More's tracts and narratives; 'The Pilgrim's Progress'...and the New England Primer which we did not devour with much avidity. There was a degree of gloomy satisfaction in the picture of John Rogers at the stake, with his wife and numerous progeny surrounding him, as they all looked quite comfortable, but the little poem which followed, beginning with the words

> In the burying ground I see
> Graves there shorter than I

illustrated by the view of a graveyard crowded to its utmost capacity, did not serve to inspire me with any sentiment but horror and fear, and this was intensified by an awful dialogue between 'Youth, Death and the Devil' which it was an outrage to put into a little child's mouth.[1]

And he went on to comment on the advantages he felt the children of 1895 enjoyed, with their 'Sunday school libraries and periodicals, and processions and banners and entertainments', all of which were unknown in his own childhood 'in the straitest fold of the Presbyterian Church' seventy-five years before, when Sunday schools were only just beginning. (He had, in fact, changed allegiance and had long been an Episcopalian – the 'processions and banners' would have played no part in a little Presbyterian's experience, at that period or at any other.) Clark was a kindly and optimistic man who, even if he had reservations about the quality of Sunday school fiction in the 1890s, would not have expressed them; he was merely gratified that Sunday was now

made pleasant for children. The Calvinist teaching of his youth – the single-minded stress on the achievement of saving grace, the terrifying warnings of what would happen if one failed – had tormented him as it had Mary Livermore (see page 18); long after he left the Presbyterians he was still troubled by fears.

But to Calvinists of his time fear and despair were an essential part of the process of salvation. 'Oh most merciful Father, hear my little groanings which I utter for the precious Redeemer's sake,' ran a tract with the title *A New Heart the Child's Best Portion* which the Philadelphia Female Tract Society published in 1817. Urgent as seventeenth-century preachers had been to impress the need of 'new hearts' upon the youth of their congregations (discussed in chapter 1), their message had been conveyed with reasoned doctrine, whereas after the Great Awakening of the 1730s and 40s revivalist preachers relied on emotion and fear. 'The God that holds you over the pit of hell, much as one holds a spider or some loathsome insect, over the fire, abhors you and is dreadfully provoked,' Jonathan Edwards told his listeners in 1741. 'You are ten thousand times so abominable in his eyes, as the most hateful and venomous serpent is in ours.'[2] The impact of preaching such as this was heightened by the diphtheria epidemic which began in New Hampshire in May 1735 and by the end of 1741 had spread over nearly all the settled region of New England – the most frightful epidemic of any childhood disease in American history.[3] Variously known as cynanche, squinancy, quinsy, angina, canker, bladders in the windpipe, rattles, hives, throat ail, it was over and over again called a new disease, for no one could recall having seen the like of it before. It frequently carried off whole families, such as the eight children of John and Marcy Wilson of Andover who died within a week in 1738. A broadside printed in Boston about 1736 warned children of their spiritual peril:

Though you are young, yet you must die
and hasten to the Pit.
O therefore don't forgetfull be
but always think of it.
Your loving Parents you must leave
whenever God shall call,
Your Brothers dear and Sisters too,
and bid adieu to all.
With weeping Eyes they will lament,
to see your little Breast,
Heaving and panting up and down
while you can find no Rest.

Like James Janeway seventy years earlier, Jonathan Edwards recorded instances of precocious piety. There was four-year-old Phebe Bartlett who, after much anguish of spirit and fear of hell, announced, 'Mother, the kingdom of God is come to me', and then began weeping for the peril of her sisters and the neighbours.[4] (Phebe was apparently so enthralled by his preaching that she could hardly wait for the Sabbath.) But whereas there had seemed to be total acquiescence in the preachers' message to the young in the seventeenth century, there were many in the next who disapproved of the revivalist methods. Charles Chauncy (1705-87), minister of the First Church in Boston, writing about the Great Awakening, deplored the disrespect and insubordination that it had induced in young people, instancing a girl of fifteen who had spent four hours exhorting and censuring her family, telling her father she could see the image of the Devil in his face and that he was going post-haste to hell.[5]

By the mid-nineteenth century there was a substantial body of theologians and teachers who saw great danger in trying to force an emotional experience in a child. Jacob Abbott in *Early Piety* (1838) warned parents that to press their children too zealously to show piety could be counterproductive: 'We often weary our children with the subject, or alienate their hearts from it, not by the fidelity of our religious instruction, but by pressing them too eagerly for an admission that they feel their force.' And he warned that parents could easily be deceived: 'If your children express strong interest in religious truth and duty for a time, be pleased with it, but place little confidence in it.' It was unwise, he said, to focus exclusively on trying to secure a change of heart; much better to cultivate children's good qualities. *The Mothers' Journal* in 1868 commented on preachers whose message was

only of God's wrath, never of his love, and children's perplexity at hearing a minister affirm that God hated even infants.

In New England many previously orthodox Congregationalists had by this time reacted against Calvinism and had become Unitarians. One writer recorded how in 1824 a congregation in Northampton, Massachusetts – where the Great Awakening had begun – had 'signed off' from the Old Church and had, under a more liberal preacher, re-established themselves as Unitarians. And she recalled the distaste her mother (born 1789) had felt, as a young bride from a very different milieu, for 'the cloud of Calvinism that enwrapped the whole valley of the Connecticut in spiritual gloom'.

In revival times, the evidences of conversion were discussed, much as the symptoms of a fever would be; and the deep things of God, – the soul's union with Christ, the 'obtaining of a hope', as it was called, – were bandied about without reserve, and without joy. In infant schools, babies wept over their 'wicked hearts'; and the children in older schools were separated into 'sheep and goats', and sat on 'anxious seats'. If they died early, the little prigs had their memoirs written, in which they implored good, old people, who had borne the burden and heat of the day in faith and patience, 'to come to Christ'.[6]

But the most influential words on the subject were those of Horace Bushnell (1802-76) who, when he was still a Congregational pastor, attacked the harshness of Calvinism. *Christian Nurture* (1847) set out his own views on religious education. He was at his most emphatic when writing about conversion, which he referred to as a mere 'technical experience'. It was wrong, he said, to teach that children grow up in sin, to be converted when they come to maturity. Rather, maturity should bring a spiritual renewal to people who, if properly nurtured, have loved good from their earliest years. In a chapter prefaced with a verse from Zechariah, 'And the streets shall be full of boys and girls playing in the streets', he insists that play is the symbol of Christian liberty, and that one of the first duties of a Christian parent is to show a generous sympathy with children's play. He is sympathetic to young children who play instead of attending to their devotions: 'Which is worse and more fatal, the child's undue possession by the spirit of play, or the man's by the spirit of gain?' And he denounces the zealots who hedge Sunday

FRONTISPIECE.

LIGHT ON LITTLE GRAVES.

Suffer little children, and forbid them not, to come unto me: for of such is the kingdom of heaven. MATT. xix. 14.

Take heed that ye despise not one of these little ones; for I say unto you, That in heaven their angels do always behold the face of my Father which is in heaven. MATT. xviii. 10.

Is it well with the child? And she answered, It is well. 2 KINGS iv. 26.

PREPARED FOR THE AMERICAN SUNDAY-SCHOOL UNION, AND REVISED BY THE COMMITTEE OF PUBLICATION.

Philadelphia:
AMERICAN SUNDAY-SCHOOL UNION,
No. 146 CHESTNUT STREET.

LIGHT ON LITTLE GRAVES.

From a Sunday school publication of 1848.

round with the 'strict police regulations' of the Jewish Sabbath:

What can a poor child do that is cut off thus, for a whole twenty-four hours, from any right to vent his exuberant feelings? ... What conception does he get of religion, by such kind of treatment, but that it comes to the world as fee to every bright thing in it, a burden, a weariness, a tariff, on the other six days of life?

A tract of 1819 directed at children 'who are sorry when the Sabbath comes' furnishes a vivid little cameo of such weariness:

They are unwilling to leave their sports to read the Bible, and learn the catechism. Instead of sitting quietly like little Henrietta, they are very uneasy. They often say, 'Pa, isn't it most night?' 'Ma, I am tired, do let me go out.' And sometimes these wicked children get away from under the eye of their parents and begin their play before the end of the Sabbath.[7]

Many children from a Calvinist background were tormented by the same fears as Betty Sewall (born 1682) and Mary Livermore (born 1820). Charles Dudley Warner (1829–1900) in *Being a Boy* (1877) described how revivals could affect the most ordinary boy. 'Sunday meeting and Sunday school he didn't mind; they were a part of regular life, and only temporarily interrupted a boy's pleasures. But when there began to be evening meetings at the different houses, a new element came into affairs.' He began to get frightened; all the talk was of 'getting religion', and he realized that unless he got it now the chances were he never would; he would be given over to hardness of heart, and his obstinacy would show that he was not one of the elect. He heard all the time that he only had to repent and believe, which he was perfectly willing to do if he could think of anything to repent of. It was essential that he should have a 'conviction of sin'; other people no better than he had it, and he began to feel panicky and lonely:

If ever a boy honestly tried to work himself into a conviction of sin, John tried. And what made him feel miserable was that he couldn't feel miserable when everybody else was miserable. He even began to pretend to be so. He put on a serious and anxious look like the others. He pretended he didn't care for play... Every day and night he heard that the spirit of the Lord would probably quit striving with him, and leave him out. The phrase was that he would 'grieve away the Holy Spirit'.

He never did achieve the desired state, and when the revival receded and the world resumed its normal course, 'John had an uneasy apprehension of his own separateness from other people in his insensibility to the revival'.

He would hardly have been comforted if he had read the available tracts on the subject. This 'insensibility' was invariably denounced as the most culpable of all failings; Christian virtues counted as nothing if the heart was not moved. What was more, it was so easy to deceive onself over the matter of conversion. Jonathan Edwards himself had passed through a religious phase as a boy, when 'I used to pray five times a day in secret, and to spend much time in religious talk with other boys; and used to meet with them to pray together. I experienced I know not what kind of delight in religion.'[8] But this was a false dawn. His true conversion came at college, when 'it pleased God to seize me with a pleurisy, in which he brought me nigh to the grave, and shook me over the pit of hell'. A sombre little tract put out by the American Tract Society with the title *The Importance of Distinguishing between True and False Conversion* confined itself to the latter. 'The devil knows Scripture and can quote it,' the author reminds readers who might think that the sound of a Bible text ringing in their ears was the sound of grace. Godly behaviour was far from enough, and indeed dangerous, for it might persuade people they were saved. In *Kitty Brown Beginning to Think*, an American Sunday School Union publication of about 1853, Kitty, a good, conscientious girl, teaches poor children, earns money for charity by reading Doddridge's *Rise and Progress of Religion* to a worthy woman, learns Bible verses, goes to prayer meetings, prepares to die. But none of this, nor 'trying to do all the good she could in the world', can make her a Christian. 'That treacherous and deceitful heart must be *changed*, and God alone had power to change it.'

But the dominance of Calvinism was already diminishing by the time *Kitty Brown* was published. Already by the late 1840s there is far less stress on conversion and death. The theological content of a child's Sunday reading dwindled, to be replaced with vaguely improving little fables – to the sorrow of an older generation who had wrestled with Doddridge and Richard Baxter. One commentator writing in 1870[9] thought that the modern Sunday school library was deplorable, not because so much of it was fiction but because the content was so often 'bad morality and bad religion'. But since this was often the only fiction that young America encountered, its influence on the national culture cannot be discounted.

SUNDAY SCHOOLS AND TRACT SOCIETIES

In 1905 the German Hugo Münsterberg observed that in the parts of the United States that he had visited, especially the small cities and rural areas, the church was a social centre in a way that it was not in his own country, and that 'a person who moves to a new part of the town or to an entirely new village, allies himself to some congregation if he is of the middle classes, in order to form social connections'.[10] And when the Lynds wrote *Middletown* some twenty-five years later[11] Sunday schools were still an important part of young Protestants' lives, and the religious activities were much the same as their parents would have known. But the Sabbatarianism was less strict: 'When we girls in our family missed Sunday school we weren't allowed to go out in the evening all the following week,' says one mother, remembering the 1890s. The difference was that the Sunday schools of her daughters' generation were also trying to accommodate themselves to their members' secular interests. *Middletown* illustrates change in other areas too: 'Our Sunday School class is *some* class,' one high school senior said enthusiastically; 'Our teacher is Mrs – and she gives some slick parties out at her place. Two of the girls in our class got kicked out of their clubs a year ago for smoking – that's the kind of class we have!' It had been very different for earlier generations.

The beginnings of the English Sunday school movement are always associated with Robert Raikes, a Gloucester printer, who in the 1780s, disturbed by the sight of so many filthy ragamuffins idling around on Sundays, wished to take them off the streets and tame them by teaching them to read, so that they could study the Bible and the Church catechism. Hannah More, similarly, had ambitions to help the rural poor in Somerset, and Sarah Trimmer to provide charity schools in Brentford, Middlesex. The English Sunday school throughout the nineteenth century was thus always associated with the poor and deprived; the clergymen's and squires' children might teach in them – and sometimes did at a very early age – but they themselves would not be taught there, it being assumed that their parents would give them proper religious instruction. (The whole system of English state education, having been devised by Victorian legislators who regarded it as a charity hand-out for the less privileged, has never shaken itself clear of these beginnings.) An English visitor to America in 1852 noticed how *all* parents sent their children to Sunday school and how different this was from England, where Raikes had exclusively 'filled his benches with the uncared-for'.[12] And though some of the earliest schools, such as those founded by the Philadelphia First Day Society, the first *permanent* American Sunday school organization, did devote themselves to teaching the poor to read and write, this could hardly last in a country that prided itself on its equality. Thus Lyman Beecher (1775–1863), realizing that the poor and ignorant who most needed Sunday schools would never attend them if they suspected class distinction, himself went to the best families in his parish and begged them to send their children there. Hence 'what had begun as an exercise in charity was converted into a prep school for the whole of evangelical America';[13] Sunday schools augmented what was taught in church, and prepared the young for adult membership of the congregation.

The earliest American schools sprang up in Philadelphia, Boston and New York, initiated by people who had seen the British models.[14] As in eighteenth-century England, where the establishment of a Sunday school was often reported as having transformed whole villages, wonderful things were told of the communities where schools were set up. They were held to have become God-fearing and decent, orderly and diligent; profane swearing and intemperance and Sabbath-breaking apparently ceased, and in the early accounts we come across plenty of tributes such as this:

I am sometimes inclined to believe, that the conversion of the whole world is far more intimately connected with the Sabbath school system, than is generally apprehended by the church. However *little*, in their own eyes, the teachers and scholars may look, yet in the sight of some of our wisest and best men, they appear like *standard bearers* in the army of King Immanuel.[15]

And early tract-writers had plenty of remorseful youths in the condemned cell exclaiming: 'Oh! if I had gone to that Sabbath school, and learned to read, and regarded the Bible, I should not have been a murderer.'

There was some opposition. There were those who held it was a breach of the Sabbath; some disliked the use of the meeting-house as a school; others felt it would interfere with family religious training. The New Jersey *Sunday School Journal* reported in 1827 that some of their schools had had to be closed because of local opposition. In one neighbourhood near Princeton the local schoolmaster stood at the door with a cane, threatening Sunday school pupils and teachers alike: 'a majority of the inhabitants of the neighbourhood, passively acquiesced in the disgraceful transaction, and the school is discontinued!!!' Nor, in fact, were the schools so all-embracing in their intake as the American Sunday School Union would have liked to think. There were always difficulties about black pupils. In the North, once the movement became middle-class, the presence of black children became embarrassing, while the South was slow to adopt Sunday schools because they were equated with black education; 'generally speaking, the American Sunday school movement faithfully observed the culture's caste demarcations just as the English evangelicals reflected the class lines there'.[16]

The teaching in the Sunday schools in the early days was very simple. Thomas Clark, the bishop quoted at the beginning of the chapter, had himself been instructed by a maker of blocks and pumps. This elderly instructor heard his pupils recite scripture texts and hymns, and then left them to their own devices. Another writer, also remembering the 1820s, said:

When the meeting was out in the morning, the school came together, each class with its teacher in a separate pew, and then the first one called upon, in each class, stood up and said some verses which they had learned in the Bible, or some hymn out of Watts's Hymns for Infant Minds, and after they had said what they had learned, they might go out.[17]

At this date fiction was regarded with the deepest suspicion by most of the Protestant orthodox, and the American Tract Society fought hard against it in their publications, averring in their report of 1836 that the moral effect could only be injurious.

The origins of this society lay in an organization formed in 1814 by Ebenezer Porter, a Massachusetts minister, to distribute Christian tracts at a low price. In 1825 it merged with the New York Religious Tract Society and took on the new name. Its aim was to supply evangelical literature to the entire accessible population of the United States, and its phenomenal success in achieving this was largely due to the zeal and entrepreneurial skills of its first president, S. V. S. Wilder. The salesmen were also missionaries (often college students), and were employed to carry the Gospel to new immigrants, to Indians, to churchless settlers on the frontiers, to the blind, to prisons, poor-houses and orphan asylums. They taught much about salvation and damnation, the observation of the Sabbath and church attendance. They sought to convert Roman Catholics, to correct the doctrine of Universalists, Unitarians, Deists and freethinkers, and to put down drinking, gambling, dancing, novel-reading, the theatre, fashionable amusements and swearing. But it was not part of their concern to deal with humanitarian topics, and slavery was never touched upon.[18]

The Society began publishing tracts for children in 1827, and by the end of May 1828 had put out 239,000 copies. At first many were English imports such as the Cheap Repository Tracts, and the Rev. Legh Richmond's amazingly popular *The Dairyman's Daughter* (1809).* But by 1834 they had started to commission American authors. Jacob Abbott wrote for them, as did his brother John, and Thomas Hopkins Gallaudet (1787–1851), remembered for his work for the deaf and for *The Child's Book on the Soul*, a kindly work in which a five-year-old is taught to reason his way into Christian belief. Wilder and his colleagues were diligently searching for material that would engage children's

interest without telling them lies, while trying to counteract the prevailing thirst for fiction.[19]

The guiding spirits of the ATS were for the most part Presbyterians and Congregationalists. ('Austere disciples of the gloomy Calvin,' commented a French visitor – 'According to their doctrine, all men, without distinction, have been created to be damned, and deserve it richly for the crime of being born.'[20]) Many other denominations were to have their own publishing houses, notably the Methodists, Baptists and Unitarians. And Sunday school books also poured from the commercial presses, who had never needed reminding how much profit was to be derived from godliness.

But the king of them all was undoubtedly the American Sunday School Union, the interdenominational organization which took on this name in 1824,[†] with its headquarters in Philadelphia. Its objectives were stated in the constitution: to concentrate the efforts of the Sabbath school societies, to disseminate useful information, circulate moral and religious publications, and endeavour to plant a Sabbath school wherever there was a population.[21] Their efforts to promote religious education seem to have been far more successful than any comparable evangelizing in industrial England. Anthony Trollope in 1862 remarked on how freely religious subjects were discussed in the United States, adding that the English visitor would rarely find 'that utter absence of all knowledge on the subject – that total darkness, which is still so common among the lower orders in our own country'.[22]

The teaching in the early Sunday schools was based, as we have seen, on the catechism, on memorizing Bible texts, on Watts and on the *New England Primer*. By the 1820s there was a growing realization that something more was needed, and so a broader-based scheme of instruction was devised with a system of reward tickets by which tracts and bibles could be earned. (This system is set out, with details of how to manipulate it, in the fourth chapter of *Tom Sawyer*.) There were also to be libraries. These were the earliest children's libraries, and for thirty years or more were a dominant cultural force. Some of the well established ones carried as many as a thousand volumes, others as few as a hundred; but limited though

---

* The success of this book is unaccountable. It describes in Janeway style but at far greater length the edifying death of one of this Isle of Wight clergyman's parishioners. The circulation in England and America was reckoned at 500,000. It was translated into nineteen languages.
† It had its origins in the Sunday and Adult School Union set up in 1817.

they might be in numbers and scope, they had much influence.

By 1830 the ASSU could claim that six million copies of their publications had been sold. It also put out periodicals – the *Youth's Friend and Scholar's Magazine* (which had begun in 1823 as the *Teacher's Offering or Sabbath Scholar's Magazine*), and, for the younger child, the *Infant's Magazine*, which ran from 1829 to 1842. Its early publications were austere and confined to doctrinal teaching, classics such as Alleine's (see page 28), and memoirs of youthful piety. But by 1849 fiction was acceptable enough for there to be many examples among the sets of books marketed as the Sunday School and Family Library, the Juvenile Library, and the like. The Child's Cabinet Library, for instance, a set of seventy small volumes, included biography, biblical history, geography, the inevitable *Dairyman's Daughter*, plus moral tales with American settings, by American authors – this being an important principle with the ASSU. But it was only to be expected, given the Calvinist insistence that anything that was not a fact must be a lie, that the appearance of fiction in Sunday school libraries should give pain to many.

THE BEGINNINGS OF FICTION: PIETY REWARDED

The American Tract Society resisted fiction longer than most, and in *The Bud of Promise* commended an exemplary boy, Richard Cleveland Allen, who died in Buffalo, NY, on 14 December 1855, having not only steadfastly avoided fiction but having always punctually returned his books. In addition: 'He manifested his love of Sabbath School by punctuality and perfect lessons . . . He always confessed his faults, was diligent in study, sympathetic to the poor and needy, knew his Bible and catechism . . . felt himself to be a sinner, delighted in the Sabbath, the conversion of sinners was an object very near his heart.'

The Rev. Heman Humphrey (1779–1861), whose hostility to fiction has already been mentioned in chapter 1, was one of those uncompromisingly orthodox churchmen who felt that the new availability of religious tales was one of the reasons why the children of the 1840s did not take up 'solid, practical, doctrinal reading' with the same zest as his own generation. Just when they should be

reading Richard Baxter or Jonathan Edwards, they were poring over storybooks. He also felt that it was the thin end of the wedge, that it would lead to a demand for less innocent fiction: 'Our unconverted children will not discriminate. We cannot expect it.'[23] Others, who did not take such a rigorous view, still saw storybooks as a dangerous temptation. There were many such warning tales as the one about Marion, aged six, who cannot resist reading during service the book she has just borrowed from the library: 'As they walked home from church Mrs Howard talked much to her little daughter about her wicked conduct.'[24]

But there were many who found Sunday school fiction obnoxious for very different reasons. 'Virtuous twaddle,' said the Rev. George B. Bacon, writing in the journal *Hours at Home* in 1870 – 'stale and mouldy', and very poorly done. His own feeling was that there should be far more factual works in the libraries, and that fiction should be fanciful tales 'making their appeal to the imagination, and moving in the unreal world of fancy'. He would not object, he said, if these were the only books in the libraries, as long as they drove out the present ones. *Appleton's Journal* in 1874 was similarly trenchant: 'When we say that *The Neptune Outward Bound* is a hopeless specimen of the dreariest class of children's literature, all experienced small boys who have spent profitless hours in the selection of books from the average Sunday school library, will know what we mean.'[25] 'Sanctimonious selections, which devout old dames consider amazingly proper and wholesome for the rising generation are repudiated with a kind of ferocious disdain by the rising generation in question,' claimed the *Overland Monthly*.[26] And of a book published by the Congregational Publishing Society in 1881 the *Atlantic Monthly* said that it was 'one of those fictions which go a long way towards putting the reader out of patience with propriety'. But in fact few of the literary journals that reviewed children's books bothered with religious fiction; there was too much of it, and the standard was deplorably low. Indeed, the Unitarian Ladies' Commission set up in 1865 to assess Sunday school books found that of those examined only a quarter was adequate; the rest were rejected, for literary rather than doctrinal reasons.[27]

The earliest collection of juvenile religious narratives was, as noted in chapter 1, the work of James Janeway in the early 1670s. The short lives

The death of an eight-year-old. Frontispiece from
Triumphs of Divine Grace, exemplified in the life and
death of Marshall A. Chappell *(New York, 1855).*

and lingering deaths of good children were to be
standard Sunday reading for many decades. It was
a comfort for bereaved parents to piece together
the life of a departed child, and sometimes children
like Hannah Hill of Philadelphia (see page 33) had
left instructions to that effect. It was a type of
literature that provoked one child to say, when his
aunt gave him *The Memoirs of a Sunday-School
Scholar,* ' "Pshaw! just as I thought; nothing but
early piety! early piety! Why couldn't she have sent
me some story about wars, or pirates, or even
Indians? I am tired to death of early piety." '[28]

The image of short graves in the churchyard,
which Bishop Thomas Clark had been haunted by
in childhood, was a theme much dwelt upon then,
and was not necessarily used in an admonitory
way. 'It is pleasant for little children to go, on a
Sunday evening, or between the hours of worship,
into the graveyards,' said a Sunday school magazine
of 1830; it helped make children serious and sober,
and more easily to believe what their teachers and
the Bible told them about death.[29] The subject of
death was an essential part of evangelical education.
While infant mortality was declining in Europe in
the early nineteenth century, it was increasing in
the United States, as a result, no doubt, of rapidly
increasing urbanization. Few homes were spared,
according to the author of *Light on Little Graves*
(1848), a book of poems on the subject: 'There is
but here and there a household that the angel of
death has not visited, to select some lovely flower
(perhaps the fairest and sweetest) and transplant
it to the world above.'

Time was so short, eternity beckoned, and no
preacher could afford to miss an opportunity of
driving this home. The methods used by the Puritans, described earlier, had changed little in two
hundred years. The Massachusetts Sabbath School
Society – who represented orthodox Congregational
belief at a time when the Church was splintered
by Unitarianism, whose adherents accused the tradi-
tionalists of an unChristian rigour and a narrow
and slavish outlook – were publishing in the 1840s
many books with death as the central theme. ' "Are
you prepared to die, Jane?" ' says a tract-distributor
to a young servant who has told her that her duties
leave her very little time for reading. ' "There is
one thing you must find time for – you must find
time to die." '[30] In *The Young Christian*, an uncharacteristic work which Jacob Abbott wrote for the
American Tract Society in 1832, Louisa leaves her
preparation for death too late. ' "I think I want to
repent," ' she tells the pastor, ' "but I cannot. I want
to love God, but I do not know how." ' She dies in
mental agony: 'no rays of peace beamed upon that
departing soul'. All the pastor could hope was that
'the sad spectacle might not be lost upon any of
us'.

Visits to the dying and the dead were part of this
education for death. In *The Teacher's Gem, or Stories
for my Class*, an MSSS publication of 1850, quarrelling sisters are taken to the poor-house to see
a boy, now raving mad, who has killed his brother
by pushing him under a train:

Then the matron opened a door and told the visitors to
enter and look at Tom's body. The little girls shrank back.
They would have avoided the sight; but their aunt thought
they needed a painful lesson ... 'Come,' she said gently,
and walking into the overseer's room, they saw, stretched
on a board, the form of a little boy. The face was quite
purple, and one of the hands was crushed out of all shape.

But the MSSS was a survival, and exceptional in
its repressive severity. Nowhere among the juvenile
publications of the period do we find loftier precepts
or sterner warnings than in their publications. The
Rev. Harvey Newcomb, who wrote many of their
tracts, in *Practical Directory for Young Christian
Females* (1833) describes how a girl should conduct
her life. Much time had to be devoted to Bible
study, prayer and fasting. Besides the ordinary meetings for worship, she should attend prayer meetings,
and work for the Bible Society and the Tract Society,

THE SISTERS.   69

THE SISTERS.

"Now, Jane, see, you have knocked down my shawl and bonnet," said Charlotte in a very cross voice.

"Well, pick them up, then," answered Jane.

"Pick them up this minute, yourself, or I'll tell aunt Mary, that I will," said Charlotte, still more crossly than before.

"Tell away," said Jane, "as fast as you like; I wonder who cares for your telling."

The conversation would doubtless have proceeded in this amiable manner, but now aunt Mary, who had heard what the little girls were saying, called them into her sitting-room and told them

THE SISTERS.

Two quarrelling sisters are taken to see a boy who has killed his brother. From The Teacher's Gem: or Stories for my class *(Massachusetts Sabbath School Society, 1850).*

for missionary causes and for the poor. She should be cautious in friendship, pray for guidance before going into society, and practise self-examination. In conclusion the reader is reminded that she can observe all this, 'and still deceive herself'. It was indeed difficult for the serious-minded to move in secular society at all, another tract, *Taking Up the Cross*,[31] pointed out: true Christians must eschew all subjects 'usually interesting to frivolous or worldly minds' – politics, literature, amusements, the weather, health, friends – and summon up the moral courage to introduce the subject of religion, indicating that for them 'it is the great topic of interest'.

One writer of a later generation was still carrying this austere standard at the end of the century – Isabella MacDonald Alden (1841–1930) who called herself 'Pansy' from her childhood name. Extraordinarily popular with Sunday schools on both sides of the Atlantic, she spent her whole life in a rarefied religious atmosphere; her family was zealously pious, and at the age of twenty-five she married a young Presbyterian minister. She was still in her early thirties, but an established author of Sunday fiction, when Daniel Lothrop made her the editor of a new periodical, the *Pansy*, a non-denominational Sunday school paper for younger readers, and this she ran from 1874 to 1896. The *Pansy*, whose cover was adorned with a wreath of purple pansies, concentrated on self-improvement; readers grappled with their besetting sins, wrote in to report progress, and formed their own 'Pansy societies'.

It was, as may be deduced, an earnest journal, and earnestness was the keynote of her writing. She was the author of some seventy-five books, of which *Chrissie's Endeavor* (1889) is a fair example. Chrissie is shamed into joining the Christian Endeavour Society by being told that the logical alternative to not joining is to pledge herself *not* to serve Christ. She enthusiastically founds her own branch, but is seduced into supposing that organizing religious tableaux is godly. Her error is brought home to her, she repents, helps nurse her brother through a dangerous illness and brings about his conversion. 'A Christian woman who would not accompany him to the theatre or opera, who declined to dance, even with him, who frowned on all games of cards, even for social entertainment, who broke loose from the ordinary Church entertainments,' muses a man who wants to marry her. Admiringly, he proposes, but she refuses him: ' "Do you not know that your life is not in accord with the One to whom I owe allegiance?" '

However, it is noticeable that after the 1840s American writers did not use the deaths of children as a literary device to the same extent as English writers still did. Perhaps the natural American optimism was proof against even the influence of Dickens, whose account of the deaths of Paul Dombey and Little Nell compelled so many lesser writers to try to imitate him. Victorians liked children in their books (Dickens' admirers found *Martin Chuzzlewit* disappointing because it had none), but they apparently derived morbid pleasure from contemplating their slow and lingering extinction.[32] American writers for the young could be equally mawkish, but were usually more positive, and saw no point in wasting young life for mere literary effect. Lachrymose ladies like Susan Warner and Martha Finley (author of the *Elsie Dinsmore* books) created heroines who went through frequent agonies of tears, but the reader could always be confident they would survive – just as the perceptive reader of their English contemporaries could guess the outcome if a child was said, for example, to have an 'old-fashioned' air or was found singing 'Home, sweet home' when left by herself.

The Sunday school hero was not, on the whole, an appealing child. Mark Twain wrote two squibs

early in his career satirizing the stories prevalent in his youth. While acknowledging that they are crude, one has to admit they are also fair comment. In 'The Story of the Bad Little Boy' (written about 1865), Jim steals and someone else is blamed, and his mother doesn't die of grief any more than he does; he even goes boating on a Sunday and isn't drowned: 'Nothing like it ever happened in those mild little books with marbled backs, and with pictures in them of men with swallow-tailed coats and bell-crowned hats, and pantaloons that are short in the legs, and women with the waists of their dresses under their arms, and no hoops on.' What is more, the boy who is wrongly blamed for Jim's misdemeanours does *not* get adopted by a venerable justice and told 'to sweep out the office, and make fires, and run errands, and chop wood, and study law, and help his wife do household labors, and have all the balance of the time to play, and get forty cents a month and be happy'. Instead, he gets the thrashing that Jim escapes:

[Jim] ran off and went to sea at last, and didn't come back and find himself sad and alone in the world, his loved ones sleeping in the quiet churchyard, and the vine-embowered home of his boyhood tumbled down and gone to decay. Ah, no; he came home as drunk as a piper, and got into the station-house the first thing.

And having prospered in his rascality, 'now he is the infernalest wickedest scoundrel in his native village, and is universally respected, and belongs to the legislature'.

The even more exuberant 'Story of the Good Little Boy' (written about the same time) concerns one Jacob Blivens, who longs to meet a Sunday school book hero,

but it wasn't any use; that good little boy always died in the last chapter, and there was a picture of the funeral, with all his relations and the Sunday-school children standing around the grave in pantaloons that were too short, and bonnets that were too large, and everybody crying into handkerchiefs that had as much as a yard and a half of stuff in them.

And then he longs to be put into a book himself. It seems possible, for he does all the right things: he learns his book, is never late at Sabbath school, will not lie or play marbles on Sunday or rob birds' nests. But he never gets a chance to make a dying

The Good Little Boy's final reward: the hand of his master's daughter:

And just as Henry Brown arose / To be both good and great / Can every little lad become / Who emulates his fate.

From Henry Brown, *in the series Grandfather Lovechild's Nursery Stories (Philadelphia, 1847).*

speech as such a hero should, for he is blown up along with a string of dogs that some wicked boys, in spite of his earnest words to them, detonate with nitroglycerine – 'You never saw a boy scattered so ... Thus perished the good little boy who did the best he could, but didn't come out according to the books.'

These two stories summarize fairly accurately the habitual themes of the genre, and the traditional punishments and rewards that the writers of moral tales held out as deterrents and baits. The good little boy pictured in a New Hampshire tract of 1843 bears out all that Mark Twain was to say about the type:

This boy loves his book. He will be wise and rich in all the good things of this world. He rises with the lark, at the dawn of day, studies well his lesson, and then off he goes to school. He pays such attention to his studies, that he is at the head of his class most of the time ... He is very much delighted, when he gets home, to show his parents the rewards which his teachers give him, and very often his parents make him the present of a new book to reward him for his industry and good conduct.

He never stops to play on the way, or disturb birds' nests, neither does he quarrel with his playmates.[33]

Tract literature offers innumerable examples of virtue bringing good fortune, as it so provokingly failed to do for the Good Little Boy. The *Well-Spring*, the MSSS's magazine, alone recorded scores of instances: from Johnnie, an orphan, who stops a horse running away and is taken on as an errand-boy by the horse's grateful owner, is sent to Sabbath school, and becomes a partner in the firm,[34] to the successful businessmen who remind each other that they owe their prosperity to a tea-party fifty years before when they had heard some good old ladies talk of 'a new heart'.[35]

But there is one story that would have awed even Mark Twain. *The Bible Boy*, though published in Baltimore, has an English background and may indeed have been of English origin. George Good, who has 'the noble ambition of striving to be like Jesus Christ' and an inexhaustible stream of Bible texts at his fingertips, one Sunday, after making a pious remark to a gentleman, is given a halfpenny. Naturally he does not spend it that day, but on the Monday hurries out to buy a tract. The bookseller is so astounded by his piety that he refunds the money. George bestows this on a blind boy, at which a gentleman who witnesses his generosity gives him a shilling. George gives this to his mother, and unselfishly lends the tract to Will Wicked. George is adopted by his first benefactor, a wealthy merchant who is deeply moved by his godliness; he inherits his whole estate when his patron drops dead in the street, and becomes Lord Mayor of London, never ceasing to reflect, 'If I had not gone to the Sunday School, I should not have known my Bible; and if I had never known my Bible, I should never have known how to direct that gentleman to heaven who gave me the halfpenny.'

FAVOURITE SUNDAY SCHOOL THEMES

By the 1850s the stress in the Sunday school book was less on conversion and spiritual qualities and more on the matters of this world: godliness and prosperity march hand in hand; diligence, a prime virtue, inevitably leads to material success (special profit being attached to keeping the Sabbath). In this, American Sunday school books differed markedly from their English contemporaries. The books which Church of England Sunday schools gave away as prizes and put in their libraries – though their library system was never so developed as in the States – put much stress on the lowliness of their readers' station, the necessity for being content with it, and above all for staying there.

In the 1790s Hannah More with her Cheap Repository Tracts had (as in *The Shepherd of Salisbury Plain*) preached contentment with one's lot, however wretched. But she had not hesitated to denounce greedy and hard-hearted farmers – she had come across too many of them herself in Somerset – and the cottagers in her books are far more forthright, independent and outspoken than in the Victorian books given to the poor. The mid-century Church of England Sunday school book was aimed at children who might well become domestic servants; thus neatness, modesty, truth-telling and meekness were the important virtues. Ambition and a desire to move out of their social station were condemned. This was partly a wish on the part of the lady authors to preserve the class barriers, but there was also in their minds a great fear – which could never be put into words – of the terrible fate that might befall young servant-girls who had romantic hopes about becoming 'ladies' and attracting the attention of a 'gentleman'.

'The less book-learning the labourer's lad got stuffed into him, the better for him and the safer for those above him, was what those in authority believed and acted up to,' wrote Joseph Arch, a rebel from early boyhood, who was later to organize agricultural labourers into their first trade union. 'These gentry did not want him to know; they did not want him to think; they only wanted him to work.[36] There was a certain amount of truth in Arch's assertions, and the attitude he described was reflected in the books given to the children of agricultural labourers in country parishes dominated by the Great House and the vicarage. Nor was much earthly hope offered by the books given to the church-going urban poor. The stories of London street waifs by Hesba Stretton and her school, so popular in the 1860s and 70s, did not end in material success. Their heroes, if they lived, might be rescued from a life of vagrancy and taught a trade, and sometimes (though rarely) rise to the responsibility of being superintendent of a Sunday school. But in general spiritual rewards were all that were offered, and though there were plenty of real-life examples of rags to riches, notably among mid-Victorian railway contractors, English Sunday school writers chose to avert their eyes.

But for American youth the possibilities for advancement seemed unlimited; the world was there to be conquered. Writers did not look back wistfully at the past, but concentrated on present achievement and expectation for the future. The mills that Blake had seen as satanic, polluting England's green and pleasant land, were here seen as 'improvement':

In all these years the village of Holly had not been standing still amid the general march of American improvement. New buildings were springing up and a large cotton-factory had been erected on the bank of the little stream that had once supplied Daniel Adams' grist-mill, and a dense population of industrious and enterprising people was the result of this undertaking.[37]

There was a romance in industrial development which to the English novelists represented only blighted country and enslaved workers:

Clang! clang! went the great bell in the cupola of the large woolen factory, which more than anything else made the village of Hillsborough the busy, thriving place it was ... What a rushing to and fro there was in the main building, where the looms were driven by the vast steam engine,

which, with its steady 'throb, throb' was like the heart to the body, giving forth the vital energy that was needed for the whole system.[38]

Machines were seen as bringing prosperity, and prosperity could only bring good:

'Father, why didn't you be a minister? I think you'd make real nice sermons.'
'Why didn't I?... There was a time when I thought I should spend my life in that way, but I found I was not quite strong enough, so I took to making machines instead; and perhaps the machines have done as much good as the sermons would.'[39]

For the young American who was prepared to work and to learn, there were no limits, though undirected labour was not enough; plenty of books pointed out that a boy had to have enterprise and he had to acquire a schooling. Mrs C. M. Edwards' *Benjie and his Friends* (1860), with its well observed details of farming and pioneering life, shows an industrious man, full of goodwill, but who is fated to be poor all his life: 'He would not count or in any way reckon fractions, or understand or see a thing the least out of sight. He hated calculation, and said, verbally and practically, "let the morrow take care of itself".' As a result his farm has broken fences and fallen gates, an unstoned well covered with a rotten plank, an empty barn with 'a leaky roof and great doors hanging by one hinge each, a roofless wood-shed without any wood in it, and sorry-looking cows, and ragged dirty sheep ... and the "discontented pig" who rooted in the barn-yard'. Even more telling, his wife turns into 'a sad little emaciated woman, with scanty hair, knitted brow, sallow complexion, sharp features, and alas! a sharper tongue'.

The ideal child of the later Sunday school books was orderly, thrifty and diligent. Given this, godliness would follow. If you want to grow rich, put by a penny a day, the *Youth's Casket*[40] told children in 1853: 'Little will get much, and much more, and a rich man you must be. But mind, *never borrow*.' After which, readers were hastily reminded that 'there is no real happiness without a well-grounded hope of a better world'.

Many books grappled with the feckless and improvident. 'Aunt Hattie' (Mrs Harriett Newell Woods Baker) dedicated *The Hole in the Pocket* (1881) to 'Young America, in order to make the fast moderate, the prodigal prudent, the spendthrift an economist, the poor rich, and the rich happy'. One of the characters is told: ' "There's a hole in your pocket, and you're likely to lose all your earnings out of it . . . Your habit of going out to refresh yourself with a glass of drink, or to take an ice-cream, when there was no real occasion for such expenditure, proved it to me." ' Admonished thus, Frank keeps accounts and sees for himself how large the hole is:

Monday, for peanuts, candy and lemonade	.10
Tuesday, for peanuts, raisins and ice-cream	.12
Wednesday, for one cocoa-nut, and dates	.12
Thursday, for three oranges and one ice-cream	.18
Friday, for lozenges and figs	.11
Saturday, for candy and cloves	.08
	.71

Prudent George's accounts, on the other hand, are impeccable, and he has money in hand: 'After putting down the sum for board and washing, there was fifty cents given at the monthly concert of prayer, twenty-five to a lame boy, ten at the Sabbath-school, five for a loaf of bread for a hungry girl, and two dollars subscription to a religious monthly.'

In stories of this type, piety followed inevitably in the wake of thrift – take care of the pence, and your soul will take care of itself. 'At home there were three boys younger than Dick, all of whom were daily taking lessons of industry and thrift, as well as lessons in practical godliness,' wrote 'Aunt Hattie' in *Diligent Dick, or the Young Farmer* (1871). Dick, aged twelve, presents himself to Mr Jones in his New York office one blazing August day and asks for a contract to supply Christmas evergreens to Mr Jones' church, showing thus not only persistence but foresight and imagination. Ingenuity in making money for worthy causes was a prominent theme in the Sunday school book. In *Self-Denial; or Alice Wood and her Missionary Society*, an ASSU story, the little girls put forward their schemes: one says she has been promised a quarter for having a tooth drawn, another half a dollar if she will stop biting her nails; Jane Prime says her

father will give three cents a quart for peach and plum stones, and Sally Bright can milk for a neighbour at a penny a time.

Whereas in England poverty tended to be regarded as ordained by God for the unfortunate to endure and for the wealthier to succour, the nineteenth-century American mostly saw it as the result of idleness and drink. The first sermon preached on New England soil had condemned beggars: 'so may it truely be sayd of a man, that when he hath lost his modestie and puts on a begging face, he hath lost his maiestie, and the Image of that noble creature, and man should not begge and crave of man but onely of God.[41] And two hundred years later Catharine Sedgwick (see page 86) could see no need for poverty or sickness in New England. Beggary was a feature of the Old World; it had no place in the New World, where anyone with a will could succeed. 'I think of the poor when the wind howls round our house in the winter,' began an ATS tract of 1854 with the title *First Lessons in Gentleness and Truth*. 'Mother says the reason why some persons in the country are poor is, because they are not willing to work. They waste their time, in the summer, in idleness, instead of providing for the coming winter.' The writer, 'Aunt Alice', concedes that while most families are poor because the parents like drink, or dislike work, there are cases where people meet with accidents or lose their money through no fault of their own, and that it would be wrong to feel unkindly towards a poor person. However, 'my father always says, if you will learn to be prompt in every thing, you will not be very likely to be poor'. The Massachusetts Sabbath School Society, of course, took a robust view:

It is a mistake to suppose that poverty and hardship must crush the spirit of the young. There may be an amount of suffering, long continued, which shall prove ruinous – as, for example, in the condition of the Irish peasantry. But in our New England, there is no depth of poverty to produce such a result. Here, when natures are crushed . . . it is by the indulgence of evil passions; because there is strife, and hatred, and malice, discontent, and envy and indolence, bitter words and bitter feelings found in these homes; not because there is poverty and toil.[42]

References to the Irish poor are frequent. Their lack of achievement in a land of promise was noticed by an eighteenth-century observer, J. H. St

John de Crèvecoeur, who reckoned that while nine out of twelve German immigrant families would succeed, and seven out of twelve Scots, only four Irish families could be expected to do so: 'They love to drink and to quarrel; they are litigious, and soon take to the gun, which is the ruin of everything; they seem beside to labour under a greater degree of ignorance in husbandry than the others.'[43]

The impact of the Irish became much greater in the 1840s, when famine drove so many out of Ireland. Their destitution upon arrival, the filth and squalor in which they were prepared to live, was a terrible shock to a nation that prided itself on having left poverty behind. ' "You don't mean to say you are going to take another of those street savages from the city into this house," ' says one outraged woman in *Irish Amy*,[44] a story that sets out to interest children in street waifs. Some tales dwelt on the need to be kind to Irish children, others on their conversion to Bible Christianity; but denunciation of the errors and iniquities of the Roman Church seems not to have played such a large part in American Sunday school books as it did in England. The Episcopal Church, however, was frequently identified with slack religious habits, particularly in the South. 'How different, thought I to myself, from the manner of keeping the Sabbath in the region where I was brought up,' mourned the New Englander William Alcott after a visit to Virginia.[45] Episcopalians broke the Sabbath and were negligent about the 'domestic altar' (family worship). 'They were not *religious* according to our sense of the word,' said one book,[46] which also complained about their disparagement of Methodists and 'the orthodox' (Congregationalists), whom they called narrow and self-righteous.

The Episcopal Church was also suspect because it countenanced the vices against which the orthodox set their face: dancing, the theatre, novel-reading, card games and gambling, which had all been outlawed by the Puritans; and drinking and smoking, which were both bound up with the nineteenth-century temperance movement. The American Tract Society was only echoing traditional Puritan teaching when it said in Tract 130, *Theatrical Exhibitions*, that the theatre was a criminal waste of time, unprofitable, a school of vice and profligacy, and that the general moral was detestable: 'Pride, revenge, false honour, duelling, suicide, the indulgence of unhallowed love, conjugal infidelity, and making the applause of men the governing rule of life ... are depicted.' It accused those who went to the theatre of contributing to the encouragement and support of licentious play-actors. (This was a more decorous rendering of William Prynne's assertion two hundred years before, in a denunciation of theatrical performance 1,006 pages long, that 'stage-playes ... are the common Nurseries, Schooles, and Seminaries of Adulterers, Adulteresses, Whore-masters, Whores, and such - polluted creatures'.[47] The Scottish Anne Grant, whose *Memoirs of an American Lady* records early-eighteenth-century life in Albany, NY, described the outrage that residents had felt when British army officers had staged a play. It was said that they

had not only spent a whole night in telling lies in a counterfeited place, the reality of which had never existed, but that they themselves were a lie, and had degraded manhood, and broke through an express prohibition in Scripture by assuming female habits; that they had not only told lies, but cursed and swore the whole night, and assumed the characters of knaves, fools and robbers.

Theatres, of course, were only to be found in towns and so would not be encountered by the country population, but 'there are scenes of amusement very nearly related to theatres,' William Alcott warned boy readers,[48] such as 'the exhibition of puppets, wax-figures, rope-dancing, circus-riding', which he thought nearly as undesirable. Alcott (1798–1859), a pioneer of education, was no stern moralist but an enlightened and humane teacher. Nor was Fanny Fern (Sara P. W. Parton, 1811–72), who also disliked circuses, and expressed ladylike distaste for their coarseness: so much better if the acrobats had learned to do something useful, and how stupid their jokes were, 'how badly they pronounce, how ungrammatically they express themselves'. But, she admitted, 'if there is anything that drives a boy crazy it is a circus'.[49] Warnings about the evils of circuses were common in mid-century Sunday school stories; some deplored the drinking and gambling that took place in the vicinity; one or two were concerned about the cruelty to the animals, but many more about the danger that boys might be tempted to go to the theatre, even to join a circus themselves – 'and then there is no hope of their making useful men'.[50]

> I ruther go to the Circus show
> But 'cause my parunts told me so,

I ruther go to the Sund'y school,
'Cause there I learn the goldun rule.

Say, Pa, – what is the goldun rule,
'At's allus at the Sund'y school?

as James Whitcomb Riley put it.[51]

Dancing, too, was prohibited by the Puritans and their heirs. In 1639 William Ames had called it 'a certain madnesse of the mind ... A kind of defiling of that dignity, which ought to bee kept by all Christians'.[52] 'The virtuous woman does not dance,' Cotton Mather said;[53] 'Such a madness is left to the pagans or the monkeys.' A hundred and fifty years later the MSSS thought much the same, but tried to make the prohibition more acceptable by stressing the bad effect it had upon the health: education is neglected, and in the end dancing may cause one's death, as in the case of Julia, who caught cold at a ball and died reproaching her mother for having let her go.[54]

Reading the directives of the religious in the ante-bellum period, one feels that they permitted very little in the way of recreation. *Letters to a Younger Brother*, an ASSU tract of 1838, for instance, finds objections to most pastimes. Draughts is deprecated for keeping boys indoors – and boys should in general abstain from all games that keep them sitting still. Chess wastes time; and those who become expert often go on to other games, and may even be tempted to gamble – 'Besides, I could never find it so beneficial to the mind as has been pretended.' Wrestling and boxing may lead to a disposition to fighting. Fishing and fowling are cruel, and the latter dangerous. Riding is a noble sport, but walking often fatigues before it has sufficiently excited the circulation. Swimming, rowing and skating are permissible, but of ball games the writer will say nothing, because 'the danger is the reader already does too much'. His conclusion is that manual labour appears to be the one and only true recreation.

The *American Quarterly Review* in September 1832 had remarked, in an otherwise hostile review of Frances Trollope's *Domestic Manners of the Americans*, that she was right in her comments about the undue influence that the clergy had upon American women. It went on to say:

She might have traced to the influence of sectarianism, the absence of all popular amusements in America – those

excepted which are brutal. The rigid exactions of the clergy, who set their face studiously against everything that savours of pleasantry and play, have driven thousands from the enjoyment of less dangerous luxuries, to the gambling table and tavern; and until we shall provide for our youth of both sexes places of common resort, where innocent recreations ... shall satisfy the demand which nature herself appears to make for such indulgencies, we shall continue to see thousands of the one falling victim to the merest cant and the most drivelling fanaticism, and an even greater proportion of the other class prostrating the noblest faculties of mind and body alike to the excess of the brothel and the bottle.

Indeed, English visitors at this time could find none of the interest in games that was so much a feature of the English schoolboy, and the strictures of the *Quarterly* reviewer are endorsed by an observer a quarter of a century later. A Boston boy, he said sadly, was a melancholy picture of prematurity: 'the principal business of life seems to be to grow old as soon as possible ... athletic games and the bolder field-sports being unknown ... all that is left is chewing, smoking, drinking, driving hired horses in wretched gigs'.[55]

Of all the prohibited pastimes, card-playing was perhaps the worst. 'I should wish you never to know even the name of a playing card,' William Alcott had said in *The Boy's Guide*. 'In the old New England,' Charles Dudley Warner wrote in his memoir of boyhood, a person could not better express his contempt of all holy and orderly life than by playing cards:

John knew a couple of desperately bad boys who were reported to play 'seven-up' in a barn, on the hay-mow, and the enormity of this practice made him shudder. He had once seen a pack of greasy 'playing-cards' and it seemed to him to contain the quintessence of sin. If he had desired to defy all Divine law and outrage all human society, he felt that he could do it by shuffling them.

In seventeenth-century New England, tobacco and drink had been accepted. But the destructive power of rum was to become apparent to responsible observers, and in 1799 *The Pennsylvania Spelling Book*, compiled by the Quaker Anthony Benezet, warned about the danger of liquors distilled from molasses, grain and fruit: they destroy the human frame, parch the stomach and rot the entrails – and the guts of hogs fed on distillers' wash are not fit for puddings. 'In early times, the diseases of the inhabitants of these provinces were few, when their drink was chiefly water.' Thirty-six years later, in a sermon entitled 'Intemperance a national evil', Benjamin Wadsworth spoke of the rapid progress of the United States 'in the vices of old countries'. The immoderate use of ardent spirits had, he said, increased since the American Revolution, beyond parallel in the annals of the world.

The evil had been sufficiently recognized for churches to have introduced an abstinence pledge as early as 1800. The first temperance organizations seem to have been those founded at Saratoga, NY, in 1808 and in Massachusetts in 1813: a movement that spread rapidly, so that by 1833 there were six thousand local societies. Every juvenile periodical of the time, secular or religious, hammered home the message, and what must surprise us now is the youth of the children who were held to be in danger. In fact, no child was too young to be warned about the dangers of strong drink and tobacco. In a little tract called *The Glass of Whiskey* the ASSU told its readers:

There is a bottle. It has something in it which is called whiskey. Little reader, I hope you will never taste any as long as you live. It is a poison. So is brandy, so is rum, so is gin, and many other drinks. They are called strong drink. They are so strong that they knock people down and kill them.

An ASSU publication of 1844[56] could assert that the temperance movement had made a great impact: 'It is so great that you can have little idea how much drunkenness there was, even so short a time ago.' (But the most eloquent temperance works, those of T. S. Arthur, were yet to come, and suggest that ten years later the problem was worse, rather than better.) The approach varied: there were the bright little characters who bravely resisted the proffered glass of wine, asserting that they were soldiers in the Cold Water Army; there were the terrible warnings about the possibility of spontaneous combustion in an MSSS tract, *Female Influence, or The Temperance Girl*, in 1851, where a man was described as like the wick of a burning candle in the midst of its own flame: 'His flesh fell off in dressing, leaving the bones almost bare. The poor miserable wretch lingered along several days, in the most terrible agony.' *The Child's Book on Intemperance*[57] gave accounts of 'the widespread

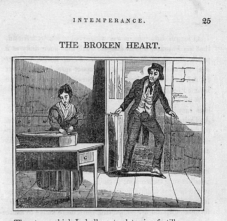

INTEMPERANCE. 25

THE BROKEN HEART.

The story which I shall next relate, is of still more appalling interest. A man, whom I shall call L——, some years since, became united to an amiable and virtuous young woman, as his wife. At the time of their marriage, he was in the enjoyment of a competent income; and the prospect of peace and happiness naturally and rightfully cheered her heart.

A drunken father staggers home to pawn the table on which his child's coffin is lying. From Charles A. Goodrich: The Child's Book on Intemperance *(Boston, 1835).*

evils of that vice in true but affecting tales of woe'. These included the often repeated story of the man who staggers home to pawn the table on which his dead child is lying, and the account of the fatal sideboard in a father's home – ' "My God! my son! where did you learn to be a drunkard?" "At the sideboard in your own parlor." '

The temperance message in America was a far more universal one than in England, where it was aimed mostly at the lower orders, and not at the social wine-drinking of the upper classes. In Louisa Alcott's *Good Wives* (1869), for instance, Mr March sees to it that the wine given for Meg's wedding is sent to the Soldiers' Home instead. Meg tells Laurie: ' "He thinks wine should be used only in illness, and mother says that neither she nor her daughters will ever offer it to any young man under her roof." ' And she exacts a promise that he will never drink it: ' "Come, Laurie, promise, and give me one more reason to call this the happiest day of my life." ' And though he comes from a household where wine is customarily served with meals, he agrees.

In England temperance was to become a central plank with Methodists and Baptists, and Cardinal Manning, seeing the destruction wrought by alcohol among the London poor, gave it up himself. But though the Church of England might deprecate the evils of drink so far as the poor were concerned, in general it expected its clergy to drink a glass of wine at the dinner-table at social gatherings. He who refused to do so was regarded as both unsociable and ungentlemanly. 'The parson whom the archdeacon feared most of all parsons was the parson who wouldn't fill his glass,' said Trollope when Archdeacon Grantly was entertaining Mr Crawley, the poor perpetual curate whose daughter was about to marry his own son.[58]

The English poor, however, though they could do themselves a great deal of harm with beer and gin, did not generally have access to rum, and whisky and brandy were beyond their means. Nor did they start so young. Faced with rum-drinking toddlers, the American temperance movement felt they had to work towards a society in which drink would be totally outlawed, and temperance literature, in spite of the name, invariably advocated total abstinence – a fact about which the *Nation* complained, calling the publications of the National Temperance Society 'foolishly and laughably bad'.[59] 'There is no moderation but that of total abstinence to be followed,' pronounced an MSSS book describing a community where the ministers and deacons had at first merely counselled moderation and caution.[60] 'It is not enough for a man to say "I shall never be a drunkard." He must say "I will never drink rum," ' said the *Youth's Casket* in 1853, pointing to the terrible consequences that could befall the man who thought he had self-control enough to be a moderate drinker.

And it is the respectability of Simon Slade's tavern, the Sickle and Sheaf, that is responsible for the destruction of Cedarville in the most famous temperance story of all, T. S. Arthur's *Ten Nights in a Bar-Room* (1854). Timothy Shay Arthur (1809–85), dull and a slow learner, was taken out of school early and apprenticed to a watchmaker. His eyes were not good enough; but he became a voracious reader and a fluent scribbler who poured out magazine articles and stories, mostly with a didactic slant, many of them about ideal marriage, and many about temperance (he also edited temperance magazines). He was one of the few of his kind who wrote about the dangers of ambition – *Making Haste to be Rich, Keeping up Appearances* and *Rising in the World* are all moral tales aimed at the worldly. *Home Heroines* describes women who by thoughtlessness bring disaster. One of its stories, 'Little Martyrs', tells of children whom their mothers have killed by a combination of heedlessness and foolish theories about child-raising. He is particularly severe on those who fail to breast-feed their infants.

But the temperance cause made him famous. *Ten Nights* was his greatest success, and its sales in the 1850s were second only to *Uncle Tom's Cabin*. Few Sunday school libraries were without it; Arthur had the supreme good fortune to produce a satisfyingly lurid and sensational work that had the full approval of the godly.

When Simon Slade abandons his trade of miller to open a tavern, it is held to be a great boon to the community, but a few years later . . . 'An eating cancer was on the community, and so far as the eye could mark its destructive progress, the wages were fearful.' But because of the tavern's seeming respectability, leading members of the community give it their approval: 'At all times of the day and evening you could see the flower of our young men going in and out.' From drinking they are led to gambling, and from gambling to brawling, riot and murder. A child is killed, delirium tremens takes hold of some, and several violent deaths are described with much savagery – ' "The doctor saw him this morning, and says the eye was fairly gouged out and broken up. In fact, when we carried him upstairs for dead, last night, his eye was lying on his cheek. I pushed it back with my own hand!" ' On the narrator's last visit to Cedarville, there is dilapidation and ruin everywhere. Slade has been killed by the son who was so full of promise; his wife is in an insane asylum. 'The accursed traffic must cease among us,' says the narrator. 'You must cut off the fountain, if you would dry up the stream.' Finally, the signpost of the Sickle and Sheaf, 'the false emblem which had invited so many to enter the way of destruction, fell crashing to the ground'.

Other writers, also, discovered the profitability of lurid and godly books. One of the more extreme was *Ned Nevins the Newsboy* (1866) by the Rev. Henry Morgan, who designated himself PMP – Poor Man's Preacher. (He ran an independent church in Boston which he decribed as 'Congregational in polity, Methodist in doctrine, and Baptist in the ordinances'.) Ned Nevins himself makes infrequent

Title-page from T. S. Arthur's best-selling temperance shocker (Philadelphia, 1854).

"If I do nuthin' wrong, somethin' good 'l come to me."

Title-page from Henry Morgan's best-seller (Boston, 1868).

appearances in Morgan's stewpot of beatings, violence, crime and seduction. The message, though, comes over plainly:

If you want to be rich you must be truthful and honest ...There is a man walking on the Common, who, when a boy, collected grease and ashes in carts on the street. He now has command of a line of steamers. His income last year was thirty thousand dollars. He was converted in a sabbath school, and became a teacher, then superintendent; and now is among the foremost in all benevolent enterprises.

Morgan, who appears to have written his own publicity, claimed in the preface of a subsequent edition that 'never since the days of the *Lamplighter* or of *Uncle Tom's Cabin* has a book awakened such universal demands from all classes... Street boys repeat the motto, "If I do no wrong, something good will come to me." '

The literary journals, however, received it with distaste, one at least comparing it most unfavourably with Charles Loring Brace's *Short Sermons to News Boys* (1866). This last is an outstanding example of how to present a religious message to those who have never before encountered one. The book consists of addresses directed at homeless boys who had found shelter in the New York News Boys' Lodging House – independent, sceptical, lawless boys who would have made as testing an audience as could be found anywhere. The Lodging House, which Brace had founded himself, hoped to protect their health, help them in the world and ultimately to turn them from vagrancy to a settled life. They were not objects of charity but each one a lodger in Brace's own hotel, paying him six cents for a bed. Nor were there any rules except that they should keep order among themselves, and use the bath. Some boys suspected that it was a 'House-o'-Refuge trap' – or, even worse, 'a Sunday-school trap' – but in the end nobody refused to attend the voluntary religious meetings on Sundays, and all joined in the Lord's Prayer, though one lad asked if it was a Catholic or a Protestant one. The sermons are very direct, mostly about God's love, the need to be honest and truthful, the need to be thankful – though most of the boys had had such wretched beginnings that this was more difficult. Brace's vision of heaven was very powerful, with imagery that such boys could understand – light, clear skies, rest, release from prison, freedom from remorse,

tears wiped away and the exultation of winning the victor's crown. It is one of the very few Sunday school books that does not put one 'out of patience with propriety'.

From 1865 to 1884 over seven million immigrants arrived in the United States, many of them Catholic or Lutheran, who brought with them their own tradition of keeping Sunday as a holiday. But Brace took an understanding view about the keeping of Sunday. He saw that it was difficult for the poorest news boys to abstain from work on that day, when they had to earn the money for their lodging: 'But it's good for the boys to be clean and well-dressed for one day, to spend a quiet day reading their Testaments, and joining in the meetings, and thinking about their own life. Make it a cheerful, peaceful and religious day.' At the time that he was writing, the strict keeping of the Sabbath was declining. Throughout the 1870s the American evangelical Churches fought the trend, denounced it from the pulpits, and warned the faithful that keeping the Sabbath was the cornerstone of the nation. But by the 1880s even the strict realized that the days were past when the Sabbath could be kept in Puritan style. It was even possible to rebuke those who thought otherwise: ' "We have the highest authority, Margaret... for believing it is lawful to do good on any day, however sacred," ' says a mother to a friend who has expressed surprise that her daughter is allowed to go and visit a sick friend on a Sunday.[61]

Were there any Sunday school books that rose above the restrictions of their time? To convey to children the beauty of holiness was beyond the powers of most. It can perhaps best be done through imaginative writing, and George MacDonald succeeded because he never spelt out his meanings, but left his readers to find them for themselves. The vast bulk of Sunday school books had nothing spiritual about them, were unworthy of the religion they professed. They laid down inflexible laws, promised unworthy rewards, presented hopelessly unalluring virtue for emulation. And the Protestant distrust of pleasure was often evident in the ugly appearance of the books they gave to their young.

To those studying the ante-bellum Sunday school book, one omission soon becomes glaringly apparent: no mention is ever made of slavery. The issue that was to rend the nation apart might never have existed. As we have noted, the American Tract Society did not concern itself with the humanitarian issues of the day. There was great enthusiasm over missionary effort for frontier families, and some talk of missions to the Indians, but not to the black population. The ASSU had made it plain to their writers that all controversial issues must be avoided. The Eighth Annual Report, in 1832, put it bluntly: 'On the delicate question of slavery, abstain from all remarks; much injury may result from an indiscreet observation.'

Though there were individual abolitionists within the ranks, the official silence on the subject astonished English evangelicals, and English visitors to American shores invariably caused grave offence if they commented upon it. The abolitionist William Lloyd Garrison, with characteristic vehemence, denounced the various religious organizations such as the ASSU as equally culpable partners in a conspiracy of complicity rather than neutrality. In 1855 he proposed to the American Anti-slavery Society that it should pass a resolution condemning these organizations as 'being in league and fellowship with the slave-holders of the South, utterly dumb in regard to the slave system, and inflexibly hostile to the anti-slavery movement', and that they should recommend that these same organizations 'should be instantly abandoned by every one claiming to be the friend of liberty and a disciple of Christ'. But the evangelical societies that he was denouncing for the most part ignored his attacks. With a membership drawn from widely divergent backgrounds, holding totally opposed views, they knew that their very existence depended upon silence.

Americans felt then that war played no part in their new civilization, it was part of the wicked Old World. In view of what was to come, a little undated ASSU tract called *War* is particularly poignant:

'War is carried on with great cruelty by savage nations. When one army beats another they put all the people they can to death in the most cruel manner...'

'O father, how horrid that is.'

'Yes, my son, war is full of horrors.'

ROMANTIC FICTION: CHASTE EROTICISM

'I call them stories,' a biographer wrote of Susan Warner's books, 'for I well recall [her sister's] look of what seemed to me troubled surprise when I once spoke of them as Miss Susan's novels. In her younger days many persons holding strict ideas kept aloof from novels.'[62] And it is always a matter of astonishment that so many Victorian writers for the young should have supposed that their own pious romances were somehow exempt from the dreadful taint of fiction. Many would have considered episodes in Warner sagas like *The Wide, Wide World* and *Melbourne House* thoroughly unhealthy. None the less, the heroine of the first has a copy of *Blackwood's Magazine* (a sober enough journal, one would have thought) taken from her by the young man who has appointed himself her spiritual director, and is made to promise that she will never in his absence read a novel. A recent critic, musing over this strange blindness on the part of Miss Warner, has commented: 'The terrible proscriptions of nineteenth century life produced the duplicity evident in the conclusion of this best-selling book, which purveyed the erotic satisfaction customary in novels, at the same time that it outlawed the entire genre.'[63]

Heman Humphrey had complained in 1840 about writers of religious fiction, whom he divided into two categories: 'those who give a religious cast to their books to make them sell, and those who wish to allure readers to the love and practice of religion'.[64] He could not wholeheartedly approve even of the second, but naturally deplored the first, whose writing, he said, was splattered with theological terms and phrases, and scriptural quotations that were hardly ever apposite. It was a class of fiction 'more dangerous in a rising family than any other'. But this was ten years before *The Wide, Wide World*. Though it and its fellows fall into the second rather than the first category, Mr Humphrey would surely have perceived the erotic content – so obvious to the modern reader though not to Miss Warner herself – as dangerous in the highest degree.

The Wide, Wide World and Maria Susanna Cummins' *The Lamplighter* (1854), published four years later, were to be best-sellers, and were accepted in both England and America as suitable Sunday school fare, though the second had not been originally intended for children. Both are the story of female orphans, a category beloved of the sentimental novelist, with a long history (discussed in chapter 6). *The Lamplighter* follows the career of Gerty, a Boston waif, who is rescued from near destitution by an old lamplighter who begins the work of redemption, and then after his death is adopted by a wealthy young blind woman. She moves with her in fashionable society and is reunited first with her long-lost father (also wealthy and fashionable, and the stepbrother of her protectress into the bargain) and then with her childhood sweetheart, successful and prosperous likewise. But the evangelical content is remarkably small. No doubt the book entered the Sunday school lists on the strength of its opening chapters – the street waif theme was to become very popular in England in the 1860s and 70s – but though Gerty is transformed from a savage little pagan into a dutiful and responsible young woman, this happens off-stage:

'But at last there came a dawn to my seemingly everlasting night. It came in the shape of a minister of Christ, our own dear Mr Arnold, who opened the eyes of my under-standing, lit the lamp of religion in my now softened soul, taught me the way to peace, and led my feeble steps into that blessed rest, which, even on earth, remaineth to the people of God.'

In *The Wide, Wide World* the religious message is more explicit, but it is mingled with a heady love interest. Miss Warner (who wrote under the name of Elizabeth Wetherell) sought to make the latter theme chaste by representing the kisses and embraces 'Mr John' lavishes upon the pubescent heroine as brotherly tokens of affection, but she succeeds only in making the relationship suggest-ively incestuous. There is a degree of self-indulgence about her writing which can be ascribed to the wretched circumstances of her own life. The daughter of an improvident and litigious father, whose reckless investments and expensive disputes with his neighbours reduced the family to abject poverty, she began writing *The Wide, Wide World* 'upon her knees', her sister Anna was to say later.[65] (This can be taken as much as a despairing plea for success as a prayer for divine guidance.) Awk-ward and ungainly as an adolescent, 'rude when in fact I do not mean to be so', 'her head in a rosy dream of fiction most of the time', self-willed, 'a bit of a sybarite by nature', she would probably have chosen to spend her life reading and tending her imagination by a comfortable fireside ('though all her life long she liked to have someone else keep the fire up',[66] – a bitter comment from the one who was expected to supply this service). She loved to write about girls who fascinate even

the most worldly by their innate good breeding and style, who are gifted and intelligent, but are able to turn their hand to practical matters; and she had them receive the male attention and solicitude that she must have yearned for herself. In her own life male company was limited to her father and the selected West Point cadets who used to be rowed over the Hudson to the Warner home on Constitution Island for Bible-reading and ginger-bread. All her characters suffer from prostrating headaches or nervous exhaustion, and there is invariably a solicitous male presence who hovers, adjusts pillows, and is ready with cups of tea and a strong, cool hand to lay on the forehead.

The Wide, Wide World, her first and most popular book, concerns Ellen Montgomery, ten when the book opens, fourteen and a half at the end of six hundred pages of very small print. She is torn from her dying mother who is all in all to her, and sent to live with her grim Aunt Fortune in upstate New York. Aunt Fortune teaches her housewifery, and Miss Alice and Mr John, a neighbouring clergyman's son and daughter, make themselves responsible for her spiritual development. Miss Alice dies of con-sumption, and Ellen's Scottish grandmother, a wealthy noblewoman, sends for her. The book ends abruptly a few months after Ellen's arrival in Scotland – Miss Warner always had difficulty manipulating her plots and characters. Her only purpose in introducing Ellen's Scottish relations, for instance, seems to be to give her the opportunity to describe an aristocratic milieu in the Old World, which, though she had no experience of it, always fascinated her. Though virtually without plot, this immensely long book is engrossing because of its descriptions of rural life, and its sensual, even lustful, accounts of food. Even at a moment of high crisis the author pauses to tell us about the richness and seasoning of the gravy being served – but Ellen has not forgotten what else is due to her: 'What *was* the matter? Only – that Mr John had forgotten the kiss that he always gave her on coming and going. Ellen was jealous of it as a pledge of sister-ship.'

Though there is a strong atmosphere of piety, there is no church-going; all is centred on vague references to Bible study. Ellen has to learn to love God (in the opening chapters she is seen to love her mother more) and to discipline herself to endure with Christian, some would say unnatural, meek-ness Aunt Fortune's irascible nature and tyrannical behaviour. At the end, when it may be supposed that she has been purified by her tribulations and led heavenwards by Alice and John, we are told that she 'had two safeguards which effectually kept her from pride and presumption. One was her love for [John] and longing remembrance of him.' The other – seemingly an afterthought – is the daily hour that she has promised John to devote to studying her Bible. However, when he comes to see his 'sister' in Edinburgh, John is far more concerned that she should promise never to touch wine nor read a novel than he is at the prospect of leaving her to spend formative years in a nest of unsympathetic, unconverted worldlings.

Nine-year-old Daisy Randolph in Susan Warner's *Melbourne House* (1864), setting out to be 'a soldier of Christ', meets with far more opposition from her family than does Ellen Montgomery. They are worldly, cruel, oppressive and in every way unworthy of her. She encounters some who help her on her way, such as the devout West Indian Juanita and a young minister 'with eyes too full of light to let you see what colour they were', as well as some whom she wishes to convert: a handsome young captain, and the 'very fine-looking' Dr Sandford – 'there was enough about Dr Sandford to engage all Daisy's attention and interest'.

The hostility endured by Daisy – grave, meek, sweet-faced, artless – must have inflamed many readers. Her family detest all manifestations of her new-found Christianity, her grace before meals, her observance of the Sabbath. The calm certainty of this sort of child evangelist, unshakeably confident that her interpretation of the Scriptures is the only valid one, is awe-inspiring. She knows that the commandment to keep the Sabbath holy must override all else, even though her father points to the commandment to honour father and mother. Her loutish brother, who torments and even strikes her, is considered beyond Daisy's evangelizing. Her indolent, worldly father is weakly subservient to her mother, and beats Daisy when he is told to do so. Her sadistic mother, at one point incensed because Daisy refuses to sing 'a gipsy song from an opera' on a Sunday, flogs the child with a slave whip: 'In a Southern home that whip had been wont to live in Mrs Randolph's pocket. [It] was small, but it had been made for use, not play, and there was no play in Mrs Randolph's use of it.'

Dr Sandford, by contrast, tends her broken ankle,

soothes her ruffled nerves, and is always at hand to lay a cool hand on her brow and arrange her pillows, or, when she is stronger, to give her scientific instruction. In short, he is the sort of doctor that many female authors in more inhibited times than the present derived a sexual pleasure from contemplating, and though attention is usually limited to brows, pulses and ankles, he also kisses Daisy: 'And greatly to Daisy's astonishment, the doctor's moustache brushed her lip. Now Daisy had always thought to herself that she would never allow anybody that wore a moustache to kiss her; here it was done without leave asked; and if the doctor was so independent of rules as that, she thought she had best not provoke him.' His agnosticism makes him even more attractive to Daisy, but she achieves no more with him than to sow a few seeds of doubt in his mind. Indeed, conversion, except of the central character, does not play very much part in Miss Warner's novels. She habitually found it difficult to bring her books to an end, and *Melbourne House* finishes even more abruptly than *The Wide, Wide World*. Within a few hurried last pages her father has an accident, and is sent to Europe for his health. And Daisy, what will they do with her?

'Send her to a Southern plantation, under the care of a governess, as I understand.'

'It will half kill Daisy,' said Mrs Sandford.

'It takes a great deal to kill people,' said the doctor.

And there the book ends.

One young mid-Victorian, given *Melbourne House* for Sunday reading, remembered the whipping (which he reckoned was properly deserved), and the food: 'As a child I used to think I would undergo a whipping every Sunday were it only to be followed by a supper of fried oysters, ice-cream and waffles ... Unfortunately I can never remember having been asked to sing on a Sunday, or indeed on any other day.'[67] He added, on a more serious note, that he was convinced that 'these emotionally pietistic little books' produced no good effect whatever on their readers, and that he himself used to be exasperated by 'the ultra-righteous little heroines'.

In her second novel, *Queechy* (1852), Miss Warner did succeed in bringing Elfleda Ringgan, ten years old when the book opens, to the age of twenty, when at last she can melt into the arms of Mr Carleton, the aristocratic Englishman (patently modelled on Jane Austen's Mr Darcy) of immense wealth and huge estates, who has long wooed her. Fleda is able to convert him. She is immaculate: 'It is the pure gold, and it knows no tarnish; it is the true coin, and it gives what it proffers to give; it is the living plant, ever blossoming' – and it is her example that changes Mr Carleton's heart. She gives him a rose, which brings about the desired result:

'She is right and I am wrong,' he thought. 'She is by far the nobler creature – worth many such as I. *Like her* I cannot be ... But I can be something other than I am ... An All-wise Governor must look for service of me. He shall have it. Whatever my life is, it shall be to some end. If not what I would, what I can. If not the purity of the rose, that of tempered steel!'

Something of the voluptuous character of the Warner style comes through even at solemn moments: 'Fleda was *curled up among her cushions, luxuriously bending over* a little black Bible' (my italics). Though well into this century Susan Warner's books were given out freely, on the strength of her name alone as Sunday school prizes, and delighted adolescent girls by their heady emotion and the attention their heroines received from dominant males, among the adults who took the trouble to read them there were some who had reservations. In England, for instance, Charlotte Yonge, who herself provided very different reading for the schoolroom girl and whose ethic and ideals were austere and rigorous, remarked shrewdly that books such as *The Wide, Wide World* would lead girls to see a lover in anybody who was kind to them.[68]

Susan's sister Anna Warner also wrote, under the name of Amy Lothrop, but in a more robust style, and *Dollars and Cents* (1852) is a down-to-earth fictional account of her family's desperate poverty, though with a happy ending. The sisters also often collaborated on books. It is impossible to disentangle in these the two separate pens, though Anna, curiously, would seem to be the dominant partner, and the hothouse emotion characteristic of Susan's work is mostly absent. Hard as they worked, they were never to achieve the carefree, ladylike leisure for which they yearned. The money they earned evaporated in Mr Warner's lawsuits, debts and bad investments, and as long as he lived they had to resign themselves to labour.

The Warner example had a profound effect upon another writer, the Presbyterian Martha Finley (1828–1909), who wrote under the name of Martha Farquharson. She was an invalid and, like the Warners, wrote from necessity, desperate to be free from financial dependence on her stepbrother. Her first novel, *Elsie Dinsmore*, appeared in 1867. Like Ellen Montgomery and Daisy Randolph, Elsie is isolated in a household which, though it is her grandfather's, is hostile and alien. She is the sole God-fearing member of it, a faithful black servant her only friend, and is tormented and mocked by her young and worldly uncles and aunts. Elsie is a near-perfect little girl, modelled, it is said, upon Miss Finley's own niece, but even more upon Daisy Randolph. Like Daisy, Elsie also refuses to sing a secular song on a Sunday, and, forced to sit at the piano for hour after hour, eventually collapses, gashing her head as she does so. This scene has not the force of the one with the slave-whip, and indeed Elsie is a pale version of the Warner heroines. She is sweet and good and meek, but does not possess the practical abilities that made Ellen and Elfleda competent housewives and useful in a crisis. And there is none of that strong Warner sense of place; the Dinsmore chronicles – there were eventually to be some thirty of them – were set, like many other romances of the Reconstruction period, in 'an antebellum Dixie that never existed'[69] and which the author did not attempt to describe.

But in one quality Miss Finley did outdo her model – in inadvertent prurience. Perhaps shocked by the amount of kissing and caressing that Susan Warner allowed herself, but fascinated by it nevertheless, she determined to keep it within the family. Accordingly, she created Horace Dinsmore, only seventeen when he begot Elsie, who comes back to Roselands, his father's plantation, after a long sojourn in Europe. (The young mother has died long before we meet Elsie.) Initially very cold to his little daughter, he comes to treat her with alternate ferocity and lover-like possessiveness. He is ready with his riding-whip to threaten to flog her for blotting her copybook – someone else, naturally, is really responsible – but delights in straining her to his bosom, sitting her on his knee and stroking her curls, and bitterly resents her cutting one off to give to a girl cousin.

Much of the second book, *Elsie's Holidays at Roselands*, is taken up with her resistance to his order

" Pick up your flower, and leave the room ;" he said, " I have
no desire for your company." *Page* 109

Elsie Dinsmore and her father. From Martha Finley:
Holidays at Roselands *(London, 1873).*

that she should read to him on the Sabbath 'a
fictitious moral tale, without a particle of religious
truth'. Through the course of some two hundred
pages the tension grows, the family ostracizes her,
her father seems to be dying of a fever that Elsie's
obduracy has induced; she weeps until they fear
for her eyes, whereat her father forbids her to weep
any more. Recovered, he tries to tempt her into
submission, and now it is her turn to pine and
sicken. In her delirium she screams in Protestant
terror at the thought of the convent to which he
has threatened to send her, and when he finally
comes, broken, to her bedside she cannot recognize
him. Eventually, after a pseudo-death when faithful
servants 'attend to the last sad offices of love to
the dear remains of the little departed one', Elsie
comes to life and is folded in the arms of her dear
papa, who has in the meantime 'learned to know

and love Jesus' and to recognize that he has been
a very cruel father.

Thereafter they are never far apart, and though
now a Christian, he still maintains that stern authority which so fascinated Miss Finley's public,
threatening to whip her even when she is grown
up, for having inadvertently allowed another man
to kiss her. Mr Travilla, from a neighbouring plantation – very rich, very upright, a man to whom
no father could possibly object – does succeed in
marrying her in spite of Horace Dinsmore's anguish.
Miss Finley allows her to bear him children, and
then at the earnest request of her readers dispatches
him to an early grave, and Elsie returns to her
father.

Though the authority of the Bible is constantly
invoked during Elsie's early resistance to her father,
the Christian message is very thin, and the over-
riding impression is of worldliness. There was no
point in being rich unless you unfailingly displayed
it in dress and ornament, Miss Finley felt, and like
Miss Warner she was fond of food, and a lot of it.
So there is copious detail about jewels and splendid
clothes (worn even by children) and elaborate meals
– though Elsie 'as a professed Christian' thinks it
sinful to dance or go to the Opera. Indeed, this
emphasis on material possessions is to be found
in other godly books of the period, and many a
girl finds the man of her dreams to be unexpectedly
immensely wealthy. In *Faith Gartney's Girlhood*
(1863) by Mrs Adeline Dutton Train Whitney (1824–
1906), for example, the heroine is saved from a
fire by the young minister who has long loved her,
and she breaks off her engagement to a wealthy
manufacturer only to find that the minister too has
inherited great riches.

It is pleasant to be able to record that the public
could also be discriminating. *Stepping Heavenward*
(1869) by Elizabeth Prentiss (1818–78) was a very
popular piece of evangelical fiction that it is hard
to fault. Written in the form of a journal, it charts
with passionate sincerity, but also with humour,
a young woman's spiritual progress from self-
absorbed adolescent always at odds with her mother,
through courtship, marriage and motherhood, finally to awareness that death is approaching. In
this there is no trace of self-indulgence; it is written
with good sense and an understanding of human
nature, as well as with a genuinely religious insight
that is sadly lacking in so many of her contemporaries.

NOTES

ASSU American Sunday School Union
MSSS Massachusetts Sabbath School Society

1. Thomas M. Clark: *Reminiscences* (New York, 1895), 7.

2. Jonathan Edwards: sermon preached at Enfield, 8 July 1741. Published as 'Sinners in the hand of an Angry God', in *Works of President Edwards* (Worcester, Mass. 1808-9) IV, 313-21.

3. Ernest Caulfield: 'Some Common Diseases of Colonial Children', *Colonial Society of Massachusetts Transactions*, 35 (Boston, 1951).

4. Jonathan Edwards: *A Faithful Narrative of the Surprising Works of God* (London, 1737), 111.

5. Charles Chauncy: *Seasonable Thoughts on the State of Religion in New England* (Boston, 1743).

6. Susan I. Lesley: *Recollections of My Mother* (Boston, 1886).

7. *The Infant Preacher, or the story of Henrietta Smith* (New Haven, Conn., 1819).

8. 'Memoirs of the late Rev. Jonathan Edwards', in *Works of President Edwards*, 46.

9. George Bacon: 'The Literature of our Sunday Schools', *Hours at Home*, 1870. Quoted in Richard Darling: *The Rise of Children's Book Reviewing in America, 1865-1881* (New York, 1968).

10. Hugo Münsterberg: *The Americans* (trans. Edwin B. Holt, London, 1905), 504.

11. Robert S. Lynd and Helen Merrell Lynd: *Middletown* (New York, 1929).

12. Mary Lundie Duncan: *America as I Found It* (London, 1852), 50.

13. Robert W. Lyn and Elliott Wright: *The Big Little School* (New York, 1971).

14. Robert Kelley: *The Transatlantic Persuasion* (New York, 1969).

15. [Sarah Tuttle]: *Letters on the Chickasaw and Osage Missions* (MSSS, Boston, 1833).

16. Lyn and Wright: op. cit.

17. [Increase N. Tarbox]: *Winnie and Walter's Evening Talks with their Father about Old Times* (Boston, 1861).

18. Stephen Elmer Slocum: 'The American Tract Society' (Ph.D. thesis, New York University, University Microfilms, Ann Arbor, 1975), 73.

19. ibid., 76.

20. Achille Murat: *A Moral and Political Sketch of the United States of North America* (London, 1833).

21. Edwin Wilbur Rice: *The Sunday School Movement* (Philadelphia, 1917).

22. Anthony Trollope: *North America* (London, 1862), I, 425.

23. Heman Humphrey: *Domestic Education* (Amherst, Mass., 1840), 101.

24. *Children's Magazine*, General Protestant Episcopal Sunday School Union, New York, vol. 31 (1859), p. 31.

25. *Appleton's Journal* vol. 11 (New York, 27 June 1874).

26. *Overland Monthly* vol. 8 (San Francisco, January 1872).

27. Darling: op. cit., 77.

28. Grace Greenwood [Sarah Jane (Clarke) Lippincott]: *Recollections of My Childhood and other stories* (Boston, 1852).

29. *Children's Magazine*, General Protestant Episcopal Sunday School Union, New York, vol. 2 (1830), p. 163.

30. Harvey Newcomb: *The Tract Distributor* (MSSS, Boston, 1839).

31. J. B. Waterbury: *Taking Up the Cross* (MSSS, Boston, 1855).

32. The literary treatment of the death of children is discussed in Peter Coveney: *The Image of Childhood* (rev. edn, London, 1967).

33. *A Pleasing Toy for Children* (Concord, NH, 1843).

34. *The Well-Spring* (MSSS, Boston, 1885), vol. 22, no. 18.

35. ibid., vol. 43, no. 34 (1886).

36. Joseph Arch: *Autobiography* [1898] (London, 1966), 28.

37. Mary D. R. Boyd: *Wat Adams, the Young Machinist and his Proverbs* (Presbyterian Board of Publication, Philadelphia, 1875).

38. Mary D. R. Boyd: *The Three Rules* (Presbyterian Board of Publication, Philadelphia, 1871).

39. Anna E. Appleton: *Stories for Eva* (American Unitarian Association, Boston, 1871).

40. This monthly, published from Buffalo, NY, which ran from 1852 to 1857, was the first publication of Erastus F. Beadle, later famous for the dime novels which he and his brother Irwin, together with Robert Adams, began publishing in the 1860s.

41. Robert Cushman: *A Sermon Preached at Plimmoth in New England, December 9, 1621* (London, 1622), 14.

42. *Amelia Sheldon, as a daughter, sister, wife and mother* (2nd edn, MSSS, Boston, 1851).

43. J. Hector St John de Crèvecoeur: *Letters from an American Farmer* [1782] (London and New York, 1981), 85.

44. Lucy Ellen Guernsey: *Irish Amy* (ASSU, Philadelphia, 1854).

45. 'Father William' [William A. Alcott]: *Recollections of Rambles at the South* (New York, 1854).

46. Mrs Lucy H. Dickinson: *Family Scenes* (MSSS, Boston, 1848).

47. William Prynne: *Histrio-Mastix: the Players Scourge or Actors Tragedie* (London, 1633), 445.

48. William A. Alcott: *The Boy's Guide* (Boston, 1845).

49. Fanny Fern [Sara P. W. Parton]: *The Play-Day Book* (New York, 1857).

50. *The Circus*, Child's Cabinet Library (ASSU, Philadelphia, n.d.).

51. James Whitcomb Riley: *The Boy Lives on Our Farm* (Indianapolis, 1892).

52. William Ames: *Conscience with the Power and Cases Thereof* (London, 1639), 214.

53. Cotton Mather: *Ornaments for the Daughters of Zion* (London, 1694), 16.

54. *The Governess* (MSSS, Boston, 1849).

55. Thomas Grattan: *Civilised America* (London, 1859), II, 312.

56. *My Native Village* (ASSU, Philadelphia, 1844).

57. Charles A. Goodrich: *The Child's Book of Intemperance* (Boston, 1835).

58. Anthony Trollope: *The Last Chronicle of Barset*, ch. 83 (London, 1867).

59. Darling: op. cit., 77.

60. Ann E. Porter: *The Little Cider Merchant, or Mr Plimpton and his neighbours* (2nd edn, Boston, 1856).

61. Appleton: op. cit.

62. Olivia Egleston Phelps Stokes: *Letters and Memories of Susan Bartlett Warner* (New York, 1925), 14.

63. Alfred Habegger: *Gender, Fantasy and Realism in American Literature* (New York, 1982), 14.

64. Humphrey: op. cit., 99.

65. Anna B. Warner: *Susan Warner ('Elizabeth Wetherell')* (New York, 1909), 264.

66. ibid., 88.

67. Lord Frederic Hamilton: *Here, There and Everywhere*, in coll. edn, *The Vanished World of Yesterday* (London, 1950), 749.

68. Charlotte M. Yonge: *What Books to Lend and What to Give* (London, 1887).

69. Helen Waite Papashvily: *All the Happy Endings: a study of the domestic novel in America* (New York, 1956), 174.

5. Liberty of Thought

A NEW ERA

'Fruitful as America has been and is in children's books, we have not yet apparently added a single one to the first rank of juvenile classics,' lamented Samuel Osgood in 1865.[1] In the article that followed he spoke about the nature of the American child, to which he attributed some of the reason for this state of affairs:

Reading begins very early with us; and the universal hurry of the American mind crowds children forward, and tempts them in pleasure, as in study and work, to rebel at the usual limitations of years, and push infancy prematurely into childhood, childhood into youth, and youth into maturity...Our heads are apt to be much older than our shoulders, and English critics of our juvenile literature say that much of it seems written for the market and counting-room rather than for the nursery and playground.

And the contents of *Oliver Optic's Magazine*, which Lee & Shepard of Boston, the pre-eminent publishers of juvenile books in the post-bellum period, launched in January 1867, would seem to confirm this. The second number, for instance, contains a description of the sights to be seen in the Paris morgue, and miscellaneous items of information such as the fact that 'Wisconsin sold over three millions dollars of butter last year' and 'The total cost of A. T. Stewart's mansion in New York with its furniture will not be less than $1,500,000.' A later issue carries an article on how to make a will. 'Why, "Young America" wears patent leathers, smokes a meerschaum, twirls a cane, flirts with the girls, drives horses,' announced a boy in the magazine *Demorest's Young America* in 1873, thereby confirming the gloomiest observations of the visitors from Britain.

There was, however, in the 1860s a new attempt to write for the very young. The writer who called herself 'Sophie May' (Rebecca Sophia Clarke, 1833–1906)* wrote five series for 'little folks', about Little Prudy (her first book in 1863), Dotty Dimple, Flaxie Frizzle and others. Like Jacob Abbott she was a Maine author, and there are similarities of approach, though Abbott would never have allowed the baby-talk. But like him she is notable for her calm good sense and understanding of young children; and, as in his books, nothing very much ever happens. Her children have minor mishaps, they grow older, their characters and their sense of responsibility develop, and by the time we reach the last series we are reading about Little Prudy's children. 'From her correspondence it seems that Miss Clarke's heart was not in these books; she would have preferred to write for adults. But she undoubtedly had a talent for humorous observation – as in *Dotty Dimple out West* (1869), where the little girl sets out on an expedition alone with her papa and boasts about the fact ecstatically to a boy she meets on the train: ' "Did you ever hear of a girl that travelled out West?...I mean a girl as little as me, 'thout anybody but my papa; and he don't know how to part my hair in the middle." '

Jane Andrews (1833–87), a Massachusetts schoolteacher, also wrote for young children, but with more imagination and invention. *Seven Little Sisters Who Live on the Round Ball that Floats in the Air* (1861) is remarkable for being possibly the first American children's fiction with exotic settings. With engaging simplicity the stories describe the lives of Agoonack the Eskimo, Gemila of the Arabian desert, Jeanette in Switzerland, Pen-se in China, Louise on the Rhine, Manenko in Africa, and a Pacific island baby. They combine a sense of distant places and strange customs with reassuring details about happy family life and parents' love, which the young reader learns are the same the world over. She wrote more in the same vein, imparting geography, history (*Ten Boys Who Lived on the*

Road from Long Ago to Now, 1885) and natural history in the guise of fiction, but with a commendably light touch.

Mary Mapes Dodge's *Hans Brinker, or the Silver Skates* (1865) gives us another glimpse of how horizons were expanding in the 1860s. It cannot be claimed as a work of great literary distinction – it reads too much like a guidebook. But what was remarkable about it, as with *Seven Little Sisters*, is the move to a setting outside America. Her publishers had asked her for a Civil War story, and were dubious about her suggestion of a book about Holland instead. Certainly, Goodrich had been brilliantly successful with Parley books about far-flung countries, but would the public be interested in a *story* about Holland? The public was, and its sales in 1865 apparently topped three hundred thousand.

Hans Brinker and his sister Gretel (known to their more prosperous contemporaries as the 'rag-pickers') are the children of a poor labourer, brain-damaged from a fall. The main plot concerns their efforts to find a doctor to cure their father. Mrs Dodge offers much information about the Dutch landscape, architecture, history and way of life; an English boy, Ben, is introduced so that the country can be seen through his eyes. But though the book is overburdened with facts, the story captivated young readers, whose impressions of Holland must at one time have been largely formed by it. It also contains the wholly fictitious legend of 'the hero of Haarlem', the boy who plugs the dyke with his finger, which was to become so much a part of the American perception of Holland that the Dutch eventually erected a statue to him. *Hans Brinker* was the best of Mrs Dodge's books. She wrote a few other stories for children, including *Donald and Dorothy* (1883) about two children's search for their true identity, and a quantity of pleasant but undistinguished verse. She was to achieve far more as an editor, and the thirty-two years she spent with the magazine *St Nicholas* (discussed later in the chapter) were important ones in the history of children's books.

Three years after *Hans Brinker* came *Little Women*, and in December 1868 *Putnam's Magazine* was able to announce a new era in books for children, a movement away from the Sunday school type of literature which had up till then been paramount. Despite the Civil War, children's books in the later

1860s were beginning to provide more entertainment than their predecessors, and were being written with a conspicuously lighter touch. And, it seems, there was a more general desire to keep children young. Some remarkable magazines were founded in that decade, including the *Riverside Magazine for Young People* (1867–70), the literary and artistic excellence of which has probably never been equalled. Humour was making an appearance, too, as in Lucretia Hale's solemn saga about the hilarious obtuseness of the Peterkin family. In New York the McLoughlin brothers (see pages 125–6) were putting out their brightly coloured toy books* which aimed only to please, and the firms of Charles S. Francis and James Miller were producing choice editions of fairy-tales for the top end of the market. Nathaniel Hawthorne's 1850s retellings of Greek myths helped to make tales of imagination respectable, and the *Riverside Magazine* was to feature new stories by Hans Andersen. Above all, Louisa Alcott's *Little Women*, escaping from the atmosphere of febrile romance and strained piety that marked the books of Susan Warner and her kind, had established a new American tradition of robust families with ordinary failings, living ordinary lives. In February 1871 the *Overland Monthly* felt that a corner had been turned:

The old-fashioned stories, with a moral or pious reflection impending at the close of every sentence, or the clumsily adjusted mixture of didactic truth and saccharine rhetoric administered like sulphur and treacle for the moral health of the unhappy infant, are happily long since abandoned. The idea of pleasing children by writing down to their suppositious level, and flavoring the work with a bland imbecility, has also exploded.

F. J. Harvey Darton had hailed the publication of the first of Lewis Carroll's *Alice* books in 1865 as the English watershed: 'It was the first unapologetic, undocumented appearance in print, for readers who sorely needed it, of liberty of thought in children's books. Henceforth . . . there was to be in hours of pleasure no more dread about the moral value.'[2] As with all generalizations, this pronouncement needs to be qualified. *Alice's Adventures in Wonderland*, though few English reviewers that Christmas saw anything remarkable in it, was certainly to become a landmark, and by the time of

---

* A trade term for short coloured picture-books.

the appearance of *Through the Looking-Glass* in 1871 it was already regarded as a classic. But there had been earlier books for the young that stood apart from any moral code or educational practice – Raspe's *Baron Munchausen*, for instance, published in 1785. And firms such as John Harris, John Marshall, and Dean & Munday at the beginning of the next century were publishing delectably illustrated inconsequential verse such as 'Old Mother Hubbard' and 'Dame Wiggins of Lee', in which there was not a vestige of a moral and often a great deal of slapstick humour. Edward Lear's first *Book of Nonsense* had appeared in 1846, and *The Rose and the Ring*, Thackeray's burlesque fairy-story, in 1855 – both containing the anarchic violence that children find supremely funny, and which naturally excludes all didacticism.

But the later Victorian period in England was not all gaiety, as Darton's remarks might have suggested. 'I'm sick of books for young people,' says one of the children in Juliana Horatia Ewing's 1880s story *Mary's Meadow*,[3] 'there's so much *stuff* in them.' The 'stuff' might be information (though the fashion for this was diminishing somewhat), or moralizing, of which there was still a great deal, or the deathbeds to which English writers (including even Mrs Ewing herself) became, in the wake of Dickens, so peculiarly addicted. And for sternness and didacticism, and sheer volume of output of 'stuff', the pre-*Alice* writers are easily outstripped by the energetic Charlotte Maria Tucker (1821–93), whose pseudonym was A.L.O.E. – A Lady of England. From the 1850s until her death she dispensed scientific information and evangelical precepts with a liberal hand, producing over 150 volumes and dominating the Sunday school and reward book market for a whole generation.

THE FAIRY-TALE: PROMOTERS AND OPPONENTS

Through much of the nineteenth century there was on both sides of the Atlantic a great cultural divide between what was read by children from literary homes and what was read by those whose main contact with leisure books was through a Sunday school. In England Charlotte Yonge, in her reading list *What Books to Lend and What to Give* (1887), categorized the two classes as 'drawing room' and 'cottage', implying that the books aimed at the one could not be read with any profit by the other. In particular, the fantastic and imaginative – the *Alices* were an important example – were beyond the reach of cottage children, who in her experience with the local parish school required stories with a familiar background and a direct message. In her grandfather's time the traditional fairy-stories had been kept alive by chapbooks aimed at the cottage home. These had been eschewed by the responsible middle-class parent, who equated them with all that was ignorant and coarse, feeling that they belonged to a peasant culture and had no place in the lives of children who were being reared to be rational and well informed. But among Charlotte Yonge's generation there had been a reaction: fairy-tales were rediscovered, and, gentrified and put out in up-market editions, were now part of Victorian nursery culture. Conversely, the oral tradition among the poorer classes seemed to have withered away, so that Miss Yonge found many children in her parish school who had never heard of such tales as *Cinderella*.

In America the difference was between the elite with literary tastes, and those whose reading was dominated by the Puritan tradition with its anxious denunciations of all the pleasures of life – from dram-drinking and tobacco to theatres, circuses and fairy-tales – indeed, anything at all that might interfere with a serious approach to life. And in between these were such as Twain's Tom Sawyer, steeped in dime novels. To Horace Scudder, editor of the *Riverside Magazine* and a writer of fairy-stories himself, Hans Andersen was one of childhood's greatest benefactors, whose stories fed and stimulated the imagination of children.[4] Caroline Hewins, from a prosperous and cultured family living near Boston, who was to become a pioneer children's librarian, remembered her childhood reading with the keenest affection.[5] It had been catholic and unrestricted, and ranged from the journal *Godey's Lady's Book* (which she had been found reading when she was four and a half) to the *Arabian Nights*, from Aesop to Hawthorne's *Wonder Book*, and when she came to draw up her *Books for the Young* in 1883 she included many fairy-stories both modern and traditional, citing distinguished opinion in their favour. Said one of her supporters:

What I want for the young are books and stories which do not simply deal with our daily life. I prefer *Alice in*

Wonderland as a book for children, to those little stories of 'Tommies' and 'Freddies', who read the books. I like Grimm's *Fairy Tales* better than those little nursery novelties. I like the fancy even of little children to have some larger food than images of their own little lives.[6]

And Caroline Hewins herself had said in the *North American Review* in 1866 that a child was injured as much by being debarred his proper rations of fancy as those of fact.

In stark contrast was the attitude conveyed in *Wat Adams, the Young Machinist* (see page 56). Resolutely against all fancy, the Presbyterian author appears to regard it as a form of pornography. The bad boy of the story tries to corrupt good little Wat (whose own library consists only of Goodrich's *Peter Parley* and Jacob Abbott's *Rollo*) not with dime novels but with fairy-tales, which even the tempter regards as such suspect material that he dare not name their titles. Wat resists, but is sufficiently off his guard to accept *Robinson Crusoe*, which makes him inattentive to his work for some days. Wat's creator suffers the perennial Puritan problem concerning the imagination – even if not inherently evil, it deflects man from more profitable matters. In 1905, some thirty years later, the editor of *Fairy Tales Every Child Should Know*[7] was to denounce this philosophy: 'we are so engrossed in getting rich that we forget that by and by, when we have become rich, we shall have to learn how to live'. He wrote passionately of the fundamental importance of fairy-tales in the development of the imagination, without which nothing else that children read could be comprehensible.

There was undoubtedly in the last century an American unease about fairy-tales. Though the literary might take them for granted – for instance, the genre received much attention from reviewers in the post Civil War period[8] – publishers were often wary of offending those with strict views, concealing fairy legends or Grimm stories under titles such as *Wonder-World Stories* or *Tales of Adventure*. Even those who supported them were often apologetic or defensive. 'There exists, in the minds of some parents, a strong and reasonable prejudice against Fairy Tales for children,' wrote one mid-century author who showed her readers a family of children steeped in such stories; 'As

the extravagant imagery and improbable incidents, in which they generally abound, often mislead or bewilder the youthful imagination'.[9] And the stories which she herself chose to relate to this fictional audience were self-consciously edifying, composed 'to awaken a reasoning thought, leading ultimately to an active principle'. ('They deal in allegory and little episodic sermons,' Andrew Lang was to say contemptuously of stories in this vein that affected to be fairy-tales.[10])

Even in 1905 James Baldwin, the author of many popular retellings of legends, was to warn in his introduction to *The Fairy Reader* that not all fairy-stories were suitable for use in well conducted American schools, and that there was nothing to be gained in reading some of them – the implication being that profit and improvement should be the motive for reading. And in 1908 – in case children should be tempted to stray into forbidden pastures – *Little Prudy's Story Book*[11] began thus:

'Don't you s'pose I know what fairy stories mean? They don't mean anything! You didn't feel afraid I'd believe 'em, did you? I wouldn't believe 'em, I *promise* I wouldn't...'

'Indeed, I hope you would not, little Prudy; for I made 'em up as I went along. There are no fairies but those we have in our hearts.'

But, mercifully, there were parents who did not take their responsibilities so earnestly and who did not ponder on where 'idle tales' might lead their young. For instance, though the Midwest 1840s childhood home of William Henry Venable was pervaded by the maxims of 'Poor Richard' (see page 54), there was an unusually wide range of reading. His father read *Oliver Twist* to the family, his three-year-old sister possessed a tattered library which included 'Mother Goose', 'Timothy Dump', and 'Dame Wiggins of Lee', and the seven-year-old Cynthia read 'with some disdain for its wishy-washiness' Lydia Sigourney's *Pictorial Primer* (see page 161). The boy himself read books of adventure such as the travels of Mungo Park and Captain Cook, *The Immortal Mentor* by Mason Locke Weems, Plutarch's *Lives* and Rollin's *Universal History*;* 'It goes without saying that *Robinson Crusoe*, *The Pilgrim's Progress*, *The Arabian Nights* and *Gulliver's Travels* found a welcome in the cottage,

---

* The writings of the French historian Charles Rollin, 1661–1741, are frequently referred to in the nineteenth century as standard textbooks of ancient history.

and that their convincing characters, mingling together in a common intercourse of enchantment, were hospitably entertained in the reception-hall of imagination.'

The McLoughlin firm must have had such families as this in mind – eclectic readers who had not the money for expensive editions – when they began putting out their toy books in the middle years of the century. Like Solomon King before them (see page 76) they had a great fondness for fairy-tales, and since to make any profit on these low-priced publications there had to be a huge print run, they must have found quite early on that there was a ready market for them, in New York at any rate. 'Had we the revenues of a multi-millionaire we should send each Christmas Day our personal cheque for ten thousand dollars to the Messrs McLoughlin of this city,' wrote Harry Thurston, critic and classical scholar, in December 1896, in the *Bookman* of which he was then the editor; '[They] still put forth those good old classics whose pages show the very subtlest literary gifts and which have long ago secured a glorious immortality.' Like so many literary figures before him, he deplored the theories of 'educationalists' who, he said, had thrown out nursery rhymes and fairy-tales, and he praised the McLoughlin brothers for keeping 'the sacred flame alight'.

The firm had been founded by John McLoughlin, a printer of Scottish origins, sometime in the 1820s, but it did not acquire its idiosyncratic character – nor indeed its success and prosperity – until his son John (1827–1905) had succeeded and taken his brother Edmund into partnership. From the early days of this second phase the firm published tales such as *Johnnie Gilpin, Hans in Luck, The Three Bears, The Ugly Little Duck, Rip Van Winkle, Goody Two-Shoes, Cinderella* and *Tom Thumb*, always with lots of pictures. Up to the early 1860s these were laboriously hand-coloured, using stencils, but then John II introduced the innovatory process of printing from relief-etched zinc plates, which gave him a head start over all rivals. From then onwards McLoughlin led the rest in the production of toy books.

At worst, the illustrations are strident. The firm had no scruples, for instance, about pirating the work of English illustrators such as Randolph Cal-

decott, Kate Greenaway and Walter Crane, and hotting up the colours. But many books are delectably attractive. The famous Thomas Nast illustrations to *Santa Claus and his Works* establishes the saint (a rotund little fellow in a woolly suit) at the North Pole. We see him in his workshop making the toys, and inspecting his ledger for the names of well conducted girls and boys 'who never disturb Pa and Ma with their noise'. *A Christmas Alphabet*, a later book by a different hand, is another very evocative piece of work, showing Kriss Kringle's* brownies making the toys, his arrival on the house-top, the filling of the stockings (see page 3), and the decking of the tree.

Few of the McLoughlin illustrators are ever named. Thomas Nast (1840–1902) also illustrated *The Fat Boy* (an episode from the *Pickwick Papers*) and a few more, including *Yankee Doodle*; Palmer Cox (1840–1924), a few. But in one of the very best, *The Wonderful Leaps of Sam Patch*, neither the artist nor the versifier is named. Mixing fact and fantasy, this story deals with the career of an American folk-hero, Sam Patch (1807–29), renowned for his spectacular leaps, the last one of which killed him. The illustrations record the American scene to an extent unusual in this sort of book. We see Sam in his mother's yard as a child, leaping from the henhouse; as a barefoot boy jumping from the hayloft; then leaping from a steeple (see frontispiece). He makes a brief excursion to England, and comes back to find Washington completely buried in the debris left by the people who have assembled to see him leap from the Capitol. And then, at the Falls of Genesee, he makes his last leap:

> He looks around on earth and sky,
> As though he bade the world good-bye.
> He takes his kerchief from his neck,
> And barely can emotion check.
> 'Here, Tom,' he said, 'You bear on this
> 'To my poor mother, Sam's last kiss.'
> He jumps! He sinks! The waters roar
> Above him, and he's seen no more;
> And as their breath the people catch,
> They sigh, 'Alas! brave, foolish Patch!'

Other American subjects included *A Peep at Buffalo Bill's Wild West* and *Camptown Races*. The firm

---

* Kriss Kringle, an alternative name for Santa Claus, is derived from the German *Christkindl*, the Christ Child, who was also associated with the giving of gifts.

put out a wide variety of titles, moral tales among them, though in these children's foibles are generally dealt with in comic style; the chattering girl, Polly Patter, for instance, in *Naughty Children*, a 'Transformation Toy Book', becomes a parrot when the book's hinged flaps are raised.* Only religious books were lacking. John McLoughlin was an active member of the Episcopal Church, but apparently took no interest in the Sunday school type of publication. (On both sides of the Atlantic this was always chiefly in the hands of the evangelicals.) Other firms, notably in Philadelphia, aimed at the same market, but never succeeded in staying the course as long as McLoughlin. In the late 1840s, for instance, Robert F. Simpson and Keller & Bright of that city were advertising Grandfather Lovechild's Series (McLoughlin had a series called Mamma Lovechild) which included unexpected versions of those English favourites from ancient romances, *Valentine and Orson* and *Guy of Warwick*, so execrated by the seventeenth-century moralists. The Philadelphia illustrators could sometimes compete with McLoughlin's, as in *Henry Brown*, the tale of a nineteenth-century Dick Whittington (see page 103) whose exemplary behaviour leads to a distinguished legal career, a seat in Congress, and the hand of his employer's daughter.

TRADITIONAL MYTHS AND LEGENDS

It is Charles Perrault's (1628–1703) retellings of such stories as *Cinderella*, *Blue Beard* and *The Sleeping Beauty* that have long been the best-known versions of these traditional tales. He adapted them from popular sources to suit the mood of French society of his time, and they have remained in the state in which he cast them, a memorial to a culture long past, reflecting the aristocratic ethic of late-seventeenth-century France. And what Perrault did for these stories, so Nathaniel Hawthorne did for Greek myths, though in a far more drastic manner – resiting them in New England, taming and emasculating them, and in certain instances creating something entirely new.

In *A Wonder Book*, as originally published in 1852, the chosen stories – 'The Gorgon's Head',

'The Golden Touch', 'The Paradise of Children', 'The Three Golden Apples', 'The Miraculous Pitcher' and 'The Chimaera' – are all told against the background of the Berkshire Hills, where a group of children of assorted ages 'at the country-seat called Tanglewood' listen to the stories of Cousin Eustace. In 1850 Hawthorne had taken a house on the Tappan estate at Lenox. We catch a glimpse of him in his own text: ' "That silent man, who lives in the old red house, near Tanglewood avenue," ' says one of the Tanglewood children, ' "and whom we sometimes meet with two children by his side, in the woods or at the lake." '

The two children were Una aged seven and Julian, five, and Hawthorne's concern to shield and protect their innocence has clearly influenced the manner in which he has chosen to tell the stories. His starting point is the landscape that they see around them, and though by the time he was composing the sequel, *Tanglewood Tales*,[12] he was shuddering at the thought of another winter up in the mountains, in 1851 he was still rapturous at the beauty of the scene. In the preamble we move from a golden day in October, with the children impatiently waiting for the mist to clear so that they can set off on a nutting expedition, through snowy December, to May and spring flowers. The narrator, Eustace Bright, is only eighteen (though the younger children feel that this is almost to be a grandfather), and it is Eustace who is made to defend the cavalier way in which Hawthorne has handled the legends, disregarding 'all classical authorities, whenever the vagrant audacity of his imagination impelled him to do so'. Hawthorne even disarmingly sends him to confront the children's father, a classical scholar who might be expected to disapprove of his 'attempt to render the fables of classical antiquity into the idiom of modern fancy and feeling'. ' "You are not exactly the auditor that I should have chosen, Sir," observes the student, "for fantasies of this nature." '

Nevertheless, he relates his version of Hercules' quest for the golden apples of the Hesperides, of which Mr Pringle is sternly critical: ' "Pray let me advise you never more to meddle with a classical myth. Your imagination is altogether Gothic, and will inevitably gothicise everything you touch. The effect is like bedaubing a marble statue with paint." '

---

* This book was in fact plagiarized from a London publication of 1858, *The Sad History of Greedy Jem and all his Little Brothers*, illustrated by Charles Bennett. Here it was Talkative Toby who gradually turned into a parrot.

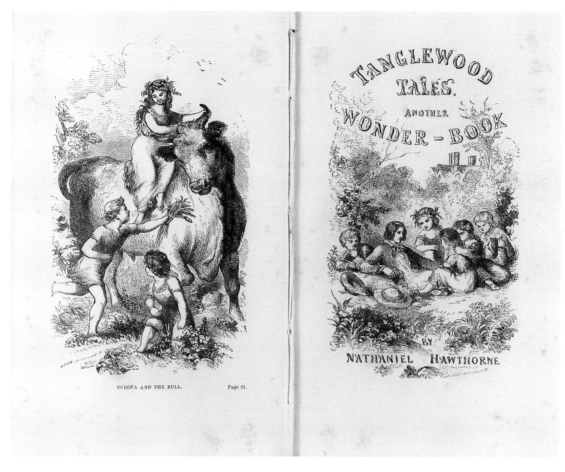

Greek legend prettified. The children 'at the country seat called Tanglewood' listen to the stories of Cousin Eustace.

To which Eustace, piqued, retorts that a modern Yankee has just as much right to remodel the ancient fables as an old Greek had: ' "They are the common property of the world, and of all time. The ancient poets remodelled them at pleasure, and held them plastic in their hands; and why should they not be plastic in my hands as well?" ' And with mounting vehemence he claims that the Greeks, by taking possession of the legends, which belonged to all mankind, ' "and putting them into shapes of indestructible beauty, indeed, but cold and heartless, have done all subsequent ages an incalculable injury" '.

The use of the term 'Gothic' (which subsequent commentators have taken up in connection with the tales) is puzzling, since in literature it is associated with the gloomy and supernatural – the antithesis of the sunlit simplicity of these tales. One

might have thought that Hawthorne was using it in its early pejorative sense when Goths were the equivalent of Vandals – 'bedaubing a marble statue with paint' suggests as much – were it not for the fact that in the preface to *A Wonder Book* he equates the term with 'romantic', stating that this is the guise in which he has chosen to present his versions: 'They are legitimate subjects for every age to clothe with its own garniture of manners and sentiment.' There is, of course, much in what he says: myth and legend are a common heritage, to be moulded by the artist into the shape his imagination dictates, but the transformation of these savage sagas of incest, rape, cannibalism and murder into gentle tales about children is unique, and his evaluation of Greek mythology curiously naive if he can describe these records of man's most primitive emotions as 'cold and heartless'.

' "I will tell you one of the nursery-tales that were made for the amusement of our great, old grand-mother, the Earth, when she was a child in frock and pin-a-fore," ' Cousin Eustace tells the little flock on whom Hawthorne has bestowed fairy names like Primrose, Periwinkle, Sweet Fern, Cowslip and But-ter-cup. ' "There are a hundred such; and it is a wonder to me, that they have not long ago been put into picture-books for little girls and boys." ' And, continuing this analogy in the introduction to *Tanglewood Tales*, Eustace Bright is made to speak of the essential purity of the tales; of how their objectionable characteristics seem to be 'a parasit-ical growth' unconnected with the original fables, and that told to children they re-assume the shapes they had in the childhood of the world, the Golden Age, when 'evil had never existed; and sorrow, misfortune, crime were mere shadows which the mind fancifully created for itself'.

'With what bright and joyous playfulness he re-peats the old stories,' Horace Scudder wrote. 'There is no opening of dark passages, no peering into recesses, but a happy generous spirit reigns throughout.'[13] Such cruelty and evil as Hawthorne has included (though he left out as much as he could – Theseus' desertion of Ariadne for instance) have been softened, and described in nursery fashion: 'Oh, the mischief, and mischief, and mis-chief, that this naughty creature did!' he says of the Chimaera. The Minotaur was 'such a hideous sort of a creature, that it was really disagreeable to think of him'. 'Upon my word, [of the dragon that guards the Golden Fleece] it was a very hideous and uncomfortable sight!' And for all Hawthorne's assertion that the stories he relates date from the beginning of time, he has in many cases drawn on the versions told by Ovid in *Metamorphoses*, a late and decadent Latin rendering.

The selection of 'nursery-tales' is a random one, with no connecting thread, and the only recurrent character is 'Quicksilver', as Hawthorne chooses to call Hermes. The gods and, indeed, all the super-natural events are markedly lacking in mystery, and Hermes–Quicksilver takes on the character of a genial though authoritative uncle. Some of the stories are reasonably close to Greek legend, such as 'The Gorgon's Head' which deals with Perseus' destruction of Medusa, though this has been con-siderably simplified – shorn, for instance, of the manner of Perseus' begetting, and more notably of Andromeda. It ends on a note particularly designed

to appeal to American readers, for Perseus, like a good son, carries back the Medusa head to 'his dear mother'.

Hawthorne had never been to Greece, and he made no attempt to evoke a landscape he did not know. What must interest us is how he contrived to make the stories attractive to American children with no background of this sort of mythology. To begin with, he settled for those stories that celebrate domesticity and the family affections (qualities which, it should be said, are somewhat hard to find in Greek legend). So we find that famous story of hospitality, 'The Miraculous Pitcher', about the kindly old couple, Baucis and Philemon, who en-tertain the gods unawares. Ovid himself had turned a Greek legend into a genre picture of peasant life, and had included a considerable amount of domestic detail which Hawthorne, curiously, omitted or al-tered. Thus the homely supper of bacon and vege-tables and roast eggs, and the dessert of dates and figs washed down by wine, become brown bread and milk, and there is much moral reflection about the surliness of Baucis and Philemon's neighbours.

'The Pomegranate-Seeds', describing the rape of Proserpina, was also a predictable choice, a moving account of a mother's quest for her lost child, and follows Ovid without much digression. But in 'The Golden Touch' Hawthorne created an entirely new story. Ovid had included in *Metamorphoses* a brief account of Midas, a legendary king of Phrygia who wished to turn all that he touched to gold, though this was only a prelude to an account of how he earned ass's ears. Hawthorne expanded those few lines into a pretty domestic tale, not only giving it a Victorian setting (and notable details of a Victorian breakfast), but, no doubt with his own daughter in mind, adding a character entirely of his own, Mary-gold, the king's small daughter. And although he added the rider that 'nobody but myself' ever heard of her, the story of Marygold's transformation into a golden statue and the anguish of her father is so compelling that nobody who has read the story in youth can disentangle her from the original legend:

The moment the lips of Midas touched Marygold's forehead, a change had taken place. Her sweet, rosy face, so full of affection as it had been, assumed a glittering yellow color, with yellow tear-drops congealing on her cheeks. Her beautiful brown ringlets took the same tint. Her soft and tender little form grew hard and inflexible within her father's encircling arms. Oh, terrible misfortune! The victim of his insatiable desire for wealth, little Marygold, was a human child no longer, but a golden statue!

Wherever Hawthorne could use child characters he did so, sometimes, as in 'The Golden Touch', introducing them where none were before, in others transforming the protagonists into children. Europa (the inamorata of Zeus) becomes a little girl; so does Pandora, and the evil that she and Epimetheus, the Greek equivalent of Adam and Eve, loose into the world is allowed to seem trivial. In any case, there is fairy help at hand.

> 'Pray, who are you, beautiful creature?' inquired Pandora.
> 'I am to be called Hope,' answered the sunshiny figure. 'And because I am such a cheery little body, I was packed into the box, to make amends to the human race for that swarm of ugly Troubles, which was destined to be let loose among them. Never fear! we shall do pretty well, in spite of them all.'

Charles Kingsley found this treatment of the legends 'distressingly vulgar', and full of indignation set out to make his own version. (In *The Heroes* (1856) he told the stories of Perseus, the Argonauts and Theseus without any of Hawthorne's prettification.) But there are moments when Hawthorne could detach himself from his role as protective father and allow himself to catch something of the darkness and terror of the old myths, notably in *Tanglewood Tales* with the description of Theseus' search in the maze for the Minotaur:

> But still he went on, now creeping through a low arch, now ascending a flight of steps, now in one crooked passage, and now in another, with here a door opening before him, and there one banging behind; until it really seemed as if the walls spun round, and whirled him round with them. And, all the while, through these hollow avenues, now nearer, now further off again, resounded the cry of the Minotaur, and the sound was so fierce, so cruel, so ugly – so like a bull's roar, and withal so like a human voice, and yet like neither of them – that the brave heart of Theseus grew sterner and angrier at every step.

But into this he felt bound to interpose reflections on the Minotaur aspect of human beings, who allow evil to enter their nature. Perhaps if Hawthorne had written these stories before he had children of his own they would not have been fettered by this sort of conscientious didacticism. As it is, they are very much of their period, but so potent in their fresh and happy optimism that anybody who encounters them early finds it hard to shake off this highly idiosyncratic version of Greek myth.

Perhaps spurred on by the Hawthorne renderings, Thomas Bulfinch (1796–1867) produced *The Age of Fable* in 1855. He was a gentle and amiable man, devoted to his parents, and 'used his leisure to supply young readers or busy readers with culture in a nutshell'.[14] He was far more faithful to the original than Hawthorne and far less discursive – the Midas story is reduced to a paragraph. He managed to compress Greek, Roman, Nordic, Middle Eastern and Hindu mythology into some forty-one chapters, but he too preferred domesticity to more violent themes: the detail allowed in the Baucis and Philemon story contrasts oddly with the scant two pages devoted to Agamemnon, Orestes and Electra and the ten to the *Iliad*. Sidney Lanier (1842–81), editor of *The Boy's Froissart* (1879), *The Boy's King Arthur* (1880), *The Boy's Mabinogion* (1881) and *The Boy's Percy* (1882) – retellings of the ballads in Percy's *Reliques of Ancient Poetry* – also stuck closely to the texts. *King Arthur*, in particular, achieved the status of a minor classic, and with the N. C. Wyeth illustrations of the 1917 edition was still being reprinted in the 1930s. James Baldwin (1841–1925), well known for his graded school readers, also presented versions of European legend. *The Story of Siegfried* (1882) was illustrated by Howard Pyle (see page 138), and there was also *The Story of Roland* (1883) and *A Story of the Golden Age* (1887).

It might seem perverse that European myth and folk-story should have preceded the native American legends by so many years. For there was, of course, a substantial body of these waiting to be discovered – the tales of the American Indians, and those that the slaves had brought with them. Henry Rowe Schoolcraft (1793–1864) had included legends in his voluminous ethnological studies of North American Indians, which Longfellow drew on for *The Song of Hiawatha* (1855), but the stories were apparently not retold for children until Cornelius Mathews put together *The Indian Fairy Book* in 1869, in which he acknowledged Schoolcraft as the source. Two years later Richard Meade Bache of Philadelphia – also, it would seem, using Schoolcraft, though this is never acknowledged – compiled *American Wonderland*. This includes many of the same stories, though differently worked.

There is some splendid material in these tales of heroic hunters, giants, ill-starred lovers, wicked magicians, wizards, magic arrows and seven-leagued moccasins. There is pity in them, as in Bache's story of the two spirits who come back to test the strength of the sorrow of the living for the departed, and also terror – the fearful Mudjee Mone-do, 'the most frightful ogre that the world had ever seen. His neckless head rested on a clumsy body supported by gnarled bandy-legs; his face hung in flabby ashen folds around his tusky mouth; and his crafty green eyes lurked below bat-winged brows, over which fell a maze of grizzled hair.' We also find a memorable sense of the North American landscape – the forests, lakes and plains – and humour, as in Bache's 'The Boy that Snared the Sun', where the petulant child gets his coat shrunk by the heat of the sun and in revenge sets out to

UNCLE REMUS

HIS SONGS AND HIS SAYINGS

THE FOLK-LORE OF THE OLD PLANTATION

By JOEL CHANDLER HARRIS

*WITH ILLUSTRATIONS BY FREDERICK S. CHURCH AND
JAMES H. MOSER*

NEW YORK
D. APPLETON AND COMPANY
1, 3, AND 5 BOND STREET
1881

The first appearance of Uncle Remus.

snare it with his sister's hair. Appalled by the consequent darkness, the council of beasts sends the dormouse, then the largest animal in the world, to release the sun, but the heat shrinks the creature until it diminishes to nearly nothing. 'What became of the little boy was never known, but he was never heard of afterward. Some persons say he was almost too bright to live, and shortly afterwards died; others that, in revenge, he was devoured by the wild beasts. However, nothing is positively known of his fate: neither of the stories is probably quite true.'

Though neither Bache's nor Mathews' style can be said to scintillate, the former's is marginally the more dramatic. But their stories appear to have made little impact, perhaps because of the drab appearance of the books – Bache was unillustrated, and the few plates in Mathews add nothing to the text – or through lack of interest in native Americans or in fairy-tales. It is a curious fact that Caroline Hewins did not include any Indian legends in her myths and legends list for *Books for the Young* (1883); nor did Marie Pabke and Margery Deane in their very recondite *Wonder-World Stories* (1877), which had Chinese, Hebrew, Hungarian, Irish, Turkish and Japanese examples as well as French and German.

The fame of the Uncle Remus stories, in contrast, is undoubtedly due to their humour, and indeed the first collection was included in the publishing firm Appleton's humorous books catalogue. Joel Chandler Harris (1848–1908) admitted that his early stories, which appeared in the *Atlanta Constitution*, were not intended to be contributions to folklore: 'I had no more conception of that than the man in the moon. The first one was written out almost by accident, and as a study in dialect.'[15] He was the only child of his mother's brief relationship with an Irish labourer. When he was fourteen he was apprenticed to a plantation newspaper, the *Country-man*,

and it was on this and neighboring plantations that I became familiar with the curious myths and animal stories that form the basis of the volumes accredited to 'Uncle Remus'. I absorbed the stories, songs and myths that I heard, but had no idea of their literary value, until, some time in the seventies, Lippincott's magazine published an article on the subject of negro folklore, containing some rough outlines of some of the stories. This article gave me my cue, and the legends told by 'Uncle Remus' are the result.[16]

In this introduction to *Uncle Remus, his songs and his sayings: the folk-lore of the old plantation* (1880) Harris gave some account of the close parallels of the African stories with the myths of other races, from Siam to the Amazon (by this time he was something of a folklorist himself). The triumph of the weak has always been a favourite theme of popular legend, and, as Harris said, it needed no scientific investigation to show why the Southern negro 'selects as his hero the weakest and most harmless of all animals, and brings him out victorious in contests with the bear, the wolf and the fox. It is not virtue that triumphs, but helplessness; it is not malice but mischievousness.' However desperate the predicaments of Brer Rabbit – as in the account of him sticking fast to the Tar Baby that Brer Fox has set as a decoy – he always manages to wriggle out of them. ' " 'Fo' you begins fer ter wipe yo' eyes 'bout Brer Rabbit," ' Uncle Remus tells the little boy sitting on his knee, ' "you wait en see wha'bouts Brer Rabbit gwineter fetch up at." ' Childlike, Brer Rabbit plays tricks on the other animals whom he considers his aggressors without troubling himself with such tiresome considerations as whether they deserve it, or whether they cause them pain. And there is mischievous humour in the way the stories are related, as when the assembly of the animals (in 'The Story of the Deluge and how it came about') ' "spoke speeches, en hollered, en cusst, en flung der langwidge 'roun' des like w'en yo' daddy wuz gwineter run fer de legislater en got lef." '

Harris was always modest about his own contribution to narratives, which, he said, came 'fresh and direct from the negroes'.[17] Nevertheless, in their adroit shaping, their elegant conciseness, they do bear distinctively his mark. He was particularly successful with the dialect. James Wood Davidson said of *Uncle Remus* that it was 'the only *true* negro dialect I ever saw printed. It marks an era in its line – the first successful attempt to write what the negro has actually said, in his own peculiar way.'[18] And Harris himself said of the first Uncle Remus collection that, if the language failed

to give vivid hints of the really poetic imagination of the negro; if it fails to embody the quaint and homely humour which was his prominent characteristic; if it does not suggest a certain picturesque sensitiveness – a curious exaltation of mind and temperament not to be defined by

words – then I have reproduced the form of the dialect merely, and not the essence.

He had not intended this first collection necessarily for children, but it was taken over by them, and later books such as *Nights with Uncle Remus* (1883), *Told by Uncle Remus* (1905) and *Uncle Remus and the Little Boy* (in which the child who listens to the stories is the son of the original auditor) address themselves more to the child reader. He did attempt original writing, but this is not nearly so successful. *Little Mr Thimblefinger and his Queer Country*, in which stories about a diminutive fairy being are told within a frame story, and *Willy Wanderoon and his Story-telling Machine*, are flat and unconvincing. Harris was at his best when he spoke with the voice of Uncle Remus, and it is sad that American–Indian stories never found a teller of his calibre.

FANTASY AND IMAGINATION

'Even those who are willing to acknowledge the existence of fairies in the Old World, sturdily deny that they have ever yet honoured the New with their presence. Absurd and foolish incredulity!' James Kirke Paulding (1778–1860), collaborator of Washington Irving, wrote thus in the preamble to a remarkable quartet of fairy-stories published anonymously under the title of *A Christmas Gift from Fairyland in* 1838.[19]

As has been noted earlier, there was from the middle years of the last century a marked difference between the American and the English styles of writing for the young. The American mainstream continued in the direction indicated by Samuel Goodrich and Jacob Abbott and the Sunday school writers, and developed such distinctive genres as the travelogue and the domestic chronicle. In England the fantasy and nonsense which were to dominate the first three decades of the twentieth century had already established themselves; Victorian children's literature was to be remembered for such writers as Edward Lear, Lewis Carroll, Charles Kingsley, George MacDonald and Andrew Lang rather than for tales of the everyday. Like Paulding, the editor of *The Fairy Book* in 1836 (see page 69) had rebuked those Americans who denied there were fairies in the New World. But the fact was that with the honourable exception of Santa Claus who accompanied the Dutch settlers to New Amsterdam, the 'little people' invoked or feared by the cottager in the Old World did not follow him when he emigrated, and, as has been said, native myths and legends were little known. Washington Irving's Rip Van Winkle tells the village children stories of ghosts, witches and Indians – not fairies – and the ancients that he encounters in the Kaatskill mountains are the shades of the old explorer Hendrick Hudson and his crew. Similarly in Irving's 'The Legend of Sleepy Hollow' – a mock-cautionary tale about the folly of credulity – Ichabod Crane finds fearful pleasure in listening to the old wives telling of 'ghosts and goblins, and haunted fields, and haunted brooks, and haunted bridges, and haunted houses', while he would delight them in his turn by 'his anecdotes of witchcraft, and of the direful omens and portentous sights and sounds in the air'. Another difficulty that faced the American writer was the monarchical tradition in the fairy-tales of the Old World. These had evolved among people used to absolute rule; there are kings and queens, princes and princesses, and very often a court setting, and though the sharp-witted peasant boy is often the hero, his reward is the hand of the princess and perhaps the chance of absolute rule himself – not, as it should be in a republic, the office of president with the inevitability of standing down later.

All this makes Paulding's achievement the more remarkable. *A Christmas Gift from Fairyland* was probably only partly aimed at children. Described as one of the most beautifully illustrated books of its time,[20] it is an exquisite piece of book production, with its rococo title-page printed in black and red, and its delicate copper engravings. (The anonymous artist was John G. Chapman.) Paulding, who had collaborated with Irving in *Salmagundi* (1807–8), used the same humorous, mock-learned style of those papers; as there, he coined for himself an Addisonian pseudonym – in this case, Sampson Fairlawn of Chicago. Having begun with a denunciation of those who boast 'that science and knowledge have banished superstition and credulity from the world', he proceeds to construct an elaborate frame in which to display his four stories: 'Sometime in the year 1818, or 1819 ... Mr Simeon Starkweather emigrated from Buncombe county, North Carolina to the great West, in search of better land.' He settles down 'where Evansville now stands', and earns his bread by shooting and trapping, but is infuriated to find that his traps are constantly being sprung:

Going out in the morning of the twenty-first of December, 1833, about sunrise, with his gun, and followed by his two dogs, Thunder and Lightning, he found that a new trap was sprung. 'Thinks I, I've got the varmint now,' says Sim, 'and if I don't split him into shingles, I'm a triflin' feller. So you see, I creeps up as quiet as a dumb adder, motioned Thunder and Lightning to lie still, got close up to the trap, and listened with both ears, I reckon. But I heard nothin' at all ...

'Well, at last, I thought I'd lift the trap, as there seemed nothin' under it, when! I wish I may be shot flyin' – a thing which we Kentucky boys can't stomach by no means – if there didn't fly out a flock of the queerest little vermint women I ever did see. I was pretty well stomped, you may depend, but kinder by instinct I cocked my gun, and let fly at them; but they gave a scream, and were out of sight before my buckshot could overtake them.'

And in the trap Simeon Starkweather finds a roll of birch bark on which, says the author, the tales that follow were inscribed. There are four of these, all reflecting Paulding's passionately felt views about the value of imagination on the one hand, and the God-given freedom of the New World on the other. In the first, the heroine, the child of a proud and powerful king, is carried by fairy means to the New World and is so entranced by the freedom she finds there that she elects to stay. The last is an allegory. A band of fairies take refuge 'from the persecutions of science and philosophy' in a beautiful New World valley. Their king and queen default and fly back to the Old World to spread calumnies about the New. Shaken by this perfidy, the fairies agree to establish a republic and, finding that the traditional rewards that they have hitherto offered merely encourage human avarice, they decide that henceforward they will bestow only 'the inestimable blessing, of a blameless conscience, a benevolent heart and a contented mind'. There is also a satirical account of a philosopher who refuses to believe in fairies, despite their indignant efforts to convert him. They disappear, declaring that not even a missionary society could accomplish it.

But the most interesting is 'The Nameless Old Woman', with its New Amsterdam and New England background. This exuberant narrative so successfully makes use of American elements like Indians and witches and St Nicholas that inevitably one wonders

IN
a certain
year which
has been unac=
countably lost in the
confusion brought about
by the New Style; in a cer=
tain month not to be found in
the Calender, and on a cer=
tain day which a long
time ago slipped
out of the week
and ran
away;

when the great CITY OF GOTHAM was so little
that a man once walked over without seeing it,—

The first American fairy-tale. The opening page of 'The Nameless Old Woman' from James Kirke Paulding's A Christmas Gift from Fairyland, *illustrated by John G. Chapman (New York, 1838).*

why others did not follow suit. Rinier, a parsimonious and churlish householder, with affection only for his vegetable garden, falls out with his neighbour who, intent on his destruction, determines to seek advice about becoming a witch. It is her adventures, ranging from New Amsterdam to Connecticut, with which the narrative is chiefly concerned. She embarks from Martha's Vineyard on the good sloop *Puttaquappounckquame*, but the ship is wrecked and there are various adventures with Indians before she reaches her goal and is initiated into the sorority. The description of the witches' revels is a mixture of the humorous and the macabre, in the style of Robert Burns' 'Tam O'Shanter' (1791):

One came on a broomstick; another mounted on a great tom-cat; a third had put a bridle on a three-legged stool, and came cantering up at a fine rate; a fourth had stolen a farmer's pig, and was urging him on tail foremost, by which cunning expedient, the obstinate animal was persuaded he was going homeward, instead of directly the contrary; a fifth bestrode a rail, the ends of which were sticking into the posts, which performed the duties of legs in the most surprising manner; and a sixth came on an old cock-turkey.

Now endowed with witch's powers, the old woman comes back to New Amsterdam to plague her neighbour and transform all his vegetables into weeds and worse, and his ducats into shin plasters. But next arrives a *deus ex machina* in the person of St Nicholas, who, informing Rinier that he is now sufficiently punished for his avarice and lack of charity, banishes the witch. Rinier thenceforward becomes the friend of the unfortunate and the comforter of the wretched. For humour and pace and use of an indigenous background, this story is hard to fault, but it is remarkably little known and had no imitators. It was to be more than sixty years, with *The Wonderful Wizard of Oz* (1900), that an American fantasy became part of the national consciousness.

Two stories written and illustrated by Christopher Pearse Cranch (1813–92), *The Last of the Huggermuggers* (1855) and its sequel *Kobboltozo* (1857), met with a similarly undeserved fate. The Huggermuggers are giants, the last of their kind, who evade Yankee schemes for exploiting them in Barnum's circus, but by dying. *The Last of the Huggermuggers* is a genial story, though its sad ending is said always to have made Cranch's small son cry.

(However, it is ironical that William Wetmore Story, calling the tale lachrymose, apparently told Cranch to read Andersen,[21] whose wistful melancholy was, in fact, to be far too avidly imitated by his admirers.)

Jacky Cable, the lad who discovers the two Huggermuggers, is 'a brave little fellow, as well as a true Yankee in his smartness and ingenuity' – the heir, indeed, of Jack the Giantkiller, the Valiant Little Tailor and those other folk-heroes who outwit the large and powerful. In fact, this sort of courage is not needed, for the Huggermugger husband and wife are a kindly, affectionate pair who beam at the party of sailors Jacky brings to the island and want to adopt them as children. But alas, one of the party, Zebedee Nabbum, is an agent of Barnum and intent on collecting the male giant to add to the menagerie ("If only we could catch him, and get him to Ameriky alive, or only his skeleton, my fortune's made, I cal'late" '). Betrayed by the malicious dwarf, Kobboltozo, the Huggermuggers sicken and die – the wife on the island, the husband on the ship taking him to America.

Nothing is clearly known, strange to say, as to what became of this skeleton. In the museum, at Philadelphia, there are some great bones, which are usually supposed to be those of the Great Mastodon. It is the opinion, however, that they are none other than those of the great Huggermugger – all that remains of the last of the giants.

The sequel *Kobboltozo* has a more serious theme: the folly of ambition. But though it shows invention and there are memorable imaginative passages, it lacks organization as well as the impetus of the first book. Jacky and Zebedee Nabbum go back to the Huggermuggers' island – the description of the deserted Huggermugger Hall is genuinely moving – and here the last of the island's dwarfs tells the story of what happened after the giants left, and of the dwarf Kobboltozo's quest for giant stature. From the directions given by the Mer King – the drawing of the Mer King's head rising from the sea which appeared as the book's frontispiece was one of Cranch's best illustrations – the dwarfs gain the impression that they can become giants by eating shellfish. So the whole colony becomes obsessed by the search for the right sort – a search that destroys them, leaving only the dwarf narrator and Kobboltozo, who retreats to a cave where he lives in perfect contentment, for he believes he is growing larger and more handsome every day,

THE MER-KING. See page 67.

Illustration by Christopher Cranch for his book Kobboltozo *(Boston, 1857).*

though in reality he is 'dwindling away to a mere insect. In a year from this time, I calculate that he will be just about the size of a pin's head.'

Cranch's two fairy-stories did not survive their time. It is always impossible to predict what literature will be important to future generations, and often difficult to account for the reason why some books have achieved the status of classics. Why, for instance, should *The Water Babies*, so thoroughly rooted in its own time and its author's personal fads and enthusiasms, and with so many of its topical allusions beyond the comprehension of any but the Victorian specialist, still be remembered when Cranch is forgotten? The sad end of the Huggermuggers, though treated lightly, may have been a contributory reason; but the suspicion is that the book was too innovatory, that American readers were not, in the 1850s, ready for fantasy.

The same obscurity overtook another mid-century book of fantasy, *Fairy Dreams* (1859), a collection of tales by Jane Goodwin Austin (1831–94), a *Mayflower* descendant, though these lack the strength and the originality of Cranch's work and have overmuch Andersen in them. They are, however, noteworthy for the emphasis put on the importance of imagination. In one story, 'The Frost-Maiden', the hero even perishes for the sake of his dreams. In spite of warnings that he will meet his death thereby, he pursues the vision he has first seen in frost pictures on the window panes. The frost-maiden whom he at last finds in the frozen far north tells him that henceforward he and she will spend their lives making such pictures: 'Then, together we will roam over sea and land, borne upon the broad wings of the north wind, and passing by the curtained, shuttered windows of the rich, we will draw our fairest pictures on the lowly casement where dwell those who have none save those we give them.' In 'König Tolv's Bride' a child is told: ' "So much religion and so many pious works are truly edifying, dear little one, but I think for my part, it will do you no harm to read a little of something more amusing; so take this volume of fairy tales, which I have all by heart, and put it in the bosom of your frock." '

Though Jane Austin wrote elsewhere about New England life, she used little of this background in her fairy-stories. But a contemporary, Mrs Mary Wentworth Newman, very successfully used California as a setting. Into *Fairy Tales from Gold Lands* (1867) she introduced dwarfs and giants – beings traditionally associated with the mining and guarding of treasure, and therefore by analogy with gold prospectors. By treating them easily and unselfconsciously, she made it seem as though they had sprung out of the native soil. All the stories touch on the quest for treasure of one sort or another, but in very different ways: 'Ching Chong Chinaman' tells of a Chinese boy who seals up in his own cave the giant who seeks to enslave him, and is rewarded for refusing to take the giant's treasure by finding 'a large tract of the richest placer-diggings ever known'; 'The Strong Man of Santa Barbara' is about a Spaniard of heroic strength who builds the church of Grand San Pedro single-handed, until he is finally so irked by the priest's rapacious demands that he makes everything crash to the ground in an earthquake.

The most interesting is 'Emperor Norton', which grafts the German peasant tradition that we meet in Grimm on to a thoroughly contemporary setting: 'Once upon a time there lived near a small village on the shore of the Atlantic, an honest farmer named Norton, who had three sons. The two elder were smart, active lads, but the youngest [Dumpy] was quiet, and so much given to dreaming that his brothers ridiculed and often slighted him.' Dumpy sets off to seek his fortune in New York, and then ships before the mast in a merchant vessel for California. At San Francisco, working in the mines, he has the good fortune to do a kindness to the king of the little people who guard the mountain treasures, and they make him their emperor: ' "As long as you preserve this crown and scepter from moth or rust, dew or fog, you shall be the true emperor of all the mines in California and Nevada." ' But failure to do so will mean that all his honours will be taken from him. Highly elated, he rushes away to show his splendour to his companions; but he loses his way, and his regalia grows damp and finally disappears into the mists of the night.

Here [in San Francisco] for years he has lived, always wearing a well-worn suit of blue, with epaulettes upon the shoulders. At the tables of all restaurants and hotels he is a free and welcome guest, and all places of amusement are open to him; in fact, wherever you go in San Francisco, you are almost sure to meet the Emperor Norton.

Horace Scudder's championship of imaginative writing has already been mentioned. Although he was the author of original works for both adults and children, it was as an editor that he was most influential, and he played a large part in establishing an outstanding children's list at Houghton Mifflin, the Boston firm with whom he was associated for nearly forty years. From his journals it would seem that he had moments of disappointment about the direction his career had taken: 'I hope I am not selling my birthright for a mess of pottage,' he wrote on 3 December 1886, after a long discussion of his decision to devote himself to publishing rather than creative writing. He reflected that it was God's will, that 'my Master has opened the way for me and ... He will lead me in it, giving me to live something more of His life, enlarging my nature, bringing me into more unselfish relations, using me to work out His own blessed ends.'[22] Despite this sense of dedication, it was high *literary* standards that he considered of paramount importance during his publishing career, and this was his first aim as editor of the *Riverside Magazine for Young People*. From early days he possessed wide-ranging literary tastes; at Williams College he had had a classical education, and among his contributions to the *Williams Quarterly* (of which he became editor when he was only seventeen) were articles on the seventeenth-century mystical poets Francis Quarles and George Herbert, on Knights of the Round Table, and on 'The Old Romance'. He spent a few years tutoring children in New York, and during this early period contributed children's stories to various periodicals. These were collected under three titles: *Seven Little People and their Friends* (published in 1862 while he was still in his early twenties), *Dream Children* (1864) and *Stories from my Attic* (1869). They are all elegantly told, often poignant, but not markedly original.

He was, as has been mentioned, a passionate admirer of Andersen who had made, in his words, the 'most unique contribution not only to the literature which children read, but to that which is illustrative of childhood', and we find echoes of Andersen in his own work, as well as of George MacDonald, and sometimes of Dickens. Unlike Howard Pyle (see page 138) and Frank Stockton (see page 140), who moved in the traditional landscape of the European fairy-tale, Scudder presented an American scene. 'A Christmas Stocking with a Hole in it' (in *Seven Little People and their Friends*), though the style is influenced by Andersen and the plot may remind us of *A Christmas Carol*, is a story about New York. Using the Santa Claus legend, it

describes how little Peter Mit's stocking is filled at the last moment by his dead father's partner, a sombre, tight-fisted man whom the spirit of Christmas has made genial. 'The Widow Dorothy's New Year's Eve' (*Dream Children*) is also set in an American city, where an old lady waits in vain for her long-dispersed family to come and see in the New Year with her, and fills the parlour with her memories. Scudder is at his best when he evokes the Cape Cod landscape (he came from a family which had settled there in the early eighteenth century), as in 'Carl's Voyaging':

A bleak land is this of Cape Cod ... The coast has few harbors; the sand lies in dunes, and rocks jut out into the sea. Houses stand boldly on the edge of the coast, and gardens huddle about the house-walls, where flowers are coaxed to grow, while the sun, blazing down upon the spiky grass, calls out in the summer-time myriads of snapping grasshoppers, that jump up and down with a sizzing sound, as if the earth were too burning to alight on, and the air too hot to stay in. The dwellers in the houses lead a strange life. One may sometimes find almost a village full of sailors' wives and families, while the sailors themselves are fishing on the banks, or wandering over the sea. Sometimes, also, the desolate crumbling houses stand alone in unplanted fields. The great ocean which washes up on the beach, and falls back at every tide, seems to entice the brown boys, and one after another they yield and sail away.

He uses the same setting for one of his finest stories, 'The Pot of Gold', from the same collection. 'Upon the edge of a marsh, lying near the sea, and fed from it by tidal creeks, stood a weather-battered house that went by the name of the Red Inn.' Here Rhoda and Crif live with Rhoda's grandmother in tranquil happiness, until Crif becomes restless and departs in pursuit of the pot of gold that an old crone tells him lies at the foot of the rainbow. Throughout his subsequent wanderings memories of home return to haunt him. Finally, when the object of so many perilous adventures lies before him, he has a vision of the Red Inn deserted, and he turns his back on the gold and follows the shape of Rhoda safely home.

Crif's quest through a dream-like landscape is strongly reminiscent of George MacDonald's 'faerie romance' *Phantastes*, but whereas MacDonald's Anados is searching for a vision of holiness, and returns reluctantly, feeling that he has left behind him an ideal that he can never know in this life, Crif turns his back on the fairy lands, longing for home. The difference is significant: the idea of home, always so powerful in American children's books, has here been elevated by Scudder into a spiritual force that can bring wandering feet back to a safe haven.

His chronicles of the travels of the Bodley family are garlanded with stories and legends and verses such as 'John Gilpin' and 'The Pied Piper of Hamelin', which clearly made far more appeal to him than the usual travelogue geographical information. The opening volume, *The Doings of the Bodley Family in Town and Country* (1875), with its account of the home life of Nathan, Philippa and Lucy Bodley, their father and mother, the hired man Martin and his brother Hen, Nathan's pig, the dog Neptune, Lucy's kitten and her doll and Mr Bottom the horse is a re-creation of his own childhood. In *The Children's Book*, published in 1881 by Houghton Mifflin, he gathered together examples of the imaginative literature that he felt was vital to the proper development of the child. There are fables, fairy-tales, legends, ballads, lyric and narrative verse, and though there is one Edgeworth story ('Waste Not, Want Not') there is markedly little in what might be termed the Goodrich / self-improvement vein.

Whereas Scudder could step beyond his literary models, Howard Pyle's work has, with a few exceptions, the air of pastiche – extensions of the European fairy-tales, particularly those of Grimm and Andersen. Indeed, sometimes he is so close to the original that it might be termed plagiarism. 'Once upon a time there came a soldier marching along the road, kicking up a little cloud of dust at each step...Tramp! tramp! tramp! he marched, whistling as he jogged along, though he carried a heavy musket over his shoulder' begins one of the stories in *Twilight Land* (1895), an opening uncomfortably near to Andersen's 'The Tinderbox'. Much of his early illustrative work has a similarly derivative air. For instance, *Yankee Doodle* (1881), delectably pretty as it is, is a close imitation of a Randolph Caldecott picture-book, from the style of the drawings down to actual layout.

The child of Quakers who were both descended from Pennsylvania's first settlers, Pyle was encouraged early on by his mother in his literary and artistic ambitions, and from her he inherited his love of literature and his interest in the great English illustrators such as Tenniel, Leech and Doyle. He studied for three years at a small art school in Philadelphia, and then went to New York in 1876, hoping to earn his living with magazine contributions. After an initial struggle, in 1881 he felt secure enough to marry. His most famous book, *The Merry Adventures of Robin Hood*, a retelling of the ballads decorated with his own illustrations, appeared two years later. It is a version with too much of the pseudo-archaic for English taste – ' "Ha," cried Robin, "I wot the wager were mine were it a hundred pounds." ' But the elegant, uncluttered drawings, pre-Raphaelite with suggestions of Dürer, make it a beautiful book, and the one which has lasted best of all his works. He was later to produce four volumes of Arthurian legend, beginning with *King Arthur and his Knights* in 1903, where the mock-archaisms are even more marked. He also had what might be termed an obsessive interest in pirates; *Howard Pyle's Book of Pirates* appeared in 1921, after his death.

His books of original tales were equally beautiful productions. Both the stories and the illustrations look towards Europe. There are kings and castles and millers' sons who marry princesses; there is talk of thalers. The illustrations are mostly medieval-picturesque, with town walls and gatehouses and lattice-windowed cottages. There may also be a grenadier in eighteenth-century uniform – Pyle went in for an eclectic mixture of periods. But there is no whimsy in his narratives, and often a refreshing earthy realism and ruthlessness. In the Grimm-type 'How Three Went Out Into The Wide World' (*The Wonder Clock*, 1888) where the Grey Goose, the Sausage and the Great Red Fox are travelling companions, the last eats the other two: 'Now this is true that I tell you: when a great red fox and a grey goose marry, and hard times come, one must make it soft for the other – mostly it is the grey goose who does that.' But accomplished though the stories are, one has the feeling that he is speaking all the time – no doubt unconsciously – with other men's voices, that he was in effect imprisoned in his own reading.

Sometimes, however, he could escape. *The Garden behind the Moon* (1895), his only full-length fantasy, inspired by the death of one of his own children, is the story of a mentally handicapped child. Though there are obvious links with MacDonald's *At the Back of the North Wind*, one feels that here is Pyle himself: 'There once was a little boy called David

David the 'mooncalf' with Hans Krout the moonstruck cobbler. Illustration by Howard Pyle for his book
The Garden Behind the Moon *(London, 1895).*

who never had any other name that I know of, unless it was "Silly" David. For he was a moon-calf, and all the other children laughed at him.' The illustrations are also markedly original and for once do not suggest other artists; one of the most powerful is that of David, vacant-faced, walking down the village street with Hans Krout the cobbler, also moon-struck and with wild, visionary eyes. Hans shows David how to walk along the moon-path over the sea, and in the moon he encounters the moon-angel (the angel of death) and looks out over the world from the moon's different storeys.

Then the angel allows him into a garden where only children can play. Pyle here was writing of a garden that he remembered from his own childhood: it is a pleasant one with its sun-dial and rose-bushes, and there is an old brick house topped with a weather-vane, but the beauties are only of this world. David grows too old for the garden, where no one can stay after the age of twelve. There is a princess there, seemingly autistic, and so that he can marry her he is sent to the Iron Castle of the Iron Man to find the Wonder-Box and the Know-All Book which will unlock her mind. Here Pyle's vision is perhaps unequal to the task he has set himself, though there are memorable moments, such as the destruction of the Iron Man, and some of his finest illustrations, including the picture of David mounting the Black Horse that will take him to the castle. When David returns it is with the key to the princess's mind.

Yes; and this that I have told you is not nonsense. The hero David did indeed bring back the Wonder-Box and the Know-All Book just exactly as I have told you – he did – he did . . .

Do you not understand? Well, well; some day you may – but first you have to bathe your eyes with moonshine and then read again.

Though it is a patchy book, we must value it because Pyle here does throw off his many disguises and speak as himself.

His best book, though, is *Otto of the Silver Hand* (1888), an extraordinarily powerful and compassionate historical tale about medieval Germany, torn apart by power struggles between rival warlords. Its hero, little Otto (son of one of these last), has something of David the moon-calf about him in that, brought up among monks, he is remote from the ways of the world. He is dismayed by the brutish

atmosphere he finds outside the monastery, and, while loyal and affectionate towards his father, cannot comprehend his violence and lust for revenge. Captured by his father's deadly enemy, he has his hand cut off while in prison, and is rescued only to see his father fight a desperate action with his captor, in which both die. The story and its splendid illustrations have great imaginative insight, as well as a feeling for history.

Frank Stockton's exuberant fairy-tales, collected under the titles *Ting-a-Ling* (1870), *The Floating Prince* (1881) and *The Bee-Man of Orn* (1887), featured in both the *Riverside Magazine* and later in *St Nicholas*, of which he was assistant editor from its foundation in 1873 until he left in 1881 to devote himself full-time to writing. Born in 1834 of an old New Jersey family, he was a child of an eminent Methodist whose offspring inclined 'less to theology than to literature', as the *Dictionary of American Biography* puts it, adding that Stockton's imagination 'worked in a world of cheerful impossibility, as

How Baron Conrad held the bridge. Illustration by Howard Pyle for his book Otto of the Silver Hand *(London 1888).*

easy-going as a fairy tale or a Gilbert and Sullivan opera'.

He used the monarchic trappings of the European fairy-tale, but in a spirit of burlesque and knock-about farce. In 'Ting-a-Ling' the prince and princess are imprisoned side by side in a giant cheese and the lady-in-waiting accidentally loses her head, which is restored to her but the wrong way round. Whereupon a little girl shouts joyfully, ' "Good! good! Now she can see to fasten her own frock behind!" ' His stories are fast-moving, funny and inventive, though sometimes the humour and the inventiveness get out of control, and he finds himself with a situation impossible to develop within the scope of a short story. And sometimes he throws away opportunities because he cannot resist buffoonery.

Stockton's best piece, and the first American fairy-story to survive into the modern period, is undoubtedly 'The Griffin and the Minor Canon', written in an unwontedly serious style. A griffin, hearing that there is a carved likeness of himself on an old church, comes flying to see it, so terrifying the town's inhabitants that they threaten to destroy the carving. But instead they send out the Minor Canon to interview him, a young man who always undertakes the tasks that others are unwilling to perform. The Minor Canon conducts the griffin to the church and shows him his likeness over the door. By now the griffin has become very attached to the Minor Canon. To those apprehensive about his eating habits he says: ' "At the vernal and the autumnal equinox I take a good meal, and that lasts me for half a year." ' The townspeople become increasingly agitated as the equinox approaches, and drive the Minor Canon out of the town, hoping that the griffin will follow. But he stays behind and takes over the young man's duties. When he hears how the young man has been treated he is furious. He harangues the people, tears down the image of himself and flies off with it to the Canon, whom he escorts back to the town. The Canon is appointed to the highest offices, but the griffin, gazing mournfully at his likeness, and because of his love for the Canon deprived of the only person who was fit for him to eat, droops and dies. Here is Stockton in an unusually subdued mood, but the story has a shape and symmetry that most of his others lack.

Humour, as has been said, has been described as America's most popular creative achievement, and perhaps nineteenth-century readers felt that this was lacking in the fantasy of their own time. Fairy-stories in the Old World style certainly made little impact; but humour did appeal. Lucretia Hale (1820–1900) is still remembered for *The Peterkin Papers*, originally contributed to the magazine *Our Young Folks* from 1868 onwards, then to *St Nicholas*. They are her only writings, and it would seem that she was inspired by Abby Morton Diaz' *Chronicles of the Stimpcett Family* (published by Lothrop of Boston in 1862), which, though not so lunatic or inventive, catalogue the disasters of a similarly accident-prone family. The Peterkins, like the Stimpcetts, are incapable of coping in an ordinarily rational manner with any domestic problem. It is not for want of thought – they use a great deal of that, especially Agamemnon who has been to college – but rather through inability to see the obvious. ' "If," said Mrs Peterkin, "we could only be more wise as a family!" ' But it is always the Lady from Philadelphia who supplies a solution, suggesting, for example, that Elizabeth Eliza need not practise the piano through the open window all through the winter, that the instrument could in fact be turned round.

And the writing of Laura Richards (1850–1943) illustrates the liberating power of humour. Her stories are preposterously sentimental, featuring charismatic little saints with names like Star Bright or Melody, but her nonsense verse has the amoral anarchy and violence of Lewis Carroll. Take Mrs Snipkin and Mrs Wobblechin, in the poem of that name, arguing about whether the window should be open or shut:

> Skinny Mrs Snipkin
> Took her little pipkin,
> Threw it straight across the room as hard
>   as she could throw.
> Hit Mrs Wobblechin
> On her little doublechin
> And out of the window a-tumble she did go.

Sometimes there are echoes of Edward Lear, as in 'The Owl, the Eel, and the Warming-pan':

> The owl, the eel and the warming-pan,
> They went to call on the soap-fat man.
> The soap-fat man, he was not within;
> He'd gone for a ride on his rolling-pin;
> So they all came back by the way of the town,
> And turned the meeting-house upside down.

This sort of unconsidered, flippant irreverence is entirely lacking in her prose. It is as if the ease with which she wrote verse lulled her into forgetting the emotions which clogged her prose pen.

Alice's Adventures in Wonderland had reached English children in November 1865, and America the following year. (Appleton of New York had bought up the bound copies and unbound sheets, which Macmillan in London had been obliged to scrap because of Tenniel's complaints about the quality of the printing.) In England it was reviewed among a welter of books for the Christmas season; only one or two of the notices considered it in any way outstanding. While few were hostile, most were lukewarm, and paid more attention to the illustrations.[23] Fewer American journals noticed *Wonderland*, and those that did mostly waited until the second edition in 1869.

The *Nation*, however, gave it a long and perceptive review in December 1866, praising the delineation of character and the puns that made one laugh out loud. The same journal, reviewing *Looking-Glass* on 8 February 1872, admitted to disappointment that there was nothing in the book as funny as the Mad Tea Party. And indeed we notice with all the American reviewers the emphasis on Carroll's humour, a quality not nearly so much stressed by the English critics, who picked out for commendation the 'nonsense', 'fancy-work', 'invention' and 'whimsical fancies'. Carroll was later to receive an unusual degree of reverent admiration in America; indeed, as a literary import one might put him in the same class as Shakespeare, Dickens, Beatrix Potter and Tolkien. But his work mercifully inspired fewer American imitators than in England, where weak fantasy was more marketable and where for the next forty or fifty years authors used children's dreams as a convenient excuse for ill-organized, inconsequential adventures. Charles Carryl (1841–1920), a New York stockbroker, was the best-known of the American writers in this style. Both *Davy and the Goblin* and *The Admiral's Caravan* had been serialized in *St Nicholas* before they appeared in book form in 1884 and 1891 respectively. There are echoes of Carroll in both. *Davy and the Goblin* has more of an improvised air – perhaps in the shape in which it may have been originally told to his daughter Constance – and there are such favourite characters as Mother Hubbard, Robinson Crusoe, Robin Hood and Sinbad. *The Admiral's Caravan* is a more finished piece of work, and the Carrollian echoes are stronger. The heroine, Dorothy, is a serious little girl very much like Alice, given to trying to express herself in language she hasn't fully mastered, and wrestling to bring some sort of order into the lives of the strange creatures who surround her. Carryl incorporates changes into his story, as well as the device of standing logic on its head, which Carroll had initiated and which all his disciples seized upon:

'What makes you quarrel so? You ought to be ashamed of yourselves.'

'We're all ashamed of one another, if *that* will do any good,' said the Admiral.

'And, you see, that gives each of us two persons to be ashamed of,' added Sir Walter, with an air of great satisfaction.

'But that isn't what I mean at all,' said Dorothy. 'I mean that each one of you ought to be ashamed of *himself*.'

'Why, we're each being ashamed of two persons already,' said the Admiral peevishly. 'I should think *that* was enough to satisfy anybody.'

Undoubtedly the most interesting part of the book, though the author might not have suspected this, are the introductory pages, setting the scene in a decaying, sleepy seaport where Dorothy lives with her Uncle Porticle in the Blue Admiral Inn; and, indeed, as we survey the struggle of American fairy-tales to establish themselves we find that authors are often at their best when constructing the domestic frame in which the stories are related.

But there was one outstanding work, now unaccountably forgotten, which is American through and through and both fast-moving and very funny. *John Whopper the Newsboy* (1871) is the work of Thomas March Clark, whom we met in the previous chapter. He became bishop of Rhode Island in 1854 (apparently, much to his astonishment), and there he continued for the next forty-nine years, much loved for his irenic qualities and his wit and humour. The last shines forth in *John Whopper*, which is gently and lovingly satirical. One might guess that it began as a tale improvised to amuse grandchildren, and was then honed into the fine piece that it is. (It was originally published anonymously, and sometimes attributed to Edward Everett Hale.)

John Whopper, a smart little newsboy, while out on his morning round falls through a hole – 'How thankful I felt that I had been taught to practise gymnastics at the school at Roxbury!' – and finds himself in China, which he has little trouble in identifying as soon as he meets one of the inhabitants. With Yankee business acumen he instantly decides to take advantage of his good luck: 'Your fortune is made, old fellow! Here you have thirty or forty Boston newspapers, not twenty-four hours old, strapped round your neck; and I rather think they will be in some demand in Canton.' He sells his papers at five dollars apiece to delighted American businessmen and, having carefully marked the chasm through which he emerged, has no difficulty in returning home. He presents his magnificent earnings to his dear old widowed mother (of course), and resolves to go into business purveying newspapers to businessmen exiled in China.

But his next attempt to return home from the Far East miscarries and he finds himself stranded in the centre of the earth, swinging like a pendulum on the earth's axis. Much pseudo-scientific information follows – 'I am afraid that some of my readers may think that there is a tone of exaggeration in my story' – and finally John emerges, not in Roxbury, but at the North Pole. Here he finds a fully equipped but abandoned wrecked ship, with all its food conveniently and naturally refrigerated, and makes himself perfectly comfortable. It being summer, he cultivates a garden, even sows an Arctic lawn, until the ice melts and frees the ship. Thereupon he hoists the Stars and Stripes and floats home. At New Bedford 'I took the cars for Roxbury, via the Boston and Providence Road . . . I found all well at home and very much relieved by my arrival.' Its starting point may have been suggested by Alice's fall through the rabbit-hole, but that is Clark's only debt to Carroll; the deadpan humour is all his own.

Similarly in a category by itself is Albert Bigelow Paine's *The Arkansaw Bear* (1898). Paine was Mark Twain's secretary, but his work owes little to his employer; and though one might say that his Hollow Tree stories (*How Mr Dog Got Even*, *How Mr Rabbit Lost his Tail* – about the tricks Mr Dog, Jack Rabbit, the Coon and the Possum play on each other) are reminiscent of *Uncle Remus*, *The Arkansaw Bear* is entirely original. It is a touching and delightful story of how Bosephus, a homeless boy, is adopted by Horatio, a fiddle-playing bear – ' "Look here, Bo," [Horatio] said, "if you'll teach me to play and sing that tune, we'll forget all about that sort o' personal supper I was planning on, and I'll take you home all in one piece." ' They wander, dancing and fiddling for their keep; Horatio's

violin has the effect of filling all who hear it, however hostile, with goodwill, and Bosephus succeeds in persuading him to forgo ' "you know – dinners" '. Horatio forms a bear colony in the Arkansas woods, but when Bosephus decides to go back to Louisiana to school, the bear goes with him. 'And with a joyful scrape of the strings and a sweet burst of melody, the friends set their faces once more to the South' – rather inadequate as a conclusion, perhaps, and of course the reader would have liked to know what future there was in Louisiana for the endearing Horatio.

The most popular fantasy with American children in the pre-Oz period was undoubtedly Palmer Cox's Brownie world. His Brownies are comic rather than fairy beings, and their adventures in a contemporary setting were much loved by American children but little known in England. Cox (1840–1924) was born in Granby, Canada, of Scottish parents, and in 1863 took himself to San Francisco where he contributed humorous verses and cartoons to California newspapers while working as a railroad employee and a ship's carpenter. Later he moved to New York and worked on a comic paper, *Wild Oats*, which folded after five years. At the age of forty he began illustrating for *St Nicholas* and also contributing verse with his own illustrations.

The Brownies were suggested by the Scottish tales he had heard in childhood. They were adapted to appeal to young Americans, and in truth bear very little resemblance to the Scottish house-elf of that name, a shy and solitary creature who supposedly helps the householder at night in return for gifts of food or clothes, and is seldom if ever seen. Cox's Brownies, in contrast, are boisterous, gregarious, pleasure-loving and adventurous, and the only characteristic that they share with the brownie of folklore is their nocturnal habits. There is very little that is unearthly or faery about these rotund little mannikins with their spindly legs (it should be noted that they are invariably male), and though they have the ability to be where they want when they want – 'only Brownies have the skill / Or gift to go thus where they will' – the reader recognizes that this is merely a convenience for their creator, who wants to take them exploring historical monuments and foreign countries and to confront them with nineteenth-century technology and diversions. For high imagination plays little part in these books; the versifying is mechanical, and the appeal must have lain in the elaborate drawings and in the

The Brownies hunted for an hour
To gain a view of London Tower;
50

Palmer Cox's Brownies in London. From The Brownies round the World *(London, 1899).*

conservative appetite of young readers who, when they like something, want it repeated for ever. They were also eye-catching, with their large format and glazed cream-coloured boards.

The Brownies: Their Book, the first in the series, appeared in 1887. Their opening adventure is a visit to a school, which mystifies and delights them and which they set topsy-turvy until sunrise startles them and they know they must be off: 'It took an hour of morning prime / According to the teacher's time / To get the books in place once more.' In subsequent episodes they try their hand at skating, bicycling, gymnastics, tobogganing, ballooning and canoeing. In *Another Brownie Book* they discover Hallowe'en and candy-pulling. As their popularity grew – a million copies of the thirteen Brownie books were sold during Cox's lifetime – he ran out of American possibilities and had to take his little heroes abroad, travelogue fashion. They not only visited European sites but ventured as far as the Philippines, and their experiences were inevitably

happy and carefree: Cox had resolved that there should be no pain and no crime – only laughter – in his books, and his formula was so successful that he was able to return to Canada and build himself a huge house which he called Brownie Castle.

And so we come – reluctantly, it has to be confessed – to *The Wonderful Wizard of Oz*. Frank Baum (1856–1919) aimed to do the same as Palmer Cox – to exclude 'all disagreeable incidents . . . heartaches and nightmares' and to retain only 'wonderment and joy'. Of all American classics this is the most difficult for a foreigner to appraise. (*The Wind in the Willows*, though a very different book, might by its Englishness also present problems.) Those who have been reared from earliest childhood on the traditional European tales expect shadow as well as light, are used to violence and the suffering endured by the heroes and heroines as well as by the villains, and do not expect these to be glossed over or eliminated – even when presented to children; they also, in a literary classic, look for some subtlety of style. But it has been shown, in Samuel Goodrich's abhorrence of the Perrault fairy-tales, how those outside this tradition might well react to them. *The Wizard of Oz* has the easy optimism that is a feature of so many of the books already discussed: the message that nothing is unpleasant if you don't want it to be; together with a blandness that the European reader finds cloying.

But it was a highly successful recipe; the first edition of ten thousand copies sold out within a few weeks of publication day in May 1900, and by the following January one hundred thousand had been sold. This may have been partly due to the illustrations by W. W. Denslow – in the art nouveau style, strongly influenced by Walter Crane. There were over a hundred text illustrations in black and one other colour, and twenty-four three-colour plates. But undoubtedly it was the MGM film version in 1939 that made the book part of American folklore. It is a rare instance of a film that improves a book, and most people now know it only through the former.

The son of an oil magnate and theatre-owner, Baum had tried his hand at several careers before he became a full-time writer; he had experimented with acting, with the family oil business, with storekeeping, journalism, and selling china and glassware. His first book for children was *Mother Goose in Prose* (1897) with illustrations by the young Maxfield Parrish – sober and gentle stories based on the rhymes, and originally told to his small sons. Baum had collaborated with Denslow in three picture-books before the first *Oz* appeared; they did one further book together, and then fell out over financial matters. (Baum's finances were never stable; at one stage, in 1911, he was rich enough to build a house called 'Ozcot' in California, but he was bankrupted the next year, and worked hard to the end of his life.)

Baum's talent was for inventing personalities – the Cowardly Lion who is searching for courage, the Scarecrow who lacks brains, the Tin Woodman without a heart. All three characters, despite their respective deficiencies, are invariably, and indistinguishably, kind, resourceful and loyal, and all each needs to become cured is faith in himself. Potentially

painful factors are smoothed over. Although Oz the Great and Terrible initially appears to the orphan Dorothy and her three companions in a variety of frightening guises, he is revealed to be in reality a little old man, a self-admitted humbug who has fooled the Land of Oz with the aid of a talent for ventriloquism. The Wicked Witch of the West melts away into nothing the moment Dorothy throws a bucket of cold water over her, and though the witch has seemingly destroyed the Tin Woodman and the Scarecrow they are soon patched up again. Dorothy herself is restored to her home on the Kansas prairie (from which the cyclone had blown her away) as soon as she learns to knock the heels of her silver shoes together. The ending is perfunctory. Dorothy has reappeared from the dead, having been away so long that a new farmhouse has been built in the place of the one whirled off by the cyclone, but the reunion with her uncle and aunt is disposed of in a quarter of a page:

Aunt Em had just come out of the house to water the cabbages when she looked up and saw Dorothy running towards her.

'My darling child!' she cried, folding the little girl in her arms and covering her face with kisses. 'Where in the world did you come from?'

'From the Land of Oz,' Dorothy said gravely. 'And here is Toto too. And oh, Aunt Em! I'm so glad to be at home again.'

This final chapter is perplexing. Home on the Kansas prairie is a wretched place where nobody has the heart to laugh or even to smile, and Dorothy's aunt and uncle have been made grim and grey by the bare struggle to exist; the opening pages that describe the harsh life of a farmer are the most interesting in the book. But this promising theme is never developed. How Uncle Henry found the resources to rebuild the farm after the disaster of the hurricane is not explained, nor whether the quality of life improves. In the Land of Oz sequences Baum had prettified the issues; here he seems just to have turned his back on them. *The Wizard of Oz* is often held to be the great breakthrough of American fantasy.* In one sense this is true; the public was ready for fairy-tales, and here was one

---

* 'It is in *The Wizard of Oz* that we might meet the first distinctive attempt to construct a fairyland out of American materials' – Edward Wagenknecht: *Utopia Americana* (Washington, DC, 1929), 17. '[It] is unquestionably the best original American fantasy to be written up to 1900' – Humphrey Carpenter and Mari Prichard: *Oxford Companion to English Children's Literature* (Oxford, 1984), 579.

whose undemanding cheerfulness and lavish illustration made an immediate appeal. But as has been
seen, from Paulding onwards there had been some
distinguished fantasy. Baum's success seems to
have been due to lucky timing and a perceptive
publisher.

Oz became a series, continued after Baum's death
by Ruth Plumly Thompson, who produced an annual
volume until 1939, and then by John R. Neill (who
illustrated the Oz books after the first). The series
grew both mechanical and repetitive, but others of
Baum's works were more inventive. *A New Wonderland* (1900, reissued as *The Surprising Adventures
of the Magical Monarch of Mo* in 1903), for instance,
is a collection of nonsensical stories with some
zanily original touches, such as the fate of the
Purple Dragon who terrorizes the kingdom.

It has been difficult to know what to do with this
dragon; there are drawbacks to cutting off his legs
or putting out his eyes, and he is so long that if a
tin can were tied to his tail he would never hear
it. The people finally settle on pulling out his teeth,
and the dragon is stretched like elastic as a com-
mando force struggles with them. Eventually the
forceps-holders have retreated far into the mountains and can go no further. Exhausted, they tie
their end of the now string-sized dragon round a
tree, and snip up the rest of him to make fiddle
strings: 'And that was not only the end of the Purple
Dragon, but there were two other ends of him; one
tied to a tree in the mountains, and the other tied
to a post in the castle.'

Children have enormous appetite for violence,
which they rarely associate with pain, and here
again Baum has succeeded in making *Grand Gui-
gnol* into gentle comedy.

CHILDREN'S PERIODICALS: A UNIVERSAL APPEAL

'For several years we have believed that the Young
People of the United States wanted and needed a
magazine which would visit them every week, instead of every month,' said the opening number of
Oliver Optic's Magazine in January 1867; 'We know
what pleasure the older members of the family
derive from the weekly coming of the religious,
agricultural, and literary papers.' Given the place
of newspapers in American culture, it is not surprising that throughout the last century American

youth was far better provided with periodicals than
the British. Gordon Kelly, the authority on American
juvenile journals, counted some seventy-five that
were begun between 1802 and the outbreak of the
Civil War,[24] though he reckoned that fewer than
one in five managed to continue publication for as
long as ten years. The mid-century years were the
peak years: over 130 juvenile journals were launched
between 1840 and 1870, and 105 in the period up
to 1900. The distinction of their contributors, particularly in the last decades of the century, is
impressive, and a large proportion of the best-
known books for children first appeared in serial
form in their pages. Take just one, *Our Young
Folks*, published by Ticknor & Fields of Boston from
1865 until 1873 (when it was absorbed into *St
Nicholas*). Its editors were John Townsend Trowbridge and Lucy Larcom (Gail Hamilton, the third,
resigned in 1868); its contributors included Thomas
Bailey Aldrich, Louisa Alcott, Jane Andrews, Lydia
Maria Child, Abby Morton Diaz, Charles Dickens,
Lucretia Hale, Elizabeth Stuart Phelps, Mayne Reid,
Harriet Beecher Stowe. Though occasionally sentimental and didactic in the style of the past, it
established a standard for others to follow.

Journals such as this were a uniquely American
phenomenon. No English equivalent had the universal appeal of the best American magazines such
as *St Nicholas* and *Harper's Young People*; indeed,
in England they only attempted to cater for carefully
selected corners of the market. At one extreme
were the blood-and-thunder boys' papers; at the
other, the cheap Sunday school weeklies, whose
ugliness outraged Ruskin. In between were journals
with a limited circulation which hoped to improve
young readers with advice, exhortation and a certain
amount of fiction. The declared intention of Charlotte Yonge's *Monthly Packet* (1851–98), whose full
title was *The Monthly Packet of Evening Readings
for Members of the English Church*, was to train
young ladies to be 'more steadfast and dutiful
daughters of our beloved Catholic Church of England'. Its readership was essentially upper-class, as
was that of *Aunt Judy's Magazine* (1866–85). This
sixpenny monthly (the Sunday school magazines
cost a penny or a halfpenny) was edited by Mrs
Gatty, the wife of a Yorkshire clergyman, and was
an altogether more genial publication than Miss
Yonge's. Though most of its contributions came
from the Gatty circle, they were often of high
quality, especially those by Juliana Horatia Ewing,

Mrs Gatty's daughter, who took over the editorship for a time after her mother's death, and much of whose work made its original appearance there. But its readership, though loyal and affectionate, was limited. *Aunt Judy* eschewed all 'sensational' tales, and in effect confined itself to the demure domestic sagas that only girls cared for. Illustrations were sparse and drawn from the publisher's stock (the circulation was clearly so small that they were not prepared for any outlay on these).

The two English magazines that succeeded best in attracting a large readership over a broad class range were the *Boy's Own Paper* (1879–1967) and the *Girl's Own Paper*, founded in 1880 and continuing under changed titles until 1956. These were published by the Religious Tract Society, and were apparently the most lucrative of any of their periodicals. Though the illustrations were undistinguished, at least they were specially drawn for each number. By the 1880s these two were the papers most popular with adolescents. (Adolescence in those days lasted a long time, and in an 1891 competition in the *Girl's Own Paper* ages ranged from eleven to thirty-eight.) They catered for the more privileged boy, but also for the wage-earning clerk; for the leisured girl and for those of 'a less high position' – even servants – who would receive instruction in 'economical cookery, plain needlework, home education and health'. Though both papers became less didactic over the years and the readership became younger, they never had the gaiety that was the mark of *St Nicholas* and *Harper's*, nor did the quality of the contributions begin to approach these.

The contents of American juvenile magazines show an increasing lightness of spirit. *Oliver Optic's Magazine* in March 1872 told parents of the folly of providing books of information only:

Do not look for science, for history, for biography, as a general rule; do not seek to cover up a pill of knowledge with a sugar-coating of entertainment; but let the child really enjoy himself... Do not be afraid of 'sensation' if it is not overdone, and too rank; let mental work and mental play alternate, and then there will be less cause for anxiety over the evils of our school system.

The 'sensational' element that its editor, William Taylor Adams (Oliver Optic) thus guardedly referred to was in fact what the cautious most deplored about his own prolific output; many librarians

banned him, and Miss Alcott made a forceful attack, much to his indignation, in *Eight Cousins*. However, the sensationalism of his paper was tame indeed compared to that of the immensely popular *Frank Leslie's Boy's and Girl's Weekly* (1866–84), with its dime-novel-style content and lurid pictures. Of this Gordon Kelly said: 'The brutality and violence evident in the *Weekly* have no counterpart in the other magazines.'[25]

The change in approach coincides with the Civil War. Similarly, it is noticeable that English children never seemed so sheltered from harsh reality as in the years that succeeded the First World War, and it may be that adults feel an especially protective instinct at the time of great national disaster, a desire to ensure that their children should lead normal lives even if the adult world lies in ruins. Whatever the reason, juvenile periodicals flourished in the 1860s, and though there were the usual clutch of Sunday school publications such as *Youth Temperance Visitor*, *Young Evangelist*, *Young Christian Soldier* and *Youth's Temperance Banner*, which trod the same paths as their predecessors, there were innovatory ones such as the *Riverside Magazine* whose aim was above all high literary standards.

These years also saw journals that strove to preserve the traditional American values against what they regarded as a new, insidious movement towards the fantastic. This was the avowed aim of *Demorest's Young America* (1866–75), started by William J. Demorest in New York to counteract the 'low and demoralizing class of literature, prepared expressly to gratify that love of the marvellous, the absurd, and the unnatural that is fostered in the young.'[26] It focused on the concrete rather than on abstractions, and took a strong temperance line, but there was a curious bias in favour of fashions and the fashionable world (his wife ran Madame Demorest's Emporium in New York). However, the lighter touch that marked juvenile productions, even didactic ones, in this period is evident in the 'Alpha Betical Constitution' with which the 1867 volume advertised its contents: 'A Beautiful Combination Delineating Engravings Funny Games Historical Items Joyous Kaleidoscopes Learning Music Notable Oddities Piquant Queries Riddles Stories Teaching Useful Virtues While Xuberant Youthful Zealous'. And the informality of one of its fan letters in that volume is reminiscent of those in *St Nicholas*:

I like your YOUNG AMERICA magazine very much. I have read most all of the stories in it. I am going to show it to all my young friends and ask them to take it...I have learned to make some of those shadows on the walls, but I could not make out those rebuses. I am eight years old, and I had a real nice party on my last birthday. I live in Chicago...and my name is Virginia.

There are also anecdotes of children who outsmart the adults – Visitor: 'I suppose you think I have staid long enough.' Child: 'I thought that a long time ago.'

The temperance message was prominent in many juvenile periodicals of the traditional sort. And though deathbeds were no longer used in attempts to batter children into early piety, nor were they a prominent feature of fiction, deaths of children were still sadly frequent in real life. The *Little Corporal* in an editorial of January 1868 reported: 'Almost every week a letter comes and says to us, "Willie is dead"; "Our darling Minnie has gone to live among the angels"; "The pale boatman has come and ferried little Frankie over to the shining shore"; "The Savior sent His angels down, and our Birdie has found her wings."' This children's journal, published from Chicago between 1865 and 1875 (when it was absorbed into the very different *St Nicholas*), was started as a patriotic venture by publisher Alfred Sewell, and was the first to achieve a national circulation.

Sewell, who in 1865 had raised over $16,000 for wounded soldiers at the Northwest Sanitary Fair by enrolling children in his Army of the American Eagle, decided to continue the good work by involving them in a magazine. The *Little Corporal*'s motto was 'Fighting Against Wrong, and for the Good, the True and the Beautiful'. The mood was to remain a military one throughout its history. The readers were referred to as 'soldiers' or 'volunteers'; long-term readers were called 'veterans', and were urged to enlist for another 'campaign'. They were also encouraged, by a system of rewards, to boost the circulation by recruiting friends. The magazine aimed at a wholesome moral atmosphere rather than at high literary standards, and its readers tended to be serious-minded and bent upon improvement; one letter of 1870, from a fifteen-year-old, told the editor that it had been 'an instrument, in the hand of God, of bringing my soul to Christ'. Its most distinguished contributor was Edward Eggleston (1837-1902), author of *The Hoosier*

Schoolmaster and *The Hoosier Schoolboy*, who at one stage acted as assistant editor. It attracted readers who might have found *St Nicholas* not adult enough:

Dear Aunt Prudy: Some boys try to be men by chewing tobacco, others by drinking whiskey. I thought I would try to become a man by getting up a club for the LITTLE CORPORAL. I want to get enough to get a watch. I am thirteen years old, and I think a watch is about all I lack of being a man.

Dear Aunt Prudy: I am telegraph operator here. Am getting a salary of twenty-five dollars a month and board; will get a better salary next month I guess; don't you think that is pretty good for a boy twelve years old?

Two Southern papers were launched in the Reconstruction period. *Burke's Weekly for Boys and Girls* (1867-70), published from Georgia, was an ambitious compilation – probably too ambitious, given the difficulties of the times – which turned itself into a monthly in 1870 and lasted only one year after that. *Southern Boys' and Girls' Monthly*, founded in Richmond, Virginia, in January 1867, lasted for only eighteen months, and its failure was blamed on problems with transport and the post. 'The many failures of the United States Post Office to fulfil its important trusts in the Southern States is becoming a very serious matter to publishers and businessmen,' said one of the last editorials.

The *Riverside Magazine for Young People* was also short-lived, but its name is synonymous with excellence. As has been said, it was unusual in that it did not advertise any particular purpose or take up any moral stance; it set out to provide a high level of entertainment for children of literary tastes. It is always associated with the name of Horace Scudder, who was only twenty-eight when he was appointed editor, but credit also has to go to Henry Houghton, proprietor of the Riverside Press at Cambridge, Massachusetts (which was to develop into the firm of Houghton Mifflin). He recognized the quality of young Scudder, who was then working for his firm, and entrusted him with this new venture. That Scudder saw the potential of children's books at a time when they were not taken seriously as a literary form is evident from an article, 'Books for Young People', in the first number: 'a literature is forming which is destined to act powerfully upon general letters; hitherto it has been little disturbed by critics,

FIVE LITTLE PIGS.

This little Pig went to market.

This little Pig stayed at home.

This little Pig had roast beef.

This little Pig had none.

And this little Pig cried " Wee !
wee ! can't find my way home."

Silhouettes by Courtland Hoppin for the Riverside Magazine, *March 1867.*

but the time must soon come, if it has not already come, when students of literature must consider the character and tendency of *Children's Letters*.'

In that the *Riverside Magazine* had an end in view, it was to stimulate the imagination. The second number's 'Books for Young People' warmly recommended Shakespeare who possessed, Scudder told his readers, 'what no other writer has in like measure, the power of furnishing material to the imagination'. It was thus the antithesis of Parleyism, and as if to drive this home, the magazine featured throughout 1867 and into 1868 full-page illustrations of nursery rhymes drawn by H. L. Stephens, including 'Hey Diddle Diddle' and 'The sow came in with the saddle', which Samuel Goodrich in his memoirs had mentioned with particular abhorrence. (The first of these illustrations, perhaps significantly, was of the 'Three Wise Men of Gotham'.) Scudder was to refer to nursery rhymes (March 1867) as 'the jingle of bright nonsense – the rhymes of Mother Goose and her sister-in-law (few enough sisters has the dame)'. They were infinitely to be preferred, he thought, to the sort of pious twaddle to be found in *Songs for Little Ones at Home*, an American Tract Society publication: 'In every such case we feel that the writer is not in sympathy with children, does not walk with them to the beckoning Saviour, but goes behind and pushes them, lecturing them meanwhile in a half-understood language.'

Henry Houghton was generous in his outlay on the *Riverside Magazine*. It had none of the meanly cramped appearance of so many of its contemporaries: the format was large, it was printed in double columns, and there was an abundance of attractive illustration – for the first time in a children's magazine, these were taken seriously. F. O. C. Darley, Winslow Homer, John La Farge and Thomas Nast all contributed to the 1867 issues, and one remembers the engaging silhouettes accompanying the 'Five Little Pigs' by Courtland Hoppin, who contributed other pages in the same vein. There were stories, factual articles, well known poetry and ballads, but Scudder's greatest editorial triumph was to secure ten new stories by Hans Andersen. Financially it was not a success; perhaps even Boston had not a sufficient number of literary children to keep it afloat – the existence of a high-quality magazine is always precarious, and Scudder made no concessions. But it stands out in the history of children's periodicals as the greatest thoroughbred of them all.

If *Our Young Folks* had occasional lapses into the manner of the past, and *Riverside* appealed to too limited a readership, *St Nicholas* struck from the start exactly the right note. It built on their foundations; without their example and their achievements it would have had to move more cautiously. But by 1873, when it began as an off-shoot of *Scribner's Monthly*, a tradition of informal entertainment for children was well established. *Scribner's* (a literary magazine successful from the beginning) had had three years' start, and Roswell Smith of the Scribner firm approached Mary Mapes Dodge with the idea of establishing a junior periodical. The subtitle initially was *Scribner's Illustrated Magazine for Girls and Boys*.

Its first number appeared in November 1873. Like Scudder, Mrs Dodge had a burning sense of commitment, a certainty that children should be given only the very best, but she added to this the common touch that perhaps he lacked. She had written in *Scribner's* in July of that year that a children's magazine had to be stronger and more uncompromising than an adult one. She believed that there should be a firm moral stance, but that the message should be implied rather than preached:

Doubtless a great deal of instruction and good moral teaching may be inculcated in the pages of a magazine; but it must be by hints dropped incidentally here and there; by a few brisk hearty statements of the difference between right and wrong; a sharp, clean thrust at falsehood, a sunny recognition of truth, a gracious application of politeness, an unwilling glimpse of the odious doings of the uncharitable and base.

The style must be natural and there must be no talking down: 'Its cheer must be the cheer of the bird-song, not of condescending editorial babble. If it *mean* freshness and heartiness, and life and joy, and its words are simply, directly, and musically put together, it will trill its own way.'

But this sort of artless spontaneity is easier to prescribe than to achieve, and it is a remarkable tribute to Mrs Dodge that she managed to address herself to her young readers in a style that for all its intense enthusiasm never seemed gushing or affected. She established her editorial persona from the very first:

Here they come! There they come! Near by, far off, everywhere, we can see them – coming by dozens, hundreds, thousands, troops on troops, and all pressing closer and closer.

Why, this is delightful. And how fresh, eager, and hearty you look! Glad to see us? Thank you. The same to you, and many happy returns.

It was an extraordinarily confident assertion for the first number of a new venture, but it was to prove well founded. Readers all over the earth – wherever English was spoken – took it to their hearts. It was more popular in England than any English equivalent (except for the *Boy's Own Paper* and the *Girl's Own Paper*, but these had yet to be founded). In the 1896 issues, for instance, we find letters from Austria, France, Germany, Italy, Scotland, Canada, China, Japan, South Africa, Brazil, Colombia, Ecuador, Nicaragua. 'I hope you will be printed forever,' said one correspondent. 'Dear St Nicholas,' wrote another, 'I have taken you for almost seven years, and during those years I don't think anything has given me so much pleasure as your magazine.'

It catered for a wide age range, and stories in large type for the younger were included. One child wrote in 1916: 'Dear St Nicholas, I was five years old Feb 5th. I had a cake with five candles on it and Mama gave me the pretty bound volumes of St Nicholas for 1913. I just love them, and wish I had all the St Nicholases you have ever published.'

Scribner did not stint, and Mrs Dodge was able to pay well, attracting the best-known writers of the day. Kipling, who had loved *St Nicholas* dearly as a child, let her have stories from *The Just So Stories* and the first *Jungle Book*. Among other English contributors were R. L. Stevenson and G. A. Henty; in the United States every children's author of any standing at some time wrote for her. Louisa Alcott's *Eight Cousins* and *Jack and Jill* were serialized there, as were Frances Hodgson Burnett's *Sara Crewe* and *Little Lord Fauntleroy*, Mark Twain's *Tom Sawyer Abroad*, Edward Eggleston's *The Hoosier Schoolboy* and Joel Chandler Harris's *Daddy Jakes the Runaway*. Jack London, Noah Brooks, Howard Pyle, Frank Baum, Frank Stockton (who was also, like Trowbridge, on the editorial staff), Hezekiah Butterworth, Palmer Cox, Laura Richards, Susan Coolidge, Lucretia Hale, Kate Douglas Wiggin, Horace Scudder and John Trowbridge all wrote for it.

St Nicholas was eclectic in its outlook. *Two Little Confederates*, Thomas Nelson Page's chivalric story

of the South during the Civil War, was published in it in 1888, and there were plenty of stories based on European history. Its factual articles covered a wide range of interests, from conjuring to the Olympic Games, from 'How the Stone-Age Children Played' to speculation on the possibilities of flying machines. There was a league of Bird-Defenders, and the Agassiz Association promoted an interest in ecological studies. An important feature was the material supplied by the readers themselves: the 'Letter-Box' began in 1874, the 'Young Contributors' Department' in 1876. A development of the latter was the 'St Nicholas League', begun in 1899, which assessed readers' contributions – whether illustrative or literary – and awarded medals and certificates. Among winners who later achieved distinction were Eudora Welty, Stephen Vincent Benét and Cornelia Otis Skinner. 'Within those red covers,' wrote Alice Jordan, 'lies the very kernel of American books for children.'[27]

Mary Mapes Dodge died in 1905, and her successor William Fayal Clarke, who had worked with her from the beginning, took over as editor, continuing until 1927. But circulation was declining, and in 1930 the Century Company, who had owned it since 1881, sold it to a firm in Columbus, Ohio. It was to change hands twice after that, and though it limped on until 1943 its last days, as Alice Jordan said sadly, are best forgotten.

Harper's Young People, which was inaugurated in 1879 and after changing its name to *Harper's Round Table* in 1895 continued until 1899, rivalled *St Nicholas* in popularity; but in effect, since it was always a fairly close imitation, all it did was to follow where the older paper had led. Many of its authors were also *St Nicholas* authors, and the contents were very similar, though they did not on the whole achieve the same literary distinction. One gets an impression of a readership of prosperous, frequently well travelled children with indulgent parents. They wrote – often from far-flung places – to 'the Post Mistress' (for many years Margaret Elizabeth Munson Sangster), whose cheerful, informal comments on their letters encouraged them to be expansive about their brothers and sisters, their friends, their pets (particularly) and the books they enjoyed, and about how they had spent their holidays:

At Christmas Santa Claus dropped down the chimney for me, on his way to other places, HARPER'S YOUNG PEOPLE (bound), a nice fur muff, a pair of skates, a box of writing-paper, a box of candy, two pairs of stockings, a pair of shoes, a pearl-handled knife, two booklets, a book with golden texts for the year 1891, a new piano stool, a new handkerchief, music lessons, and a book of selections. Don't you think he was pretty generous?

'I am fifteen, and very tall, but I enjoy your paper immensely, though I am an English girl. I often wonder what marshmallows are like when I read of them in the letters to the Post-Office Box,' wrote another reader. To which the Post Mistress replied: 'If you would call on me I would like to give you some.'

It was responses like this, and indeed the genial informality of the best post-bellum American children's books, that made them distinctive and so endeared them to English readers. In contrast, one might append the reply that the editor of the *Girl's Own Paper* gave in 1880 to an unfortunate reader: 'We do not know to what letter you refer, nor the question asked, nor who you are. What you are we do know, viz., a rude little girl, who does not know how to spell and sends a poor specimen of scribbling.'

NOTES

1. 'Books for our Children', *Atlantic Monthly*, vol. 16 (Dec. 1865).

2. F. J. Harvey Darton: *Children's Books in England* (3rd edn, Cambridge, UK, 1982), 260.

3. Published in *Aunt Judy's Magazine*, Nov. 1883–March 1884; in book form, London, 1886.

4. Horace Scudder: *Childhood in Literature and Art* (Cambridge, Mass., 1894), 216.

5. 'A Mid-century Child and her Books', in *Caroline M. Hewins: Her Book* (Boston, 1954).

6. Caroline Hewins: *Books for the Young* (Boston, 1883).

7. *Fairy Tales Every Child Should Know*, ed. Hamilton Wright Mabie (New York, 1903).

8. See Richard Darling: *The Rise of Children's Book Reviewing in America 1865–1881* (New York, 1968).

9. Susan Pindar: *Fireside Fairies, or Christmas at Aunt Elsie's* (New York, n.d. [c. 1849]).

10. *Illustrated London News*, 3 Dec. 1892, p. 714.

11. By 'Sophie May' [Rebecca Sophie Clarke], 1833–1906; published posthumously.

12. This contains 'The Minotaur', 'The Pygmies', 'The Dragon's Teeth', 'Circe's Palace', 'The Pomegranate-Seeds', 'The Golden Fleece'. The sources from which Hawthorne took his tales are discussed in Roger Lancelyn Green's postscript to *The Complete Greek Stories of Nathaniel Hawthorne* (London, 1964).

13. Scudder: op. cit., 208.

14. Ernest Rhys: introduction to the Everyman edn of *The Age of Fable* (London, 1910).

15. Julia Collier Harris: *The Life and Letters of Joel Chandler Harris* (London, 1919), 155.

16. ibid., 142.

17. ibid., 163.

18. Walter Blair and Hamlin Hill: *America's Humor* (New York, 1978), vii.

19. It was reissued the following year under the title of *A Gift from Fairyland*.

20. Sinclair Hamilton: *Early American Book Illustrators and Wood Engravers* (Princeton, NJ, 1958).

21. See Cornelia Meigs, Anne Thaxter Eaton, Elizabeth Nesbitt and Ruth Hill Viguers: *A Critical History of Children's Literature* (New York, 1958), 208.

22. Harvard, Houghton Library *58M-231, Scudder, Horace E., Box 3.

23. The English reviews have been reprinted in *Jabberwocky*, the journal of the Lewis Carroll Society, vol. 9, nos 1, 2, 3 (London, 1979-80). They are summarized by Elizabeth Cripps in 'Alice and the Reviewers', *Children's Literature*, vol. 11 (New Haven, Conn., 1983).

24. R. Gordon Kelly: *Mother was a Lady* (Westport, Conn., 1974).

25. ibid., 29.

26. *Demorest's Young America*, vol. 7 (Aug. 1873).

27. Alice M. Jordan: *From Rollo to Tom Sawyer* (Boston, 1948), 131.

Part Three

DIFFERING IDEALS

6. Homes and Heroines

ENGLISH CONSTRAINT, AMERICAN LATITUDE

The liberated atmosphere of American family books in the nineteenth century, and the robust and confident children, from Jacob Abbott's Rollo to the little friends-of-all-the-world like Eleanor Porter's Pollyanna and Kate Douglas Wiggin's Rebecca of Sunnybrook Farm, fascinated young Britons, who could find nothing comparable in their own books. In England, until the advent of E. Nesbit's more independent children, the characters in family stories moved always under the watchful and anxious eyes of parents. It is ironical, in view of what visitors thought about the lack of childhood in the New World, that young American readers apparently pitied their English contemporaries for their rigorous upbringing. 'We did not think those English children had so good a time as we did,' wrote Lucy Larcom of her Massachusetts childhood in the 1830s. 'They had to be so prim and methodical. It seemed to us that the little folks across the water were never allowed to romp and run wild; some of us may have held a vague idea that this freedom of ours was the natural inheritance of republican children only.'[1]

Lucy Larcom's childhood, however, stopped abruptly upon the death of her father when she was eleven and she was sent to work in a mill. This was not an option that would have been open to a middle-class English contemporary, whose girlhood would have continued, however penurious the background, until she was seventeen or so. English girls were carefully chaperoned, and rarely left the family circle. Nor might they mix with any class lower than their own. Contamination would be the result if they did; they could pick up not only bad manners and a bad style and thereby become *déclassé*, but possibly – if one is to go by Charlotte Yonge who specialized in books for the young upper-class person – a devious outlook and lack of regard for truth. Nothing better demonstrates the elaborate Victorian class stratification than the history of girls' education in England in that century where, even within the same foundation, there could be separate sections for upper-, middle-, and lower-middle-class girls, who would never be allowed to meet. (Ironically, this was at its most marked in church schools.) The new high schools that were founded from the 1870s onwards and which did set out to be classless had to counter parental prejudice by ensuring, with rules of silence, that the children did not speak to each other, and that no girl walked home with another unless the parents had given written permission.

With this sort of prohibition in force the content of the English family story, and girls' books especially, was inevitably severely constrained, and limited in its appeal. The subtle punctilios and taboos which were a rich source of material for novelists such as Trollope had a paralysing effect on children's books. Many of the Victorian women who wrote for children appeared to be fighting a desperate rearguard action against new money and mercantile values. Their instinct was that disinterested and honourable conduct and truth-telling were the birthright of the land-owning classes and those descended from them, and that commercial instincts and lack of straightforwardness must be expected from those who were in contact with money. Charlotte Yonge (1823–1901) and Mary Louisa Molesworth (1839–1921) were both particularly concerned with demarcation of class territory. Miss Yonge, whose father owned a small estate in Hampshire, felt passionately that the Church of England and the English squirearchy were the guardians of religious truth and the right way of living. Mrs Molesworth's father, on the other hand, though he came from the right sort of family, had left the army to become a Manchester businessman, which no doubt accounts for his daughter's intense preoccupation with social status and self-conscious identification with the upper classes. It has meant that the entire output of these two writers is now dead as far as children are concerned – though their books may still be read with pleasure by readers with the taste for social minutiae of a bygone age.

The family stories of Juliana Horatia Ewing (1841–85) had less of this rarefied outlook, but her style – leisurely, discursive, and given to abstraction – could only be appreciated by those with a good literary background, and her books were intended for families such as her own, upper-middle-class with wide-ranging intellectual interests. Unlike the works of such American contemporaries as Louisa Alcott, Susan Coolidge, Margaret Sidney and Kate Douglas Wiggin, all authors much loved by English children, the English domestic tale was little known across the Atlantic and, significantly, was never a feature of periodicals like *St Nicholas* and *Harper's*.

It is interesting in this connection to look at *Sara Crewe* and *Little Lord Fauntleroy*, both serialized in *St Nicholas* and both very popular with English and American children. Their author, Frances Hodgson Burnett, is claimed as a national by both Britain and the US, but since she left England when she was a child, and both her marriages were to Americans, the latter has the stronger claim (though after she became rich and famous she was to spend long periods in her various English homes). Despite the English setting of nearly all her stories, her child characters have a confidence and self-sufficiency that could only be American. *Sara Crewe, or what happened at Miss Minchin's* (first published in 1887, and expanded in 1905 as *A Little Princess*) describes how a little girl at a boarding school is victimized by Miss Minchin the proprietress when her father dies and the fees can no longer be paid, and comforts herself by pretending she is a princess. Dramatically rescued by a wealthy friend of her father's, she learns that she is the heiress to diamond mines and unimaginable wealth. (For all this expansive optimism so alien to the English tradition, the author's instincts about class differences remained rooted in the Old World: Miss Minchin's little kitchen maid whom Sara has befriended is rescued too, but only to be Sara's personal attendant.)

Little Lord Fauntleroy is the story of a young American who becomes heir to an earldom, and turns his winning ways on the English in general and his cantankerous old grandfather in particular. Cedric Errol, with his confiding friendliness, has an assurance and a sense of equality that sets him apart from any English boy. The dry old English lawyer sent out to New York to fetch him is fascinated; he has known plenty of English children 'strictly taken care of by their tutors and governesses, and who were sometimes shy, and sometimes a trifle boisterous, but never very interesting'. (Sara Crewe, too, has a grave dignity and natural authority that infuriates Miss Minchin.) Even in Mrs Burnett's *The Secret Garden* (1911), about two disagreeable, self-willed children who in bringing a neglected garden to life effect a transformation on themselves, the change is wrought by the children alone, without adult intervention. This concept of children as masters of their own destiny, which was not at all how Victorians in England saw them, naturally appealed to young readers, who also warmed to the fairy-tale outcome of so many American stories. Who would not prefer to read of little Fauntleroy, lapped in luxury and doted on by all, rather than of Charlotte Yonge's shy, awkward Countess Kate,[2] who has to be beaten out on the anvil of a stern and repressive regime to shape her for her new station in life?

The English family stories reflected the rigours, moral and physical, then thought appropriate for the nursery and schoolroom. Often strikingly well written, with deft characterization, they seem oppressive now in the lofty demands that they make on the child, and the reader notices the degree of moral responsibility expected even of the youngest. No initiative was expected or allowed, but children were the custodians of their consciences, and many stories dwelt on the agony of mind suffered when some small wrong had been committed. Later Victorians, remembering the sternness of their own upbringing and the moral pressure put upon them, often tried to make amends by peopling their books with irresponsible nursery scamps and pickles. But their mischievous escapades nearly always took place against a secure background of protective and understanding parents and nurses, and there were people to clear up the mess and mend the torn clothes; young Americans would still have found them amazingly helpless and childish.

But, whatever Lucy Larcom and her friends thought, English children did play. Isolated in their nurseries, if they were upper- or middle-class, they became absorbed in their own make-believe in a way that was impossible for children living cheek by jowl with adults, under pressure to be self-sufficient and to contribute to the common weal. English memoirs and autobiographies are full of imagined worlds, which by the end of the last century had become part of the adult vision of childhood. Kenneth Grahame in the opening chapter of *The Golden Age* (1895) describes with affected contempt the 'pale phantasms of reality' to which adults devote their attention, the social and political inanities they discuss at meals – whereas children, 'we *illuminati*, eating silently, our heads full of plans and conspiracies, could have told them what real life was. We had just left it outside, and were all on fire to get back to it.' It was an attitude that the Edwardian writers, from Barrie to E. Nesbit, were to take up, and children who could not see buccaneers lurking at the bottom of their suburban gardens, or who did not believe in fairies, were regarded as an inferior species. So potent indeed were Barrie's memories of his own childhood games of pirates and Red Indians and shipwrecks that in middle age he was to play them out with another generation of boys, the pond in a Surrey cottage serving as a pirate-infested lagoon. In Robert Louis Stevenson's *A Child's Garden of Verses* (1885) the child is shown voyaging and exploring in dream worlds: 'Let the sofa be mountains, the carpet be sea, / There I'll establish a city for me,' says the little boy building with his blocks. In the evening, while his parents sit by the fire he is crawling with his gun round the forest track behind the sofa. And if he is bored by adult company he only has to shut his eyes:

> To go sailing far away
> To the pleasant Land of Play;
> To the fairy land afar
> Where the Little People are;

For the everyday world is a very drab one:

> High bare walls, great bare floor;
> Great big knobs on drawer and door;
> Great big people perched on chairs,
> Stitching tucks and mending tears,
> Each a hill that I could climb,
> And talking nonsense all the time.

But this real world, where tucks were stitched and tears mended, was the one that American children were encouraged to inhabit, and the games that they played, as recorded in memoirs and in the juvenile stories of the last century, were down to earth. Susan Coolidge in *Nine Little Goslings* (1875) spoke of 'running races, spinning tops, flying kites, going downhill on sleds, and making a noise in the open air'. Louisa Alcott makes the grandmother in *An Old-Fashioned Girl* (1870) look back wistfully to a time when girls were not fashion-plates by the age of fourteen: ' "We were little folks till eighteen or so; worked and studied, dressed and played, like children ... we all learned to make bread and cook, and wore little chintz gowns, and were as gay and hearty as kittens." ' By which it will be seen that childhood was expected to be purposeful and practical. Curiously, the lifestyle that did most resemble English childhood was to be found in the South; young Victorians would have understood the games played by the three small girls in Louise-Clarke Pyrnelle's nostalgic evocation of ante-bellum life in Mississippi, *Diddie, Dumps and Tot* (1882):

'We're goin' ter play Injuns! We're goin' ter make out we're travellin' in the big rockin'-cheer, goin' ter New Orleans, an' the little niggers is got ter be Injuns, hid all behin' the trunks an' beds an' door; an' after we rock an' rock er *lo-o-ong* time, and we're goin' ter make out it's night, an' stretch mamma's big shawl over two cheers an' make er tent, and be cookin' supper in our little pots an' kittles, an' the little niggers is got ter holler, "Who-ee, who-eee," an' jump out on us, an' cut off our heads with er billycrow.'

One has, of course, to discount the indulged plantation ways which permitted each white child a little black attendant. English children would certainly not have had unlimited pie and cake, either ('Their mother always let them have whatever they wanted to have tea-parties with').

The difference between what English and American children ate was marked. In 1693 in *Some Thoughts Concerning Education* (a book whose influence seems to have been restricted to England) the philosopher John Locke laid down principles for child-rearing, and among them rules for feeding the young. It was a largely farinaceous diet, low-fat, salt-restricted, very plain indeed, with meat only once a day, little fruit, no sugar or high seasoning, and only milk and water to drink. To this regime the English upper classes largely adhered for at least two hundred and fifty years – for as long, in effect, as circumstances permitted the more prosperous to give children their meals separately. The Second World War and the general levelling of diet finally put an end to it.

Rose learns to make bread. From Louisa M. Alcott:
Eight Cousins, *serialized in* St Nicholas, *1875.*

Locke was forgotten as the initiator of the regime; it became a hallowed English tradition. It was not just mothers and nurses that knew it had to be so. Anthony Trollope, for instance, watched American infants ordering their fish or beef-steak at breakfast and demanding pickles to accompany them, and compared it with himself at the same age, eating bread and milk under the supervision of a nursery-maid.[3] Plenty of other visitors catalogued with amazement what American children were allowed to eat: the fruit, the salads, the oysters, johnny cakes, toast swimming in butter; fish, flesh and game at breakfast; jellies and ices at night; tea and coffee. On the other side of the Atlantic the Locke diet seems to have become as much a character-building principle as a medical one, and it was fundamental to English nursery and schoolroom life. Thus for children brought up austerely on a diet in which boiled mutton, potatoes, rice pudding and bread and milk played the most prominent part it was entrancing to read about what their American contemporaries apparently took as a matter of course. Susan Warner in *The Wide, Wide World* describes 'splitters' – apparently, butter shortcake served hot with plenty more butter – with such eloquence that salivating readers wrote to ask for the recipe. (But it should be recorded that there were occasional misgivings about this lavishness, and not only among the visitors. Louisa Alcott's Dr

Alec, for instance, in *Eight Cousins*, throws away his niece's strong coffee and makes her drink milk; he also substitutes porridge and brown bread at breakfast for her hot white rolls. Likewise Elsie Dinsmore's father, newly returned from Europe, imposes an English-style regime on his small daughter.)

Food was remembered by many in their accounts of childhood with almost erotic satisfaction. It could be used as a method of redemption. In *The Secret Garden* the metamorphosis of Mary and Colin is brought about partly by the food; the breakfasts of 'home-made bread and fresh butter, snow-white eggs, raspberry jam and clotted cream' with 'delicate slices of sizzling ham' betray Mrs Hodgson Burnett's American background. In reality, English children would have been given bread and milk – ham and eggs being thought indigestible, butter and cream too rich, raspberry jam debilitating to the character. And Harriet Beecher Stowe's Pussy Willow[4] similarly transforms a peevish, wilting New York girl. We know from the first breakfast she gives Emily how matters will turn out:

First there was a large saucer of strawberries, delightfully arranged on green vine-leaves; then there was a small glass pitcher full of the thickest and richest cream, that was just the colour of a saffrano rose-leaf... Then there was the most charming little cake of golden butter you ever saw, shaped with a flower on it and arranged upon

The kitchen hearth. From Jacob Abbott: Stuyvesant, *illustrated by Carl Emil Doepler (New York, 1853).*

The Thanksgiving turkeys. Drawing by Winslow Homer, from Harper's Weekly, *1858.*

two large strawberry-leaves, that actually had a little round pearl of dew on each of their points... Then there were some white, tender little biscuits, and some nice round muffins of a bright yellow color, made of corn meal, by a very choice receipt on which Pussy prided herself.

To the English mind, if children were indulged over their food it was a sign of an ill-bred family. In Mrs Molesworth's *Mary* (1893), a mother visiting a confectioner's shop orders, as a very great treat, a glass of milk and a bun for her small daughter ('little Miss Bertram of the Priory'). But a stout lady coming in with her children says: ' "Now, what will you have, my loveys? Puffs, cheesecakes, macaroons?" ' The English reader is instantly aware that the family is a vulgar one, and is prepared for their subsequent boorish behaviour.

The kitchen played a vital part in stories of American family life, especially when it was in a farmhouse. It is the centre of the busy purposefulness that Americans prized far more highly than

leisure. 'There is a kind of sentiment about the kitchen in New England, a sentiment not provoked by other rooms,' said Kate Douglas Wiggin in *Rose o' the River* (1905):

Here the farmer drops in to spend a few minutes when he comes back from the barn or field on an errand. Here, in the great, clean, sweet, comfortable place, the busy housewife lives, sometimes rocking the cradle, sometimes opening and shutting the oven door, sometimes stirring the pot, darning stockings, paring vegetables, or mixing goodies in a yellow bowl. The children sit on the steps, stringing beans, shelling peas, or hulling berries; the cat sleeps on the floor near the wood-box; and the visitor feels exiled if he stays in sitting room or parlor, for here, where the mother is always busy, is the heart of the farm-house.

Thanksgiving – about which the English read wistfully – was an especially kitchen-centred festival (the nearest English equivalent was the harvest home supper, which some farmers gave to those who had helped bring in the harvest):

November had come, the crops were in, and barn, buttery, and bin were overflowing with the harvest that rewarded the summer's hard work. The big kitchen was a jolly place just now, for in the great fire-place roared a cheerful fire; on the walls hung garlands of dried apples, onions and corn; up aloft from the beams shone crook-necked squashes, juicy hams and dried venison ... Savoury smells were in the air; on the crane hung steaming kettles, and down among the red embers copper sauce-pans simmered, all suggestive of some approaching feast ... Two small boys sat on the wooden settle shelling corn for popping, and picking out the biggest nuts from the goodly store their own hands had gathered in October. Four young girls stood at the long dresser, busily chopping meat, pounding spice, and slicing apples.[5]

The kitchen played little part in the equivalent English story of the period, and it was a long time before it did. Even in E. Nesbit's books the children accept the meals placed before them without any thought of how they are prepared; however pinched the circumstances – as in *The Railway Children* – there is always someone to stew the mutton. It is an above-stairs culture, and the habitual baize-covered door shuts off the kitchen regions. But it is the kitchen dimension that gives such a pleasurable sense of warmth and well-being to American books; the hearth and the food on the table represent comfort and security. Kenneth Grahame knew what he was about when the Rat and the Mole, lost in the Wild Wood, stumble upon Badger's home and are brought in to 'all the glow and warmth of a large fire-lit kitchen'. Few of Grahame's compatriots have been able to achieve the same effect in a real-world setting, and the most appealing English kitchens are peopled not by human families, but by hobbits or moles, by Mrs Tiggy-Winkle and Mrs Tabitha Twitchit and their kind. It might even be significant that the most memorable of all, the Duchess's kitchen in *Alice*, is a symbol of anarchy.

THE AMERICAN HOME

' "I do think that families are the most beautiful things in all the world!" ' exclaims Jo in Louisa Alcott's *Good Wives*. A generation before, an undated little New York chapbook, *The Good Child's Present*,

had said the same: 'There is not a more beautiful sight on earth, than that of a happy family.' Early settlers felt that in its perfection it could only be experienced in the New World. The French immigrant J. H. St John de Crèvecoeur (1735–1813) had seen the life of the American farmer as paradise on earth: 'Where is that station which can confer a more substantial system of felicity than that of an American farmer possessing freedom of action, freedom of thoughts, ruled by a mode of government which requires but little of us?'[6] He concluded with a paean of thanksgiving: 'I bless God for all the good He has given me; I envy no man's prosperity, and wish no other portion of happiness than that I may live to teach the same philosophy to my children and give each of them a farm, show them how to cultivate it, and be like their father, good, substantial, independent American farmers.'[7]

Another eighteenth-century writer described the supposed responses of an admiring European traveller, who is passing the night in a log-house on a site which only six years before had been a wilderness but which is now sown with crops and stocked with cattle. The owner is self-sufficient, providing meat, dairy products and clothes for his family. The visitor notices that 'each one in the family filled his own place, and contentment, and satisfaction reigned through the whole'. After family prayers he retires to rest and reflection:

I fancied myself to have fallen upon a discovery, after which the sages of antiquity had sought in vain. And that

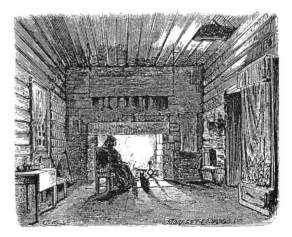

At home in the log house. From Jacob Abbott:
The Studio *(New York, 1855).*

here in the wilderness, I had found in what the greatest happiness of life consisted. For here was religion without colour of superstition – here was civil and religious liberty in perfection – here was independence – and the whole shut out from the disagreeable noise and bustle of the world.[8]

It was a sentiment that was to persist, and which can be encountered over and over again in the children's books of the last century. Lydia Sigourney, for instance, in *The Pictorial Primer* (1844) makes the pioneer's house epitomize the American achievement: 'You see a house built of logs. Large trees are growing near it, and a small brook runs by. It stands alone. Few people pass that way. It is in one of the new states where there are but few inhabitants.' The family in this one-room house have come from New England, and are to face a hard life before they can feel established. And beyond the immediate need to cut down trees and clear the ground lies their determination to build a church and a schoolhouse as soon as practicable. Meanwhile, they live contentedly in harmonious and godly simplicity, upon their own produce: 'Bowls of fresh milk are upon [the table], and bread that the mother has just baked, and eggs from their own poultry, and a cup of maple molasses. The father asks Heaven's blessing upon their food. Then, seated around, they partake of it with cheerful hearts.' During the day, while the father is out at work in the fields, the mother instructs the children from the books, few but highly prized, that they have brought with them: 'The one which they most value is the Bible, the Book of their Father in heaven. They teach its blessed words to their little ones. They read it together, before they retire to rest, and then the father prays God to protect and bless his family, and make them at last a family in heaven.'

Long after a more urban culture had become the lot of the majority, the instinct remained that in the log-house lay true happiness. It was romantic, as William Dean Howells' father felt when he took his family back to the simple life: 'It was like renewing the wild romance of [boyhood] days to take up once again the life in a log cabin interrupted by many years' sojourn in matter-of-fact dwellings of frame and bricks.'[9] It also taught true values, as many children's authors were to point out: 'Cheerfulness and innocence are connected with the life of a farmer. Large cities abound with countless temptations, with extravagance and vice. Vagrant and idle people gather there, desiring to be rich without labour, and thus opening the door to crimes, which, in an agricultural community, are unknown. Our farmers are our true nobility.'[10]

Some writers, like Louisa Tuthill, attacked the lust for money which drove young men from their homes in the country to seek their fortune in cities:

Alas! for our country...this insane craving for wealth which breaks up our pleasant country homes and sends our young men to the 'ends of the earth' or engulfs them in the maelstrom of city life! Is there no voice of warning loud and strong enough to reach the young, fresh, comparatively innocent, thousands of boys, who are still sheltered beneath the parental roof, in the blessed country - the quiet, health-promoting, peace-promoting country![11]

Other books described the transformation that could be effected by country life. Take only one example, Laura Richards' *Queen Hildegarde* (1889), in which a pampered heroine is sent from a luxurious city home for a character-forming three months on a farm. At home she is wont to sit nibbling caramels all day, discussing fashion and gossiping with equally empty-headed friends. On the farm she learns domestic skills and begins to take an interest in others. She comes back to town to 'one round of hospitals and tenement-houses and *sloughs of horror*', as a former friend dolefully put it. In other stories, fathers, suddenly aware of the corrupting influence of urban life, remove their families to an untainted existence on the land, where there is no room for idlers. Sons and daughters alike, purged and purified by the experience, have to learn practical skills and pull their weight. In this century, Dorothy Canfield's over-protected Betsy in *Understood Betsy* (1916) learns self-reliance when she leaves her sheltered city home to live on a Vermont farm.

The earliest novelist to celebrate the American domestic virtues was Catharine Maria Sedgwick, whose influence on subsequent writers is discussed later in the chapter. Like de Crèvecoeur, she was confident that the noblest and best way of life was to be found on the New England farm, and in her most famous novel, *Redwood*, it is shown to exert a formative influence on the characters of the wealthy family from Virginia who find themselves unwilling guests at the Lenoxes' farm. Catharine

Sedgwick was irked that foreign visitors could not see American perfection, and devoted much space in her books in trying to eradicate the sort of behaviour that might excite their scorn. (The American habit of spitting was a subject she returned to over and over again – 'a vulgarity in our national manners which cannot be passed over'.[12])

Home (1835), one of her stories for young people, is a triumphant celebration of the superiority of the New World, and of country life. To begin with, Mr Barclay, part-owner of a printing press, has married at the age of twenty-two – 'Thankful ought we to be, that in our favored land a working man need not wait until he be bald or grey before he may, with prudence, avail himself of the blessed institution of marriage... In Europe, ay, in what *was* "merry England" it is not so.' Confident that true equality, and life as an American ought to lead it, are far more easily attainable in the country where there are no artificial manners, he leaves New York, selling his fashionable ornaments and laying out $25 on a solid library of English and American history and literature. Of this, of course, the Bible is the foundation. Within fourteen years there are seven children, who all have their duties in the home since there is only one servant. We see the girls at work, in a scene that might have come out of Alcott or Beecher Stowe:

Martha, the queen bee, in her kitchen, as clean as any parlour... her little handmaids in her school of mutual aid and instruction, with their sleeves rolled up from their fat, fair arms, their curls tucked under their caps, and their gingham aprons, learning the mysteries of cake and pastry manufacture, pickling, preserving and other coarser arts; while another little maiden, her eyes sparkling, and her cheeks flushed with exercise, might be heard plying her broom 'up stairs and down stairs and in the lady's chamber', and warbling songs that might soothe the savage breast...

Nor were they in the least disqualified by these household duties for more refined employments; and when they assembled in the evening, with their pretty work boxes and fancy-work, their books and drawing, they formed a group to grace any drawing-room in the land.

Another such scene, in Miss Sedgwick's *The Poor Rich Man, and the Rich Poor Man*, pictures the Aikin family (rich in health and contentment, though lacking worldly wealth) employing themselves profitably:

Uncle Phil is sitting by the half-opened window with a year-old baby on his lap, telling over on its toes that charming lyric, 'This little pig went to market, and that pig staid at home'; aunt Charlotte was preparing a pot of wholesome soup... a little girl, six years old, was tacking worsted binding together for Venetian blinds whereby she got from a manufacturer... two shillings a week, and at the same time teaching a sister, something more than two years younger, the multiplication table.

And Mr Aikin thinks how right he was to choose a healthy life. The lawyers and merchants that he knows are falling prey to disease; the hair of one, once so black and glossy, has fallen out and he is reduced to wearing a wig, his eyes are buried in fat, his skin is mottled, and he lives in continued dread of an apoplexy. As for the rest, 'how many Pearl-street merchants over five-and-thirty are dyspeptics!'

The Aikin husband and wife are equal partners, as were the Barclays in *Home*, but this is a rarity with Catharine Sedgwick, and in *Redwood* we notice a significant departure from the Puritan concept of the family as a community ruled by the father and husband. Mr Lenox is not a worthless wastrel – he 'belonged to the mass of New-England farmers, was industrious and frugal, sober and temperate' – but his wife is his superior: 'intelligent, well-informed, enterprising and efficient'. She is the driving force, a formidable combination of practical skills and high intelligence:

Her husband and sons wore the finest cloth that was manufactured in the county... [Her] table was covered with the handsomest and the whitest diaper. Her butter and cheese commanded the highest price in the market. Besides these home-bred virtues, she possessed the almost universal passion of her country for intellectual pleasures. She read with avidity herself, and eagerly seized every opportunity for the improvement of her children.

The Sedgwick family life was apparently a happy and loving one, though the father allowed no dissent – 'Jove's thunder was to a pagan believer but a summer day's drifting cloud to it,' his daughter said of his awful frown.[13] But Sedgwick novels are remarkable for their number of degraded fathers. Sometimes, as in *The Boy of Mount Rhigi* (1847), they are vicious and brutalized – ' "He a father! He makes me lie for him, and steal for him; and if I don't, he tries to drown me." ' Some are self-indulgent voluptuaries, like Fanny's father in 'Fanny and

PHIL READING THE BIBLE TO HIS FATHER. Page 212.

Trying to redeem an errant father. A son reading the Bible to his drunken father. From Oliver Optic: Plane and Plank *(Boston, 1870).*

her Dog Neptune',[14] who while his wife and daughter are living under a regime of the strictest self-denial, is running up restaurant bills ('for sundry bottles of champagne and burgundy, for paties, omelets, soufflés &c. &c.'), so that Fanny's beloved dog has to be sold.

George Wilbur Peck was only expanding on this contempt when, a generation later, in *Peck's Bad Boy* (1883), he held up for derision the most abject father of all. Pa is a cowardly buffoon with a roving eye and an inability to hold his liquor, his son's whole purpose in life being to ridicule and humiliate him. ' "Some men can get full and not show it, but when Pa gets full, he gets so full his back teeth float, and the liquor crowds his eyes out, and wiggles all over his face, and he laughs all the time." ' The boy puts cayenne pepper on his father's beard, red ants in his clothes. To shock pious

acquaintances he fills Pa's pockets with playing cards and soaks his handkerchief in rum, and sees to it that Mrs Peck suspects him of adultery. 'For right down solid fun this book has never been equaled,' says the blurb.

Pa can at least be said to be a presence in the Peck household, but Huckleberry Finn's father (*The Adventures of Huckleberry Finn*, 1889) has so little significance that Huck's friends count him as having no family.

'Well, hain't he got a father?' [says Tom Sawyer]
'Yes, he's got a father, but you can't never find him these days. He used to lay drunk with the hogs in the tanyard, but he hain't been seen in these parts for a year or more.'

Pap 'always used to whale me when he was sober and could get his hands on me'; and when it is reported that his body has been found in the river, Huck is disbelieving and feels a shudder of apprehension: 'I judged the old man would turn up again by and by, though I wished he wouldn't.' Pap does turn up, a more degraded sight than even Peck's Pa:

His hair was long and tangled and greasy, and hung down, and you could see his eyes shining through like he was behind vines. It was all black, no grey; so was his long, mixed-up whiskers. There wasn't no colour in his face, where his face showed; it was white; not like another man's white, but a white to make a body's flesh crawl – a tree-toad white, a fish-belly white. As for his clothes – just rags, that was all.

Pap is incensed that his son is improving himself, looks clean and is going to school; ' "First you know you'll get religion too." ' He takes Huck over for a time and keeps him locked up, till the boy escapes. After that we hear no more of him; he is apparently regarded as beneath contempt, an irrelevance that no one can be bothered to remember.

But most often the fathers are feebly unable to cope, not mocked so much as brushed aside: 'He used to drink, and though not otherwise vicious, he was what the country people call "a poor shack".'[15] Another – a Pollyanna-like character who always sees the bright side – succeeds in drowning his daughter, but accepts the disaster manfully: 'It was a wonderful providence Ellen was drowned that day, for the very next he calculated on enclosing the cistern; but it was meant to be so – he always felt that Ellen was not long for this world'![16]

As early as 1836 the *Mothers' Monthly Journal* had castigated American fathers and accused them of dereliction of duty:

Fathers! How much is comprehended in that name ... And yet, how frequently is it pronounced without striking a single chord of affection in the heart – without recalling one pleasant emotion to the mind ... Do they always *appear* to their children, in the richly combined character of protector, provider, father, and friend? It is much to be feared that many do not, and that for this neglect only specious excuses can be furnished – the cares of the world, the pressure of business, the thirst for wealth!

At about this time, an Austrian immigrant to Boston was saying the same. The young men, he considered, were 'industrious, persevering, but not an amiable race of beings ... Money-making is the principal pursuit to which they are devoted; and which so completely absorbs their time that, between business and politics, they hardly find time for the cultivation of affection.'[17]

And contempt for the father is curiously prevalent in the American family story. He may be a 'poor shack', or selfish and indolent like Ellen Montgomery's father in *The Wide, Wide World*, who is lost at sea without any emotion being expended on him by either the heroine or the author. He may, by his ill-fortune or ill-health, provide a convenient spur for a hero or heroine to learn self-sufficiency and ultimately take over the reins: 'It was a common story. Large speculations, though undertaken in full prospect of success, had brought failure; and disappointment had brought paralysis. A week, and the struggle was over, and a broken-hearted family, gathered in the father's library, talked of future plans.'[18] Faith's father in *Faith Gartney's Girlhood* (1863) by Mrs Adeline Dutton Train Whitney (1824–1906) is an overworked businessman forever trying, like Maria Edgeworth's Rosamond in 'The Birthday Present', to pull paper over a basket that is too big. He is 'a man of no method in his expenditure. When money chanced to be plenty with him it was very apt to go as might happen – for French clocks, or whatsoever; and then, suddenly, the paper fell short elsewhere, and lo! a corner was left uncovered.' Worry and work make him ill, and Faith sees that she must take over the family finances.

The father may be dead, though unregretted, as in Alice Hegan Rice's story: 'When Mr Wiggs travelled to eternity by the alcohol route, [Mrs Wiggs] buried his faults with him, and for want of better virtues to extol she always laid stress on the fine hand he wrote.'[19] But the son in John Trowbridge's *Phil and his Friends* (1884) can find nothing good to say about his feckless parent; his grief at his death is because he had hoped to reclaim him. Sometimes the father is merely irrelevant, an absentee. It is a curious fact that although there are three families of cousins in Louisa Alcott's *Eight Cousins* (1875), no fathers are ever seen. Uncle Jem and Uncle Steve are at sea, and 'Uncle Mac was in such a minority ... he dared not open his lips, and let his wife rule undisturbed.' In *Little Women*, 'Marmee's' influence is supreme, for Father is away in the war. And in *Good Wives* her dominance continues. Though to the outsider, the author says resolutely, 'the five energetic women seemed to rule the house',

Illustration by Lizbeth B. Comins for Little Women,
from Ednah Dow Cheney: Louisa May Alcott, the
Children's Friend *(Boston, 1888).*

'the quiet scholar, sitting among his books, was still head of the family'; but Alcott fails to project him as a character, and he is superfluous to the story. (With the sons-in-law it is different: both John Brooke and Fritz Bhaer are shown as dominant husbands and fathers.) She must have had in mind the disruptive family role played in her childhood by her own father, to whom she became close only in later years. But the errant, absent or expendable father was a commonplace in American books of the last century, and the solid, affectionate presence such as Laura Ingalls Wilder's 'Pa' a rarity. Even where the father is loved and respected he is a secondary figure. ' "It's just this way," ' the heroine says to a close family friend in Kate Douglas Wiggin's *Mother Carey's Chickens* (1911); ' "First there's mother, and then all round mother there's a wide, wide space; and then father and you come next the space." '

The American mother presided over the hearth. 'She is the arch on which the law reposes, and on her depends its fulfilment,' said a Polish visitor in 1857, noting that the male preoccupation with business made her the mainspring of the family. 'The husband, the father, acts under her advice; he is the deacon where she is the high-priest. The woman,

wife, mother, or even daughter, exercises in all these wordly relations an omnipresence and latitude nowhere conceded to them in Europe.'[20] 'The very soul of the family,' an English travel book had commented a generation earlier; she had 'more sweetness, more goodness, at least as much courage, but more sensibility than the men'.[21] She was to maintain this role all through the century, so far as domestic fiction was concerned. She might be totally absent, as in the stories of female orphans to be considered later, but if she was there she ruled with never-failing spirit, courage and resourcefulness. No English storybook mother – even if she is, as in E. Nesbit's *The Railway Children*, effectively a single parent – plays the pivotal role of 'Marmee', or the valiant Mrs Wiggs of the Cabbage Patch, or Margaret Sidney's Mrs Pepper of *Five Little Peppers*[22] (both the latter books were dedicated to the authors' own mothers). They immolate self; they buoy up failing spirits, however great the adversity. ' "Here's the very thing," ' says Mrs Wiggs, at her wits' end to know how to keep her dying son warm. ' "It's my dress skirt. I don't need it a mite, settin' up here so close to the fire. See how nice it tucks in all 'round!" '

They keep their finger on the family pulse, receive confidences and confessions, soothe and advise: 'The mother's room! What family knows not that sociable spot – that *heart* of the house? To it go the weary, the sick, the sad, and the happy, all sure of sympathy and aid – all secure in their expectations of meeting there the cheering word, the comforting smile, and the loving friend.'[23]

The New England housewife added an extra dimension: she found time to pursue intellectual interests. Susan Sedgwick (1789?–1867), who wrote domestic fiction in the tradition of her more famous sister-in-law Catharine, shows us 'a sample of a good New England wife and mother' in *Alida, or, Town and Country* (1844). Mrs Tyler is seen making tarts, while she supervises the lessons of two of her children and rocks the cradle with her foot. Nevertheless, she is able to converse with a visitor

in the most agreeable manner of Miss Edgeworth, with whose works she appeared perfectly familiar; of different systems of education, then of Scott, Byron, and Heaven knows of whom besides, till I forgot myself entirely, and stayed till her tarts were snugly tucked in, the oven door closed, and she must have been in a fidget to get to her sick children.

In what at first sight seems a send-up but was not apparently intended as such, Frances Trego Montgomery transferred the idealized mother and the peccant father to a goat family. *Billy Whiskers; the autobiography of a goat* (1902) was the first in a series of stories about a goat who causes as much mayhem as any of the Bad Boys discussed in the next chapter. He marries Nanny – 'poor little meek Nanny with her gentle ways' – but after only two weeks of wedded bliss joins a circus where he achieves star status, but is also locked up to prevent further mischief: ' "How I wish Nanny was here to comfort me," thought Billy. "She was always so patient and cheerful." How like a man that was for Billy to forget all about Nanny while he was free and having a good time, but the minute he was in trouble to think of her.' Meanwhile Nanny has given birth to two kids, and has not forgotten her Billy, 'though all the young Billy Goats in the herd tried to make her do so'. (Billy, for his part, has been philandering with a donkey and lustfully eyeing a llama.) But when the scapegrace father escapes from the circus and painfully makes his way home he supposes, when he sees the happy family, that Nanny has married again: 'He watched her wash the kids' little faces for the night with her soft tongue and give them a good-night kiss on their little noses before they cuddled down to sleep beside her. It made Billy groan with lonesomeness to see it all.' Nanny can, of course, reassure him that her love has never faded: ' "Ever since you have been gone, I have walked to the fence every night and looked and waited for you to come back and it nearly broke my heart when night after night went by and you did not come." ' And the story ends happily, with the proud parents admiring their young.

In the contemporary English storybooks the father is a dignified figure, the unquestioned source of authority, very often occupying the position of bishop of his little flock as the Puritan writers had seen him. Evangelical fathers sometimes even told their children that they stood in place of God to them. Charlotte Yonge, though no Puritan, saw the father as priest, with the right to make all spiritual decisions for his children, to rule when they should be confirmed, whether they might go to particular church services, even whether or not they should take holy orders. She was prepared to acknowledge faults in them, but their word was law. Victorian fathers might see comparatively little of their chil-

dren, but with the English tradition of inherited wealth and the resultant upper-class leisure (a way of life that the middle classes sought to emulate), they spent much time in the home and writers represented their presence as remote, perhaps, but certainly pervasive.

English mothers, on the other hand, were rarely shown as having the energy and drive of their American counterparts. (The huge families that were the norm in the Victorian period often meant in real life that over a period of twenty years or more women were permanently pregnant, recovering from a confinement, or lactating.) They had little in the way of domestic duties, and the ordinary care of the children, even in a modest middle-class household, was undertaken by nurses. The early and mid-Victorian writers showed them as guardian angels who did not scold or punish, but whose look of grief could speedily bring remorseful tears to the eyes of the errant. However, they could be very demanding, and in the novels of Charlotte Yonge, whose message to girl readers was that their first duty lay at home, they consumed the lives of their daughters, who had to help teach younger siblings and – which seemed equally important – undertake a multitude of trivial social duties; upper- and middle-class women, in the absence of practical housework, felt a stern obligation to fill their time with elaborate social ritual. The late Victorian storybook mother had fewer children, was more light-hearted and looked on social life as entertainment rather than as solemn duty, but she delegated even more to servants, and seldom ate a meal with her children. ' "Why, Ann, did you never invite me before? You train these children to behave so nicely that I really must come sometimes, now that I have once found my way up," ' says one mother, who has been persuaded to make an appearance at nursery tea.[24]

The American boy's bond with his mother had no parallel in English books, where the tradition of the stiff upper lip (inculcated by the boarding-school system) precluded the expressions of devotion which were commonplace in American storybooks. Whereas an English boy might claim to have been influenced by the ethos of his school, Americans asserted that all the moral and religious training had come from the mother: 'I have an abiding faith that the best school on earth in which to start young ideas to shoot is a farmhouse with a mother in it as a teacher who possesses a good deal of ambition and grit enough to use the plum switch as well.'[25] Even when very young, the English boy liked to think himself emancipated from petticoat government; he would have been embarrassed to be reminded of the sort of dependence upon mother described by Mary Mapes Dodge:

Although he thought himself quite a big boy, as he strutted about in his home-made jacket and trousers, one thing would sorely trouble him – and that was to be away from Mother, even for an hour. There was something in Mother's way of singing, Mother's way of kissing hurt little hands and fingers, Mother's way of sprinkling sugar upon bread, and Mother's way of rocking tired little boys.[26]

William Dean Howells referred to mothers in much the same way in *A Boy's Town* and *The Flight of Pony Baker*, though, since he is writing from boy perspective – the pre-adolescent – he affects to be rueful. Mothers are first-rate when you are sick, and they do try to see your point of view, but they are tiresome about things like guns, about going swimming before you can swim, and they make fathers lay down the law when, left to themselves, fathers would turn a blind eye. It was acceptable to attribute yearnings for one's mother to much older boys – to West Point cadets, indeed: 'Homesickness had broken out in the fourth class of late, and had become epidemic. These boys were but boys, and the manliest of them all would – many a day – have given up his hopes of being a brigadier just to lay his head down on his mother's apron, and have her pet him and comfort him.'[27] Thus wrote Anna Warner, who with her sister regularly entertained the cadets at their home on Constitution Island. The young men, it may be supposed, sometimes confided such feelings to their sympathetic hostesses over the tea and gingerbread. It does not follow that they would have publicly admitted to them, but it is interesting that it was permissible at this date (1903) to refer to them in a boys' story.

Any boy who is tempted to cut away from the thraldom of domestic chores is soon repentant. One hero has a sagacious mother who, when she discovers that her son plans to stow away on a fishing schooner, decides to cure him once for all by arranging that the captain should make him work his passage. It was not a comfortable experience, as he tells his friends afterwards:

'Boys ... when I was on the Swiftsure I found out how lonesome a boy can be without his mother; I never knew before. Just as long as I can I shall stay where I can see my mother and speak to her; and if at any time one of you thinks that his mother isn't the best and dearest friend a boy can have, just do as I did, and it won't take you very long to find out that you are mistaken.'[28]

And it was also possible for young Americans to make a public affirmation of their feeling for their mothers. Edward Hale described Class Day at Harvard, when the Seniors were carried on the shoulders of their friends so as to pull flowers from the trees and present them to the girl of their choice: 'I chanced to see Hamilton, with his hands filled with flowers, looking about everywhere for someone. At last his face lighted up, and he made his way through the crowd, not to a pretty girl, but to his mother, whose eyes filled with tears as he threw his roses on her lap.'[29] Howells summed it up: 'She was not only the center of home to me; she was home itself, and in the years before I made a home of my own, absence from her was the homesickness, or the fear of it, which was always haunting me.'[30]

The English boy of the ruling classes was reared in a very different tradition. From the age of eight onwards he spent the greater part of the year away from home, in an exclusively male environment, where the prime desideratum was that he should learn to stand on his own feet and eventually exercise authority, and thus be prepared for a life of governing others. The image of a mother is sometimes evoked as a talisman, to keep a boy from impure thoughts or actions. Squire Brown says to young Tom, who is being dispatched to Rugby at the age of ten or so:

'If schools are what they were in my time, you'll see a great many cruel blackguard things done, and hear a deal of foul bad talk. But never fear. You tell the truth, keep a brave and kind heart, and never listen to or say anything you wouldn't have your mother or sister hear, and you'll never feel ashamed to come home, or we to see you.'[31]

Though we are shown a touching relationship between the delicate George Arthur and his widowed mother, Tom Brown's own mother faces the departure of her small son from home with equanimity, merely wondering whether he is old enough to manage the long cross-country coach journey by himself. She plays no subsequent recorded part in the boy's life; it is his headmaster, the great Dr Arnold, who he feels has moulded his character. And it is school, university, the regiment, which the English writers invoked as the focus of male loyalty. At the end of *The Bending of a Twig* (1906), a novel by Desmond Coke about the experiences of a boy at Shrewsbury School, the hero feels profound emotion at the thought of leaving: 'Slowly, surely, in the six long years, Shrewsbury had woven her spell round Lycidas, until she formed, and always would form as no other place (except perhaps Oxford) could ever form, a real part of his life.' Home, it will be noted, is irrelevant, and Coke dedicates the book 'To my house-master, to whom I owe all'.

The focus of home remains in the American writing for the young. It dominated Laura Ingalls Wilder's account of her childhood and youth. However daunting the circumstances in this chronicle of a pioneering family in the 1870s and 1880s, the resourceful and courageous mother sets up the few cherished household possessions that she has brought with her from Wisconsin, and rapidly creates a stable and secure home. We read with relish about the food that she lays before the family, the ordinary meals as well as the red-letter occasions; as we have seen in earlier books, food seems to serve to bind the family together. It is Ma that is the linchpin of the household; Pa, though loving and much loved, is at heart a boy, a little irresponsible and perennially restless. And in a very different book, Cynthia Voigt's *Homecoming* (1981), we are shown four children, illegitimate and with no memory of their father, abandoned by their sick and distraught mother, who are doggedly searching for a home. Until they can find the grandmother who may or may not accept them and take them in, the eldest sister who leads them nightly creates a home and provides food (which the author invariably carefully details) wherever they happen to have reached in their weary travelling.

CLASSIC FAMILY STORIES

Young Victorians in England – and many subsequently – derived their ideas of American family life from a handful of authors. Some of the earlier generations would have encountered Jacob Abbott's robust and purposeful Rollo and his friends. The three Katy books by Susan Coolidge (Sarah Chauncey Woolsey, 1835–1905) have less of an American flavour than these, and, perhaps significantly, have always been better known in England – where they are in the same league of popularity as *Heidi* and *Pinocchio* – than in their country of origin. Two books about poor families, *Mrs Wiggs of the Cabbage Patch* by Alice Hegan Rice (1870–1942) and *Five Little Peppers and How They Grew* by Margaret Sidney (Harriet M. Lothrop, 1844–1924), gave readers a more cheerful picture of poverty than anything they might encounter in England. But best-known of all, of course, was Louisa Alcott, whose *Little Women* (1867) 'has a place in American culture along with taffy pulling and Flag Day', as her biographer Martha Saxton proclaimed, but which is also on a different plane from the others, and can be regarded as a minor literary masterpiece.

What Katy Did (1872) and *What Katy Did at School* (1873) have remained continuously in print in England ever since their first publication, and even now are available in a variety of different editions. (The final *What Katy Did Next* is an unmemorable travelogue culminating in Katy's engagement to a young naval officer.) Few young Americans, on the other hand, have ever encountered them. When one examines them beside, say, *Little Women*, or such later favourites as Eleanor Porter's *Pollyanna* or Kate Douglas Wiggin's *Rebecca of Sunnybrook Farm*, one realizes that they are much closer to the English style of family story, and it is perhaps significant that all the books that Susan Coolidge's Carr family read are English ones – *Robinson Crusoe* and *Alice*, plus works by Mrs Sherwood, Maria Edgeworth, Elizabeth Sewell (*Amy Herbert*) and Mary Howitt (*Strive and Thrive*). And though it is often said that the first *Katy* was inspired by *Little Women* of five years before, it is in fact more like Charlotte Yonge's *The Daisy Chain* (1856). It is not just that two widowed fathers (both, by coincidence, medical men) are left to rear a large family, but also that the children themselves experience the sort of sheltered, leisurely childhood that, as has been said, is rare in American stories. There is a nurse, devoted family servants, and an aunt to oversee the household. In addition, life for Katy, Clover, Elsie, Dorry, Joanna and Phil Carr takes on the 'us' and 'them' aspect that was a commonplace in English books, where children felt that they were not so much part of a republic as ranged up against an immutable dictatorship whose directives were always arbitrary and unpredictable.

And like English children, the little Carrs play with single-minded absorption, knowing that there will be someone to mend the torn clothes and clear up the chaos when the day is over.

Katy herself, initially a headstrong tomboy with literary leanings, is a type of heroine that more than one female author, remembering her own youthful self, inclined towards. But, in a development unusual in an American book of that period – though much favoured by English writers – Katy injures her spine, and the 'Great Teacher' enrols her as a pupil in His own school, 'the School of Pain'. Led by the saintly Cousin Helen (a character whose charisma fails to convince most readers), she leaves wilful childhood behind her and becomes a thoughtful young woman – so thoughtful and responsible at the age of fourteen, indeed, that Dr Carr feels it necessary to send her away to boarding school to learn to frisk like a girl again.

And in *What Katy Did at School* we have one of the earliest examples of a genre that, though it was always a rarity in America, was to become enormously popular with English girls – popular enough to dominate the juvenile publishing scene in the 1920s and 30s – the school story. It contains ingredients which later were to become very familiar: the unjust accusation made by a purblind and obtuse headmistress, the naughty harum-scarum with a heart of gold, the oppressive and unfair teacher. The one element foreign to the English school story is the pupils' preoccupation with the boys in the neighbouring Arrowmouth College; Katy and Clover are as innocently unaware that there is another sex as any girls in a pre-1960 English story (brothers, naturally, come into a category of their own). But their companions are obsessed.

European observers would not have been surprised: 'From the earliest age at which these "Misses" begin their preparation for their career as "young ladies"...a never-ceasing series of what they call flirtations, but which takes the most decided form of coquetry, is carried on with intense ardour.'[32] Coolidge, rather than lecturing her readers about the folly of this practice, introduces a diversion to take the pupils' minds off the boys next door. Katy invents the Society for the Suppression of Unladylike Conduct, a literary group whose members spend Saturday afternoons composing comic verse.

If the Katy books seemed not so very different from home to the English reader, then the five chronicles of the Pepper family made up for it. Stories about the Victorian poor in England were designed either to teach moral or religious truths to the working class, or to awaken pity in the hearts of the more prosperous. One or two writers, such as Maria Louisa Charlesworth (1818–80), the author of *Ministering Children* (1854), even implied that it was necessary for the poor to suffer so that the charitable could earn spiritual bonus points by relieving them. It can be seen, therefore, that light-heartedness had no place in any story of English poverty, so that the merry laughter of the Pepper family and the happy outcome of their troubles seemed to belong to another world. 'Times were always hard with them now-a-days', we are told in the first chapter, and 'Mrs Pepper had had hard work to scrape together money enough to put bread into her children's mouths, and to pay the rent of the little brown house.' Nevertheless, she is unfailingly cheerful, and her 'noisy happy brood' make 'the little brown house fairly ring with jollity and fun'. There is a bad patch when the children have measles, but the cloud passes and soon 'the old, sunny cheerfulness began to creep [back again], and to bubble over as of yore'.

And now a fairy-tale element takes over. The doctor who cures Polly Pepper's eyes provides a new stove; but more than that – a rich family, enraptured by the Peppers and the spirit in the brown house, showers benefits on them. Their Christmas presents are particularly remarkable. In an English story, blankets, stout shoes and flannel petticoats would be thought appropriate for the poor. But though the Peppers do receive sensible gifts such as a shawl, a work-basket and a cookery manual, there are frivolous luxuries as well, of a sort usually only given to the wealthy: a cage with a singing bird, a large wax doll, and, most extravagant and useless of all, quantities of out-of-season flowers – heliotropes, pinks and roses.

Even more astonishing to children accustomed to the rigid Victorian class stratification, Polly Pepper is taken into this rich household, and settles down with no apparent social unease. And when she becomes lonely, the whole Pepper family is sent for, and joins her as a permanency. As with Polly, there is no problem of adjustment, and the two households integrate with perfect harmony. It is an outcome that all child readers must find completely satisfying, but that no English writer would have been able to provide.

Mrs Wiggs of the Cabbage Patch, in contrast, has its feet more firmly on the ground. Indeed, it has its sombre moments, and probably, given its subplot about the 'Christmas Lady' and the lover she has spurned, was never originally intended as a children's book, though it has long been classified as one. The Wiggses are desperately poor, and the little boy who is the breadwinner dies, cold, hungry, and overpowered by his responsibilities. But Mrs Wiggs' philosophy has always been that 'ever'thing in the world comes right, if we jes' wait long enough', and the episode is somewhat out of key with the comedy which Alice Hegan Rice finds in Cabbage Patch life, and indeed with Mrs Wiggs' account of Mr Wiggs' death:

'...and I kep sayin', "Oh, Mr Wiggs! You don't think you are dyin', do you?" an' he answered up jes' as natural an' fretful-like, "Good lan', Nancy! How do I know? I ain't never died before." An' them was the very las' words he ever spoke.'

'Was he a church member, Miss Wiggs?' inquired Miss Hazy.

'Well, no, not exactly,' admitted Mrs Wiggs reluctantly. 'But he was what you might say a well-wisher.'

It is the comedy that is remembered: the preparations in the Cabbage Patch on the red-letter day when the Wiggs family are given tickets for the theatre, with the one good dress divided between two little girls – ' "They do look kinder mixed, but I reckon it don't matter, so long as they're both happy," ' – and with everyone having her plaits ironed. But just as with the good things showered upon the Peppers, such a treat as the theatre (let alone the restaurant meal that follows) would have been undreamt of in the stories about the English poor. It was not so much that the theatre would have been considered evil in itself (plenty of American writers of the stricter evangelical school took that line) but that it was inappropriate for people of the Wiggses' station. A Sunday school treat, a penny reading organized by the church – these were in order; but there, in the Sunday school book, it must stop, lest The Poor (as Miss Charlesworth's *Ministering Children* always referred to them) should be tempted into a ruinously luxurious way of life.

Despite acute poverty, Mrs Wiggs and Mrs Pepper (both mothers of the dominant type that one associates with American stories) have succeeded in build-

ing warm and loving homes, and the families' affection and loyalty shine through the misfortunes. The same spirit pervades *Little Women*, a much greater book. Indeed, when one considers the fiction available for girls before 1868 we recognize it as a work of extraordinary achievement. Here Alcott broke away from high-flown sentiments and pious admonitions, from the overwrought emotion of Susan Warner, and presented attractive, credible, strongly differentiated characters with recognizable failings. Moreover, she credited her readers with enough intelligence to perceive these last for themselves, and forbore to point a finger or to lecture. Since it was her own background that she was depicting, she concentrated on characters and episodes in Alcott family life rather than on any story line. Written with little revision or reworking, in only six weeks, the book has an uncontrived spontaneity that is entirely lacking in the more pretentious *Moods* (1864) – the novel for which Alcott would have chosen to be remembered – and indeed in any of the domestic fiction that preceded her.

Little Women was not, of course, the full story of the Alcott girls' youth. Loyalty to her father, Bronson Alcott, a feeling that since she was writing for the young she should suppress the sadder episodes, made her present a security that had been lacking in a childhood haunted by the direst poverty, and, when she was eleven, by the threatened departure from the home of her father, fired by Shaker views about celibacy. Ardent and idealistic (Emerson described him as 'very tedious and prosing and egoistical and narrow'[33]), he existed in a ferment of inchoate theories about how life should be lived – which inevitably resulted in much suffering for those near him. His wife wrote with some bitterness in her journal in 1843:

A woman may perform the most disinterested duties – she may 'die' daily in the cause of truth and righteousness. She lives neglected, dies forgotten. But a man who never performed in his whole life one self-denying act, but who has accidental gifts of genius, is celebrated by his contemporaries, while his name and works live on from age to age.

To this a female friend added: 'A woman may live a whole life of sacrifice, and at her death meekly says "I die a woman". A man passes a few years in experiments in self-denial and simple life, and says "Behold a God." '[34]

They all drew to the fire, mother in the big chair, with Beth at her feet; Meg and Amy perched on either arm of the chair, and Jo leaning on the back. — PAGE 12.

'Marmee' with her children. Louisa May Alcott's drawing for the frontispiece of the first edition of Little Women *(1868).*

It says much for the sweetness of his daughter's nature that she not only maintained a deep affection for this wayward parent, but – unusually, as we have seen, among American female authors – did not write him off as a 'poor shack'. Indeed, she consistently presented fathers as wise and loving. True, they may be absent, but if we are allowed to meet them we know that they are stable presences. She believed that women should be capable of independence (there had been a moment when her mother had thought that she would be left to support the family, and the young Louisa had vowed to turn all her talents to the same purpose). ' "Being of age, I'm going to take care of myself, and not be a burden any longer," ' says Christie in *Work: a story of experience* (1873). ' "I'm old enough to take care of myself; and if I'd been a boy, I should have been told to do it long ago." '

But Louisa Alcott was no strident feminist. She thought that women were the primary domestic influence, the peacemakers who held families together and kept men on the right path: 'It was a pretty sight to see the one earnest, sweet-faced girl among the flock of tall boys, trying to understand, to help and to please them with a patient affection that worked many a small miracle unperceived,' she says of Rose in *Eight Cousins*. This was a role favoured by both American and English writers. 'It is woman's work to make ... homes, as the safeguard and earthly anchor of the men she is connected with,' said Charlotte Yonge.[35] And the ideal girl of Yonge's novels is one who waits on fathers and brothers and, by keeping them happy at home, prevents their feet from straying.

Alcott's own responsibilities were not only domestic; like Susan Warner before her she was the financial prop of the whole household. By the time she wrote *Jo's Boys* (1886) she was confident enough of herself in this role to write of the possibility of careers for women. In the final book of the quartet, the school of twelve boys run by Jo and her husband in *Little Men* has become Laurence College for both girls and boys. Here the girls are taught about women's rights, and the possibility that they too can have a career is put before them; Nan, indeed, is studying medicine, 'and at twenty was getting on bravely; for now, thanks to other intelligent women, colleges and hospitals were open to her'. There was nothing comparable in English girls' fiction at this date; Charlotte Yonge, in fact, punished one of her girls who wished to become a doctor by marrying her off to a charlatan Greek. (He soon abandons her, and when her family at last find her, in America, she is desperately trying to keep herself alive as a cheapjack photographer.[36]

The March girls from the start are independent. Meg, aged sixteen, is already a governess; Jo, fifteen, is a companion to her aunt, and only the twelve-year-old Amy is still at school. They are also, by English standards, extraordinarily free from chaperonage – a feature of American girlhood which had been remarked upon, disapprovingly, by European visitors. ('Their intercourse with men is without restraint. They invite them to their homes, receive their visits, walk with them and ride with them alone ... They go to parties and return home in the same carriage with any man of their acquaintance, quite unattended by any female relative or friend,' said one disconcerted Englishman.[37]) It is stressed that the March girls are 'simple-hearted' and innocent, and it is implied that they are young for their age and so can accept the fifteen-year-old Laurie from next door as one of themselves, without foolish thoughts of his being a beau. The relationship between the boy and the four sisters was, indeed, most unusual to English eyes. Girls living at home rarely met boys, unless brothers or cousins, until they 'came out' at the age of eighteen or so. And it would have been an uncommon adolescent English male who could have made himself so acceptable and companionable to a bevy of females (perhaps an uncommon American one, too, if one is to go by the boorish and bullying brothers who make frequent appearances in girls' stories).

But the home-made music, the theatricals, the Pickwick Club and Pickwick Portfolio, and the post office for communications between the March and the Laurence households, were instantly familiar. These were pastimes that large Victorian families in England loved to devise, and which American stories – more often than not about farm life where there was never a moment of leisure – rarely featured. Nor are Meg, Jo, Beth and Amy as deftly practical as most American heroines were shown to be. The Marches have a maid, and though all have their appointed domestic chores, cooking remains an arcane mystery. ' "Isn't bread 'riz' enough when it runs over the pans?" ' asks Jo, distraught, one day when as an experiment the girls have undertaken the housekeeping. The lunch they try to prepare is a disaster, and they have to fall back on bread and butter and olives, but it is treated as a joke, not as a serious failure of a woman's role.

The three sequels to *Little Women* are remarkable for an insight into happy marriage as keen as if the author had experienced it herself. Charlotte Yonge's viewpoint in her many domestic chronicles was always that of the unmarried daughter. In *Good Wives* Alcott can not only give a convincing picture of the early months of Meg and John Brooke's marriage, but also describe the despairing pangs of Jo, her *alter ego*, when she supposes Professor Bhaer is indifferent to her. Her incredulous joy when she discovers that he is not, and the subsequent half-comic trudge home in the rain under the same umbrella, are presented with such conviction that one could almost fancy she was writing from experience. The concluding paragraph of this chapter expresses the intensity of the author's feeling for home. Their mutual love now acknowledged, Jo leads her Fritz back to the March household: 'Though it came in such a very simple guise, that was the crowning moment of both their lives, when, turning from the night and storm and loneliness to the household light and warmth and peace waiting to receive them, with a glad "Welcome home!" Jo led her lover in, and shut the door.' And it is Louisa herself speaking when she has Beth say, acknowledging that she has not long to live, ' "It seems as if I should be homesick for you even in heaven" ', a declaration which encapsulates everything that her contemporaries were trying to convey about the primacy of home and family.

Little Women brought instant success, and the money that was so desperately needed for the Alcott family. But it might be said in the end to have become an albatross round the neck of its creator, sending her in a direction that she would not necessarily have chosen for herself. *Little Men* (1871) helped pay for 'the furnace and all the bills', she said in her journal in January 1872, and had been written, largely while she was on holiday in Rome, with some degree of enjoyment. By the time she came to *Jo's Boys* she was bored and exhausted, and longed, she wrote in the final chapter, to sink 'Plumfield and its environs so deeply in the bowels of the earth that no youthful Schliemann could ever find a vestige of it'. She put into Jo's mouth what she felt about her own career. She was glad that she had been able to make her mother's last years 'happy and serene', but she was tired of the fame, and resented the loss of liberty. Rueful about the voracious appetite of her juvenile readers for 'more stories; more right away', she described herself as 'a literary nursery-maid who provides moral pap for the young'.

Certainly the books outside the *Little Women* cycle seem limp and tired, and it is difficult to distinguish them from their contemporaries. *An Old-Fashioned Girl* (1869) was written while she could still take some pleasure in literary effort, and Polly's efforts to earn a living in Boston reflect some of her creator's own experiences. *Eight Cousins* (1874) is enjoyable, though over-sweet. But with *Under the Lilacs* (1878), the story – in which nothing much ever happens – of a lost circus boy adopted by a kindly but dull family, it is hard for the reader to plod on to the end. *Jack and Jill* (1880) is curiously reminiscent of *What Katy Did*, with its headstrong heroine learning lessons in 'the School of Pain' after an accident incurred through her wilfulness.

Nor can the many short stories be anything but a disappointment for those who only know *Little Women*. Jo, the successful author, feels that she has 'offered herself up on the altar of juvenile literature'. For Louisa Alcott, as for others who have written for children, this could only be second best.

A HUNDRED YEARS OF AMERICAN HEROINES

The nineteenth-century ideal for American young womanhood differed, then, in many respects from the English one. The girls we meet in American fiction are sturdier, more independent, freer in manner. They are also far more versed in practical housewifery. Writer after writer stressed that the 'accomplishments of the kitchen' were as important as those of the parlour. Even though Susan Warner herself did not take kindly to domestic duties (and on her sister's evidence tried to avoid them), she saw to it that Ellen Montgomery was drilled in housewifery by her Aunt Fortune, to become almost as competent (Ellen was also accomplished and ladylike, and able to impress aristocratic Scots in Edinburgh drawing-rooms). For one thing, efficient servants were hard to find. And for another, life was uncertain:

> The wants of American life, and the fluctuations of American fortune, call for a plan of female education, differing, in some respects, from the best arranged models of Europe. The girl who in January invites her little friends to a party in a superb mansion, may, in February, be compelled to cook her own dinner; and in March may have no dinner to cook. The daughter of a wealthy merchant... may be the bride of a backwoodsman; and a 'lodge in the wilderness' of the Great West, is like anything but a cottage orné.[38]

The sensible New England mother saw to it that her daughters, however affluent the family circumstances, were trained to be useful. ' "Here, Jane, come and sit down on this stool, and I will try to learn you to sew," ' opens one little book for Connecticut beginner readers in the 1840s.[39] Children of Jane's age were too young to stitch shirts and household linen, but were in 'the primary department of sampler and patchwork', as a Massachusetts Sabbath School Society publication put it.[40] Caroline

Gilman (1794–1888), brought up in Massachusetts (she later went to live in the South), remembered that though 'our pecuniary circumstances enabled us to indulge in the luxuries of life', her own mother was proud of the way the young Caroline could stitch a frilled shirt in two days, make her own bed, sweep and dust, and bake cakes and puddings.[41] 'If the arrangements of your father's household make it desirable and proper that you should assist at the ironing table, or in making cakes and pies, or in clear-starching your own muslins, or in making preserves or cleaning silver,' the *Young Lady's Friend* told its readers in 1837, they should no more be ashamed of it than they would be of combing their hair.

The same message can be found in countless other books of the period: domestic duties must come first. In Mrs A. J. Graves' *The Young Lady's Book of Good Examples* (1848), Sarah returns from boarding school to find her family has advanced in prosperity and now lives in a splendid mansion. Her father has filled her bookshelves with what her mother describes contemptuously as 'poetry, philosophy, history, and such useless things, and not one cookery book among them'. She is told that now her schooling is over she must make herself useful:

> But it cost her many a struggle. Often when she took the broom or duster in her hand to go through the daily routine of household occupations, or when her delicately formed fingers were soiled by her labor in burnishing the brass ornaments and iron castings of the parlor stove, the sight of an unfinished book lying open on the parlor table ... [was] to her temptation hard to be resisted.

Mary Livermore, whose Calvinist upbringing in early-nineteenth-century Boston has already been described in chapter 1, was a girl with strong intellectual leanings. (She was later to become a lecturer and author.) Her mother warned her that no amount of reading or learning would atone for ignorance of domestic affairs, and that no man would marry such a shiftless creature.

In a similar way, Charlotte Yonge was telling her girl readers that their obligations to their families were paramount; all intellectual interests must come a poor second to, say, amusing fathers or brothers. ' "I get time, one way or another," ' says spirited little Meta in *The Daisy Chain* (1856), motherless daughter of a wealthy landowner, who knows that

The tidy sister and the slattern. From Bourne H. Draper: 'The Busy Bee'. The Sunday School Story Book
(Philadelphia, 1831).

her primary duty is to keep her spoilt and indolent brother contented at home; ' "There is the evening, very often, when I have sung both him and papa to sleep. I had two hours, all to myself, yesterday night . . . and I had a famous reading of Thirlwall's *Greece.*" ' A Charlotte Yonge heroine might contrive time for this sort of dilettante reading, but serious study was treated as self-indulgence, and fifteen-year-old Ethel May, the central character in *The Daisy Chain*, who has a passion for Greek and Latin, is gently warned by her sister that it is preventing her from becoming ' "the sort of woman that dear mamma wished to make you" ', while her brother tells her more robustly that she ' "would

get into a regular learned lady, and be good for nothing" '. More than that, her father, though a doctor, dislikes her wearing glasses to correct her short sight, because they make her look odd. Femininity was the unquestioned desideratum on either side of the Atlantic, and however affluent the circumstances they portrayed, the American writers for girls insisted that their heroines must devote themselves to domesticity. Only Louisa Alcott ventured to suggest that there might be alternatives.

The nature of true gentility was something that preoccupied many of the earlier American writers for girls. Catharine Sedgwick, as has already been seen, was especially concerned to inculcate good manners, and for her as for many of those who wrote after her the natural ways of the country-dweller were infinitely to be preferred to the self-conscious posturing of the fine city ladies. True ladies were unashamed of menial tasks. They also dressed simply; there was much finger-wagging at those who aped high fashion – ' "O! Fashion, Fashion! what a deceiver and destroyer thou art! What a mockery, to call thy votaries friends!" ' groans one father whose daughters' lives are ruined by their vanity and folly.[42] Above all, true ladies were unaffected, and many American writers were resentful of the criticisms made by the more carping English commentators.

'I like [our] manners when they are not spoiled by affectation, and an attempt to imitate foreigners. I wish our people would be more independent in that respect. They ought not to despise themselves because, forsooth, every Englishman who darts through the country sees fit to ridicule their manners for differing from his own.' Thus spake Mrs Louisa Tuthill (1798–1879) in *I Will Be a Lady*, a story which contrasted, in a style which long continued to be popular, the virtues of the artless country-bred Beulah with the mincing, affected town girl who screams at the sight of a cow because she thinks this is ladylike, and calls all animal food 'meat' because she is afraid that if she gave the proper names she would be mistaken in New York for a butcher's daughter.

However, America was a land of equality, and Lydia Child emphasized in her preface to *The Girl's Own Book* (*c.* 1831) that though every girl 'in this land of precarious fortunes' should learn to be useful, daughters should be educated 'to fulfil the duties of a humble station, or to dignify and adorn the highest'. She therefore included something of everything in her book – an engaging compilation, very popular on both sides of the Atlantic – in which practical instructions for such matters as plain sewing and mending mingle with suggestions for amusements and games.

Mrs Child was one of many writers who stressed that the health of American girls of the period suffered from lack of sufficient open-air exercise; she therefore included some fairly boisterous games. Fanny Fern (Sara P. Parton) too in 1857 was urging her little girls to romp: 'I say fly kites; play ball; drive hoop; climb sheds and fences; tear your aprons (mind you mend them yourself); soil your hands and faces, tangle your hair, do anything that's innocent, but *don't* grow up with crooked backs, flat chests, sallow faces, dull eyes, and diseased brains.'[43] And perhaps with the idea of offsetting the city miss whose ideas circled round the latest fashions and who eschewed all outdoor activity – this type makes frequent appearances in mid-century girls' books – American writers introduced the 'romp' type of heroine. In English school stories of the 1920s and 30s she was to become very popular; often represented as Irish, and described as a mad-cap or a harum-scarum, she invariably had a heart of gold. Her mischievous escapades were held to be innocent, and were used to show up the sly and devious ways of the villainesses of the stories. But to the more sedate Victorians, such American tearaways as Rose Red in *What Katy Did at School* were dangerously near being hoydenish. Rose Red (her real name is Rosamond Redding) is 'the greatest witch in the school; not exactly pretty, you know, but sort of killing and fascinating. She's always getting into the most awful scrapes.' The scrapes are imaginative – Rose Red has a droll sense of humour and walks in crocodile to the bath house wearing her towel, soap and sponge as adornments – but without a vestige of malice or ill-breeding. And this is what the mother of Elizabeth Stuart Phelps' mid-century heroine, Gypsy Breynton, means when she says to her daughter, ' "Be sure you are a perfect lady" ', as she dispatches her to boarding school. Gypsy (whose first set of adventures in a series of four appeared in 1866) is a tomboy, styled 'Regular Romp' by her brother – a far healthier type, girls' writers pointed out, than citified fashion-plates. But it will be noted that she has a ladylike sense of decorum: 'There was not a trout-brook for miles that she had not fished. There was hardly a tree she had not climbed, or a fence or a stone-wall – provided, of course, that it was away from the main road and people's eyes – that she had not walked.'

If they had grown out of this sort of activities, then romps would fall back upon a spirit of raillery that never degenerated into unkindness. Mrs A. D. T. Whitney's Sin Saxon (her real name is Asenath Saxon)[44] is full of imaginative pranks, and has a literary talent. She may tease the spinster lady with whom she finds herself holidaying, but she perceives her goodness: ' "She helps one to feel what the higher – the Highest – must be." ' Elizabeth W. Champney made a similar prankster the heroine of *Witch Winnie* (1889), a serious book with a

The type of fashion-plate child denounced in storybooks. James H. Cafferty. Portrait of a Young Girl, c. *1850.*

religious message. Witch Winnie is high-spirited and full of fun, but fundamentally serious. She and her boon-companions try to fit themselves for heaven by enrolling themselves as 'King's Daughters', bound together by the common purpose of doing good, and evolve a scheme for giving poor city children vacations in the country. The dedication runs

> All their jokes the brownies lend her,
> She's a merry, mischief thing;
> But her heart is very tender –
> She's a Daughter of the King.

Out of these different elements – the practical little housewife, the irrepressible romp, the country girl and lover of nature – evolved a favourite type of American child heroine who lasted into this century and can be found in Mrs Wiggin's *Rebecca of Sunnybrook Farm* and the Canadian prototype, L. M. Montgomery's *Anne of Green Gables* (1908), as well as in Gene Stratton Porter's *A Girl of the Limberlost* (1909), in which Elnora collects rare moths to pay her way through high school and redeems her sour, unloving mother (a role usually filled in such fiction by the figure of a spinster aunt) by the sweetness of her nature.

These young women, often orphans, had a long history, and their manners changed to suit the taste of the times. In the 1850s they were, though fundamentally independent spirits, meeker and more soulful. 'First take a young and not-too-pretty child about ten years old,' wrote a historian of the mid-nineteenth-century sentimental novel.[45] 'Make sure the child is, or is shortly to be, an orphan... Now put the child under the care of a shrewish aunt, who resents being obliged to take care of her dead brother's brat.' The author, who was writing some forty years before recent feminist efforts to rehabilitate such novels,[46] goes on to summarize the pattern of so many of the sagas penned by such women's authors as Susan Warner, Maria Cummins, Jane Augusta Evans Wilson, Mrs E. D. E. N. Southworth, Ann Sophia Stephens, Caroline Lee Hentz, Mrs H. B. Goodwin, Marion Harland, E. P. Roe and others writing between 1850 and 1872. The orphan would be spirited; she might even 'sass' her aunt. Her pride, therefore, has to be subdued, usually with the aid of a saintly female spiritual mentor who tends to be an invalid, if not consumptive and doomed for early demise. The orphan is befriended

in her loneliness by 'an eccentric (Barkis-like) teamster and a wealthy (Cheeryble-like) merchant who now and then gives her a lollipop', and comes to spread light and gladness to all about her. 'You may end your story here if you will, with the child on the verge of adolescence; but it is preferable to carry on a few years in order that the heroine may be menaced by a proud, handsome, Rochester-like man aged about thirty who has traveled and sinned (very vaguely) in the Orient.' After being initially spurned, Mr Rochester proposes again and is accepted: 'Don't be alarmed at this: his pride has been humbled too, and he is now reformed. He may even become a minister, but he has plenty of money. For her part, the heroine now drops all fantastic notions of female independence, for she realizes that a woman's greatest glory is wifely submission.'

With the exception of Susan Warner, the writers cited above were not addressing themselves to children. But from 1850 – the date of *The Wide, Wide World* – until well on into the twentieth century, elements from this scenario keep recurring in American girls' books, and indeed were associated with them by English readers. The female orphan and the abrasive spinster aunt are to be found in scores of American stories. Among the better known, apart from *The Wide, Wide World*, *Rebecca of Sunnybrook Farm* and *Anne of Green Gables*, are Mrs A. D. T. Whitney's *Faith Gartney's Girlhood* (1863) and Eleanor Porter's *Pollyanna* (1913). Susan Coolidge's Katy has such an aunt, though it is the benign influence of Cousin Helen which helps to break her of her wilful ways. Even the 'Barkis-like teamster' who takes Ellen Montgomery to Aunt Fortune's farm in *The Wide, Wide World* is, in the person of Jeremiah Cobb, performing a similar mission for Mrs Wiggin's Rebecca Randall fifty-three years later. Matthew, who brings Anne back to his tart spinster sister at the Green Gables farmstead, is another such. The Cheeryble-style merchant is often present too; Rebecca calls hers 'Mr Aladdin' (his real name is Alan Ladd), and by the end of the book, when he opposes the idea that she should have a career, we realize that she is destined to marry him, just as Jerusha Abbott (another orphan) marries her benefactor in Jean Webster's *Daddy Long-Legs* (1912). The 'proud, handsome, Rochester-like man' is, in fact, not such a common element in children's books. Though Susan Warner made Elfleda's suitor in *Queechy* (1852) a Byronic English

The farmer's daughter comes to town. Lithograph by Augustus Kollner in Common Sights in Town and Country
(American Sunday School Union, n.d, c. 1850).

landowner of fabulous wealth, we are assured that he 'had pride enough to keep from low company, and make him abhor low pursuits'. And Elfleda has succeeded in converting him to a proper religious state of mind by the end of the novel.

Conversion plays a dominant part in these heroines' lives, but after the 1850s it tends to be of a secular sort: instead, orphans bring warmth and light where there has hitherto been cold and dark. Sometimes they are set from the start to irradiate the lives of others; sometimes, like Ellen Montgomery, they have first to pass through a fiery furnace. The pattern – one can hardly call it a plot – of *The Wide, Wide World* was to produce Rebecca, Anne and Pollyanna fifty and sixty years later. But where did Ellen, and indeed the whole genre of charismatic orphans, spring from? Richardson's *Pamela* (published 1740–1) is an obvious starting point for novels about unattached young persons

accumulating experience in a hostile world. There was also Susanna Rowson's *Charlotte Temple* (published in England in 1791, in the US 1794), which was a runaway American best-seller for decades. Designed for 'the perusal of the young and thoughtless of the fair sex', this is a moral story about a girl who, unlike the strong-willed and calculating Pamela, does *not* resist seduction, and elopes from England to New York where she gives birth to a daughter and dies.

Fatherless Fanny, or The Memoirs of a Little Mendicant (1811), a tale by an unidentified English author about a girl of immaculate virtue, staggering beauty, winning personality and unknown parentage, was another romance very popular with susceptible females and contains many ingredients to be found in later works. Fanny is left in a young ladies' seminary where she is treated by the proprietress with crawling deference or cruel contempt, according to how recently the school fees have been paid. (Frances Hodgson Burnett was to use the same situation in *Sara Crewe*.) She is adopted by a dashing young nobleman (because of a hoax he thinks Fanny is a lost dog), and experiences many a vicissitude and attempted seduction before she discovers her parents and marries a duke. Like Ellen Montgomery two generations later, Fatherless Fanny, 'lovely, artless Fanny', has her guardian angel, a young woman who teaches her about religion: 'With what rapture did the amiable instructress awaken, in the docile mind of her beloved Fanny, the first conceptions of the Deity, and teach her guileless lips to pronounce the first word of praise and gratitude.'

Jane Eyre (1847) also made a deep impression. There was not only the never failing attraction of the orphan buffeted by uncaring society, but also the sardonically masterful Mr Rochester. In *Beulah* (1859) Augusta Evans Wilson, an Alabama author whose later *St Elmo* was to be a best-seller, followed Charlotte Brontë's model with unabashed faithfulness. Beulah, from the orphan asylum, is adopted by the stern Dr Guy Hartwell, embittered by his loveless marriage to a heartless flirt who is also insane, and after many a mishap she becomes his wife. The author's emotions were so inflamed by the thought of Jane Eyre demurely kissing her blind master and accepting his proposal of marriage while still addressing him as 'sir' that she reproduced the situation in her own book:

'Give me your hand, Beulah...There, is it mine?'
'Yes, sir, if you want it.'
'And may I claim it as I choose?'
'Yes, sir.'

But leaving aside Mr Rochester and his creator, the author who seems to have exerted much influence on the development of the American storybook heroine, and upon Susan Warner's in particular, was Catharine Sedgwick. In her first work, *A New-England Tale* (1822) – a book begun as a Sunday school story but expanded to novel length and set in the Berkshire Hills, whose scenery she describes with much feeling (Susan Warner was to imitate this with her descriptions of upstate New York) – we meet a heroine who is going to become very familiar: Jane Elton, meek, demure, long-suffering, and an orphan. She is sent to live with her aunt Wilson who uses Jane like a servant. Jane endures all with Christian fortitude, and the

good that she does is contrasted with the cant and lack of charity of her aunt. ' "It seems to me, Jane ...you pick fruit from every good tree, no matter whose vineyard it grows in," ' says the aunt, exasperated by her niece's ability to see virtues in everyone. Ellen Bruce, the orphan heroine of Sedgwick's second novel, *Redwood*, is even more the prototype of the Ellen of *The Wide, Wide World* and many subsequent girly romances. She is of flawless virtue, prone to tearfulness, but 'the natural gaiety of childhood, though sometimes intermitted, was not impaired', and she can gambol with her kitten and chase a butterfly like the artless child she is. Thanks to her female guardian angel she is accomplished in drawing, French and Italian, history and poetry, but she is also a practical little housewife and a good sick nurse.

Above all, she is a potent force for good. In an episode which made a great impression on Miss Warner, Ellen gives her Bible to the godless Mr Redwood with a shy note asking him to treasure it for her sake. Miss Warner was to use the episode in *Melbourne House*, where Daisy Randolph puts on to her father's shaving soap this note: 'Dear papa, wont you think about being a Christian? Do not be displeased with "Daisy".' Both Ellens, and indeed all Miss Warner's heroines in spite of their rustic backgrounds, possess natural and graceful manners which are the admiration of even the most sophisticated. ' "She is a fascinating child," ' says one of Ellen Montgomery's well born Scottish relations, though reluctant to concede thus much to a Yankee: ' "the best-bred child in the world".'

Virtuous orphans, as has been shown, had long been popular with authors and readers alike, but in *A New-England Tale* and *Redwood* we do seem to encounter for the first time what was to become a standard character in American girls' stories – the granite-hewn New England aunt. Perhaps the climate did not favour the type in Old England – at any rate, they are creatures uniquely of the New World, highly capable, furiously energetic, self-sufficient and houseproud; able to set broken arms with the same efficiency as they salt a pig or make butter. They are always down to earth – faced with a niece's ardent outpourings about 'high and holy work of love', the aunt in Mrs Whitney's *Faith Gartney's Girlhood* tells her not to be 'fine and transcendental', and adds 'There's your mother's mending basket, brimful of stockings.' The warmth of their hearts varies: Aunt Wilson in *A New-England*

Tale is a Calvinistic virago, but Miss Debby in *Redwood*, on the other hand, is benevolent under the craggy exterior. She is over six foot tall, bushy-eyebrowed with weather-beaten skin and grizzled hair worn in a long braid which 'did not require, in her judgement, more than a weekly adjustment'. But her kind expression humanizes the hard features, and affects bystanders like sun on a November day.

Rebecca of Sunnybrook Farm has two aunts; the gentle kindness of Aunt Jane is offset by the harsh practicality of Aunt Miranda, of whom we are told that she uses her heart only for the pumping and circulating of blood: 'She was just, conscientious, economical, industrious, a regular attendant at church and Sunday-school, and a member of the State Missionary and Bible societies but in the presence of all these chilly virtues you longed for one warm little fault.' Ellen Montgomery's Aunt Fortune is much the same: brusque and abrasive, 'sharp all over'. She takes a poor view of the child

The ideal of girlhood – 'twelve years old, with a face like a flower', 1893.

that her improvident brother has foisted upon her and, practical as ever, at once dyes the girl's white stockings to a more sensible shade. Her heart takes a lot of melting, and compared to Pollyanna who thaws out Aunt Polly fairly quickly, and to Anne of Green Gables who has the same effect on Marilla Cuthbert, Ellen has a Herculean task.

But in showing this interest in aunts, American writers gave a prominence and a status to spinsters that is lacking in English books for girls. Nor did they always have to be relations. In *Faith Gartney's Girlhood*, for example, there are two girls who will never marry, to whom 'earthly having and holding should never come. God puts such souls, oftener than we think, into such life. These are his Vestals.' A third character is a middle-aged nurse – to unsympathetic eyes 'a scrawny, sour-looking old maid' – who dedicates herself to those who are desperately ill: ' "*Somebody's* got to nurse small-pox, and yellow fever, and raving-distracted people; and I *know* the Lord made me fit to do just that very work." ' She didn't marry, she says, because ' "the Lord gave me a pretty plain indication that He hadn't laid out that kind of life for me. So I just looked round to find out what better he had for me to do." ' She goes through life choosing, metaphorically and in fact, what she calls 'the drumsticks of the chicken' – in other words, what other people reject. Spinsterdom, as Mrs Whitney saw it, was a vocation, not forced upon women but taken up as an act of self-abnegation.

When Martha Finley's last Elsie Dinsmore book appeared in 1905 the taste in heroines had changed. Elsie is not an orphan – indeed, as has been seen in chapter 4 she is unwholesomely over-fathered – but she belonged to the artless, demure, effortlessly good type of heroine encountered in the earlier American girls' story. Although *Little Women* and *What Katy Did* had shown that heroines need not be orphans to be popular, writers still hankered after them and continued to weave fantasies about wistful girl waifs. But by the turn of the century there was a new style. They still won all hearts (except their aunts'), just as the Ellens and Elfleda and Daisy Randolph and Elsie Dinsmore had done, but they did not seek to convert those around them by the truths of the Bible so much as by their own personality.

Kate Douglas Wiggin's *Rebecca of Sunnybrook Farm* – Rebecca is not in strict fact an orphan, but fatherless and adopted by her mother's two spinster sisters – depicts the most attractive heroine in this tradition. Published two years before the final Elsie book, it is the beginning of a new trend heralding the joyful, highly articulate little girl with a non-stop tongue. An important element is that she is imaginative and can rise high above the everyday practicalities which for so many writers of the past had been the be-all and end-all of a woman's life:

The bare little farmhouse was a fixed fact, but she had many a palace into which she now and then withdrew – palaces peopled with stirring and gallant figures belonging to the world of romance; palaces not without their heavenly apparitions, too, breathing celestical counsel. Every time she retired to her citadel of dreams she came forth radiant and refreshed, as one who has seen the evening star, or heard sweet music, or smelled the Rose of Joy.

But though Rebecca's teacher plans a career for her, and the 'Barkis-like teamster' admiringly predicts that she will be ' "somethin' remarkable – a singer, or a writer, or a lady doctor" ', we guess she is ultimately destined to marry the Cheeryble merchant, and that this represents for the author a woman's greatest happiness.

When we first meet her, 'a little brown elf in buff calico' with eyes like 'stars of twilight fair' (Mrs Wiggin here quotes Wordsworth), Rebecca is sitting by the side of Mr Jeremiah Cobb on his stage-coach and exercising her powers of enchantment on him. (He tells his wife later that 'whenever the child looked at him she knocked him galley west'.) We leave her, now seventeen, having finished with high school and won many more hearts, giving up her plans for a teaching career to nurse her sick mother. But the grim Aunt Miranda has died and left her the house, so that she now has a home to offer her family.

Five years later L. M. Montgomery produced a Canadian version of the prattling, imaginative orphan. *Anne of Green Gables*, set in Prince Edward Island, is unashamedly derived from *Rebecca*, and it is difficult to distinguish between the two girls. Anne Shirley (who, if people won't call her 'Cordelia' as she would so dearly love, insists that they spell her name with an 'e') arrives at Avonlea sitting beside another Barkis – only this 'time he and his spinster sister are going to adopt her, in spite of the fact that they really wanted a boy orphan. She says to him on the journey: ' "Would you rather I didn't talk? If you say so, I'll stop. I *can* stop when I make up my mind to it, although it's difficult." '

But Matthew Cuthbert is knocked sideways by 'this freckled witch' who asks him such questions as ' "Have you ever imagined what it must feel like to be divinely beautiful?" '; and soon everybody in Avonlea is, too, even those initially hostile. 'The good stars met in your horoscope,' says the author on the title-page, quoting Browning this time, 'Made you of spirit and fire and dew'. The first book was followed by five others dealing with Anne growing and grown-up, but qualities that are attractive in a child become tiresomely fey in an adult.

Jean Webster's orphan Judy – Jerusha Abbott, named from a tombstone and a telephone directory – in *Daddy Long-Legs* is handled better. She is seventeen when we first meet her, and has never received a letter or a birthday present nor even travelled on a train. A rich and well disposed (and youngish) trustee at her orphanage offers to send her to college, stipulating that in return she should write him a monthly letter recording her progress, though he intends to stay unseen and shelters under the name of 'John Smith'. These letters, artlessly laying bare all her experiences and hopes and secrets as well as expatiating upon the subjects she is learning, form the substance of the book. In spite of her disadvantaged background she has the assurance and ease of all American heroines, and these never fail her when she comes to 'room' with patrician contemporaries or goes to stay in their homes. 'John Smith' naturally loves her as much as we do; and finally, 'Reader, I married him.'

In contrast to these two, Eleanor Porter's Pollyanna seems cast in an older mould. She is the little evangelist, albeit secular, spreading light all round her. She arrives at the house of a cold, unfeeling aunt who does not want her, but by playing the 'just being glad' game melts that icy heart and many others: ' "For long years I have been a cross, crabbed, unlovable, unloved old man ... Then one day, like one of the prisms that you love so well, little girl, you danced into my life and flecked my dreary old world with dashes of the purple and gold and scarlet of your own bright cheeriness." ' The whole community is indebted to her. She shows a despairing minister the way he must tread, and her shining eyes inspire the doctor with 'new-found exaltation' in his profession. She cements marriages, cheers invalids and widows, finds a home for all the homeless – whether puppies, kittens or boys. We cannot wonder when we hear in *Pollyanna Grows Up* (1915) that ' "Dr Ames says he hears she's revolutionized the whole town where she came from." '

To the sceptical reader the once famous diary of Opal Whiteley seems to have been written by an adult strongly influenced by such books as *Rebecca* and *Anne of Green Gables*. First published in 1920, it purports to be the work of a waif of six or seven reared in a lumber camp in Oregon by harsh foster-parents. (In fact we know now that Opal Whiteley was schizophrenic, which explains much, and that in reality she was brought up in a normal way by her own family who suffered greatly from the publicity at the time of the diary's first publication.) The author's theme is Wordsworthian wonder at the world that lies around her: 'So many thoughts do abide near with us. They come from heaven and live among the flowers and the ferns and often I find them in the trees. I do so love to go on searches for the thoughts that do dwell near about.' The writer is full of whimsical, anthropomorphic imaginings; all the animals in her life – there are many and she is always in trouble for the attention she lavishes upon them – are given names like Louis II, le Grand Condé ('a wood-mouse with [*sic*] likes to travel in the sleeve of my red dress') and Menander Euripides Theocritus Thucydides ('a most dear lamb that had needs to be mothered'). And there is a hint of the Cheeryble figure – of Adam Ladd or Daddy Long-Legs – in 'the man who wears grey neckties and is kind to mice'. The diary is a curious last echo of the orphan theme, which had engaged so many female writers.

NOTES

1. Lucy Larcom: *A New England Girlhood* (Boston, 1889), 104.
2. Charlotte Yonge: *Countess Kate* (London, 1862).
3. Anthony Trollope: *North America* (London, 1862), I, 37.
4. *Little Pussy Willow* appeared in *Our Young Folks*, 1866–7.
5. Louisa Alcott: 'An Old-Fashioned Thanksgiving', *Aunt Jo's Scrap-Bag* (Boston, 1882), VI.
6. J. Hector St John de Crèvecoeur: *Letters from an American Farmer* [1782], ed. Albert E. Stone (Penguin American Library, Harmondsworth, UK, and New York, 1981), 52.
7. ibid., 65.
8. [Thomas Brockway]: *The European Traveller in America* (Hartford, Conn., 1785).
9. William Dean Howells: *Years of My Youth* (New York, 1916), 45.
10. Lydia Sigourney: *The Boy's Book* (New York, 1843).
11. Louisa Tuthill: *Get Money* (New York, 1858).
12. Catharine Sedgwick: *Morals of Manners, or Hints for Our Young People* (New York, n.d. [*c.* 1846]).
13. Seth Curtis Beach: *Daughters of the Puritans* (London, 1967), 10.
14. This appeared in *Stories for Young Persons* (New York, 1840) and *Pleasant Words in Tales and Stories* (London, 1853).
15. Catharine Sedgwick: *Facts and Fancies for School-day Reading* (New York, 1848).
16. Catharine Sedgwick: *The Poor Rich Man and the Rich Poor Man* (New York, 1836).
17. Francis Grund: *Aristocracy in America* [1839] (Harper Torchbook edn, New York, 1959), 64.
18. *In the Clearings* (American Unitarian Association, Boston, 1873).
19. Alice Hegan Rice: *Mrs Wiggs of the Cabbage Patch* (New York, 1901).
20. Adam G. de Gurowski: *America and Europe* (New York, 1857), 392.
21. J. Goldsmith: *A View of the Character, Manners and Customs of the North Americans* (Philadelphia, 1810), 22.
22. Margaret Sidney [Harriet M. Lothrop]: *The Five Little Peppers and How They Grew* (Boston, 1881).
23. *Life in the West, or The Moreton Family* (ASSU, Philadelphia, 1851).
24. L. B. Walford: 'Such a Little Thing', *Atlanta*, Dec. 1888, p. 216.
25. Louis Albert Banks: *An Oregon Boyhood* (Boston, 1898).
26. Mary Mapes Dodge: 'Trapper Joe', in *The Land of Pluck* (New York, 1894).
27. Anna B. Warner: *West Point Colors* (New York, 1903).
28. 'Tom's Troubles', in *Fifty-Two Stories of Boy-Life at Home and Abroad* (London, 1894).
29. Edward Hale: *Sunday School Stories*, Part II (Boston, 1889).
30. Howells: op. cit., 23.
31. Thomas Hughes: *Tom Brown's Schooldays* (London, 1857).
32. Thomas Colley Grattan: *Civilized America* (London, 1859), II, 57.
33. Quoted by Martha Saxton: *Louisa May, a modern biography of Louisa M. Alcott* (Boston, 1977), 151.
34. ibid., 144.
35. Charlotte Yonge: *Womankind* (London, 1877), 257.
36. Charlotte Yonge: *Magnum Bonum* (London, 1879).
37. Grattan: op. cit., II, 57.
38. Anna Bache: *Little Clara* (Philadelphia, 1842).
39. *Little Lessons for Little Learners. In Words of One Syllable* (New Haven, Conn., 1840).

40. *The Truant Girl* (Boston, 1847).

41. Caroline Gilman: *Recollections of a Housekeeper* (New York, 1834).

42. Aunt Hattie [Harriette Newell Baker]: *Fashion and Folly* (Chicago, 1883).

43. Fanny Fern [Sara Payson Parton]: *The Play-Day Book* (New York, 1857).

44. Mrs A. D. T. Whitney: *A Summer in Leslie Goldthwaite's Life* (Boston, 1866).

45. Alexander Cowie: 'The Vogue of the Domestic Novel', *South Atlantic Quarterly*, Vol. 41 (Oct. 1942).

46. Notably by Jane Tompkins in *Sensational Designs: the cultural work of American fiction 1790–1860* (Oxford, 1985).

7. Frank and Manly: Ideals of Boyhood

STORIES FOR BOYS: BRITISH AND AMERICAN COMPARED

'The mild tales that girls read simply to pass away the time are ineffective with [British boys],' wrote Charlotte Yonge in 1887. 'Many will not read at all. Those who will read require something either solid, droll, or exciting.'[1] She suggested various adventure stories that fulfilled male demand for 'a pretty book with plenty of killing', remarking that if boys could be kept away from penny dreadfuls while they were growing up there was some hope for the future. The authors she recommended – Jules Verne, George Manville Fenn, W. H. G. Kingston, Captain Mayne Reid, George Henty, Robert Ballantyne (with reservations about the orthodoxy of his religious views) – provided adventure mingled with information and a certain amount of preaching. But the last was a variable quantity. While, for instance, the religious message was strong in Kingston's books, Captain Mayne Reid, who described himself in the preface to his second book, *The Scalp Hunters* (1851), as 'a coarse, crude and careless writer', usually forgot or did not bother to include any in the welter of bloodshed and violence. Since Mayne Reid provided an abundance of detail about natural history, Charlotte Yonge seems to have thought it was safe to include him in her list of recommended reading, though she could not have known his more lurid romances, which can be both sadistic and erotic.

Similarly in America, it was recognized that boys required something more robust than the usual style of Sunday school moral tale, and in their efforts to keep them from the dime novel, certain establishment authors such as Oliver Optic and Captain Mayne Reid sometimes produced books that were nearly as sensational. But though both countries had ostensibly the same vision for their boys – a desire that they should be frank and manly – and though both turned out thousands of stories about perilous and patriotic adventures, their eco-nomic and social circumstances during the last century were so very different that there seems to have been little exchange of this type of tale. For, while British authors were addressing themselves to boys who must always be reminded that they were part of a whole infinitely more important than themselves – whether it was the team or the school, or the workforce or regiment that lay in the future – American authors were stressing that individual effort was what counted, and that every boy had it within him to be a Franklin or a Lincoln.

Thus the Victorian boys' book in England, while inculcating the manly virtues, insisted on the need for self-abnegation. Little boys, when they arrived at school (and stories of boarding-school life were very popular in the later years of the century), had to be taught – harshly, very often – that they were insignificant worms, that what mattered was the school, their house, the cricket or football team. As they progressed up the school they would be able to contribute more, to bear responsibility, but it was only what they could give that mattered, not they themselves. At the end of Desmond Coke's *The Bending of the Twig*, an account of experiences at Shrewsbury School already touched upon in the previous chapter, Lycidas Marsh – his extravagant first name is a symbol of the individuality that he has to cast from him – has a last encounter with his housemaster before he leaves school. Mr Alton tells him that although he started with strange ideas, notably the one that he could do anything, he has in fact done well, has given real help as head of his house and set a good example of duty:

'I must say just this: when you get to Oxford, try to cultivate a belief that you *can* do what you *ought* to do. I don't mean you to go back to your old preposterous belief in yourself; self-confidence is quite different from self-conceit. And another thing: both at Oxford and afterwards, remember how much Shrewsbury has done for you, and do all you can for her. I want your School –

Frontispiece by E. W. Kemble for the first edition of The Adventures of Huckleberry Finn, *1884.*

and of course, your 'Varsity – to be a kind of minor religion with you, ranked by the side of patriotism.'

And it was this message that rang out from chapel pulpits, in school assembly halls, in house masters' studies, both in real life and in fiction, and which, seeping down into Sunday school prize books and into magazines and comics, affected boys at every level of English society. The same spirit held regiments, even the British Empire, together, and must have played an important part in the enduring of four years' slaughter on the Western Front during the First World War.

But belief in oneself, in the individual as sole arbiter of his destiny, is the message of the American boys' book. 'Tout soldat français porte dans sa giberne le bâton de maréchal de France,' Napoleon is supposed to have said, and the example of Franklin stirred many heroes of fiction – as *A Present from New York*, published by Mahlon Day in 1828, succinctly put it:

What lad is there who has not heard of Dr Benjamin Franklin, the great American Philosopher and Statesman? He was once a poor boy, wandering up and down in the earth; and by very careful attention to his manners, and industrious and studious conduct, he stored his mind with a fund of useful knowledge, and rose, by degrees, to the most honourable stations amongst men.

Some fifty years later Horatio Alger has the hero of *Bound to Rise* say much the same: ' "I'm poor now, but so was Franklin. He worked hard, and tried to learn all he could. That's the way he succeeded, I'm going to do the same." ' And at the library he takes out Rollin's *Universal History*. ' "I like stories very much, but I have only a little time to read, and I must try to learn something." ' This emphasis on self-improvement through books is to be found in many stories by Alger and his kind. ' "You see, my lad, my studious habits paid me in money," ' the eponymous hero of Alger's *Ragged Dick* (1867) is told; ' "If you ever expect to do anything in the world you must know something of books." ' Religion helps too: ' "Well, Dick," ' muses the same hero, ' "you're gettin' up in the world. You've got money invested and are goin' to attend church." '

Study plays far less part in the English books, and in the school stories, indeed, it is only sport that matters; to be known as a 'swot', 'sap' or 'grind'

Ragged Dick was originally serialized in the Student and Schoolmate *in 1867. It was published in book form the following year.*

– or whatever the particular school idiom was for one fond of his books – was to be condemned. Even the masters deprecated it. ' "He won't believe me when I say he will never have any influence without games," ' laments Lycidas' housemaster in *The Bending of a Twig*. The cult of athleticism dominated the English public school ethos from the 1850s onwards, the irony being that Dr Thomas Arnold, whose reforms at Rugby School in the 1830s had such a profound effect upon the entire public school system, had no interest in team games (except as a diversion from more unruly male pastimes), but sought to promote good learning and high standards of Christian behaviour and moral responsibility among his pupils.

The American boy, who often in the early days received only a few weeks' schooling in the year, was part of no team. He stood by himself. Entrepreneurial skills – which only in the later decades of this century have been at all encouraged in British youth – were all-important, indeed might come to the rescue of a family in dire need, and were much promoted in Sunday school literature, as has already been seen. The ingenious could make money out of seeming disaster. In one author's memories of his boyhood, the calf that had eaten a five-dollar bill through a boy's carelessness is promptly exhibited: 'The boys had not been born in Connecticut and of ten generations of Yankee traders for nothing.' (The show lasted more than a fortnight and brought in seventeen dollars.[2]) The trading instinct prevailed, it seemed, at all levels of society. We find it in fiction at Owen Johnson's (1878–1952) Lawrenceville, the American equivalent of an English public school. Macnooder is an Admirable Crichton, the kingpin of every school activity. In addition, he makes a profit out of it: 'He received a commission from a dozen firms to sell to his likenesses, stationery, athletic goods, choice sets of books, fin de siècle neckties, fancy waistcoats, fountain pens and safety razors, all of which articles, if report is to be credited, he sold with ease and eloquence at ten per cent above the retail price.'[3]

Americans saw commerce as infinitely romantic, something to boast about, especially if prosperity had come from individual effort and from small beginnings. Victorian England was very different. Those who became rich through trade tried to put their origins behind them as soon as they could, buying a country estate so that they could set themselves up as landed gentlemen, and sending their sons to schools where they could assimilate with the upper classes. Trade was a matter of shame, not pride, and a family that was reduced to selling commodities instantly lost caste, whatever their origins. Thus when the eldest son of Charlotte Yonge's Underwood family in *The Pillars of the House* (1873) enters a printing business so that he can support his orphaned brothers and sisters (in Miss Yonge's usual ample style there are twelve of them), he ceases to be a gentleman.

Nor, as has been said in a previous chapter, did Victorian Sunday school literature aimed at the English working boy suggest that there were fortunes to be made. Destitute boys might sweep crossings, or sell matches, but their luck could turn only when some benefactor put them in the way of learning a trade. Maria Edgeworth's little Paul in

'The Basket-Woman' (*The Parent's Assistant*) supports his grandmother by pushing stones behind the wheels of carriages to prevent them from rolling backwards as they climb a steep hill near his home. He invents a gadget that will do the job more efficiently and safely without the need for stones, and in an American book this would have set him on the ladder to a gold-studded future. But Paul is merely offered the opportunity to learn a new skill, basket-making. Trade, especially, was played down. Samuel Smiles, whose Franklin-style *Self-Help* (1859) teaching thrift, diligence and self-improvement was the gospel of so many English artisan households, might have been the son of a shopkeeper, but the examples he gave of men who had made their own way were inventors, engineers and manufacturers rather than those who bought and sold. If England was a nation of shopkeepers as Napoleon had averred, no Englishman was going to admit it.

'We are called . . . to follow step by step the progress of a lad who leaves home barefoot and penniless, with one definite purpose kept steadily in view and pursued with patient, unflinching toil.'[4] Self-advancement of this sort is the theme of one large category of American books for boys in the last century. Childhood was very short for the majority of them, and there was precious little play. The twelve-year-old telegraph operator who proudly told the editor of the *Little Corporal* in 1874 that he was earning twenty-five dollars a month (see page 148) was a typical instance. William Thayer* reminded readers in *From Log Cabin to White House* (1880) that President Garfield from the age of eight had looked after his widowed mother's farm while his older brother (who had been in charge of it since he was eleven) went out to work.

Farm boys such as he had the least leisure of all; the treadmill of their days was recorded by plenty of writers in their memoirs.

Like most country lads, he inherited the obligation (more or less shirked as a matter of self-preservation) to do innumerable chores, to weed the garden, hunt the eggs, bring in firewood, carry water to the hands in the field, drop corn, gather sheaves, stow away hay in the mow, drive the cows home from pasture, and assist in a hundred

---

* William Makepeace Thayer (1820–98) was a Congregational minister who specialized in didactic works for the young. He wrote several other books about the youth of American presidents, with such titles as *From Farm-house to the White House*, *From Pioneer Home to the White House*, *From the Tannery to the White House*.

The boy pioneer building a log cabin. Illustration by W. A. Rogers for Noah Brooks: The Boy Settlers, *serialized in St Nicholas, 1891.*

minor tasks demanded by the exacting economies of the farm,

wrote William Venable who grew up in the 1840s in Southern Ohio.[5] 'The boy comes nearer to perpetual motion than anything else in nature, only it is not altogether a voluntary motion,' said Charles Dudley Warner in *Being a Boy* (1877), remembering

how while the men of the family were allowed to lounge at the noon break or after supper, the boy, 'like a barrel of beer [was] always on draught'.

Hamlin Garland, brought up in Wisconsin, found the grinding routine even more oppressive. He and his brothers and sisters had been in bondage to the family farm from the time they were old enough to carry in the wood. They milked, sawed the logs, sowed the corn, husked it in the bitter cold of late autumn (a cruel ordeal), herded the cattle, fed the calves. The only respite was the three months that they spent at school, a relief because there were no cows.[6] (But the ferocity of some of those country schools then, often taught by men with no aptitude or liking for the work, was notorious. Edward Eggleston described one such in Indiana in *The Hoosier Schoolboy* (1883), and John Trowbridge enumerated some of the savagely inventive physical punishments that had been inflicted in his school.[7])

But this did mean that such leisure as came a country boy's way was ecstatically remembered. Garland, for instance, recorded a unique week when he and three others borrowed a wagon and a boat, and went a day's journey to a distant spot none of them knew. Here they camped in an oak grove, using their axes to cut down saplings to make the frame for a tent. 'And as Lincoln lay looking out of the tent door at the smoke curling up, hearing the horses chewing and tramping, and an owl hooting, it seemed gloriously like the stories he had read, and the dreams he had had of being free from care and free from toil, far in the wilderness.'

In all this, when it came to boys' stories Americans of course had an enormous advantage in the nineteenth century. There were pioneers pressing westward, there were Indians and gold-prospectors and cowboys, and fortunes to be made by even the youngest. The wilderness was at their doorstep, country boys had real axes and real guns, and could just step over the threshold to find adventure, whereas English writers had to send their characters overseas or into the past for theirs. Baden-Powell's *Scouting for Boys*, the Bible of the Scout movement, which remained required reading for all its members for decades, even when it was written in 1908 was a quaint exercise in boyish fantasy, with its urgent message that urban English youth should learn tracking skills, and how to make themselves comfortable in the wild. Thus while English children played at the primitive life, young Americans could experience it at first hand. In any case, it was reality that was stressed in their upbringing. According to Thayer in *From Log Cabin to White House*, an account of President Garfield's youth much favoured by Sunday schools, his hero at one time fell under the thrall of storybooks, which had deflected him from his course of self-improvement. Thayer thought that adventure stories were far more

dangerous than the company of 'deceitful and degenerate men.' Any sensible boy could see through these, but books, on the other hand, he took to his heart 'and communed with them, as friend communes with friend', not realizing how they might corrupt. Thus the story of Sinbad the sailor and the works of Captain Marryat had knocked young Garfield off course and fired him with the temporary ambition of being a sailor. Thayer did not mention Richard Dana's *Two Years Before the Mast* (1840), which the boy, who was nine when it was published, well might have read. In 1834 the nineteen-year-old Dana, then a Harvard undergraduate, had signed on as an ordinary seaman on a small merchant ship that was setting off from Boston to California, round Cape Horn, to pick up a cargo of hides. It was two years before he got back. His soberly recorded account of his experiences, always harsh and sometimes perilous, were very popular in both America and England.

Though there were many like Thayer who would have preferred that boys should read nothing to distract them from the serious business of getting on in life, stories of fictitious adventure became accepted as respectable. These seem to have been far less closely scrutinized than fiction for girls – anything with geographical and zoological information in it being, apparently, deemed improving. Thus Captain Mayne Reid (1818–83), as already mentioned, was accepted though he was far from being a Sunday school character. Reid, whose nationality at any given time depended upon the state of his finances, was the son of an Irish Presbyterian minister. He emigrated to the US in 1840, and was variously storekeeper, negro-overseer, schoolmaster and actor before he obtained a commission and went to fight in the Mexican War, where he was severely wounded. His novels, beginning with *The Rifle Rangers* (1850), at first were set in the American South and West, but later ranged all round the world. He went back to Britain but, having lost his money in grandiose building schemes, returned to the States for a further period in 1867. Here in 1869 he launched *Onward*, subtitled 'a Magazine for the Young Manhood of America', in whose pages he took many a swipe at the Old Country. He was savage about the English class system, referred to the 'dull, flat, and sodden gloom' of Britain, 'where there is no joy or gladness outside its aristocracy', and was contemptuous of British youth, whom he compared unfavourably with young Americans. In spite of these sentiments he was to spend the last few years of his life in England.

From the mid-century onwards, as juvenile publishing became an industry, what had been unisex developed into two sharply differentiated categories. Writing for boys, and writing for girls, became professions in themselves. Many authors' work suffered under the relentless demand from publishers, and was often mechanical and written to a formula. Harry Castlemon (Charles Austin Fosdick, 1842–1913), for instance, wrote some fifty-eight books in series with names such as Gunboat, Rocky Mountain, Sportsman's Club, Boy Trapper, Roughing It, Rod and Gun, Go-Ahead, Forest and Stream and War. (This marketing of books in named series was a particularly American phenomenon. Presumably it saved bulk buyers the trouble of reading any more than the title.)

John Townsend Trowbridge (1827–1916), however, though he too was forced into the series mould (Start in Life, Jack Hazard and others), produced individual work of high quality. His memoirs, *My Own Story* (1903), show that though he was brought up 'under the shadow of the Calvinism of those days' – a tradition which, as has been shown, had a deep distrust of fiction – he had been a bookish boy who had devoured history, poetry and historical romance. And this wider culture shows in his work. Many of his boys' books, it has to be admitted, have the usual theme of noble mothers and plucky young fellows who stand on their own feet. His outstanding achievement, *Cudjo's Cave* (1864), gained from not being aimed at children, though it was later taken over by them. This is a story of Tennessee just before the Civil War, with bitter and violent divisions between the Unionists and those who are for secession. A children's book would have probably simplified the issues, but here Trowbridge shows how many shades of opinion there are among the Unionists, and how widely different are the views about the status of the black man among those who oppose slavery. The central characters are a Quaker schoolmaster who vanquishes his scruples about fighting when it comes to defending his companions, and the magnificent Pomp, a black man of great physical and intellectual powers, who spares his most dangerous enemy when he is finally, after much bloodshed, at his mercy. For the book, for all its cliff- hanging excitement, is as much about compassion as about fighting, and one of the most subtly observed characters is the coward who out of fear betrays the man who has rescued him, but is later shamed into standing by him.

Elijah Kellogg (1813–1901), a New England Congregational minister whose stories about the fishermen and farmers of Maine were very popular with Sunday schools, saw life in more simplistic terms than Trowbridge. Kellogg's ideal man is huge, virile, long-enduring, heroically industrious; a doer rather than a thinker. ' "Essence of hoe-handle, if persistently taken two hours a day – or rake-handle either, especially if there's a shower rising – will cure the most aggravated case of that *disgraceful* disorder [nerves]," ' says a character in *Winning his Spurs* (1872), a story of college life based on his own student days at Bowdoin College. This robust advice comes from the hero's father, a minister, and the son is a chip off the old block, with a healthy contempt for anything that smacks of the transcendental. He remembers disparagingly a young minister who preached from his father's pulpit, bespectacled, with his hair parted in the middle. He talked about 'Goethe, Kant and the pre-existence of matter, and the soul of the universe. And every time he made a pause, he put his hand on his heart, turned up his eyes, and looked as our Margaret does when mother's going to make her take a dose of salts and senna.'

Kellogg, as might be inferred, was a more down-to-earth preacher. 'His virility, his devoutness, and his methods of using scythe and hoe, seine and boat in preaching the Gospel,' says the *Dictionary of American Biography*, won for him the affection of his parishioners. 'He could swim, sail, farm and fish with the boys in his parish, and then, at an unexpected moment, kneel down in their boat, or in the field . . . and pray with them.' He was vehement about 'the almost indestructible influence of a Christian home, of early moral training',[8] and this meant, of course, a mother's power for good. In *A Strong Arm and a Mother's Blessing*, which looks back to Maine settlers' life at the beginning of the nineteenth century, Arthur leaves home penniless, to seek his fortune. Remorseful that she has no money to give him, his mother cuts from the loom the length of cloth she had intended to make into clothing for her husband and younger sons. If all else fails in the early days and he is in need, he can sell it. But in the end he comes back with it intact.

Kellogg, a plain man himself, did not desire great

wealth for his young male characters. An outdoor life and honest work should satisfy everybody. Of the three boys on this farm, which it has nearly killed the father to establish and then work, he says: 'without luxuries, while at the same time supplied with good substantial food of the kind that makes bone and sinew, [they] were trained to industry, to begin a piece of work and carry it through, to confine their desires to the limit of their means, and to take a noble pride in mastering difficulties.' Arthur, the eldest, comes back to the farm with enough money made from trade to marry and to set himself up on a farm in Ohio. Trade for him has been only a means to an end, 'and that end was to own a piece of land, and to live on it'. He prospers in the new terrain, and in time persuades his parents to join him there, but though he and his wife in time build themselves a frame-house, '[his mother] said her happiest days were spent in a log house, and she wanted to live that part of her life over again'.

Kellogg's simple values contrasted markedly with those of Oliver Optic (William Taylor Adams, 1822–97), a New England schoolmaster and an author as prolific as Samuel Goodrich and Jacob Abbott. He wanted not just success for his heroes, but success in prodigal proportions. Louisa Alcott attacked what she called 'optical delusions' in *Eight Cousins*, which in 1875 was being serialized in *St Nicholas*. Having denounced Optic's use of slang, the scenes in police courts, counterfeiters' dens, gambling houses and drinking saloons, she turned to the outcome of his heroes' adventures:

'Now I put it to you, boys, is it natural for lads from fifteen to eighteen to command ships, defeat pirates, outwit smugglers, and so cover themselves with glory, that Admiral Farragut invites them to dinner, saying: "Noble boy, you are an honor to your country!" ... Even if the hero is an honest boy trying to get his living, he is not permitted to do so in a natural way, by hard work and years of patient effort, but is suddenly adopted by a millionaire whose pocketbook he has returned; or a rich uncle appears from the sea, just in the nick of time; or the remarkable boy earns a few dollars, speculates in peanuts or neck-ties, and grows rich so rapidly that Sinbad in the diamond valley is a pauper compared to him.'

Alcott's strictures were perverse. Of course it was not natural, and the Optic readers knew it as well as she did. But it did make for agreeable escapism. And though she and such writers as Susan Coolidge and Harriet Beecher Stowe kept their plots sober, plenty of her female contemporaries such as Mrs A. D. T. Whitney and Margaret Sidney rewarded their characters with the conventional riches beyond the dreams of avarice. William Adams was nettled. He wrote in *Oliver Optic's Magazine* in September 1875 that there were improbabilities in her own stories, and that she had charged Optic books 'with all the faults of all the juvenile books published, her own included'. This was fair comment; in addition, Adams had taught in Boston schools for twenty years, and knew even better than Charlotte Yonge that boys would not read 'mild tales'. They wanted pace and action and an undemanding style.

This Horatio Alger (1832–99) supplied in good measure. He is often cited as exemplifying the American dream, though in fact many writers both before and after him used for their heroes this combination of diligence plus luck. A very early instance is to be found in a little chapbook published in Hillsborough, Ohio, in 1820. *An Interesting Narrative of Two Pious Twin Children* (a German story) has bound in with it the American story of Charles Berry, a good son. The Berry family live in 'one of the most wild and desolate parts of the State of New-Jersey' where Berry père is hiding from his creditors. Little Charles, remembering the New Testament words, 'ask and ye shall receive', hires himself to the local baker, and finds sewing work for his mother and sisters. But though the baker is charmed with him the family's prosperity comes not from these efforts but from the timely demise of a great-uncle who leaves them 'an immense fortune'.

It was to be a formula endlessly repeated in the type of Sunday school tales that Mark Twain parodied (see pages 102–4). Readers expected something more dramatic than the chronicle of years of grinding work, and writers like Alger – who aimed his stories at the type of barely literate lads that he encountered in the New York News Boys Lodging House – therefore threw in hefty chunks of unlikely good luck. A spoof biography of Alger,* by an author who presumably never expected to be

---

* Herbert Mayes: *Alger: a biography without a hero* was published in New York by Macy-Masius in 1928. Mayes, who was to become President of the McCall Corporation, later admitted that it was nearly all fiction, and was written in response to the taste for debunking biography then prevalent. Unfortunately, it was regarded as authoritative by later writers. Edwin P. Hoyt's *Horatio's Boys* (New York, 1974) discusses the hoax.

taken seriously – at least for so long – has bedevil-
led most accounts of this writer (even that in the
Dictionary of American Biography) ever since. It
put out the legend that he was a compulsive
womanizer with a taste for luxurious living, and
Mayes even went to the lengths of inventing a diary
to bear this out. But in fact Alger was a social
inadequate whose tastes inclined towards little boys.
Ordained as a Unitarian minister, in 1864 he fled
from his first (and only) parish after a charge of
pederasty had been brought against him. There is
no evidence that he ever indulged in anything of
the sort again, but he was always to prefer the
company of boys. He had no home of his own, but
spent much of his time at the News Boys Lodging
House, and his bald style of narration must have
had their limited reading abilities in mind.

His compassion for the poor of New York was
genuine, and while indicating what he thought about
such evils as drink, tobacco and gambling, he did
not harangue his readers. Something of this tenderness comes out in *Phil the Fiddler*, an attack on
the way children from Southern Italy were sold by
their desperate parents to *padroni* who used them
to beg on the streets of New York, and in his
description of Ragged Dick, a tough shoe-shine boy,
providing fairy-stories for the little waif, Mark,
whom he has rescued from the street. Dick is one
of the most engaging of his heroes, with a pert wit
reminiscent of Sam Weller. By the time we get to
the sequel *Mark, the Match Boy* he is Richard
Hunter, a clerk in a respectable Pearl Street business
house, who has taught himself to read and who
even studies French. (Alger always has a great
respect for education, and his boys are often sent
to college by their benefactors.) But descriptions of
'years of patient effort' as advocated by Alcott would
hardly appeal to the sort of boys that Alger wrote
for, and in each of these two stories, as in so many
of his others, there is a *deus ex machina* and a
happy accident to rescue the heroes from street
life. Dick saves a rich little boy from drowning,
and is given a job by the grateful father, and Mark
finds his wealthy grandfather.

By no means all writers had Alger's respect for
learning. Charles Asbury Stephens (1844–1931), one
of the most popular and prolific of all boys' open-

air-life writers, often expressed his contempt for
college education, which was in his view no substitute for experience:

'Here we're cooped up in one little town to study year
after year. All we can get is a mere book knowledge.
Come to go out into the world, we're as green and *greener*
than before we went to college. I doubt if it would be a
good plan to stuff one's head with more printed descriptions
of things and places. A fellow ought to travel *as he studies*,
I'd say.

The boys in this book – *Camping Out* (1872) –
decide to educate themselves, and accumulate some
capital, by going on an expedition to find a lode
of lead. They fail to strike this, but discover graphite
instead. This earns them $15,000, enough to buy a
yacht for more explorations – ' "It would be a good
thing to penetrate within the polar circle. What
experience that would give us!" '

Stephens further developed the education-through-
experience theme in the Knockabout series of
travelogues.* It opened with *The Knockabout Club
in the Woods* (1883), in which six young men set
off through Maine to Canada by bicycle – 'that light
and airy hermaphrodite betwixt feet and wings
when the road isn't too sandy'. In the second book,
The Knockabout Club along Shore (published in the
same year), he expressed himself more forcefully
about the college system of education – an imitation
of the Old World model, based on the 'excessive
and disproportionate recitation of Greek and Latin,
Metaphysics, and abstruse Mathematics'. Travel is
the great educator, and he proposed that a steamship
should be fitted up as a college. He lamented that
while American youth supported this enthusiastically, their elders opposed it on the score of cost.
His account of the then pastimes of rich young
males is interesting:

Ah for the squandered millions which aristocratic empty-
headed young patriciandom is yearly spending on its
elegant vices which end in dry rot of muscle and of brain!

Three millions of dollars a year in pugs and poodles
and their blankets! Seventeen millions of dollars in fast
horses and horse racing! Twenty-three millions of dollars
in club-houses and sumptuous private *maisons de joie*! –

---

* It followed in the wake of Hezekiah Butterworth's Zig-Zag Club, whose first travels were recorded in *Zig-Zag Journeys in Europe* (1880).
Sixteen other volumes followed. Butterworth's interest was more in cultural and historical aspects of the various countries visited than in
day-to-day experiences of travelling.

Toby and his friend Mr Stubbs. Illustration by W. A. Rogers for James Otis: Toby Tyler, or Ten Weeks with a Circus *(New York, 1881).*

glamour, was a frequent theme in moral tales. But though Otis, who had himself been connected with a circus, stripped away the glamour and showed his readers the sordid, often cruel reality, this is an adventure story with both comedy (in the person of the Living Skeleton and his wife the Fat Lady) and pathos – for when Toby eventually runs away he takes with him his greatest friend, Mr Stubbs, the wilful and wayward monkey, who dies on the way home.

A later book with a less exotic background, *The Boys' Revolt* (1894), is, however, the more remarkable story, and probably the best that Otis ever wrote. In this account of New York street boys there are effectively no adult characters. Its theme is tyranny and the cowardice of the mob. Two youthful demagogues whip up their fellow-bootblacks to strike 'for ten cents a shine an' no Italians':

'If we act like other folks . . . we can chum together an' put prices way up. What'll the men do if they can't get their boots blacked less'n ten cents? Won't they have to pay it?'

'The Italians will shine all they can for a nickel a pair!' Jippy Simson said excitedly.

'That's it! That's jest it!' Baldy shouted. 'If every feller here 'grees not to take less 'n ten cents, an' to knock the head offer every Italian he sees, we can run the town . . . . If any feller works for less, fire him right outer the Union an' thump his head if he tries to do any work.'

Some of the boys nearly starve, and several are beaten up before they realize the two bosses are living high on their subscriptions. Only the finale is unconvincing; this being a children's book, Otis is unable to round it off with an account of what the mob probably would have done in such circumstances to discredited leaders, and it ends with a moral about 'how many people can be wronged in an attempt to gain a fancied right for one'.

Cudjo's Cave, as has been said, gained from not having been originally written as a children's book. The same can be said for two outstanding novels by Thomas Janvier (1849–1913), which are equal to anything by Jules Verne or Rider Haggard. *The Aztec Treasure House* (1890) is about an exploration party that sets out to search for a lost Aztec city. The members of the team have very different motives: one is a scholar, passionately interested in the history of ancient civilizations; two are hardheaded Yankees, impelled by curiosity and perhaps

tasteless beastliness. Forty-two millions of dollars for the best cigars and wines – the only known equivalent of which is a brain softened and whirling round of a morning! But not a dollar for the Steamship College.

With the exception of Trowbridge's *Cudjo's Cave*, the books mentioned so far have been competent rather than distinguished. But in the later years of the century there was to be some outstandingly original work. *Toby Tyler; or ten weeks with a circus* (1881) by James Otis (James Otis Kaler, 1848–1912) was so successful that the author gave up his work as a journalist and devoted himself full time to children's writing. With a total of 175 juvenile stories, he outstripped even Oliver Optic. Denunciation of circuses, which for country children unused to any sort of theatre had an intoxicating

a desire for gain; the saintly Fray Antonio goes
with the hope that he can spread the message of
the Gospel to the Aztecs, and the boy Pablo out of
devotion to the priest and to the little donkey El
Sabio (the Wise One), who is to be their beast of
burden. Besides the powerful descriptions of the
mountains and forgotten valleys, the dangers of the
journey and the climax when they are surrounded
by hostile Aztecs, there is the interest of the indi-
viduals themselves, who are fleshed out with far
more care than adventure writers usually take with
their characters.

In the Sargasso Sea (1898) is an even more noteworthy book, in that Janvier contrives to keep up
the pace and the tension with only one character.
The narrator is abandoned on board a ship in
Caribbean waters when a hurricane forces crew
and the rest of the passengers to the boats. The
wreck and he drift into the Sargasso Sea, 'a region
which every living ship steered clear of, and into
which never any but dead ships came'. Here are
packed tight together wrecks of many centuries,
and in his desperate efforts to find first food and
then some means of getting himself clear of the
region, he scrambles over hundreds of ships – some
so old that phosphorescent light on their rotting
timbers bathe them in unearthly radiance. One of
his most horrifying experiences is stumbling into
the hold of a slave ship and finding the chained
skeletons lying side by side; one of the most moving
is the sight of a relic of the War of 1812, the 'wreck
of an ancient sea-battle, fought out fiercely to a
finish before ever I was born'. On the decks are
scores of skeletons – 'just as they had fallen, there
they lay: with legs or arms or ribs splintered or
carried off by the shot that had struck them'. In
the cabin is the log with the final entry: 'Most of
our men are dead. All of us living are badly hurt.'
The narrator's fear, loneliness and despair are so
marvellously described that his escape (on a small
steam launch found in a recent wreck) comes almost
as an anti-climax.

Both these books come at a time of change. The
North American continent is settled, and there is
no new territory to carve out; there is a large urban
population; childhood is longer, and though they
still show enterprise and business flair, storybook
boys are no longer embarking on careers as capitalists from the age of twelve or less, nor supporting
the whole family single-handed. Nor are they gold-
prospecting or killing Indians. (In fact, Indians are

now recognized as having rights of their own, as
William Stoddard's *Little Smoke* (1891), a story
about Sioux Indians, showed.) There is far more
time for play, and for imaginative books. Howard
Pyle's *Otto of the Silver Hand* has already been
mentioned. Two other books showed the same em-
pathy with distant times, both by John Bennett
(1865–1956), a shadowy figure who also published
ballads and verse. *Master Skylark* (1897), subtitled
'a story of Shakespeare's time', has as its central
character Nick, a boy from Stratford, who is ab-
ducted because of his beautiful singing voice and
kept against his will in London, to sing as a Child
of St Paul's. The Queen hears him and offers him
a place among the court musicians. But he asks to
go back to Stratford, and it is Shakespeare himself
who eventually restores him to his home and his
mother. Though it is at moments a little too sweet
for modern taste, it carries its historical background
with exemplary ease – better, indeed, than Mark
Twain's somewhat heavy-handed treatment of
Tudor London in *The Prince and the Pauper* (1882).
Nor are the dirt and savagery of Elizabethan London
glossed over; take the episode where Nick goes
reluctantly to see his former captor, now in the
condemned cell at Newgate, having killed a fellow-
gambler:

As they came up Newgate street to the crossing of Giltspur
and the Old Bailey, the black arch of the ancient gate
loomed grimly against the sky, its squinting window-slits
peering down like the eyes of an old ogre. The bell of St
Sepulchre's was tolling, and there was a crowd about the
door, which opened, letting out a black cart in which was
a priest praying and a man in irons going to be hanged
on Tyburn Hill. His sweating face was ashen grey; and
when the cart came to the church door they gave him
mockingly a great bunch of fresh, bright flowers. Nick
could not bear to watch.

The story is told with passion and conviction; Bennett shows a remarkable feeling for the English
landscape and the passing of the seasons, and
identification with a child torn from his own surroundings and longing for home.

Bennett's *Barnaby Lee* (1902) is a more complex
story, of seventeenth-century colonial America, told
with great technical skill and an admirable sense
of place. It is set against the background of New
Amsterdam in 1664, where an English boy, Barnaby
Lee, who has escaped from the ship where he is

a reluctant apprentice, is taken in by the sheriff's family, the Van Sweringens. There are two threads to the plot. On the one hand, we have Barnaby's struggles to get out of the clutches of the villainous Captain King. On the other is the demise of the Dutch colony which, to the anguish of Van Sweringen and the others who have fought for it, has to be handed over to the British. It is a very subtle book which, most unusually for a historical novel of that date, is a study of defeat. For the Dutch it spells tragedy. For Barnaby the ending is happy in that Captain King is eventually routed, and he himself is restored to his family's Maryland estates. But that is at first a bitter-sweet experience, because he is alone there:

'Master Drew,' he said earnestly, 'do ye think that by calling a place home ye can make it homelike?'

Drew looked down. 'Nay, lad,' he said gently. 'No calling

'He was lying in a trundle-bed beside a cheery fire, in a white-walled beautiful little room.' Illustration by Clyde O. De Lande for John Bennett: Barnaby Lee *(London, 1902).*

makes a place a home. 'Tis the love that is in it which fastens on our hearts like a hook of steel.'

Like so many American books, *Barnaby Lee* and *Master Skylark* are in effect a celebration of home.

GOOD BOYS AND BAD BOYS

Previous chapters have shown various types of good boy. The morbid, over-scrupulous piety of Nathanael, Cotton Mather's young brother, described in chapter 1, and of the early Janeway-style tracts was one sort. But Nathanael and his kind became increasingly rare after the 1830s, to be replaced by Franklin disciples like little Wat Adams the Machinist (see page 56), single-minded in their devotion to the axioms of 'Poor Richard'. These diligent boys, who feature so large in the Sunday school books of the last century and in the *McGuffey Eclectic Readers*, were a type much better suited to use the opportunities of the New World: 'Industry, sobriety, thrift, propriety, modesty, conformity – these were the essential virtues, and those who practised them were sure of success. Success, too, for all the patina of morality that was brushed over it, was clearly material. It was a job, a farm, money in hand or in the bank.'[9]

Values such as these were employed to chilling effect in the accounts of precocious little capitalists like Wat and his kind, but could be made attractive by writers such as Elijah Kellogg, whose boys, with no idea of great material gain, labour to establish and support themselves in a demanding environment. Similarly, Harry Castlemon in *The Boy Trapper*, a story typical of scores of others, showed how a boy with nothing but his two hands and a rifle (which he has first had to earn by trapping quails) manages to support his destitute family – burdened, of course, with the usual useless father, who even sinks so low as to steal his son's savings.

As has been already shown, independence and self-reliance were required of both boys and girls from an early age. Anne Grant described how boys were transformed into men in colonial Albany. In 1808 she set down the reminiscences of an acquaintance some fifty years older than herself who recalled that the boys she knew in her youth had soon grown tired of a life of dependence. Their fathers would supply them with forty or fifty dollars,

Then the little boy said:
"Oh!"
Then the bank man took
the little boy into partnership, and gave him half the
profits and all the capital.

Mark Twain's parody of the Good Little Boy Story. Illustration by Nicollet for Poor Little Stephen Girard
(New York, 1981).

a negro boy and a canoe, which they would load with guns, powder, beads and spirits, and they would then set off northwards to trade with the Indians for furs. There were dangers, of course: from the Indians themselves, from rival French traders, from the hostile terrain, the rivers and lakes, and from wild animals:

It is utterly inconceivable how even a single season, spent in this manner, ripened the mind and changed the whole appearance, nay the very character of the countenance of these demi-savages, for such they seem on returning from among their friends in the forests. Lofty, sedate and collected, they seem masters of themselves, and independent of others; though, sunburnt and austere, one scarce knows them till they unbend.[10]

They were now men, she said, 'considered as active and useful members of society, possessing a stake in the common weal'.

And manliness was a recurring ideal. *I Mean to be a Man* is the title of a little homily in a collection of tales of the 1830s.[11] It is the answer given by a seven-year-old schoolboy when asked what he is going to do when he grows up; the author remarks approvingly: 'It matters very little whether he be a farmer, or a merchant, or a minister, if he be a MAN – he will be successful, and be loved and respected.' Juvenile writers devoted much space to this theme, usually adding the rider that the truly manly boy was *not* the one who strutted about with a cane, smoked and drank, but he who was disciplined and self-reliant. Self-reliance was expected of all American boys, the advantaged as well as the disadvantaged. Jane Andrews ended her *Ten Boys Who Lived on the Road from Long Ago to Now* (1885) with a fable about a young prince who has to make his own way in life, of whom his father says: 'I have treasures enough to make him rich, and pleasures enough to make him happy, but he will have to learn that, in order to enjoy riches and pleasures, he will have to earn them.' And the young prince, when he has won through, rejects them all, declaring: 'In going to seek them, I have gained something better than them all.'

This was the good side of the Franklin ethic. The reverse side has already been shown. Few writers faced the logical outcome of the obsessive quest for gain described in so many Sunday school books, and admitted that their boy heroes would surely turn into men eaten up by their business interests, or into burnt-out wrecks – in short, the absentee, ruined or useless fathers who feature so prominently in nineteenth-century juvenile fiction. The furthest they usually went was to point out the superiority of country life and the corrupting effect of cities. Thus Catharine Sedgwick directed a warning tale to ambitious boys. *Memoir of Joseph Curtis, a Model Man* features a boy who turns his back on his country home and gets a job 'in a great dry-goods shop', where he is valued by his employer for his sharpness at selling. He is well conducted and sober and 'abstains from all improper places of amusement'. He prospers, acquires his own business, marries well. 'Every year adds to his wealth and his mercantile reputation.' But 'look at his face and you will see wrinkles where dimples were. The plowshare of care has cut furrows on his brow, and his sallow sunken cheeks show that the baleful shadow of dyspepsia is settled on him.' His business fails, and '*now* he looks back at his country-home through the right end of the telescope'.

The Southern chivalric ideals were, of course, in diametric opposition to Northern business values, but children's books written from the South are sparse. The most famous example is *Two Little Confederates* (1888) by Thomas Nelson Page, of whom Edmund Wilson said, 'it was hard to make the Civil War seem cosy, but [he] did his best'.[12] A Virginian gentleman who towards the end of his life was ambassador to Italy, Page deplored the commercial spirit that he associated with the North. The 'two little confederates', who have seen their Virginia plantation home and indeed all the countryside plundered and overrun by Federal troops, are as brave and manly as any Northerner, but they add an extra quality – a high courtesy that is extended to friend and foe alike without thought of gain. They succour a dying enemy soldier and pray beside him. The soldier is buried in their garden, and when after the war his mother comes

searching for her son, she is given all the hospitality that the denuded home can provide. (It is significant that the grandson she brings with her is 'better-dressed than any boy they had ever seen', in contrast to their own patched clothing.) Frank and Willy lead her to visit the grave. ' "He was a real brave soldier," they told her consolingly.'

Many post-bellum writers from the North came to hold the same romantic view of the Old South as Page – a development that was predicted as long ago as 1888 by Albion W. Tourgée. He had forecast that the South was destined to become the Hesperidean Garden of American literature, and that a halo of romantic glory would cluster round the deposed sovereigns who once reigned there.[13] It is interesting that even in 1867 Martha Finley was using a plantation setting for her Elsie Dinsmore books, thereby making Elsie herself – beautiful, virtuous, charismatic – an early Sunday school Southern belle.

But one of the basic desiderata of the later type of Good Boy was that he should have at some stage been a bad one, and it is ironic that the Nathanael Mather ideal youth became suspect and equated with the opprobrious 'girl–boy'. A Bad Boy, on the other hand, had the ingredients of success in him. George Peck in *Peck's Bad Boy and his Pa* put it thus: 'Of course all boys are not full of tricks, but the best of them are. That is, those who are the readiest to play innocent jokes, and who are continually looking for chances to make Rome burn, are the most apt to turn out to be first-class business men.'[14] Peck enumerated the escapades that could be expected of a typical boy who is 'full of vinegar'. You might find him crawling under the canvas of a circus tent, raiding a melon patch, tying a can to a dog's tail.

But he shuffles through life until the time comes for him to make a mark in the world, and then he buckles on the harness and goes to the front, and becomes successful, and then those who said he would bring up in State Prison, remember then he always WAS a mighty smart lad, and they never tire of telling of some of his deviltry when he was a boy, though they thought he was pretty tough at the time.

'The Good Bad Boy is, of course, America's vision of itself, crude and unruly in his beginnings, but endowed by his creator with an instinctive sense of what is right', as Leslie Fiedler said,[15] and readers had no difficulty in distinguishing between the type of badness that, though they might not actually recommend it, writers described with only mock disapproval, and the reprobacy that all right-minded boys would avoid. The boy who was going to grow up to be an ornament to his country had spirit. The Victorian English, who prized unquestioning obedience in their own children, were amazed at what American parents would accept from their young. Captain Marryat described a three-year-old defying his father. ' "A sturdy republican, sir," ' says the father, smiling at the boy's resolute refusal to do as he is told. 'Be it recollected that I give this as one instance of a thousand which I witnessed during my sojourn in the country,' commented Marryat dourly, accustomed to instant obedience in the young as well as on board ship.[16] An observer a generation later noticed the same disregard for parents. ' "Remember who you are talking to, sir!" ' said one indignant father to an insubordinate son. ' "I am your father, sir." ' ' "Who's to blame for that?" said young Impertinence. "It ain't me!" '[17]

Readers in the post-bellum period were well aware that authors took a poor view of what earlier generations had regarded as Good Boys, and that there was indeed a category of Bad Good Boys. John Habberton dedicated his *The Worst Boy in Town* (1880) to 'very bad boys. And to the fine old fellows who were once called very bad boys'. He took a poor view of the ones who were law-abiding. Jack is the sort of boy to whom disaster gravitates; 'it seemed that when [he] was unoccupied even for half an hour, an indignant complaint by someone was absolutely sure to follow'. His mother cannot understand it; she says how very different her own brothers were. '[They] had lacked the vitality necessary to persistent mischief-making and had always been considered good boys, though their manliness after they reached adult years was strictly of a negative nature, and they had invariably failed in business and everything else they undertook.' When Jack, feeling he has been irredeemably bad, tries to run away, his father, having consulted the minister, forbears to punish him, but offers a builder a thousand dollars to teach him a trade. And he leaves off being the worst boy in town because 'he had something besides mischief to exercise his busy brain upon'.

Naturally there were Bad Boys, and the most commonly encountered type in the last century was the dandified lout. If Alger tells us that one of his characters claims to be 'the son of a gentleman'

and has a lofty idea of his dignity and social position, we know that he falls into this category, that he is an idle good-for-nothing with expensive tastes and dishonest practices. The species was almost invariably an urban one. A publication of 1861 for very young readers described 'the Broadway Swell': 'They are to be seen everywhere that ladies go, for these dandies generally are such brainless boobies that they think all the ladies are ready to kneel at their feet for love . . . Just take a look at . . . him smoking his cigar . . . Look at those whiskers, like a card of wool stuck to each cheek with glue.'[18] Harriet Beecher Stowe describes a Boston example, El Vinson, son of a wealthy merchant, 'one of those bright quick fellows . . . who can keep at the head of their classes with but little outlay of time and thought'. He assumes 'the air of a gentleman of elegant leisure', lounges over novels, hires what he calls 'a decent turnout' from the local livery stables, smokes cigars and keeps a flask of brandy by him. Of his schoolmasters he says: ' "If there's anything that gives a charm to life, it's a fight with these Dons. I half plagued their lives out in the Latin School." '[19]

Sometimes it is the fault of an over-indulgent mother, as in the case of Mrs Tuthill's Master Clarence, aged thirteen: 'There he stands, four feet ten in his morocco pumps, long-tailed, purple coat, plaid pantaloons, blue waistcoat, frilled shirt-bosom with turquoise studs – nothing wanting but the neck-tie to complete his elegant toilet!' And this his mother is embroidering, a crimson satin affair with gold-coloured silk.[20] The younger version of this is the 'girl–boy', who often makes an appearance in nineteenth-century American books. One of the earliest (and most extreme) personifications of this is Billy Bedlow, in a story by Eliza Leslie from an 1831 number of the *Juvenile Miscellany*:[21]

Billy Bedlow thought himself a very pretty boy, and took great pleasure in admiring his face in the glass. He had light yellow hair, which he called golden; he would not consent to have it cut, and it flowed in ringlets over his shoulders; to make it curl, he put it every night in papers. He kept in his room a bottle of Cologne-water, with which he was continually perfuming himself; and he slept all night in buckskin gloves to keep his hands white and delicate.

He is cowardly, screaming at spiders and wasps; dislikes boys' sports, preferring to sit with his sisters and dress their dolls. However, after a visit to a ship when he wears a braided frock coat and his sister's corset, another boy persuades him to abandon his effeminate ways. And, as this is a children's story, he reforms. It is a sad reversal of the early piety theme that the girl–boys of later fiction often have their sights on the ministry, like Georgie Bassett, in Booth Tarkington's *Penrod* – always clean and polite and loathed by his peers. To William Dean Howells and his friends (*A Boy's Town*), 'a fellow who brushed his hair and put on shoes and came into the parlor when there was company was looked on as a girl–boy'.

The bond between an American boy and his mother being what it was, the foolishly indulgent mother who is largely responsible for such little fops as Billy Bedlow does not come in for much stick – certainly not as much as fathers received. But we notice such mothers, and loutish sons, as peripheral characters in many books. Mary Livermore in her autobiography spoke ruefully of the latter, reporting that she was frequently entertained in homes dominated by the whims of a boy. 'Theodore Parker used to say that the average American boy, from the time he was twelve until he was eighteen, was a barbarian, and when people disputed his statement, he would answer it, "If you doubt it, ask their sisters."' In *What Katy Did at School* Lilly Page's brother plagues the life out of his sister until Katy tames him. Daisy Randolph in Susan Warner's *Melbourne House* has an even worse torment of a brother, Miss Warner's attitude seemingly being that this is boy nature, just as it is a mother's nature to spoil her sons. Ransom Randolph gets his own way in everything, and boxes the good little Daisy's ears when thwarted. His mother's response is that 'boys will do such things and it is absurd of Daisy to mind, that she deserved what she got for interfering'.

This sort of behavior is, of course, totally contrary to the code of the Good Bad Boy. Even Peck's Bad Boy, crude and spiteful as he seems to the modern reader, will fight to protect a smaller boy or a schoolgirl. There is no malice in the idealized Bad Boy; it is just that he is born to trouble, and he is resigned to the fact that the cards are stacked against him:

He had not intended to destroy the carriage-lamps. He had been merely hurling stones at a creature whose perfidy deserved such action, and the hitting of the lamps had

Thomas Bailey Aldrich: The Story of a Bad Boy, *serialized in* Our Young Folks, *April, 1869. The narrator finds he is left to pay for twelve ninepenny ties.*

been merely another move of the great conspirator Fate to force one Jimmie Trescott into dark and troublesome ways. The boy was beginning to find the world a bitter place. He couldn't win appreciation for a single virtue; he could only achieve quick rigorous punishment for his misdemeanors.[22]

'I may truthfully say,' remarks Thomas Bailey Aldrich on the opening page of the autobiographical *Story of a Bad Boy* '[that] I was an amiable, impulsive lad, blessed with fine digestive powers, and no hypocrite.' This gentle, kindly account of a small boy sent from New Orleans to be brought up in his grandfather's house in an old New England seaport, serialized in *St Nicholas* in 1869 and published the following year, was the first of the Bad Boy books. By the standards of Peck's boy or Tom Sawyer he is the cherub that he averred he most certainly was not. There are various frolics with gunpowder which he miraculously survives; he tumbles in and out of fights – an epic snow battle between the North End and the South End boys is one of them. And he admits to detesting Sundays and the sepulchral gloom that descends over the little town of Rivermouth.

The gunpowder should be noticed, for this is a recurrent theme in the sagas of Bad Boys, American youth having greater access to it and at a far earlier age than anybody in the Old World. 'I was not more than seven years old,' wrote Edward Hale (1822–1909), 'when I burned off my eyebrows by igniting gunpowder with my burning-glass. I thought it was wisest not to tell my mother.'[23] A manual of 1821, *The Art of Making Fireworks*[24] – judging by the illustrations, addressed to very young boys – gives many recipes for making explosions ('This explosion is not dangerous') and artificial earthquakes. Sometimes it concedes that some 'singular composition' is not worth making oneself, as it requires 'so much trouble, caution and exactness', but mostly it encourages readers to experiment for themselves. There are many possibilities, for instance, in fulminating silver, which can be put in the heel of a boot, under the leg of a chair, or in a drawer where 'it will explode with a loud report, to the no small discomfiture of the person at the drawer'. It can be put into tobacco pipes and 'segars' – and, most comical jape of all, it can be put into artificial spiders, 'and on any female espying it, she will naturally tread on it, to crush it, when it will make a loud report'.

It was necessary to warn even toddlers about the dangers of unskilled handling of guns, as can be seen from this primer:

See that care-less boy fir-ing off his fa-ther's gun! He has fright-ened the cow, and she has kicked Bet-ty o-ver, and spilled the pail of milk. Rob-ert's mo-ther is at the win-dow, and she seems a-larmed. Rob-ert does not know how to fire off a gun, and might have killed Bet-ty, or his bro-ther close at his side. Ma-ny boys have killed their bro-thers or sis-ters while play-ing with guns, and have had to mourn all their days for their care-less-ness and mis-chief. Lit-tle boys should not med-dle with guns.[25]

But the writer taking such a pusillanimous stance is obviously a woman. A man is more robust, as in an American Sunday School Union publication of 1864: ' "Oh, don't make cowards of the boys, mother," said grandfather. "A little smell of powder never hurt a Yankee shaver." '[26]

Explosives played a prominent part in most Bad Boy activities. The hero of Metta V. Victor's *A Bad Boy's Diary*, for instance, throws firecrackers at horses, shoots the minister with his father's pistol, puts gunpowder in the chimney, burns down the town hall and finishes by blowing up the new railroad bridge. Peck's Bad Boy and his friends use

dynamite to destroy a dog. They have considered other ways of disposing of it, but reckon that poison would be too uneventful, drowning too uncertain, starving would take too long. Dynamite is tied to its tail, and after an initial scare when it tries to run after them – it is a friendly animal – 'the sky rained dog'.[27]

Even the two infants aged five and three in John Habberton's *Helen's Babies* (1876), left in the charge of their harassed uncle, put gunpowder in the buns to make them rise. Budge and Tod, demonic, inventive, self-willed and implacable, are the stuff that the true Bad Boy is made of, and though so young have grasped that the adult world is arraigned against them: ' "I don't see what little boys was made for, anyhow; if ev'rybody gets cross with them, an' don't let 'em do what they want to." ' Or as their counterparts say in the same author's *Other People's Children*: ' "Little boysh never *can* do anyfing nysh wivout bein' made to don't." ' The author's conclusion is that the so-called right of adults to demand implicit obedience is the most vicious, debasing tyranny the world has been cursed by.

Boys will be boys, says Peck, and he reckons that his Bad Boy is the sort that has made America great. The reluctant residents of St Petersburg make a similar forecast for Tom Sawyer: 'There are some that believed he would be President yet, if he escaped hanging.' *The Adventures of Tom Sawyer* (1876) is remarkable among the Bad Boy sagas in that while they were all written from an adult perspective, Twain was able to discard his mature self and take on boy nature again – crude, anarchic, violent. Tom's age is vague. He is somewhere between six and fourteen, young enough to be losing his front milk teeth, strong enough to punt himself on a raft across the river, old enough to enjoy smoking and courting girls. Probably he is twelve, that being the golden age of boyhood as perceived by American writers. But the author's vision wavers, since on the first page he is 'a small boy' and Becky Thatcher is 'a lovely little blue-eyed creature', and by the middle of the book they have shot into adolescence.

Tom lives in the present, and dismisses the future as something that will never happen to him. His exploits are such as most boys will relish, and there is no concern for those who suffer from them – whether it be the cat or Sid the Good Boy. Even when Tom and Huck witness a murder, they are afraid only for their own skins:

'S'pose something and Injun Joe didn't hang, why he'd kill us some time or other, just as dead sure as we're lying here.'

'That's just what I was thinking to myself, Huck.'

The most unlikely jape works, as it would in a boy's fantasizing. The cat lowered through the ceiling on 'Examination' day claws off the schoolmaster's wig, as intended. Tom and his companions not only leave home and escape successfully to Jackson's Island, they also escape *from* it, and, presumed by all to be dead, make their splendid reappearance the Sunday after in church, where their own funeral is under way, in the middle of the minister's sermon before a sorrowing congregation. The treasure theme is handled with a boy's lack of moral sense. When Tom and Huck dig up the $12,000 from the cave where Injun Joe has buried them, and where he has only a couple of weeks before died a ghastly death, there are no queasy adult scruples about this being tainted money, stolen from people whom the 'half-breed' well might have murdered:

'Got it at last!' said Huck, ploughing among the tarnished coins with his hands. 'My, but we're rich, Tom!'

'Huck, I always reckoned we'd get it. It's just too good to believe, but we *have* got it, sure!'

And the Widow Douglas, Huck's guardian, puts the money out at six per cent and Judge Thatcher does the same with Tom's.

There is one feature of *Tom Sawyer* that makes it stand out among American boys' books – the dream world that Tom inhabits, nourished by copious reading of fiction. Storybook American boys, as has been seen, were presented as hard-headed and practical men in embryo who steered clear of unnecessary books. Imaginative games such as those played in Richard Jefferies' *Bevis* (1882) – where the boys act out the roles of explorers, castaways, soldiers, savages – or by the four children in Kenneth Grahame's *The Golden Age* and *Dream Days*, have no place in their purposeful lives. But Tom Sawyer lives the part of Robin Hood or his favourite pirate just as Bevis might have done. In *The Adventures of Huckleberry Finn* he persuades the boys that 'a whole parcel of Spanish merchants and rich A-rabs was going to camp in Cave Hollow with two hundred elephants, and six hundred camels, and over a thousand "sumter"

mules, all loaded down with di'monds'. The gathering turns out to be a Sunday school picnic, but he so nearly convinces them that it was the work of a magician that Huck tries rubbing an old tin lamp to see whether he can't summon a genie. He is mortified that the rescuing of the runaway slave, Jim, can be accomplished easily:

'Well, if that ain't just like you, Huck Finn. You *can* get up the infant-schooliest ways of going at a thing. Why, haven't you ever read any books at all? – Baron Trenck, nor Casanova, nor Benvenuto Challeeny, nor Henri IV, nor none of them heroes? Who ever heard of getting a prisoner loose in such an old-maidy way as [slipping the chain off]?'

For Tom, imagination transcends reality, and not just for him: he also succeeds – at any rate while they are in his company – in making his peers see life through the same glass. More than that, the boy world is dominant, adult concerns are irrelevant, and authority if not grotesque is ineffectual or degraded. The boy rules, as nowhere else in American children's literature. Twain, urged by Howells, combed a certain amount of coarseness out of *Tom Sawyer*, but it remains one of the most subversive children's books to have achieved classic status.

But Twain's ultimate exploration of the Bad Boy theme comes in *The Adventures of Huckleberry Finn* (1884). Here the actual adventures described (strange and improbable enough) seem prosaic compared to the fantasies entertained by the participants. What is really happening and what Huck thinks is happening are like two sets of fantasies running on parallel lines. The first is the author's; the other, the more luxuriant one of the characters. Similarly, Huck's and Jim's confused moral ideas and stores of historical misinformation seem like a parody of the adult delusions by which they are surrounded. The adults, like Huck and Jim, think and act in separate compartments. We are used in literature, as in life, to people who fail to live up to their principles. Here, people find it hard to be as depraved as their principles. So in chapter 32 we find this conversation between Aunt Sally, a kind-hearted soul really, and Huck:

'We blowed out a cylinder-head.'

'Good gracious! anybody hurt?'

'No'm. Killed a nigger.'

'Well, it's lucky, because sometimes people do get hurt.'

The America of Twain's youth was still talking about men being born free and equal. As Jim's excitement mounts in chapter 16 when he thinks he is nearing freedom, Huck's 'conscience' becomes more and more uneasy:

I begun to get it through my head that he *was* most free – and who was to blame for it? Why, *me*. I couldn't get that out of my conscience, no how nor no way. It got to troubling me so I couldn't rest...

It was according to the old saying, 'Give a nigger an inch and he'll take an ell.'... Here was this nigger which I had as good as helped to run away, coming right out flat-footed and saying he would steal his [Jim's] children – children that belonged to a man I didn't even know; a man that hadn't ever done me no harm.

Huck is aware of two separate principles: that Jim is his friend, but that being black Jim has no rights, while his owner's right to possess him is fundamental. He mistakes his humane feeling for temptation, and the tradition of slavery for natural right. When he pretends that Jim is not a runaway slave but his own white father with smallpox, he attributes his failure to feel guilty to bad education and a defective conscience. A hilarious parodic version of the issue of confused conscience is seen near the end, where Tom Sawyer's sense of the *right* way to release prisoners is derived from reading romances; style and principle are inextricably confused in his mind. Huck's practical sense is overcome by an admiration for Tom's weak romanticism: ' "What's the good of a plan that ain't no more trouble than that?" ' asks Tom, and Huck's agreement is sincere.

Twain is also able to insinuate into Huck's words a poetic sense of the landscape. Huck thinks he is being knowing and cynical, when he is revealing a hidden sense of wonder. The reader is not allowed to forget that he is, at most, two generations away from the virgin continent we encounter in James Fenimore Cooper (1789–1851). The civilization depicted by Twain is in some ways cruder than that of Natty Bumppo's time (in Cooper's *Leather-Stocking Tales*). So the boys Huck and Tom, the adult but childish Jim, and the adults who can be taken in by the con men's childish tricks, are all part of the same pattern. It is as if America itself was being presented as still in a state of Bad Boyhood.

THE GOLDEN PAST

'The Boy must not be judged by the standard of Childhood or Manhood,' wrote B. P. Shillaber in 1879. 'He has a sphere of his own; and all of his mischief, frolic and general deucedness belongs to his condition. The Boy has but little plan, purpose, or intention, in what he does, beyond having a good time.'[28] Shillaber, who had created the comic character of Mrs Partington, a New England matron, was now turning his attention to her mischievous small nephew, Ike. When the first article about Mrs Partington appeared in 1847 in the Boston newspaper for which he was then working, it was not the mood of the time to ruminate over the nature of children. They might be tearaways, as Ike was, but authors did not, apparently, draw on memories of themselves when young nor attempt to explain boy psychology to their readers. Thomas Bailey Aldrich's *The Story of a Bad Boy* (1869) was the first in a new field, though it was no doubt *The Adventures of Tom Sawyer* seven years later that made the wistful evocation of Bad Boyhood popular. (Twain, incidentally, is now recognized to have modelled Tom's Aunt Polly on Mrs Partington.)

The autobiographical writing of authors such as Charles Dudley Warner, Hamlin Garland and William Venable has already been mentioned. William Dean Howells (1837–1920) was another who wrote at length about his youth. In *A Boy's Town* (1890), which first appeared in *Harper's Young People*, he tried to recreate for a younger generation a landscape and a way of life that he felt had vanished with increased urbanization, and were unknown to his readers. He was unsentimental when he considered the boy that he had been, and detached in a way that the children's books of his own youth could not have countenanced, especially when it came to discussing a boy's moral code. 'A boy hardly knows what harm is,' he told his readers, 'and he does it mostly without realizing that it hurts.' A boy imitated, he did not invent, and it was easier to imitate war rather than peace; thus, boys spent most of their time plotting mischief and, far from following the lead of the best boys, they followed the worst boy as far as they dared.

Without realizing that it was evil, they meant more evil than it would have been possible for ten times as many boys to commit. If the half of it were now committed by men, the United States would be such an awful place that the decent people would all want to go and live in Canada.

I have often read in stories of boys who were fond of nature, and loved her sublimity and beauty, but I do not believe boys are ever naturally fond of nature.... A dead horse will draw a crowd of small boys, who will dwell without shrinking upon the details of his putrefaction, when they would pass by a rose-tree in bloom with indifference...

They are not cruel, that is, they have no delight in giving pain, as a general thing; but they do cruel things out of curiosity, to see how their victims will act... They acquaint themselves, at any risk, with all that is going on in the great strange world they have come into; and they do not pick or choose daintily among the facts and objects they encounter.

The boy, he concluded, was not wicked – he was merely a savage. It was not such a cliché then as might be supposed. Earlier writers had had little to say about the boy nature of their young heroes, who were far too busy carving out their place in the world for idle play, while their successors, when it became fashionable to cultivate boyhood, tended to do so in a golden haze of sentimentality. ' "Dear Lord, I've been scolded again for tryin' to do somethin' real nice for other people," ' says one of John Habberton's diabolical cherubs. ' "I guess it makes me know something about how the good prophets an' Jesus felt. Please don't let *me* have to be crucified for doin' good, for Christ's sake, Amen." ' [29]

There was also the intimations-of-immortality sort of writing. No boy in Howells' experience ever had these, but at least one writer remembered tears coming to his eyes, as 'his soul was listening to the faraway music' of the life that stretched before him:

They chattered idly... But the chatter was only a seeming. For in truth the boys were absorbing the glory of the moonlight. And the undertones of their being were sounding in unison with the gentle music of the hour. Their souls – fresher from God than are the souls of men – were a-quiver with joy, and they babbled to hide their ecstasies. [30]

This was William Allen White (1868–1944) remembering a Kansas childhood in the 1870s. It was part of a rush of literary nostalgia for the past that

marked the last decades of the century. 'A Wail in B minor', in the same book, begins:

Oh, what has become of the ornery boy,
    Who used to chew slip'ry elm, 'rosum' and wheat:
And say 'jest a coddin' ' and 'what d'ye soy?';
    And wear rolled up trousers all out at the seat?

The golden past was a boys' realm, it being only boys, seemingly, who could snatch leisure and freedom. Women wrote memoirs of their youth too, of course, but in soberer style and without the yearning for something that had irrevocably vanished; childhood for them was centred on the home and was only a foretaste of the homes they would create in adult life; they never achieved the delirious irresponsibility that was an essential part of being a boy. Yet even for him, only two or three years at most were involved – that short span when he was old enough to take advantage of the terrain around him but before he had to accept adult responsibilities. 'The disadvantage of the position is that it does not last long enough,' Charles Dudley Warner said sorrowfully, having described the state as one of the best in the world: 'Just as you get used to being a boy you have to be something else, with a good deal more work to do and not have so much fun.' [31] He would choose to be ten; 'as soon as I got any older I would quit it'.

But most writers reckoned that twelve was the pinnacle of youth, and all agreed that with adolescence the decline started:

A boy just twelve is like a Frenchman just elected to the Academy. Distinction and honour wait upon him. Younger boys show deference to a person of twelve; his experience is guaranteed, his judgment, therefore, mellow; consequently his influence is profound. Eleven is not quite satisfactory, it is only an approach... Thirteen is embarrassed by the beginnings of a new colthood; the child becomes a youth. But twelve is the top of boyhood. [32]

And once it is over, there is no return. 'Who, being recently banished from Boyville, has not sought to return?' wrote White:

We who are passing 'through the wilderness of this world' find it difficult to realize what an impenetrable wall there is around the town of Boyville. Storm it as we may with the simulation of light-heartedness, bombard it with our heavy guns, loaded with fishing-hooks and golf-sticks, and

skates and baseballs and butterfly-nets, the walls remain.
If once the clanging gates of the town shut upon a youth,
he is banished forever. From afar he may peer over the
walls at the games inside, but he may not be of them.[33]

And he shook his head over the unseeing adults:
'Grown-up people forget that their wisdom has
impaired their vision to see às boys see and to pass
judgement upon things in another sphere.' Mark
Twain alone did not lose his boy's vision. *Tom
Sawyer* has none of the long-distance perception
that other writers brought to their nostalgic evoca-
tions of a vanished past; he is back there pitching
in with Tom and Huck and their kind. He does not
explain or interpret; for him, apparently, nothing
has changed.

Turn-of-the-century writers in England, too, were
insisting that it was children who had the truth of
the matter within them. 'O children, open your
hearts to me, / And tell me your wonder thoughts!'
begged Algernon Blackwood,[34] pleading with them
also to 'open your eyes to me and tell me your
visions, too' and finishing:

> For the grown-up folk
>   Are a troublesome folk,
> And the book of their childhood is torn,
>   Is blotted, and crumpled, and torn!

The first to make this sort of statement popular
had been Kenneth Grahame with *The Golden Age*
(1895) and *Dream Days* (1898). He had attempted
a child's eye view of a world controlled by obtuse
adults whom he called Olympians, making his point
about the abyss between children and adults by
writing in consciously mannered Olympian prose
– 'I certainly did once inhabit Arcady. Can it be
that I also have become an Olympian?' The title
Dream Days is significant, for to his four child
characters the fantasy worlds that they inhabit are
far more real than their everyday surroundings,
and it is this vision that separates them from the
adult world, whose purblind inhabitants are un-
heeding of all the wonders about them. In England,
as has been seen, it was possible for the more
prosperous to extend the childhood of their offspring
to last twenty years or more. But being grown-up
was fun too, provided you were reasonably affluent;
besides, the rigours of the English nursery and
schoolroom were still fresh in the memory. So that
while Edwardian poets and belle-lettristes were

telling their readers that it was children who had
the key to the meaning of life, they did not on the
whole yearn to be back among them.

Americans, however, felt the shades of the prison-
house closing round them at a very early age. John
Greenleaf Whittier's 'The Barefoot Boy' concludes:

> All too soon these feet must hide
> In the prison cells of pride,
> Lose the freedom of the sod,
> Like a colt for work be shod,
> Made to tread the mills of toil,
> Up and down in ceaseless moil.

In Mrs Abby Morton Diaz's *The William Henry
Letters* (1872), which purport to be the letters written
home by a ten-year-old at boarding school, the
child is told by his father: 'A boy of your age is
old enough to be looking ahead some, to see what
he is aiming at...Set up your mark, and a good
high one. And be sure and remember that, as a
general thing, there is no such thing as luck.' When
he is twelve, William Henry has to leave school
and consider where he is going next. For a twelve-
year-old, English boy life had hardly begun. His
best years – those of late adolescence when he was
lording it at the top of the school, and at university
where there was a heady new freedom and irresponsibility – lay far ahead. But Mrs Diaz's little
boy already feels a greybeard: ' "I'm so old I can't
help looking ahead some sometimes, to see where
I'm coming out." ' Thomas Bailey Aldrich was more
fortunate than most in that, though he could not
go to Harvard as he had hoped, at least he did not
have to take on adult responsibilities until he was
sixteen. But William Dean Howells, from early
boyhood, was working in his father's printing business. Aged twelve, he was driven out of the paradise
that was 'Boy's Town' when the business was sold
and the family moved. 'The parting was an anguish
of bitter tears' and he pined for his old friends and
familiar surroundings, and also for the childhood
that had come to an end. He was eventually allowed
to revisit the town but, like William Allen White
trying to regain admittance to 'Boyville', he was
shut out; his old associates saw him changed and
were uneasy.

It was always a country life that was remembered
with such longing. Writers were remarkably con-
sistent in what they recalled so ecstatically. Summer
and the barefoot season seemed to last most of the

year: 'Life has a good many innocent joys for the human animal,' said Howells, 'but surely none so ecstatic as the boy feels when his bare feet first touch the breast of our mother earth in the spring.'[35] Hamlin Garland described the same marvellous moment: 'The first thing that Lincoln did was to pull off his boots, in order not to miss the delicious feeling of the warm soil, as the tender soles of his feet sank into it, burrowing like some wild thing lately returned to its native element.'[36] In the summer he and his friends wore shoes only to Sunday school, or if they were going to town; 'when ordered to wash their feet, they ran out into the tall grass, cleansed them in the dew, running backward in order to wash their heels'.

Untamed territory where one could wander freely was required. Francis Grierson described one prelapsarian paradise in the Midwest:[37]

About two miles from the town there was a place where boys used to band together to 'go in swimming', and in this spot I took my first swimming lesson.... Here [there] was a delicious shaded creek where we fished for perch and bass, and farther on, in the woods, we went in search of paw-paw trees and came across flying squirrels, strange birds, and huge flocks of wild pigeons. These were the woods of enchantment, by the border of the Father of Waters, in the soft warm autumn days when health and unadulterated joy made life worth living.

For the height of bliss a river was required. Howells, who spent some of his childhood years in Hamilton, Ohio, spoke about 'the almost unrivalled fitness' of this town to be the home of a boy, with its rivers and reservoirs, and canals for swimming and skating.[38] It stood on the Miami, 'as blue as the sky when it was not as yellow as gold', and there was also the Old River (the Miami's former channel), a canal and a canal basin, and the 'Hydraulic' which brought water for working the mills through the heart of the town. Here he and his friends fished and swam, and made little flutter-mills: 'As with everything that boys do, these mills were mostly failures, [but] . . . they met such disappointment with dauntless cheerfulness, and lightly turned from some bursting bubble to some other where the glory of the universe was still mirrored.' But the swimming was the best of all. There were signs you could make to invite your friends to come swimming. You could make appropriate movements with your arms, or you could

hold up two fingers, if you wanted to be secret, in the form of a swallow tail. Very often you had to be secret, for you well might be forbidden to go in more than once or twice a day, and 'they all had to go in at least three or four times'.

What boys wanted then were red-topped boots (but when Howells proudly acquired his they were far too big for him and the other boys jeered), marbles, candy, soda-water, striped slate pencils, fish hooks. They never had the money for them and longed to be able to earn some, unaware that when they did they would no longer be boys – only wistful onlookers. They also wanted watermelons, of which they never could have enough: 'Enough, to a boy, meant at least one entire melon, weighing from twenty to thirty pounds, for himself alone, to consume at a single sitting.'[39] Their appetite was insatiable but selective. They might consume at one sitting water-melon and chocolate creams and liquorice sticks and lemon drops and peanuts and jaw-breakers and sardines and raspberry lemonade and pickles and popcorn and ice-cream and cider and sausages and cinnamon-drops and waffles, as Booth Tarkington's Penrod did, but they were intensely suspicious of food outside their experience. They all coveted guns, and thought them 'the most valuable and enjoyable personal property on earth. We pitied boys, and even men, that lived before firearms were invented.'[40] Howells' Pony Baker will not be allowed a gun until he is twelve, which is unfair, as 'one of the fellows who was only eight was going to have a gun as soon as his brother had done with his'.[41] (Pony's mother is also unreasonable about gunpowder – 'She would never let him come near the stove with it, after one of the fellows tried to dry his powder on the stove . . . and forgot to take it off the stove quick enough, and it almost blew his mother up and did pretty nearly scare her to death.')

Circuses induced a sort of madness in boys. (The number of Sunday school stories that heavily warned them about the sin and moral dangers associated with circuses is partial testimony to that.) 'I really do not know how boys lived through the wonder and glory,' said Howells, who devoted a chapter to the circuses of his youth in *A Boy's Town*. 'For a fortnight beforehand they worked themselves up for the arrival of the circus into a fever of fear and hope' – the fear being that their fathers might not allow them to go. 'Even the Fourth of July grew pale and of small account in the "glittering, gorgeous Panorama of Polychromatic Pictures", which once a year visited the country town,' recalled Hamlin Garland.

The boy whose father refused to take him wept with no loss of dignity in the eyes of his fellows. He could even swear in his disappointment and be excused for it...

No one but a country boy can rightly measure the majesty and allurement of a circus. To go from the lonely prairie or the dusty corn-field and come face to face with the 'amazing aggregation of world-wide wonders' was like enduring the visions of the Apocalypse.[42]

American boys also fell in love. Blue eyes and a pink dress made ten-year-old knees turn to water – even the worst of Bad Boys saw no shame in this, and Peck's Bad Boy could write of his beloved:

'You see before you a shadow. I have drunk of the sweets of life and now only the dregs remain. I look back at the happiness of the last two weeks, during which I have been permitted to gaze into the fond blue eyes of my loved one, and carry her rubbers to school for her to wear home when it rained, to hear the sweet words that fell from her lips as she lovingly told me I was a terror.'

This, of course, is strained and tiresome. But there are more authentic-sounding experiences; dumb yearning for the opposite sex played an important part in turn-of-the century nostalgia, both fictitious and autobiographical. The mode of courtship may be quaint, but we recognize the intensity of the emotion in Stephen Crane's *Whilomville Stories*. Jimmie Trescott woos Abbie by following her home from school, and then, when she looks back at him, begins frantically to run and jump and fight the boy with him.

Whereupon she of course became insufferably vain in manner, and whenever Jimmie came near her she tossed her head and turned away her face and daintily swished her skirts as if he was contagion itself. But Jimmie was happy. His soul was satisfied with the mere presence of the beloved object so long as he could feel that she furtively gazed upon him from time to time and noticed his prowess.

Falling in love played a part in Bad Boy stories from the very beginning. 'If the reader supposes that I lived all this time in Rivermouth without falling a victim to one or more of the young ladies attending Miss Dorothy Gibbs's Female Institute, why, then all I have to say is the reader exhibits his ignorance of human nature,' says Aldrich towards the end of *The Story of a Bad Boy*, having devoted all his previous chapters to boy exploits. Aldrich admitted that he had originally thought girls rather tame company, but seeing his contemporaries sending and receiving mysterious epistles and leaving packets of lemon-drops in hollow trees, he felt it was the proper thing to do. He went through the motions of courtship with a couple of Miss Gibbs' pupils, but 'the conclusion was forced on me that I was not a boy likely to distinguish myself in this branch of business'. However, he did fall overwhelmingly and painfully in love with a nineteen-year-old visitor to the house, 'suffering pangs as poignant as if I had been ten feet high and as old as Methuselah'. And for two weeks after he had discovered that Miss Nelly was in fact betrothed to another, he mooned around as a 'Blighted Being'; he brooded over *The Sorrows of Werther*, and 'if I could have committed suicide without killing myself, I should certainly have done so'. Tom Sawyer – no one tougher than this boy – falls heavily in love in chapter 4; when Becky Thatcher appears for the first time at Sunday school 'his soul was all ablaze with bliss'. 'The next moment he was "showing off" with all his might – cuffing boys, pulling hair, making faces, in a word using every art that seemed likely to fascinate a girl, and win her applause.'

But as far as English storybook boys were concerned, girls might not exist; there were sisters, of course, but these were asexual objects. Kenneth Grahame in *The Golden Age* included a chapter called 'Young Adam Cupid' where Edward falls briefly in love with the farmer's nine-year-old daughter. But this is only fleeting; Edward's normal feelings about the sex are bemused contempt: ' "I can't make out what they find to talk about... They don't *know* anything; they can't *do* anything – except play the piano, and nobody would want to talk about *that*." ' He has so little use for his sisters that he wishes he could exchange them for a pair of Japanese guinea-pigs. When his inamorata hears this she sticks her tongue out at him. A man can stand much, says Grahame, but 'personal ridicule is a shaft that reaches the very vitals'. Edward works out his chagrin on his aunt's fowls, which he chases until they drop, and declares 'his unmitigable resolve to go into the army'.

A precocious awareness of femininity. Illustration by A. Dorothy Cessna for Robert Casey:
The Parson's Boys *(Denver, Colorado, 1906).*

The apparent lack of interest in the opposite sex may have partly been Victorian convention, but must also have been fostered by the single-sex system of English education. Pre-adolescents seem to have felt the indifference indicated by Grahame, and unless there were brothers and sisters, or perhaps cousins, kept apart from the other sex; adolescents secluded in boarding schools certainly fell in love, but with each other. English school fiction such as Horace Annesley Vachell's *The Hill* (1905), E. F. Benson's *David Blaize* and Hugh Walpole's *Jeremy at Crale* (1927) is full of what now seems blatantly homosexual emotion but was then seen – by the participants and by authority – as normal. Certainly, the greatest stress on romantic friendship occurs in adult novels about school life rather than in the school stories so popular from the 1880s onwards, but in the latter the often intense relationship between friends seems more marked because of the way it is taken for granted. Such friendships, both in real life and in fiction, very often lasted well into university life and beyond. 'The opposite sex is despised and hated, treated as something obscene,' Robert Graves had written of public schools before the First World War.[43] And at Oxford undergraduates until well after the Second World War seem rarely to have troubled their heads about women. 'Women were lacking from our lives,' said an Etonian who took his degree in 1938. Oxford might have women's colleges, but they played no part in male undergraduate lives. Of course, it was known that they were around, but somewhere in the outer suburbs, 'convents loosely linked to our great monastery, but unvisited, and from which no visitors came. In all those years I never once entered a woman's college, and never knew a single girl well enough to call her by her first name.'[44]

At English girls' schools there were 'crushes' on older girls, and these and 'bosom friendships' play much part in school stories. There is never any mention of boys except as 'chums' with whom one could play hearty games, and it is this, as has been already noted, that makes *What Katy Did at School* so different from the English girls' school story. Authors played down femininity and made their heroines tomboys, 'harum-scarums' or 'madcaps', and if a character was shown to be interested in her appearance the practised English reader understood at once that she would come to no good. In school fiction for both boys and girls, any interest in the opposite sex was regarded as so unspeakably low as to be unthinkable.

Perhaps the only English author to incorporate into her books the precocious awareness of feminine power that is such a marked feature of the American Bad Boy was Richmal Crompton (Richmal Crompton Lamburn, 1890–1969) whose *Just – William* stories – there were to be some forty of them – appeared between 1922 and 1970. William Brown, a scapegrace eleven-year-old forever in trouble, has the usual aggressive English contempt for womenfolk, whom he dismisses as 'soppy', but is weak as water when confronted by the femininity of Violet Elizabeth Bott, aged six, the daughter of a *nouveau riche* sauce-manufacturer. If she shakes her curls and her frilly skirts at him and threatens to 'thcream and thcream ... till I'm thick', he creeps away, unmanned.

The William series, which was immensely popular in England but which never appeared in America, seems to stem from the American Bad Boy tradition, and in particular from Tarkington's *Penrod* (1914). Even though Richmal Crompton always denied any knowledge of Penrod Schofield, the similarities between him and William are so marked that they cannot have been coincidence. Penrod and William are both clichés of boyhood, with a boundless capacity for getting into trouble, certain that they are profoundly misunderstood, and contemptuous of law-abiding boys. They are natural wreckers; under their assault all tidy adult plans fall asunder – parties, pageants, courtship. 'The serious poetry of all languages has omitted the little brother; and yet he is one of the greatest trials of love – the immemorial burden of courtship,' said Tarkington, and, like Penrod, William also has an elder sister (and a brother too) whose flirtations he sabotages. Each boy also has a faithful gang of three associates. Whole Penrod episodes are repeated; even the illustrations are uncannily similar.

While *Just – William* was aimed only at juvenile readers and never rises above farce – which becomes increasingly strained and mechanical as invention ran out – *Penrod* and its two sequels *Penrod and Sam* and *Penrod Jashber* seem partly autobiographical, and, like Howells in *A Boy's Town*, the author reflects on boy psychology and on what makes a fundamentally well-meaning boy into a powder-keg. Like other Bad Boy authors, Tarkington yearns for a paradise whose gates have closed. The first *Penrod* ends:

Penrod's fantasy world. Illustration by Gordon Grant for Booth Tarkington: Penrod, His Complete Story.

The last shaft of sunshine of that day fell graciously and like a blessing upon the boy sitting on the fence. Years afterwards a quiet sunset would recall to him sometimes the gentle evening of his twelfth birthday and bring him the picture of his boy self, sitting in rosy light upon the fence, gazing pensively down upon his wistful, scraggly, little old dog, Duke. But something else, surpassing, he would remember of that hour, for, in the side street, close by, a pink skirt flickered from behind a shade tree to the shelter of the fence, there was a gleam of amber curls, and Penrod started, as something like a tiny white wing fluttered by his head, and there came to his ears the sound of a light laugh and of light footsteps departing, the laughter tremulous, the footsteps fleet.

In the grass, between Duke's forepaws, there lay a white note, folded in the shape of a cocked hat, and the sun sent forth a final amazing glory as Penrod opened it and read:

'Your my Bow'

Penrod is both the end of an era and the beginning of a new one. It is the culmination of the Bad Boy and the Golden Past traditions, but it also shows the American boy in a relatively new role, not the pioneer or the valiant breadwinner, nor desperately snatching at pleasure before the prison-house of adult life swallows him up, but the child of prosperous suburban parents with a long youth stretching ahead of him, plenty of leisure and no responsibilities. There is even liberty for make-believe. It has been seen how fiercely this had been discouraged by previous generations, but Tarkington writes as though fantasy worlds were a commonplace:

No doubt many of us, like Penrod, live not so much in one commingled world as in two interchangeable worlds, the one able instantly to replace the other with such smooth rapidity as to produce not the slightest jar. In youth specially, the interchanging of these two worlds is so continuous, so facile, and accomplished with so quick and sleek a movement that it is like the play of light and shadow.

Indeed, Tarkington contends that of all the influences upon youth, 'those that affect the imagination [are] always the most powerful'. In this he was echoing the theme of Kenneth Grahame's essays on childhood and of so much subsequent fiction for children. It is significant that Richmal Crompton should have had her inspiration for the escapades of a naughty boy from an American source.

NOTES

1. Charlotte M. Yonge: *What Books to Give and What to Lend* (London, 1887).

2. John Habberton: *Some Boys' Doings* (Philadelphia, 1901).

3. Owen Johnson: 'The Awakening of Hickey', in *The Prodigious Hickey* (New York, 1910).

4. Elijah Kellogg: *A Strong Arm and a Mother's Blessing* (Boston, 1869).

5. William A. Venable: *A Buckeye Boyhood* (Cincinnati, 1911), 90.

6. Hamlin Garland: *Boy Life on the Prairie* (New York, 1899).

7. John Townsend Trowbridge: *My Own Story* (Boston, 1903), 40.

8. Elijah Kellogg: *John Godsoe's Legacy* (Boston, 1873).

9. Henry Steel Commager, foreword to *McGuffey Fifth Eclectic Reader* (1879 edn, Signet Classics, New York, 1962).

10. Anne Grant: *Memoirs of an American Lady* (London, 1808), I, 90.

11. *The Little Casket Filled with Pleasant Stories* (New York, n.d.).

12. Edmund Wilson: *Patriotic Gore* (New York, 1962), 614.

13. Wilson discusses Tourgée's article 'The South as a Field for Fiction' in ibid. 615.

14. George W. Peck: *Peck's Bad Boy and his Pa* (Chicago, 1883).

15. Leslie Fiedler: *Love and Death in the American Novel* (New York, 1960).

16. Frederick Marryat: *Diary in America* (Philadelphia, 1839), 216.

17. David Macrae: *The Americans at Home* (Edinburgh, 1870), I, 28.

18. *Amusing Stories for Young Folks* (Boston, 1861).

19. Harriet Beecher Stowe: 'The Minister's Watermelons', in *Stories and Sketches for the Young* (Boston, 1897).

20. Louisa C. Tuthill: *True Manliness* (Boston, 1867).

21. Eliza Leslie: 'Billy Bedlow; or the Girl–Boy', *Juvenile Miscellany*, 3rd series, vol. 1 (Boston, 1831).

22. Stephen Crane: *Whilomville Stories* (New York, 1900).

23. Edward Hale: *A New England Boyhood* (New York, 1893).

24. Christopher Grotz: *The Art of Making Fireworks* (New York, 1821).

25. *National Pictorial Primer* (New York, n.d.).

26. *The Old Flag* (American Sunday School Union, Philadelphia, 1864).

27. George W. Peck: *Peck's Red-headed Boy* (New York, 1903).

28. B. P. Shillaber: *Ike Partington; or the adventures of a human boy and his friends* (Boston, 1879).

29. John Habberton: *Other People's Children* (New York, 1877).

30. William Allen White: *The Court of Boyville* (New York, 1899).

31. Charles Dudley Warner: *Being a Boy* (Boston, 1877).

32. Booth Tarkington: *Penrod* (New York, 1914).

33. White: op. cit.

34. Algernon Blackwood: 'A Prisoner in Fairyland', in *The Fairy Lovers' Days*, ed. Eleanor Sinclair Rohde (London, 1930).

35. William Dean Howells: *Years of My Youth* (New York, 1916).

36. Garland: op. cit.

37. Francis Grierson [Benjamin Henry Jesse Francis Shepard]: *The Valley of the Shadows* (Boston and New York, 1909).

38. William Dean Howells: *A Boy's Town* (New York, 1890).

39. Habberton: *Some Boys' Doings*.

40. ibid.

41. William Dean Howells: *The Flight of Pony Baker* (New York, 1902).

42. Garland: op. cit.

43. Robert Graves: *Goodbye to All That* (London, 1929).

44. Nigel Nicolson in *My Oxford*, ed. Anne Thwaite (London, 1977).

Postscript

The fundamental difference between the American tradition of childhood and the English – at least until fifty years ago – is neatly summed up by the contrasting jackets for the *Oxford Book of Children's Verse in America* (1985) and that chosen twelve years before for the English-based *Oxford Book of Children's Verse*. The American poems lie under a picture of purposeful little citizens in a library; they are consulting card indexes, studying texts, and generally addressing themselves to the acquisition of knowledge. But on the jacket of the English anthology – showing a painting by George Romney – a group of children are dancing in an Arcadian summer, absorbed in a game that never ends. By the time the two books were published there was far less to distinguish the two cultures, but the difference in the anthologies is marked – the one closely linked with the everyday world, the other strong on fantasy.

The first three decades of this century are reckoned to be golden ones for English children's books. The mood was set in the 1890s by Kenneth Grahame's *The Golden Age* and *Dream Days*. A flood of child-orientated writing followed, and fantasy had its richest flowering yet. It was the era of *Peter Pan*, first staged in 1904, *The Wind in the Willows* (1908), of E. Nesbit, Beatrix Potter, Walter de la Mare, Hugh Lofting and A. A. Milne. The family adventure stories which became popular in the wake of Arthur Ransome's *Swallows and Amazons* (1930) are more fantasy than reality; their child characters lead a life of perpetual holiday, in a world where adults are only a peripheral and shadowy presence. On a lower literary level there was an extraordinary preoccupation with fairyland and a desire that children should believe in fairies; annuals, comics and school readers were saturated with stories and poems about them. They even reached the pages of *Punch*; Rose Fyleman's 'There are fairies at the bottom of my garden', and other of her fairy verse, made their first appearance there.

Throughout this period America kept a much closer grip on reality. (Even Eugene Field (1850–95), whose children's verse approached nearest to Rose Fyleman and her kind, had restricted his fancies to sugar plum trees and calico cats.) Some American poets, indeed, took an admirably astringent view of English literary fashions. Of the Christopher Robin type of verse Ogden Nash remarked in 'My Daddy':

> And everything that baby says,
>   My daddy's sure to tell.
> You *must* have read my daddy's verse.
>   I hope he fries in hell.

And Morris Bishop reacted thus to the prattle of 'an elf man in the woods':

> I said, 'it makes me sick.
>
> It gives me sharp and shooting pains
>   To listen to such drool.'
> I lifted up my foot and squashed
>   The God damn little fool.

There was, though, undeniably, American whimsy; the enormously prolific Thornton Burgess (1874–1965), for instance, was writing his cosy little animal tales – beginning with *Old Mother West Wind* (1910) and continuing until the mid-1960s – which ultimately derive from Potter and Grahame and Joel Chandler Harris, while carrying an added moral element of the simplistic sort so often deemed appropriate for the young. Burgess' Peter Rabbit has long ears because of his dreadful curiosity. Hooty the Owl is punished for his cruelty: Mother Nature decrees that he shall fly around only after 'round, red Mr Sun has gone to bed behind the Purple Hills'. The well conducted animals like Johnny Chuck and Danny Meadow Mouse and Prickly Porky, though, are as merry-hearted and frolicsome as the fairies in contemporary English comics and annuals.

But most of American make-believe at this period, as we have noted, went into the creation of radiant children who bring light and warmth into dried-up adult hearts. In *Rebecca of Sunnybrook Farm* (1903), one of the earliest, even the seemingly implacable Aunt Miranda cannot in the end resist her. More than thirty years after the first Bad Boy stories made their appearance, *Miss Minerva and William Green Hill* (1909) by Frances Boyd Calhoun (who died shortly after its publication) presents an interesting variant of the theme. William has an infinite penchant for mischief, but – and here lies the difference with his predecessors – he has great beauty and Fauntleroy charm (as well as the additional advantage of being an orphan). His spinster aunt wants to bring him up as a girl, 'a fine, practical, machine-like individual, moral, upright, religious', and then educate him for the ministry. William, being thoroughly masculine, thwarts all this. But his winning ways and ability to melt all hearts bring about the marriage of his aunt to the faithful major who has always loved her, and who vows that the boy will henceforth be brought up as a boy. The book enjoyed so much success that a series of sequels was commissioned from another hand. In Gene Stratton Porter's *A Girl of the Limberlost*, published in the same year, an unloving mother is transformed by a sunny daughter. Eleanor Porter in *Pollyanna* (1913) returns to the aunt theme; sour Aunt Polly becomes sweet-natured under her niece's influence, and melts into the arms of the doctor. In many of the American books of this period, children who are notably different from their English contemporaries combine imagination with shrewd practical flair. Gene Stratton Porter's Elnora sells her moth collection in order to be able to go to school. Mrs Wiggin's Rebecca may write poetry, but she can also sell soap with great aplomb. Miss Calhoun's William Green Hill sells his mumps to his young contemporaries so that they too can be cosseted with invalid delicacies; and 'grew rich in marbles, in tops, in toads, in chewing gum'.

Just as in *Penrod*, where a boy's fantasy life is set against a background of leisurely middle-class surburbia, Booth Tarkington moved the American style closer to the English, so had Eleanor Gates, in *The Poor Little Rich Girl* (published two years earlier in 1912), with a younger child. This seven-year-old, isolated and lonely in her nursery, with wealthy parents too preoccupied even to come up in the elevator to see her, consoles herself with 'pretendings', which turn into the dreams of delirium when a slapdash nursemaid nearly kills her with an overdose of what seems to have been opium. (When she recovers the doctor prescribes what we have seen to be the previous century's universal country-life panacea: 'Take two pairs of sandals, a dozen cheap gingham dresses...and a bottle of something good for wild blackberry scratches.') The story is laboured compared with *Penrod*, but shares with that book a similar starting point – one that is to be found in many English books of that period and earlier but which is a comparative rarity in America – the dreamy child detached from the adult world and, more importantly, a background in which it is possible to be dreamy and detached.

Edward Stratemeyer's series, while certainly not about young dreamers – his subjects are young New Age Americans, products of a prosperous urban middle class – might be said to share another similarity: they are about privileged young people who have plenty of leisure, and in this represent a new departure from the more purposeful heroes and heroines of earlier times. These books dominated the reading of young Americans in the twentieth century to an extraordinary extent. The career of the author himself (1862–1930) resembles a Horatio Alger story, with its combination of diligence, flair and good luck. The child of German immigrant parents, he left school after eighth grade, took a job as a clerk in a tobacco shop, wrote his first best-seller in 1898 (a patriotic novel about the Spanish–American war), and launched the first of his Rover Boy series the following year (under the name of Arthur M. Winfield). Other series, under various pseudonyms, included the Bobbsey Twins (as Laura Lee Hope), the Motor Boys (as Clarence Young), Tom Swift (as Victor Appleton) as well as scores more. The Stratemeyer Syndicate was formed in 1914 to manufacture books out of the outlines that its originator provided, and created such series as the Hardy Boys and Nancy Drew. Stratemeyer died a millionaire.

In other early-twentieth-century American writing, too, we find far more time for being young, for the cultivation of athletics – as in the sports-orientated school stories of Ralph Henry Barbour (1870–1944) – or for larking around at school untroubled by serious thoughts of one's future, as in Owen Johnson's Lawrenceville stories –

The Varmint (1910) and *The Tennessee Shad* (1911) among others.

We can single out two distinguised pieces of imaginative writing, one at the beginning and one at the end of these years. Gelett Burgess (1866–1951) is still remembered for his Goops, unmannerly children represented by drawings of quasi-human blobs, accompanying sprightly verse. These might be called descendants of the eighteenth-century moral fables; the stories in *The Lively City o' Ligg* (1899) have far more originality. Like Andersen, Burgess anthropomorphized inanimate objects, but introduced satirical humour into these accounts of runaway chairs, elevators that try to dislodge the superstructures above them, and lovesick bicycles. In the best of his stories, 'The Terrible Train' – a New World version of the traditional dragon-slaying myth – a 'fearful, fierce and furious railway train' is tamed with kindness by the little-boy hero, and thereafter follows him around the streets of Ligg, amusing tourists with its acrobatic tricks.

Carl Sandburg's *Rootabaga Stories* (1922), on the other hand, while they too are ostensibly light-hearted, have an inner seriousness. The strength of his feeling for the Midwest, its landscape, way of life and rhythms of speech, shines through these stories and their two successors, *Rootabaga Pigeons* (1923) and *Potato Face* (1930). Bearing the mark of no other writer, they have also never been imitated. His nonsense has none of the ruthless logic of Lewis Carroll; even more than Edward Lear's, it works by sound rather than meaning – ' "They are going to Kansas, to Kokomo, to Canada, to Kalamazoo, to Kamchatka, to the Chattahoochee," ' say the neighbours when they hear that Gimme the Ax and his two children Please Gimme and Ax Me No Questions are breaking away to go to the Rootabaga Country. And here, again by stringing together names, Sandburg evokes the American

landscape: 'Yang Yang and Hoo were two girls who used to live in Battle Ax, Michigan, before they moved to Wagon Wheel Gap, Colorado, and then back to Broken Doors, Ohio, and then over to Open Windows, Iowa, and at last down to Alfalfa Clover, Oklahoma, where they say "Our Oklahoma home is in Oklahoma".' Sometimes he uses an incantatory assemblage of inconsequential words, and at others he is surreal, as in the opening story, 'How They Broke Away to Go to the Rootabaga Country', where Gimme the Ax and his two children, tired of living in a house where everything is the same as it always was, sell all their possessions – pigs, pastures, pepper-pickers and pitchforks – and buy a ticket 'to ride where the rail-road tracks run off into the sky and never come back'. With their 'long slick yellow slab ticket with a blue spanch across it' they journey on and on undaunted, through strange countries, and when at last the train stops running straight and goes in zig-zags and the pigs are wearing bibs, then they know they are in Rootabaga Country. If Sandburg had found a Tenniel, these stories might have become the American equivalent of *Alice*. But the drawings by Maud and Miska Petersham are of a conventional prettiness totally at odds with the stark, anarchic originality of the text.

The Rootabaga Stories, and 1922, is a good point to end – with such a wholly American literary work, the culmination, it could be said, of the indigenous fantasy begun by James Kirke Paulding some ninety years before, which produced authors as various as Hawthorne, Christopher Cranch, Joel Chandler Harris, Frank Stockton and Frank Baum. It also launched America's own golden age, in which it was accepted that literary worth should be the criterion in what was written for children, and that pleasure was as important as moral profit. In the 1990s the pendulum is swinging back again – as pendulums are so apt to do.

Select Bibliography

The following is a short list of works that may be found generally useful. Additional material is listed under individual chapter headings.

Andrews, Siri, ed.: *The Hewins Lectures, 1947–1962* (Boston, 1963). Annual lectures on children's books in New England: the travelogue storybook; *Youth's Companion*, Mrs A. D. T. Whitney, Jacob Abbott, Eliza Orne White, Laura E. Richards, Lucretia P. Hale, Susan Coolidge, Kate Douglas Wiggin. There were later lectures, printed in the *Horn Book Magazine*, on Samuel Goodrich, Thomas Bailey Aldrich, and Susan Warner, Maria Susanna Cummins, Martha Finley ('the Lachrymose Ladies').

Arnold, Arnold: *Pictures and Stories from Forgotten Children's Books* (New York, 1969).

Avery, Gillian: *Childhood's Pattern* (London, 1975).

Barry, Florence V.: *A Century of Children's Books* (New York, 1923).

Benardete, Jane, and Phyllis Moe: *Companions of our Youth: stories by women for young people's magazines, 1865–1900* (New York, 1980).

Billman, Carol: *The Secret of the Stratemeyer Syndicate* (New York, 1986).

Bingham, Jane, ed.: Writers for Children (New York, 1988).

Bingham, Jane, and Grayce Scholt: *Fifteen Centuries of Children's Literature: an annotated chronology of British and American works in historical context* (Westport, Conn., 1980). Articles on Alcott, Baum, Burnett, Cooper, Dodge, Lucretia Hale, Harris, Hawthorne, Irving, Pyle, Richards, Sandburg, Stockton, Wiggin.

Blair, Walter, and Hamlin Hill: *America's Humor* (New York, 1978).

Blanck, Jacob: *Peter Parley to Penrod; a bibliographical description of the best-loved American juvenile books* (Cambridge, Mass., 1961).

Bremner, Robert H.: *Children and Youth in America: a documentary history* (Cambridge, Mass., 1970).

Brown, Herbert Ross: *The Sentimental Novel in America 1789–1860* (New York, 1975).

Cable, Mary: *The Little Darlings: a history of child-rearing in America* (New York, 1975).

Calhoun, Arthur W.: *A Social History of the American Family* (Cleveland, 1918).

Carpenter, Charles: *History of American Schoolbooks* (Philadelphia, 1963).

Carpenter, Humphrey, and Mari Prichard: *The Oxford Companion to Children's Literature* (Oxford, 1984).

Cawelti, John G.: *Apostles of the Self-made Man* (Chicago, 1965).

Darling, Richard L.: *The Rise of Children's Book Reviewing in America, 1865–1881* (New York, 1968).

Darton, F. J. Harvey: *Children's Books in England* (3rd edn, rev. Brian Alderson, Cambridge, UK, 1982).

deMause, Lloyd, ed.: *The History of Childhood* (New York, 1974).

Demers, Patricia, and Gordon Moyles: *From Instruction to Delight: an anthology of children's literature to 1850* (Toronto, 1982).

Earle, Alice Morse: *Child Life in Colonial Days* (New York, 1904).

Elson, Ruth Miller: *Guardians of Tradition: American schoolbooks of the nineteenth century* (Lincoln, Nebr., 1964).

Erikson, Erik H.: *Childhood and Society* (2nd edn, New York, 1963).

Estes, Glenn E., ed. *American Writers for Children before 1900, Dictionary of National Biography* (Detroit, 1985)

Fiedler, Leslie A.: *Love and Death in the American Novel* (rev. edn, New York, 1966).

Habegger, Alfred: *Gender, Fantasy and Realism in American Literature* (New York, 1982).

Halsey, Rosalie V.: *Forgotten Books of the American Nursery* (Boston, 1911).

Haviland, Virginia, ed.: *Children's Literature: a guide to reference sources* (Washington, DC, 1966).

Haviland, Virginia, and Margaret N. Coughlan: *Yankee-Doodle's Literary Sampler of Prose, Poetry, and Pictures* (New York, 1974).

Hewins, Caroline M.: *A Mid-century Child and her Books* (New York, 1926).

Hiner, N. Ray, and Joseph M. Hawes, eds: *Growing up in America: children in historical perspective* (Urbana and Chicago, 1985).

Jackson, Mary V.: *Engines of Instruction, Mischief, and Magic: children's literature in England from its beginnings to 1839* (Aldershot, Hants, 1989).

Johnson, Clifton: *Old-time Schools and School Books* (New York, 1904).

Jordan, Alice M.: *From Rollo to Tom Sawyer* (Boston, 1948).

Kelly, R. Gordon: *Mother was a Lady: self and society in selected American children's periodicals* (Westport, Conn., 1974).

Kelly, R. Gordon, ed.: *Children's Periodicals of the United States* (Westport, Conn., 1984).

Kett, Joseph: *Rites of Passage: adolescence in America: 1790 to the Present* (New York, 1977).

Kiefer, Monica: *American Children through their Books* (Philadelphia, 1948).

Kuhn, Anne L.: *The Mother's Role in Childhood Education: New England concepts* (New Haven, Conn., 1947).

Lystad, Mary: *From Dr Mather to Dr Seuss* (Boston, 1980).

McCullough, David Willis, ed.: *American Childhoods* (Boston, 1987).

MacDonald, Ruth K.: *Literature for Children in England and America from 1646 to 1774* (Troy, NY, 1982).

MacLeod, Anne Scott: *A Moral Tale: children's fiction and American culture 1820–1860* (Hamden, Conn., 1975).

McNall, Sally Allen: 'American Children's Literature, 1880–Present', in N. Ray Hiner and Joseph M. Hawes, eds: *American Childhood: a research guide and historical handbook* (Westport, Conn., 1985).

Meigs, Cornelia, Anne Thaxter Eaton, Elizabeth Nesbitt, Ruth Hill Viguers: *A Critical History of Children's Literature* (New York, 1953).

Mott, Frank Luther: *Golden Multitudes: the story of best-sellers in the United States* (New York, 1947).

Neuburg, Victor E.: *The Penny Histories* (London, 1968).

Newell, William Wells: *Games and Songs of American Children* (New York, 1884).

Nietz, John: *Old Textbooks* (Pittsburgh, 1961).

Opie, Iona and Peter, eds: *The Oxford Dictionary of Nursery Rhymes* (Oxford, 1951).

Papashivly, Helen W.: *All the Happy Endings* (New York, 1956).

Rideing, W. H.: *The Boyhood of Famous Authors* (New York, 1897).

Rosenbach, A. S. W.: *Early American Children's Books* (Portland, Me., 1933).

Sloane, William: *Children's Books in England and America in the Seventeenth Century* (New York, 1955).

Stoddard, Lothrop: *The Story of Youth* (London, 1929).

Tebbel, John: *A History of Book Publishing in the United States*, I (New York, 1972).

Thwaite, Mary F.: *From Primer to Pleasure in Reading* (rev. edn, Boston, 1972).

Townsend, John Rowe: *Written for Children: an outline of English-language children's literature* (rev. edn, Boston, 1983).

Welch, D'Alté A.: *A Bibliography of American Children's Books Printed prior to 1821* (Worcester, Mass., 1972).

Wishy, Bernard: *The Child and the Republic: the dawn of modern American child nurture* (Philadelphia, 1968).

CHAPTER 1

Baldwin, T. W.: *William Shakspere's Petty School* (Urbana, Ill., 1943).

Caldwell, Patricia: *The Puritan Conversion Narrative* (Cambridge, UK, 1983).

Eames, Wilberforce: *Early New England Catechisms* (Worcester, Mass., 1898).

Fleming, Sandford: *Children and Puritanism* (New Haven, Conn., 1933).

Ford, Paul Leicester: *The New England Primer* (New York, 1897).

Ford, Worthington Chauncey: *The Boston Book Market 1679–1730* (Boston, 1917).

Frost, J. William: *The Quaker Family in Colonial America* (New York, 1973).

Greven, Philip: *The Protestant Temperament; patterns of child-rearing, religious experience and the self in early America* (New York, 1977).

Heartman, Charles F.: *The New England Primer issued prior to 1830* (3rd edn, New York, 1934).

Hill, Christopher: *Society and Puritanism in Pre-Revolutionary England* (London, 1964).

Littlefield, George Emery: *Early Boston Booksellers* (Boston, 1900).

Livermore, George: *The Origin, History and Character of the New England Primer* (Cambridge, Mass., 1849).

Miller, Perry: *The New England Mind: the seventeenth century* (Cambridge, Mass., 1954).

Morgan, Edmund S.: *The Puritan Family* (Boston, 1944).

Morison, Samuel Eliot: *The Puritan Pronaos: studies in the intellectual life of New England in the seventeenth century* (New York, 1936).

Slater, Peter Gregg: *Children in the New England Mind* (Hamden, Conn., 1977).

Sommerville, C. John: *The Discovery of Childhood in Puritan England* (Athens, Ga., 1992).

Vaughan, Alden T., and Edward W. Clark, eds: *Puritans among the Indians: accounts of captivity and redemption 1676–1724* (Cambridge, Mass., 1981).

Wheeler, Joseph Towne: 'Books owned by Marylanders 1700–1776', *Maryland Historical Magazine*, vol. 35 (1940).

Wright, Louis B.: *The First Gentlemen of Virginia: intellectual qualities of the early colonial ruling class* (San Marino, Calif., 1940).

Wright, Thomas Goddard: *Literary Culture in Early New England 1620–1730* (New Haven, Conn., 1920).

Ziff, Larzer: *Puritanism in America* (New York, 1973).

CHAPTER 2

Bridenbaugh, Carl: *Cities in Revolt: urban life in America 1743–1776* (New York, 1955).

Bridenbaugh, Carl and Jessica: *Rebels and Gentlemen: Philadelphia in the age of Franklin* (New York, 1962).

Clark, Ronald W.: *Benjamin Franklin: a biography* (London, 1983).

Davis, Richard Beale: *A Colonial Southern Bookshelf* (Athens, Ga., 1979)

Ford, Paul Leicester: *'The Sayings of Poor Richard': the prefaces, proverbs and poems of Benjamin Franklin. Originally printed in Poor Richard's almanacs* (Brooklyn, NY, 1890).

Ford, Worthington Chauncey: *Broadsides, Ballads &c. Printed in Massachusetts 1639–1800* (Massachusetts Historical Society Collections, 75, 1922).

Ford, Worthington Chauncey: *The Isaiah Thomas Collection of Ballads* (Worcester, Mass., 1924).

Hofstadter, Richard: *America at 1750* (London, 1972).

Klein, Mindy Freedman: 'Isaiah Thomas's Contribution to Children's Literature in America' (MA thesis, Graduate Library School, University of Chicago, 1976).

Morgan, Edmund S.: *Virginians at Home; family life in the eighteenth century* (Williamsburg, Va., 1952).

Roscoe, S.: *John Newbery and his Successors 1740–1814* (Wormley, Herts., 1973).

Shipton, Clifford K.: *Isaiah Thomas, Printer, Patriot and Philanthropist, 1749–1831* (Rochester, NY, 1948).

Stone, Wilbur Macey: *The Divine and Moral Songs of Isaac Watts* (New York, 1918).

Stone, Wilbur Macey: *The Gigantick Histories of Thomas Boreman* (Portland, Me., 1933).

Straub, Jean: 'Quaker School Life in Philadelphia before 1800', *Pennsylvania Magazine of History and Biography*, 79 (1965).

Thomas, Isaiah: *The History of Printing in America* (Worcester, Mass., 1810).

Thwaite, M. F., ed.: *John Newbery: A Little Pretty Pocket Book* (London, 1968).

Tolles, Frederick B.: *Meeting House and Counting House* (Chapel Hill, NC, 1948).

Ver Steeg, Clarence L.: *The Formative Years* (New York, 1964).

Weber, Max: *The Protestant Ethic* (London, 1930).

Weiss, Harry: *American Chapbooks, 1722–1842* (New York, 1945).

Wolf II, Edwin: *The Book Culture of a Colonial American City: Philadelphia Books, Bookmen and Booksellers* (Oxford, 1988).

Wroth, Lawrence C.: *An American Bookshelf, 1755* (Philadelphia, 1934).

Wroth, Lawrence C.: *The Colonial Printer* (Portland, Me., 1938).

CHAPTER 3

Butler, Marilyn: *Maria Edgeworth: a literary biography* (Oxford, 1972).

Karcher, Carolyn: 'Lydia Maria Child and the *Juvenile Miscellany*', in Selma K. Richardson, ed.: *Research about Nineteenth Century Children and Books* (Urbana–Champaign, Ill., 1980).

Lamberton, Berenice G.: 'A Critical Biography of Lydia Maria Child' (Ph.D. thesis, University of Maryland, 1953).

Roselle, Daniel: *Samuel Griswold Goodrich, Creator of Peter Parley: a study of his life and work* (Albany, NY, 1968).

Summerfield, Geoffrey: *Fantasy and Reason: children's literature in the eighteenth century* (London, 1984).

Weiss, Harry B.: *The Printers and Publishers of Children's Books in New York City, 1698–1830* (New York, 1948). Reprinted from the *Bulletin of the New York Public Library*.

CHAPTER 4

Bode, Carl: *The Anatomy of American Popular Culture 1840–1861* (Berkeley, 1959).

Brown, Janet E.: *The Saga of Elsie Dinsmore* (University of Buffalo Studies, 17, July 1945).

Cushman, Alice B.: 'A Nineteenth Century Plan for Reading: the American Sunday school movement', in Siri Andrews, ed.: *The Hewins Lectures, 1947–1962* (Boston, 1963).

Gaustad, Edwin Scott: *The Great Awakening in New England* (New York, 1957).

Lynn, Robert W., and Elliott Wright: *The Big Little School: Sunday child of American Protestantism* (New York, 1971).

Rice, Edwin Wilbur: *The Sunday School Movement and the American Sunday School Union* (Philadelphia, 1917).

Slocum, Stephen Elmer: 'The American Tract Society' (Ph.D. thesis, New York University, 1975).

CHAPTER 5

Abbott, Charles D.: *Howard Pyle: a chronicle* (New York and London, 1923).

Baym, Nina: *The Shape of Hawthorne's Career* (Ithaca, NY, 1976).

Bickley, R. Bruce: *Joel Chandler Harris* (Boston, 1978).

Doll, Carol: 'The Children of Sophie May', in Selma K. Richardson, ed.: *Research about Nineteenth Century Children and Books* (Urbana–Champaign, Ill., 1980).

Griffin, Martin I. J.: *Frank R. Stockton: a critical biography* (Philadelphia and London, 1939).

Hearn, Michael Patrick, ed.: *The Wizard of Oz* (New York, 1983). Contains a selection of articles on Baum.

Morse, Willard Samuel, and Gertrude Brinklé: *Howard Pyle: a record of his illustrations and writings* (Wilmington, Del., 1921).

Nesbitt, Elizabeth: *Howard Pyle* (London and New York, 1966).

Stewart, Randall: *Nathaniel Hawthorne: a biography* (New Haven, Conn., 1948).

West, Mark I., ed.: *Before Oz: juvenile fantasy stories from nineteenth century America* (Hamden, Conn., 1989)

CHAPTER 6

Baym, Nina: *Woman's Fiction: a guide to novels by and about women in America, 1820–1870* (Ithaca, NY, and London, 1978).

Beach, Seth Curtis: *Daughters of the Puritans* (London, 1967).

Cowie, Alexander: 'The Vogue of the Domestic Novel, 1850–1870', *South Atlantic Quarterly*, Vol. 41 (1942).

Saxton, Martha: *Louisa May: a modern biography of Louisa May Alcott* (Boston, 1977).

Stern, Madeleine B.: *Louisa May Alcott* (2nd rev. edn, Norman, Okla., 1971).

Stern, Madeleine B.: introduction to Daniel Shealy, Madeleine B. Stern and Joel Myerson, eds: *Louisa May Alcott: selected fiction* (Boston and London, 1990).

Thwaite, Ann: *Waiting for the Party: the life of Frances Hodgson Burnett* (London and New York, 1974).

Tompkins, Jane: *Sensational Designs: the cultural work of American fiction, 1790–1860* (Oxford, 1985).

Warner, Anna B.: *Susan Warner: 'Elizabeth Wetherell'* (New York, 1909).

Welsh, Mary Michael: *Catharine Maria Sedgwick: her position in the literature and thought of her time up to 1860* (Washington, DC, 1937).

CHAPTER 7

Blair, Walter: *Mark Twain and Huck Finn* (Berkeley, 1960).

Hinz, Joseph: 'Huck and Pluck: "Bad" Boys in American fiction', *South Atlantic Quarterly*, vol. 53 (1952).

Hoyt, Edwin P.: *Horatio's Boys: the life and works of Horatio Alger, Jr.* (New York, 1974).

Quigly, Isabel: *The Heirs of Tom Brown: the English school story* (London, 1982).

Richards, Jeffrey: *Happiest Days: the public schools in English fiction* (Manchester, UK, 1988).

Stone, Albert E.: *The Innocent Eye: childhood in Mark Twain's imagination* (New Haven, Conn., 1961).

Index